RELIGION AND POLITICS IN SRI LANKA

Religion and Politics in Sri Lanka

URMILA PHADNIS

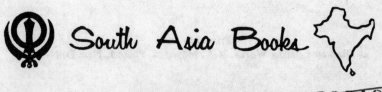

South Asia Books

© Urmila Phadnis

Published in the United States of America by
South Asia Books
Box 502
Columbia, Mo. 65201

1976

by arrangement with
MANOHAR BOOK SERVICE
2, Ansari Road, Darya Ganj,
New Delhi-110002, India

ISBN 0-88386-754-0

Printed in India
at Dhawan Printing Works, 26-A, Mayapuri, Phase I, New Delhi-110027

To

Aditi and Ashwini

PREFACE

This is a study of the evolutionary process of the structure of the Sinhalese Buddhist system which is the religion of the majority in Sri Lanka. It encompasses a historical analysis of the organisation of the Buddhist religion namely, the Sangha and the manifold functions and role of the Buddhist clergy, i.e., Bhikkhus, in urban and rural settings. The study is an attempt to analyse the interplay of the religious and political systems as they have emerged in the island in the different phases of its history.

The term "politics" has been used to connote political parties and political elites; their pronouncements and activities on various religious issues; the whole business of electioneering; party bargaining and policy pronouncements in the legislature; and, last but not the least, the manipulative strategies of the various parties on religious issues as well as their efforts to aggregate, neutralise or nullify the power of the clergy on various other issues.

As such, the study concentrates on (a) the salient features of the structure of the various orders (Nikaya) of the Buddhist clergy in order to bring out the potential resources of the clergy for elective and representational politics; the patterns of relationship the monks established with party leaders and workers in various situations; and relations worked out among themselves as they extended from their own religious organisations into organisations outside; (b) the activities of the political parties, with special reference to their interest in using religious themes and symbols in political articulation and to their efforts to elicit the support of the monks for the attainment of their objectives. This is attempted at two levels:

electoral politics and the making and implementation of public policies.

In the first three chapters I have discussed the major features of the Buddhist religious system in Sri Lanka, before moving on to a discussion of the *Sangha* and its connections with party politics. Chapter IV analyses the evolution of the Ceylonese party system, the changes in the general party positions with regard to Buddhism, the extent to which Buddhist themes and symbols feature in party documents as well as election campaigns and the responses of the various parties to the religious issues over the period. Chapter V dwells on the role of the Buddhist clergy in electoral politics since 1931.

In the next three chapters I have concetrated on those situations in which the State has tried to initiate and implement policies for reformation and reorganisation of the *Sangha* or in which Bhikkhu interest groups have tried to influence policies and governmental decision-making. These include official efforts to implement the recommendations of the Buddha Sasana Commission which was appointed by the Government and the Government's attempts at land reforms (which threatened the status of monastic landlordism); measures to strenghthen the status of Sinhala as the official language and the role of the monks therein; and finally, attempts by a section of monks to influence the government's foreign policy on particular issue such as the Chinese occupation of Tibet, the position of the "stateless" persons of Indian origin in Sri Lanka, and the Vietnam War.

These three areas of focus—the special features of the Buddhist doctrines and practices in Sri Lanka, the interaction between parties and priests, and the activities of the associations of the clergy and groups in various policy fields—should enable one to appraise criticaily the nature and character of the patterns of interaction between the religious and political orders in Sri Lanka. These have been placed in a comparative setting in the concluding chapter.

In the constitution of May 1972, Ceylon—the earlier name of the island—was changed to Sri Lanka. It this study, both the names are used interchangeably.

It is virtually impossible to acknowledge my gratitude to a large number of Ceylonese from all walks of life, particularly the Bhikkhu and Buddhist lay leaders who enlightened me on various facets of the study and the complexities therein. They not only answered all my queries with tremendous patience but also gave me access to the relevant data in their libraries and archives. I would also like to express my thanks to the staff of the "Times of Ceylon" library (where I spent long hours perusing the newspaper clippings) as well as others at the Times office who provided me with all the facilities.

The list of friends and colleagues who helped me in several ways—boosting my morale, reading and discussing various chapters—is again too long. I will, however, like in particular to express my deep indebtedness to Professor Bruce Graham, University of Sussex, discussions with whom gave concrete shape to my scattered ideas. To him as well as to my friends, Mr. and Mrs. P.H. Roberts, I am deeply grateful for going through the manuscript and offering provocative and valuable comments on the same.

Last but not the least, I owe the finalisation of the book to my husband. Mr U.N. Phadnis, who went through the various drafts of the study and played the role of a sympathetic critic as much as of a patient husband.

Jawaharlal Nehru University,   URMILA PHADNIS
New Delhi
15th Nov. 1975

CONTENTS

CONTENTS

ABBREVIATIONS

For the translation of Sinhala titles see glossary

ACBC	—	All Ceylon Buddhist Congress
ACBS	—	All Ceylon Bhikkhus Sammelanaya
BC Pact	—	Bandaranaike-Chelvanayagam Pact
BJB	—	Bauddha Jatika Balavegaya
BLP	—	Bolshevik Leninist Party
BP	—	Bhasa Peramuna
BRB	—	Bauddha Raksha Balamandalaya
BSS	—	Bauddha Sasana Samiti
CIC	—	Ceylon Indian Congress
CNC	—	Ceylon National Congress
CP	—	Communist Party
EBP	—	Eksath Bhikkhu Peramuna
FP	—	Federal Party
JVP	—	Jatika Vimukti Peramuna
LBM	—	Lanka Bauddha Mandalaya
LLP	—	Labour Party
PP	—	Lanka Prajatantravadi Pakshaya
LSP	—	Lanka Swaraj Party
LSS	—	Lanka Sangha Samvidanaya
LSSP	—	Lanka Sama Samaja Party
MEP	—	Mahajana Eksath Peramuna
MSP	—	Maha Sangha Peramuna
NMSS	—	Nikaya Maha Sangha Sabha
RP	—	Republican Party
SJS	—	Sinhala Jatika Sangamaya
SLBP	—	Samastha Lanka Bauddha Peramuna
SLBS	—	Samastha Lanka Bhikkhu Sammelanaya

SLEBM	— Sri Lanka Eksath Bhikkhus Mandalaya
SLEBBM	— Sri Lanka Eksath Bhikkhu Bala Mandalaya
SLFP	— Sri Lanka Freedom Party
SLMBS	— Sri Lanka Maha Bhikkhu Sangamaya
SLMSS	— Sri Lanka Maha Sangha Sabha
SLSS	— Sri Lanka Sangha Samvidhanaya
SMS	— Sinhala Maha Sabha
TC	— Tamil Congress
TNBMBM	— Tri Nikaya Bhikkhu Maha Bala Mandalaya
TNMSS	— Tri Nikaya Maha Sangha Sabha
TUF	— Tamil United Front
UBA	— United Buddhist Association
UF	— United Front
ULF	— United Left Front
UNP	— United National Party
YMBA	— Young Men's Buddhist Association.

Chapter I

THE SINHALESE BUDDHIST SYSTEM
A STRUCTURAL ANALYSIS

INTRODUCTION

In its canonical form, Theravada Buddhism has been a source of controversy amongst scholars who have attempted to find a general definition of religion which would be cross-culturally valid. Initially, the focal point of many definitions seemed to be 'belief in supernatural beings, god or gods'.[1] Apparently even Max Weber appears to have had in his mind this criterion when he described 'primitive' Buddhism as a 'godless creed', 'an ethical movement without a deity', and without a cult and wondered whether such a system of ethics without god could be called a 'religion'.[2]

Such an interpretation of religion would be applicable to Buddhism if it is regarded strictly as a system of thought in its canonical context. The evolution and growth of Buddhism as an ideology as much as an institution, however, indicates that canonical Buddhism is only one of its aspects. It was probably this aspect of the Buddhist system that made Durkheim object to the definitions of religion. Emphasizing the social-institutional concomitants of religion, Durkheim argued that not-

---

1. Hans-Dieter Evers, 'Buddha and the Seven Gods : The Dual Organisation of a Temple in Central Ceylon', *The Journal of Asian Studies*, Vol, 27, No. 3. May 1968, p. 541.
2. Max Weber, *The Religion of India : The Sociology of Hinduism and Buddhism*, ed. and trans. Hans H. Gerth and Don T. Martindale (Illinois, 1958), p. 206.

withstanding the absence of gods or at least the minimal role ascribed to them, Buddhism was a religion. Consequently, on empirical grounds he argued that the earlier definitions of religion needed to be modified.[3]

The study of the Buddhist religious system in Sri Lanka and elsewhere bears out Durkheim's objections to the earlier formulations. In the official Buddhist cosmos, while the existence of gods and demons is recognised, they are considered irrelevant to the achievement of the goal of Buddhism which is Nirvana (salvation).[4] In practice, however, the role of gods is made much more functional in the Buddhist system than has been made out in the canons. Consequently, the Sinhalese Buddhist Pantheon emerges as a hierarchical structure composed of the Buddha, gods, demons and other supernatural beings, so devised as to provide for a functional role for each without impairing in any manner the dominant status of the Buddha.

The Sinhalese religion, in other words, has revolved round a set of precepts which, in response to the social environment of the concerned era, have been institutionalised in concrete patterns of organisation and rituals. In functional terms, the religious behaviour and practices have tended to draw legitimisation from these precepts without always retaining their

3. Emphasising the inner logic of the religious system, Durkheim's analysis rested on the delineation of the sacred/profane categories. 'Sacred' things are those 'which the interdictions protect and isolate'; 'profane' are those to which these interdictions are applied and which must remain at a distance from the first. Religion, according to him, was a set of beliefs and practices incorporating the sacred and profane categories which, though kept apart, did maintain a subordination and superordination, leading to the formation of a 'moral community' called a Church. Emile Durkheim, *The Elementary Forms of Religious Life*, trans. Joseph Ward Swain (New York, 1975), pp. 37-63.

4. The term 'salvation' however, hardly does justice to the term 'Nirvana'; unlike the Christian beliefs there is no 'soul' in Buddhist philosophy to be saved or salvaged as is clearly expounded by the Buddhist logician Nagsena. F. Max Muller, ed., *The Sacred Books of the East* (Delhi, 1967), Vol. 35, pp. 88-89.

spirit, underlining thereby the 'transformative capabilities'[5] of Buddhism.

How can the nature of this transformation be characterised? Has it been syncretistic as E.R. Leach and Michael Ames have implied in their respective writings?[6] Or has it been 'accretive'—the process of an individual religion being added on to the religion of the group, as Gombrich puts it? "I would also like to deny", maintains Gombrich, "that the Sinhalese Buddhist religion, in any sense of the term, is syncretistic. I take it that we talk of cultural syncretism when elements from different cultures combine or fuse to produce a composite which is not normal or not acceptable in either culture."[7]

An appraisal of the nature of this change, is significant for an analysis of the dynamies of Sinhalese Buddhism as it evolved in Sri Lanka over the past 2500 years. Presented in the context of the canonical, social and political factors, such an analysis facilitates an understanding of the bases of the strength and weaknesses of the Buddhist religious system in a pluralistic social order.

THE PLURAL SOCIETY OF SRI LANKA

Situated almost in the midst of the Indian Ocean, Sri Lanka covers an area of 25,252 square miles and has a population of about 14 million (Census of 1963). Religion-wise, the population is composed of Buddhists, Hindus, Muslims and Christians. This population consists of the Sinhalese, tracing their ancestry to Prince Vijaya and his 700 followers who, according to Sinhalese chronicles, migrated to Ceylon from Eastern India in the sixth century B.C. Next in number are the Tamils, who came to the island in several migratory

5. S.N. Eisenstadt, 'The Protestant Ethic Thesis', in Ronald Robertson, ed., *Sociology of Religion* (London, 1965). pp. 293-314.

6. E.R. Leach, 'Pulleyar and the Lord Buddha : An Aspect of Religious Syncretism in Ceylon', *Psychoanalysis and Psychoanalytic Review*, Vol. 49, No. 2, 1962, pp. 80-102; and Michael M. Ames. 'Religious Syncretism in Ceylon' unpublished Ph. D., Thesis, Harvard University, 1962.

7. Richard F. Combrich, *Precept and Practice : Traditional Buddhism in the Rural Highlands of Ceylon* (London, 1971), pp. 47-49.

waves from South India, over the last 1,500 years or so. The Sinhalese and the Tamils together account for about 92 per cent of the total population.

The migratory waves of population were all from the Indian sub-continent. An exception was that of the Arab traders who came to the island mainly for trade from the West Asian countries and settled along the eastern coastline of the island. The intermingling of these trading communities with the Sinhalese and the Tamils gave birth to the Moor element with its Islamic heritage. During the Western colonial period, inter-marriages between Europeans and Sinhalese as well as Tamils led to a small Burgher community.

Table 1[8]

Population of Sri Lanka by Ethnic Category During Census Years

Race	1946		1953		1963	
	Number '000	Per-centage	Number '000	Per-centage	Number '000	Per-centage
All races	4,657	100.0	8,098	100.0	10,582	100.0
Low-country Sinhalese	2,903	43.6	3,470	42.0	4,470	42.0
Kandyan Sinhalese	1,718	26.0	2,147	26.5	3,043	28.8
Ceylon Tamils	734	11.0	885	10.9	1,165	11.0
Indian Tamils	781	11.7	974	12.0	1,125	10.6
Ceylon Moors	374	5.6	464	5.7	627	5.9
Indian Moors	36	0.5	47	0.6	55	0.5
Burghers and Eurasians	42	0.6	46	0.6	46	0.5
Malays	23	0.4	25	0.5	55	0.3
Others	49	0.6	40	0.5	20	0.2

Although these categories correspond to general linguistic and religious categories, there is some blurring at the margins. As far as religious affiliation is concerned, a detailed compari-son is only possible using the 1946 census date (the subsequent censuses of 1953 and 1963 do not give such a breakdown) but

8. Ceylon, Department of Census and Statistics, *Statistical Pocket Book of Ceylon*—1970 (Colombo, 1970), Table 10, p. 26.

because there has not been much conversion amongst the Ceylonese during the last 25 years (except the recent conversion of a few thousand low caste Tamils of the Jaffna peninsula to Buddhism), the 1946 census can be taken as fairly representative of the island's religious distribution which is as follows:

Table 2[9]

Distribution of Religious Communities by Ethnic Categories, 1946

Community	Percentage			
	Buddhists	Hindus	Muslims	Christians
Sinhalese	91.9	0.1	0.1	7.9
Ceylon Tamils	2.6	80.6	0.2	16.5
Indian Tamils	2.3	89.3	0.3	8.1
Ceylon Moors	0.7	0.3	97.7	0.3

Some conclusions may be drawn by comparing Tables 1 and 2 with Table 3 which give the proportions of the population in religious categories for the last three censuses. Nine out of ten Sinhalese are Buddhists; nine out of ten Tamils are Hindus; almost all Moors are Muslims; and Christians, although constituting the majority of the Eurasian category, form substantial minorities in the other ethnic categories.

Table 3[10]

Population of Sri Lanka by Religion in Census Years

Religion	Num-ber '000	Percen-tage	Num-ber '000	Per-centage	Num-ber '000	Per-centage
All religions	6,657	100.0	8,098	100.0	10,582	100.0
Buddhists	4,295	64.5	5,209	64.3	7,003	66.3
Hindus	1,320	19.8	1,611	19.9	1,958	18.5
Christians	603	9.1	724	8.9	885	8.4
Muslims	457	6.6	542	6.8	724	6.7
Others	2	—	12	0.1	12	0.1

9. Robert N. Kearny, *Communalism and Language in the Politics of Ceylon* (Durham, 1967), p. 9.
10. Ceylon, *Statistical Pocket Book*, n. 8, Table 9, p. 26.

As regards the linguistic distribution of the various communities in Sri Lanka, it indicates a high correlation in ethnic and linguistic categories as is evident from Table 4:

Table 4[11]

Language(s) spoken by the Ceylonese of three years of age and over

(Year 1953)

Language Spoken	Number	Percentage
Sinhalese only	4,289,957	58.9
Tamil only	1,570,084	21.6
English only	14,066	0.2
Sinhalese and Tamil	719,194	9.9
Sinhalese and English	307,570	4.2
Tamil and English	146,549	2.0
Sinhalese, Tamil and English	233,567	3.2
Total	7,280,987	100.0

In sum, it is obvious that a considerable number of Sinhalese are Sinhalese-speaking Buddhists. Similar is the case with Tamils, amongst whom the number of Tamil-speaking Hindus is fairly large. With its strong religious and linguistic overtones, community identification in Sri Lanka thus is a hallmark of its social order.

THE HISTORICAL TRADITIONS OF SINHALESE BUDDHISM

The definition of the Sinhalese as an ethnic and linguistic group rests on its identification with the long history of Buddhism in Sri Lanka. Indeed, for the Sinhalese Buddhists, Buddhism does not merely exist as a set of beliefs, rites and legends but also as the strong theme in the history of their island and culture.

Introduced to Sri Lanka in the third century B.C. Buddhism rapidly became the dominant faith of its people. Some of the major reasons for its rapid expansion were: (a) the absence of any organised religion during this period;

11. Ceylon, Department of Census and Statistics, *Census of Ceylon 1953*, (Ceylon, 1953), Vol. 3, Part I, Table 17, p. 664.

(b) the royal patronage which it acquired almost immediately after its advent in the country, and (c) the missionary zeal of the Bhikkhus (Buddhist monks).

Sri Lanka thus became the first country in Asia to come under the sway of Buddhism and to assimilate its essential attributes. In fact, so dominant has been the influence of Buddhism in Sri Lanka that the chronicled history of traditional Sri Lanka is virtually the history of Buddhism in the island.

Recorded by the monks in Pali, the Ceylonese chronicles —Dipavamsa, Mahavamsa and Culavamsa—provide a continuous narrative of historical and religious events from the fifth century B.C. to the eighteenth century A.D.[12] In the narrative, the historical events are shrouded in myths and legends. To begin with, according to the Dipavamsa—the oldest of them—the Buddha himself visited the island thrice, banishing the evil spirits and setting his footprint on the Samantakuta (Adam's peak). The Buddha had thus consecrated the island preparatory to the arrival of, Prince Vijaya the founder of the Sinhalese race. It has been said that before his death the Buddha prophesied that Sri Lanka would be the place where Buddhism would flourish. And Sri Lanka was to be the Dhammadipa (the island of Buddhist Doctrine) and the descendants of Vijaya the Defenders of the Faith.

The inextricable links between Sinhalese nationalism and the national religion—Buddhism—was heavily underscored in the chronicles. One of the heroes of this mythicised history, for instance, was Duttha-Gamini (101-77 B.C.), son of the ruler of Rohana—a principality in the southeast of the island; the other two were the principalities in western Sri Lanka called Dakkinadesa and Anuradhapura in central

12. The Dipavamsa (Chronicle of the Island) was written in the fourth or the first half of the fifth century. The Mahavamsa (Great Chronicle) was composed in four parts. The first part was written in the sixth century, the second in the thirteenth, the third in the fourteenth and the last in the eighteenth century. In the European edition edited by Wilhelm Geiger and published by the Pali Text Society, London, only the first part is called Mahavamsa. The latter parts form Culavamsa.

Sri Lanka. At this time Anuradhapura was governed by
Elara—a Tamil king from South India.

From Rohana a popular revival was initiated by Duttha-
Gamini who proclaimed that he was fighting the Tamil ruler
not 'for kingdom but for Buddhism.' With a Buddhist
relic in his spear, and leading the army which was also joined
by the Bhikkhus (Buddhist monks),[13] Duttha-Gamini attacked
Anuradhapura. The war ended when the Sinhalese prince
slew the Tamil king in single combat at the gates of
Anuradhapura. The crusade to liberate the Sinhalese nation
and save the national religion thus ended with the victory of
a Sinhalese Buddhist king over an alien political usurper.
This was the "beginning of nationalism among the
Sinhalese".[14]

Such an early political concept of the political identity of
the Sinhalese nation and national religion was "not in full
agreement with the teachings embodied in the Buddhist
scriptures".[15] Nor was the idea of the "establishment of
Sasana',[16] in a state, i.e., a politically defined territory,

13. A word needs to be added with regard to the use of the terms
monks, clergy and Bhikkhu. According to Webster's Dictionary,
the clergy is 'a body of religious officials or functionaries prepared
and authorised to conduct religious services or attend to religious
duties'. A monk, on the other hand, is one who is a member of a
monastic order, who has retired from the world to devote himself
to asceticism as a solitary or a celibate, *Webster's Third New International Dictionary* (London, 1961), pp. 421 and 1,420. Literally,
Bhikkhu means almsman or beggar. He has renounced the world
to lead a solitary life. In practice, however, the Bhikkhus, by and
large, assumed the definitional role of the clergy. Throughout this
study, the terms monk and clergy are used in their definitional
context and in a limited manner, and the term Bhikkhu, has been
used most frequently.

14. Walpola Rahula, *History of Buddhism in Ceylon—The Anuradhapura
Period—3rd Century B.C.-10th Century A.D.* (Colombo, 1956),
pp, 79-80.

15. Heinz Bechert, 'Sangha, State, Society, Nation' : Persistence of
Tradition in Post-Traditional Buddhist Societies', *Daedalus*, Vol.
102, No. 1, Winter 1973, p. 88.

16. The term *'Sasana'* connotes 'instruction', 'order'. It "refers to the
dogmatical teachings of the Buddha as well as to the disciplinary
orders given by the Buddha. In later Pali works and as a loan-word in

canonical. Buddhism was concerned in the main with the other worldly objective of Nirvana, which had to be attained through one's own efforts. In its pure form, it remained therefore not only a highly individualistic but also a "specfically unpolitical and anti-political" religion.[17] However, once it assumed the status of a state religion with a certain historical continuity and emerged as the religion of the masses, its involvement with socio-political issues inevitably followed.

It is significant to note that, in their narrative, the religious interpreters appear as much concerned with the stability of the political order as with the maintenance of the integrity of the religious organisation. With the intermittent invasions by the Tamils from South India during the first century B.C. and fifth century A.D. becoming a perennial feature during the tenth to the fifteenth century, the chroniclers record a deep sense of anxiety in maintaining order and stability in the political community to stem the intrusion of various isms and

Sinhalese, Burmese and Thai, 'Sasana' means the totality of the Buddhist institutions in a lawful unbroken succession from the time of the Buddha onwards. Therefore, the term...denotes...a valid tradition of monastic order or *upasampada*." Heinz Bechert, 'Theravada Buddhist Sangha—Some General Observations on Historical and Political Factors in its Development', *Journal of Asian Studies*, Vol. 29, No. 4, August 1970, p. 762.

Soon after his conversion and the propagation of Buddhism as a State religion, King Devanamapiya-Tissa (B.C. 227-207) asked Bhikkhu Mahinda whether Buddhism was established in the island. Mahinda answered that when a son, born in Ceylon, of Ceylonese parents, became a monk in Ceylon, studied in Ceylon and recited it in Ceylon, then the 'roots of the *Sasana* are deep set'. The affirmative though conditional answer of the Monk was significant in another context too. "The idea of the 'establishment of Buddhism' ", continues Rahula, 'in a given geographical unit with its implications is quite foreign to the teachings of the Buddha. Such a thing was never expressed by the Master. True it is that the Buddha sent forth his disciples to go about in the world preaching the Dharma for the 'good of the many'. But nowhere had he given injunctions or instructions regarding a ritual or particular method of 'establishing' the *Sasana* in a country." Rahula, n. 14, pp. 54-55.

17. Weber, n. 2, p. 206.

movements like Mahayanism in the late third century A.D.[18] An expression of this anxiety and concern is the elucidation of the close relationship between the decline or ascendancy of the Sinhalese Buddhist kingship and Sinhalese religion.

Further, if the "joy, blissfulness and satisfaction in the Doctrine of the Buddha" have been projected as the ultimate goals in the chronicles, their importance is contrasted with the stark realities of suffering and impermanence of this world. The dramatistion of the brutalities of wars and their repercussions on the religio-poiitical system of Sri Lanka emphasizes the transient character of mundane life as against the transcendental serenity of the other world. It illustrates, however, the dynamism of Buddhism in adapting itself to changes in a given social situation.

In the development of Buddhism in the island such a change did occur initially in relation to the then prevailing non-Buddhistic religious beliefs and practices and later in the face of the Hinduistic and Mahayanistic concepts and rituals, which were followed by the influence of Christianity during the colonial domination by the western powers.

The process of the containment of the 'external' influences manifested itself in the denunciation of the 'alien' and 'heretical' elements, and, at times, even in their suppression with royal support. Simultaneously, the process of adaptation and absorption found expression in the 'conversion' of the Sinhalese goblins and gods into the Sinhalese Buddhist system. The 'Buddhicisation' of the Hindu gods, for instance, led to the ascription of certain functions to them which, as will be discussed later, were markedly different from the ones ascribed to them in the Hindu pantheon.

Scholars like Paranavitane provide an explanation for such a diffusive adaptation. According to him, the intrusion of non-Buddhist beliefs and practices in the Buddhist system was due to the time factor. "All the principal changes", concluded Paranavitane in one of his papers, "in the doctrines and practices of Buddhism which took place in India were

18. For an authoritative narrative of the historical events in Sri Lanka during this period see C.W. Nicholas and S. Paranavitana, *A Concise History of Ceylon* (Colombo, 1961).

introduced in Ceylon, and though they were vigorously
opposed by the orthodox Church", in the early phases of
their introduction and the Theravadins, in due course, the
orthodox Buddhists themselves had "imbibed some of the
Mahayana doctrines, such as the worship of Avalokita, the
use of spells and mystic diagrams. Then came the Hindu
influence and the Bodhisattvas, were identified with the great
gods of the Hindu pantheon."[19]

Though the historical factors are of great significance in
the study of the evolution and growth of any religious
system, in themselves they do not provide, an adequate
framework "to account for the vital motivational factors
that lay behind sustained adherence to seemingly contradictory beliefs and systems".[20] Such motivational factors were

19. S. Paranavitane, 'Mahayanism in Ceylon', *Ceylon Journal of
    Science*, section G, vol. 2, 1928-33, pp. 35-71.

    A word might be added here about the Hinayana and Mahayana
    schools of Buddhism. The great schism is reported to have taken
    place in the Second Great Council, around 338 B.C., about 150
    years after Buddha's death. The Buddha had permitted change in
    minor rules of conduct to meet the changing social conditions. The
    divergence over the definition of the term 'minor' led to the con-
    vening of the Second Great Council (the first council was held
    shortly after Buddha's death to codify his authentic teachings). This
    led to a division. The more orthodox among the clergy, the Thera-
    vadins (those following the way of the Elders), emphasised upon
    monastic asceticism. Others decided to form another council
    and adopted rules more accommodating to mass religion.
    This became Mahayana, the Greater Vehicle, which provided for
    the concept of the Bodhisattva, a future Buddha who instead of
    seeking his own enlightenment would help others on earth to find
    the path to salvation and therefore would give some sort of
    primacy to the needs of the masses.

    Theravada Budddism, less appropriately called Hinayana or Lesser
    Vehicle Buddhism, is the majority religion in Burma, Ceylon, Laos,
    Cambodia, Thailand, Vietnam; and is also propagated in Indonesia
    and India. Mahayana Buddhism has its adherents in Japan and
    China. Jerrold Schecter, *The New Face of Buddha : Buddhism and
    Political Power in Southeast Asia* (London, 1967), p. 11.

20. K. Malalagoda, Sociological Aspects of Revival and Change
    in Buddhism in Nineteenth Century Ceylon (Thesis, Ph. D., un-
    published, Oxford, 1970), pp. 21-24.

as much in response to the political crises as to the gradually emerging feudal social order of the island.[21] Finally, the 'plebeian religious needs' was another factor which accelerated the process of adaptation and which, at times, led to innovations in the Buddhist religious system.

The 'plebeian religious needs', as aptly elucidated by Max Weber, were the needs for "emotional experience of the super worldly and for the emergency aid in external and internal distress."[22] The satisfaction of such needs could be met by two types of sorteriology: magic or saviour or both. And though 'Ancient Buddhism' was inimical to both the magic and the images, the Buddhist sorteriology accommodated them to meet specific plebeian needs. Consequently, at times the spirit of the precepts was violated and at others, innovations made.

In the course of its history, therefore, Sinhalese Buddhism became more complicated in terms of both beliefs and organisation as is evident from a brief elucidation of its basic doctrines, particularly in the manner in which they were perceived and practised by the Buddhist masses.

BUDDHISM: SOME OF ITS BASIC DOCTRINES

Buddhism, the path to *Nirvana* (Deliverance or Salvation) is shown by a Buddha, i.e., a Supremely Enlightened one. In every world cycle, there have been several Buddhas. The last Buddha, the twenty second in the series of twenty-eight in the present world cycle, was Siddhartha. Born a prince in India in the sixth century B.C., he discovered the means through which salvation could be achieved but delayed his Deliverance so that he could teach the way to his disciples. And this he did for the next 45 years before he died and attained Nirvana. Even after 2,500 years Gautama Buddha stands as the towering, indeed, the only figure in Buddhist philosophy and history.

A synoptic view of the canonical Buddhist doctrines can be found from (*a*) the scriptural standpoint on the concept

---

21. For details on this point refer to Chapter II.
22. Weber, n. 2, pp. 236-7.

of the saviour and gods, (b) the nature of the universe consisting of the Laukik (this world) and the Lokottara (the world beyond), (c) the immediate, intermediary and ultimate goals of Buddhism as they emerge from the conception of Karma (law of action and retribution), rebirth and salvation, and (d) the means and styles of such goal-pursuits by the Buddhist clergy and laity.

Although it was the Buddha who discovered the path to Nirvana, he is conceived in Theravada traditions as neither a saviour nor a god. Though both the terms find favour with the Mahayana school, it is not so with the Theravadins, who maintain that the basic principles underlying Buddha's teachings emphasized the fact that each and every individual had to strive for his own salvation. The exemplification of Buddha's life and teachings no doubt showed the path but it was left to each person to tread it himself and in a style of his own choice.

"The preponderant view concerning the Buddha in normative Buddhism", concludes Melford E. Spiro, "is that, having attained nirvana, He is no longer alive, in any sense at least in which He can serve as a Saviour. He shows the way to, but is not the agent of, salvation.[19] His function thus is not to save, a task for which the Buddhists, if they wish, can invoke the gods and the spirits, but with his authority."[23]

In *Candalakappa*, answering the question of young Brahamans whether there were gods, Buddha said : "There are. The world is loud in agreement that there are gods. However, the gods are impermanent; they are subject to birth and death. Their power is limited to the fulfilment of worldly positions; to create the world, to change its order, to bestow a good birth on a suppliant, or to grant him liberation, is not within their power."[24] They act within the

23. Melford E. Spiro, *Buddhism and Society* : *A Great Tradition and its Burmese Vicissitudes* (London, 1971), p. 35.
24. Helmuth Von Glassenapp, *Buddhism : A Nontheistic Religion* (London, 1970), p. 19. However, this needs to be done only in exceptional circumstances as the monk, by and large, is supposed to be able to fend for himself. The disparaging introductory remarks of Nagarjuna in his commentaries regarding the gods and spirits indicate this mood aptly. Ibid., p. 31.

framework of a moral order in which their function is to
reward the good-doer and to punish the evil-doer.[25] Amongst
their functions are included the veneration of the Buddha
and the propagation of his glory. It is from him that they
draw their power and authority.

Such a subordination of gods and spirits to the Buddha
(as will be discussed later) elevates him to the position of a
super-deity. In the process the invocation of gods and
spirits is scripturally legitimised. Digha Nikaya (Dialogues
of the Buddha), for instance, lists the gods and spirits in whom
monks may take refuge if necessary.[26]

Thus, contrary to general belief, the gods and spirits do
find a place in the canonical religious system, though with
limited jurisdiction and restricted powers, to help the pursuit
of the ultimate goal, i.e., salvation, which is in the realm
of Lokottara.

In this context, the Buddhist view of the world needs an
explanation. There are two worlds—the Laukika and the
Lokottara Everything is classified as belonging to either world.
Laukika, the worldly, refers to things which are "mundane,
secular, profane" as against Lokottara, which symbolises the
"supra mundane, holy sacred". The concept of Lokottara and
what it signifies constitutes the fundamental religious beliefs
and the ultimate goal—salvation.[27]

Why do the Sinhalese Buddhists want deliverance from
life? Because in a world which is transitory and therefore
perennially in a state of flux, life not only entails suffering
but *is* suffering. This is the essence of the sermon which was
preached by the Buddha to his disciples at Sarnath (India),
which deals with the 'Great Truth', namely, the nature, origin, conditions and means of destroying suffering. To
begin with, birth, decay, sickness, and death come to all
persons in their impermanent existence. And if everything

25. Ibid., p. 19.
26. Ibid., p. 21.
27. Michael M. Ames, 'Magical Animism and Buddhism : A Struc-
    tural Analysis of the Sinhalese Religious System', *Journal of Asian
    Studies*, Vol. 23, No. 3, June 1964, pp. 22-23.

is transitory, "suffering is the inevitable consequence of all experience, both pleasurable and non-pleasurable, since it then results equally from attainment of one's desires or from their frustration. Consider: everything being impermanent, one achieves a desired object only to lose it—which leads to suffering, or one worries about the possibility of losing it—which also leads to suffering. Moreover, if the self too is no more permanent than anything else—if it too is in a state of constant flux—one is never content with what one has. Having attained the object of desire, one immediately longs to satisfy yet another desire which, whether attained or unattained, is the cause of still more suffering."[28]

Suffering is thus unavoidable. So long as there is life, there is desire and desire inevitably leads to suffering. This is the import of the second Noble Truth: suffering springs from ignorant craving or attachment (Lobha) and the desire to preserve the individual ego. Suffering, therefore, is an evil which is not to be pursued (as in certain forms of Hinduism and Christianity), but to be eliminated. Suffering, teaches the third Noble Truth, can be eliminated through the extinction of desire or craving (Nirodh). This could be done, concludes the Fourth Noble Truth, by achieving an attitude of detachment which could be developed by the pursuit of the eightfold path.

The eightfold path is as follows:
(1) Right view or correct insight which begins with rational understanding and leads on to to an insight which permeates one's whole being.
(2) Right aspiration, or intention—the compassionate, wise, renunciation of all pleasures of life which are generally possible at the expense of others.
(3) Right speech—the mastery of one's passions and the avoidance of untruth.
(4) Right conduct or action.
(5) Right pursuit of livelihood.
(6) Right effort.
(7) Right mindfulness.
(8) Right concentration.

28. Spiro, n. 23, p. 37.

This is the path through which an individual can purify himself of all defiling thoughts and actions in order to improve his spiritual condition. Closely related to this path is the concept of Karma—the law of action with its own axiomatic truth: good karma leads to good (pin) and bad ones to bad (pav).

It is only through the earning of more and more merit (pinkama) that chances of a better birth can be improved in the Sansara (temporal world)—the field in which the cycle of rebirths operates.

The immediate goal for a lay Buddhist is more and more "merit making" and "meditation leading to a better birth —an intermediary goal". The cycle of rebirths may come to an end—signifying the attainment of the ultimate goal, i.e., Nirvana—after thousands and thousands of rebirths.

Thus, then, the central concept in the Buddhist cosmology is that of suffering, not sin, leading to the causality of Karma and on to a cycle of rebirths. To attain Nirvana, however, "one must escape rebirth altogether; he must transcend even the desire to perform good actions. The devotees must make a complete and fundamental break with the past. Not only must he try to escape suffering; he must also learn to renounce pleasure, the desire to live, to enjoy. This is because any desire, good or bad, leads to rebirth, and rebirth leads to suffering".[29]

To conclude, the Buddhist concept of Nirvana is conceivably the most radical form of striving for salvation,[30] ideologically as well as sociologically. Ideationally, it entails the transcendence of the entire physical temporal world. Sociologically, the transcendence of the temporal world necessitates the abandonment of the socio-political world. But physical retreat from the world is not sufficient. It is merely a sine qua non for yet another, a psychologically radical act; having abandoned the world, one must sever all ties with it.[31] This demands extreme virtuousness and total wordly renunciation.

29. Ames, n. 27 p. 24.
30. Weber, n. 2, p. 206.
31. Spiro, n. 23, p. 65.

For an ordinary Buddhist, it is evident, salvation is not only too arduous but is far too distant; redemption is far beyond immediate reach. Thus, for an average Buddhist this can only be an ultimate ideal and goal relevant to him in the pursuit of the intermediary goal, i.e., ensuring better rebirth and finding the means towards this end. His major and immediate concern is to achieve 'Proximate Salvation'.[32]

The problem of reconciling the values in the idea of ultimate salvation through Nirvana with those in- volved in the process of gradual betterment through a succession of rebirths produces elements of ambiguity and paradox in Buddhism. The particular expression of beliefs and practices will depend to some extent on the social and political contexts, and we may expect to observe the 'selective emphasis and reorganisation of the original elements'. Some doctrines may be emphasised, others ignored, and others accorded a token significance.[33] The same variability and adaptability is observed in the structure of the Sinhalese Buddhist Pantheon.

THE SINHALESE BUDDHIST PANTHEON

In their writings on the Sinhalese pantheon of deities, Leach,[34] Ames, [35] Yalman, [36] Obeyesekere,[37] Gombrich[38] and

32. Ibid., pp. 66-67.
33. Ibid., p. 68.
34. Leach, n. 6, pp. 80-102.
35. Ames, n. 27, pp. 33-49. Also see ibid, 'Buddha and the Dancing Goblins : A Theory of Magic and Religion'., *American Anthropologist*, Vol. 66, No. 1, February 1964, pp. 75-82, and 'Ritual Prestations and the Structure of the Sinhalese Pantheon', in Nash et al., *Anthropological Studies in Theravada Buddhism*, Cultural Report Series, No. 13, Southeast Asia Studies (Yale University, 1966), pp. 27-50.
36. Nur Yalman, *Under the Bo Tree : Studies in Caste, Kinship and Marriage in the Interior of Ceylon* (California, Berkeley, 1967).
37. Gananath Obeyesekere, 'The Buddhist Pantheon and its Extensions', in Nash, et al., *Anthropological Studies in Theravad Buddhism*, pp. 1-26. Also Gananath Obeyesekere, 'The Great Traditions and the Little in the Perspective of Sinhalese Buddhism', *Journal of Asian Studies*, Vol. 22, No. 2, February 1963, pp. 139-53.
38. Gombrich, n. 7.

Evers[39] describe the various components of the religious
system which, though kept apart in theory, are enmeshed in
practice. Each unit, performing a specific function for the
major religious system, induces interaction with the next and
with each other and thus establishing their mutual complemen-
tality and interdependence. The Sinhalese religious system
in practice, futher, is "hierarchically structured and in consonance with a social structure based on a hierarchy of
caste",[40] an anathema in canonical Buddhism.

What are the structural elements in the Sinhalese pantheon? It is a hierarchical system of the Buddha, deities,
demons and spirits with a parallel hierarchy of values and
functions as presented in Table 5.

TABLE 5[41]

Diagram of the Sinhalese Buddhist Pantheon

	Level	Name of the Deity	Attributes
Pan-Sinhalese deities	(1)	Buddha	Pure god
	(2)	Guardian Deities, e.g., Saman, Vishnu Skanda, and Vibhisana	Rational Puni-tiveness. "Just gods"
	(3)	District Deities	Rational Puni-tiveness 'just gods"
	(4)	Demons	Irrational Punitiveness
	(5)	Spirits, e.g., Pretas, Goblins, Ghosts	Pure evil

The hierarchical pattern is manifest in the architectural
patterns of the vihara (temple) in many cases as well as in the
mode of obeisance and types of offerings. In a typical vihara,
the main entrance leads to the image shrine of the Buddha

39. H.D. Evers, *Monks, Priests and Peasants*: *A Study of Buddhism and Social Structure in Central Ceylon* (Leiden, 1972).
40. Obeyesekere, 'The Gieat Tradition and the Little in the Perspective of Sinhalese Budhism,' n. 37, p. 142.
41. Adapted from the diagram in Obeyesekere in Nash, n. 35, p. 6. Also see Yatadolawatte Dhammavisuddhi, 'Buddhist Sangha in Ceylon, Circa 1200-1600', (unpublished thesis), Ph. D. London University, 1970, pp. 350- 411.

in which the devotee first walks in, pays his homage and makes offerings to the Buddha. From there he moves on to the temple of the gods through a side entry. The offerings to the Buddha and the gods are the same—vegetarian food, auspicious incense and flowers—but are different in the case of the lesser supernatural beings who are offered inferior food like meat, fish and eggs—a symbol of their inferior status. The mode of offering, however, varies slightly in the case of the Buddha and the gods; the Buddha is worshipped with the hand on the head or forehead; the gods are worshipped with the hand somewhat lower or with the fists clenched and placed against the chest.[42]

Holding a presiding position in the pantheon, the Buddha is worshipped virtually at every ritual, but he is not regarded as a god in the conventional sense of the term as one who intercedes on behalf of human beings and brings them reward or punishment. The prayers to the Buddha are commemorative rather than propitiatory or petitionary.[43] He does not possess a human status since he has attained salvation, and yet, the Buddha is, in a sense, 'living'. Prayers are addressed to him and to his image and dietary offerings are made to him, the idea being that though the Buddha cannot offer refuge or solace to people, the prayers to him are (a) symbolic expression of homage to a great man and his sacred teachings, and (b) manifestation of 'good deeds', facilitating 'merit-making' —the immediate goal of a Buddhist devotee leading at least ideally towards the ultimate one.

Some points of departure from canonical Buddhism emerge in bold relief in this context. The idea of images, for instance, as opposed to the Buddha's injunctions, is clearly Mahayanist. However, though the image idea was totally opposed by the Master, the veneration of his relics was not; hence the idea of

---

42. Ibid., p, 10. Also see Hans Dieter Evers, 'Buddha and the Seven Gods : The Dual Organisation of a Temple in Central Ceylon', *Journal of Asian Studies*, Vol. 27, No. 3, May 1968, pp.541-50.

43. Paranavitane, n. 19, pp. 52-64.

his presence in the relics with its underlying notions of magic.[44] But all the Buddhist temples do not have his relics, though every one of them has his image.

Further, the fact of his being omniscient and omnipotent seems to be an important part of the religious system, in which the Mahayanist concept of the Bodhisattva has been incorporated but with modifications.

Unlike the Theravadins, the Mahayanists recognise a large number of Bodhisattvas who help mankind in its unfulfilled search for enlightenment. The only Bodhisattva common to both the schools is Metteyye—Buddhist messiah. But Hinayana Buddhists in Sri Lanka attach a far greater importance to another Bodhisattva—Avalokiteswara—who originated in Mahayana and who is evoked in a crisis. Avalokiteswara, according to Paranavitane, has been worshipped by the Sinhalese Buddhist as Natha since the thirteenth century. Geiger, who disagrees with him, maintains that the worship of Natha was originally a part of the Sinhalese folk religion and that he was subsequently absorbed in the Sinhalese pantheon. In spite of the dispute about the origin of the deity, both the scholars agree that in the present Sinhalese pantheon, Natha is a Bodhisattva, identified both with Avalokiteswara and Metteyye, ranking next to the Buddha.[45] Natha, however, is not conceived as a self-sacrificing saviour who has postponed his own salvation to save the world as in Mahayanism, but is also gradually converted into a deity, granting favours or punishing his devotees for their misdeeds.

It is noteworthy that the gods and spirits—the Gods of the Four Quarters, the various Brahmas and Nagas who are often referred to in Pali texts—are ascribed a minor position in the Sinhalese rituals. Instead, gods like Vishnu, Skanda, Pattini and Natha, most of whom are worshipped by similar names

---

44. Obeyesekere, *Journal of Asian Studies*, n. 37, pp. 139-53. There are two kinds of relics, i.e, remnants of the body found in the ashes of the funeral pyre and relics of articles used personally by the Buddha. In addition to these are the relics of the senior disciples of the Buddha who had attained salvation.

45. Paranavitane, n. 19, pp. 52-64, and Wilhelm Geiger, *Culture of Ceylon in Mediaeval Times*, ed. Heinz Bechert, (Wiesbaden, 1960), pp. 170-71 and 210-11.

in Hindu mythology, play a far more significant role in the Sinhalese pantheon. Here again, the Hindu gods, in functional terms, are divested of their original attributes. They do not hold the dominant position but are subordinate to the Buddha. Divested of their capacity to save, their duty has been to protect the Holy Island, its people and most of all, their sacred religion.[46]

The above deities are 'pan-Sinhalese', i.e., their power extends all over the island. Below them are the local gods who form the third level of the hierarchy. These local gods as well as the demons and spirits forming the last two levels of the religious structure, derive their power and authority to fulfil their functions from the Buddha. As in the traditional feudal structure in which the provincial lords and district chiefs derived their authority from the king through 'warrants', the distribution of power and delegation of authority is done by the Buddha through the grant of Varans or warrants to them.

Besides linking the supernatural beings with each other and finally with the Buddha at the top, the Varans meet 'the specific religious needs' of the Buddhist masses. Although the prayers to Buddha can only be commemorative, they can also be petitionary to his subordinates who, if invoked, can help mankind in the pursuit of its goal in this world by creating an environment conductive to this goal. One of their many functions in this respect is warding off the spirits.

Why should the spirits, connoting evil, be assigned a place in the Sinhalese pantheon? "The spirit cults", explains Michael Ames, "are entirely devoted to combating misfortune and providing consolation in the present existence. By alleviating mental disturbances, they enable Buddhists to concentrate on meritorious and meditating activities, both of which involve mental development. Magical-animism, therefore, caters to both the types of Buddhists: the few virtuous and the masses."[47]

---

46. Obeyesekere, n. 37, pp. 142-3.
47. Ames, n. 27, p. 47. For a detailed exposition of the religious beliefs and practices see, Geiger n. 45 and M.B. Ariyapala, *Society in Mediaeval Ceylon* (Colombo, 1956).

The principle of hierarchy in the pantheon carries an important message: the position of the deities of the pantheon are the products of Karma. Thus, if the Buddha represents the highest goal of the Buddhist aspiration, i.e., Nirvana, the deities are the ones who have achieved their position by virtue of merit earned in their past births. Thus, salvation remains the ideal but its achievement in stages is symbolised in the position of the guardian deities who are viewed as Bodhisattvas or future Buddhas and are addressed in the rituals as "Lord who will be future Buddha".[48]

In sum, the Sinhalese Buddhist system presents a well-integrated and unitary structure with its fairly well-defined hierarchy. A remarkable feature of this system is that in terms of its basic values, it is hardly different from the canonical one. The primacy of the salvation idiom remains undisplaced from its original position in the final analysis. And so is the importance of the doctrine of Karma. However, as salvation is an ideal which is difficult to understand and even more difficult to attain, temporary ways and means must be found to combat suffering till salvation is possible. These means, aiming at the intermediary goal—better rebirth—"may even become an end in themselves rather than means to something higher".[49] And this is what happens, in effect.

The needs of the secondary goal are met in various ways: by ascribing the position of a super deity to the Buddha, by incorporating the deities—local and foreign—after 'converting' them to Buddhism and by manipulating the spirits. The Great Tradition, i.e., the culture of the reflective few—the priests, theologians and the literary men—provides the core of a cultural idiom which remains the major referent for the Little Tradition of the non-reflective many, but it is "refashioned to fit the peasant world view'.[50] At the structural and behavioural level, such refashioning becomes more and more apparent in the process. At times, this has not met with approval from the interpreters and managers—the Buddhist clergy—which at best has accepted them with a disgruntled reticence, if it was necessary to legitimise them.

48. Obeyesekere in Nash, n. 37, p. 9.
49. Ames, n. 27, p. 47.
50. Obeyesekere, n. 37, p. 153.

LEGITIMISATION OF ADAPTATION : THE PROCESS

As stated earlier, according to the decisions of the First Council of the Buddhist Sangha which met soon after the death of the Buddha, it was decided that no Vinaya rules could be changed or new ones added. The monks tried to overcome this difficulty by interpreting the rules to suit the changing needs of the times. At times such interpretations were in consonance with the letter but not with the spirit of some of the injunctions of the Buddha. Such changes were the manifestations of the challenges of the times as of the increasing involvement of the clergy in social and political affairs.

The controversy regarding the relative status of Learning (Granthas) as distinct from Meditation (Vipassana), as early as the first century A.D., was symbolic of this problem. At this time a large assembly of monks in Sri Lanka raised a question: What was the basis of Buddhism—Learning and Teaching, or Practice? The answer was provided in the Dhammapada (which incorporated the teachings of Buddha); a person of meditation, even though he had little learning, was superior to the one who was learned but had no Realisation or Practice.

The final decision, however, went against the original teaching. It was maintained that Learning and not Practice was the basis of the Sasana. Subsequent commentaries supported the same view. They declared that "there may or may not be realization (Pativedha) and practice (Patipatti); learning is enough for the perpetuation of the Sasana. The wise one, having heard the Tripitaka, will fulfil even both....Therefore, the Sasana (religion) is established when learning endures."[51]

The primacy of the Ganthadhuras (vocation of books) over the Vipasanadhuras (vocation of meditation) was the recognition of the need for its continuous socialisation at the mass level. Living in seclusion, the meditator no doubt symbolised the ascetic ideal but it was only learning and its transmission in various forms which could sustain Buddhism as a living religion. Hence there was the need for adaptations and modifications without violating the core of the ultimate ideal. A

---

51. Rahula, n. 14, pp. 158-9.

few illustrations will suffice to make the point.

Civil wars and foreign invasions at various points of Sinhalese history threatened Buddhism with total extinction. Faced
with these dangers, some of the Bhikkhus felt that in order
to sustain the intellectual traditions, not only should the Tripitaka ('books', literally meaning the three baskets), the
Vinaya Pitaka (The Book of Discipline), the Sutta Pitaka (The
Book of Formulae) and the Abbidhamma Pitaka (The Book
of Doctrine), incorporating the teachings of Buddha in Pali
be preserved but the history of Buddism in the island should
also be chronicled. But in his several Suttas (sermons) Buddha
had made it clear that the Bhikkhus should not talk about
kings, ministers, rebels, wars, and such other mundane
matters. Such 'low and mean talk' was prohibited for the
monks.

In the circumstances, when a Bhikkhu decided to write
Mahavamsa (which was to be as much the history of Buddhism in Sri Lanka as that of the Sinhalese people), a way out
was required for the purpose, and the commentaries on the
teachings of Buddha did provide one. It was maintained in
the commentaries that if at the end of the discussions about
kings and their deeds one could reflect that all these persons
were subject to decay, then the discussion became part of the
meditation, illustrative of the transitoriness of this world. It
is because of this that every chapter of the chronicle ends with
a verse emphasising the impermanence of wordly objects and
situations. The history of the Buddhist religion thus in theory
was viewed by the monks as a means of highlighting the
basic concepts of sufferings (Duka), and the impermanence of
the world.[52] In the process, however, the means at times became an end, with the monks assuming the role of the royal
scribes.

The emergence of monks as painters is an extension of the

52. Ibid., pp. 160-62. 'What better theme for meditation than the
    crimes and follies of mankind. If history had no other lesson to
    teach, scanning its pages or rather hearing its sad stories of the
    death of its kings, was to fortify oneself anew in the knowledge
    of the transiency of all things, and to savour by contrast, the joy
    of the mind directed towards the Four Noble Truths.' E.F.C. Ludo-
    wyk, *The Footprint of the Buddha* (London, 1958), pp.107-8.

same logic. Here again, Buddha prohibited monks painting men and women and specified only designs such as creepers and flowers as the proper subjects of painting. The commentators, however, decided to allow a certain latitude in this respect; painting or sculpturing of events sent from the Jataka stories (stories of the former lives of the Buddha) or events such almsgiving (which necessitated the drawing of men and women), were allowed as they were apt to "produce serene joy (passion) and emotion (Samvega)". At the same time, continues Dr. Rahula, "monks were not unaware of the reality that viharas with beautiful paintings and statues attracted multitudes of pilgrims, who made valuable offerings to the place. This was also an incentive for monks to make their viharas attractive aesthetically and artistically."[53]

Another noteworthy example of the manipulation of devices to fulfil not the spirit but the letter of the canonical doctrine was the 'religionisation' of slavery. The endowment of grants to the Buddhist temples in the form of land necessitated the employment of slaves for their management in consonance with the prevailing feudal ethos. But the Buddha had strictly prohibited such a practice. As the acceptance of slaves was against the injunctions of the Master, the *Majhimma Nikaya* commentary devised a justification: slaves could be accepted if someone promised to offer a kappiyakaraka and an aramika. Kappiyakarikas were those laymen who undertook the responsibility of providing monks with their needs. Aramika meant attendants and servants of the monastery.[54]

It is necessary to refer to two further examples of how Buddhists in Sri Lanka justified their adaptation to the needs of their society: (*a*) the indulgence of the monks in medicine, and (*b*) their role in the Paritta ceremony which is an important ritual in a ceremonial function even today. As regards the former, the Buddha had initially said that Bhikkhus were not to practise medicine, but later they were permitted to treat other monks but not laity. Even this concession was revised: the monks, if asked to treat a layman, were not sup-

53. Rahula, n. 14, p. 164.
54. Ibid., pp. 146-7.

posed to oblige but were permitted to describe how one of their fellow monks was afflicted by the disease in question and how he was treated. This of course meant that laymen could go home, without a doctor but with a prescription.

The paritta chanting ritual dates back about 1,500 years. Meaning 'protection', the ritual is invoked for various purposes such as exorcising evil spirits and dispelling diseases as well as blessing an auspicious occasion. Detailed rules are prescribed in the Paritta Pota (the Book of Paritta) and its invocation brings into bold relief the structural hierarchy as well as the functional integration amongst the various units of the religious system. If the expulsion of an evil spirit is desired, then certain sermons specified in the *Paritta Pota* should be recited by the monk for seven days. During this period, elaborate rules of what should and should not be done are detailed. The Bhikkhu, for instance, should not eat meat or any flour preparation. From the monastery to the sick man's house, he should be conducted by men carrying weapons, and during the recital too he should be protected by armed men. If, after the seven days' recital, the spirit leaves the sick man, then the affair is ended. If the spirit remains, then the gods should be told of the obstinacy of the spirits. A god, as Buddha's emissary, should then be asked to expel the spirit.[55]

The scenario is the same in the ritualised Buddhist festivals; the purpose, obvious. The popular belief in spirits is not questioned but their inferiority to deities is maintained. Buddha's paramountcy is acknowledged without his direct involvement in the action. Hence the need for guardian deities (as and when necessary). Guardian deities expel the evil spirits because until the devotee is physically and mentally fit he cannot further the immediate goal of his ultimate objective. Obviously, it has been within the compass of the Buddhist religious system to assume several functions which, in strict terms, are a-canonical.

CONCLUSION

Whereas in its country of origin Buddhism, by and large,

55. Ibid., pp. 278-80, See also Gombrich, n. 7, pp. 101-9.

emerged as an urban religion of a merchant-plebeian group, in Sri Lanka, almost from its inception, it became predominantly a peasant religion.[56] As such, the Buddhist religious system adapted itself to its host society and to the changes in that society over a period of time. Such a process of adaptation necessarily entailed changes in the system of beliefs and practices associated with the religion. It had to take into account the need to accommodate pre-Buddhist magical-animist beliefs and the need to combat challenges from rival faiths and movements, partly by absorbing some elements from them. But these processes of accommodation, adaptation and absorption were contained within limits and it is possible to detect a strong line of continuity running through the history of Sinhalese Buddhism.

Could then one agree with Dr. Gombrich's characterisation of the religious system as 'accretive'? If one views the Sinhalese Buddhist system primarily in ideational terms then such a description might be valid. However, if the religious system is perceived as a set of precepts which have been institutionalised in response to the socio-political situations in concrete organisational and ritualistic patterns and behaviour, then the religious system seems to be something more than being merely accretive. No doubt the accretive approach of growth (i.e., growth by the addition of various other units to the core so that the result is an aggregate rather than a system of units) facilitates an understanding of the structural dimensions of the system, but it does no justice to the functional and contextual dimensions—the dynamics of interaction between the various units of the religious system in the context of and in response to the pressures and influences of the other systems —social, political and economic, from time to time.

The role of such an interaction assumes an added significance when, with the ultimate ideal of the Sinhalese religious system being too intractable and distant, the intermediary

---

56. For an incisive account of the contrasts in the major characteristics of 'classical' Buddhism and Sinhalese Buddhism see Newton Gunasinghe, 'Buddhism and Economic Growth with Special Reference to Ceylon' (unpublished Master's thesis, Department of Anthropology and Sociology, Monash University, 1972), Chpaters I and II.

goal—better rebirth—becomes the goal in effect, for the many. With the secondary goal becoming, more often, an end in itself, the Buddhist institutions need to gear themselves to the needs of the proximate goal while not only keeping the ultimate ideal as little corrupted as possible but also drawing to the extent possible, sustenance from it through the canonical legitimation of adaptation and change.

What is noteworthy in this context is the intertwining of the ultimate and the actual in ritual and behavioural terms. Further, in practice, some of the 'supernatural' attributes of the Buddha endow him with a position and status in the hierarchical structure which, strictly speaking, is not wholly convergent with the spirit of the canon. To illustrate, the position of the Buddha in the Sinhalese pantheon ascribes to him attributes which make him a supreme being. More than this, it also endows him with a position under which, after the delegation of authority to the deities, the Buddha is, so to say, a 'sleeping' Buddha; it is his agents who take over and do the 'jobs'. It also needs to be noted that the primacy of the Buddha becomes further pronounced in a relational and hierarchical context; the authority and status of the Buddha, in the work-a-day life, become meaningful in relation to the attributes and functions of the hierarchy below. In effect thus, with the intermediary goal becoming more often an end and not a means especially for the laity, the powers of the gods become more relevant than they were initially. In other words, without compromising either with the major core concepts of the doctrine or with the inner structure of canonical Buddhism, the Sinhalese pantheon represents a shift in emphasis on the function of the intermediaries.

Alongside such a shift in emphasis, certain traditions and practices have prevailed in the Sinhalese Buddhist system which are either unknown to the vinaya or are clearly anti-canonical. If the establishment of 'Sasana' in the island, the preservation of Buddhism as a national inheritance and the consequent enmeshing of the political identity of the Sinhalese nation with a national religion exemplify the former, the phenomenon of 'monastic landlordism' as well as the caste and kinship bases of some of the monastic chapters demonstrate the latter.

Such a process of unification and/or reconciliation of diverse beliefs and practices, manifesting the close interaction of the religious and feudal social structure of the island and underlining discontinuities as much as continuities, have, over a period of time, led to the evolution of Sinhalese Buddhism as a systemic whole rather than an aggregate of various parts.

An analysis of the historical evolution of the Sangha brings out a blend of the universal and the unique—the strictly canonical and the truly Sinhalese features of the Buddhist monastic system—as evolved in the island over 2,500 years.

Chapter II

THE SANGHA : HISTORICAL SETTING

INTRODUCTION

Unlike Hinduism or Islam which, initially, did not conceive of an institution of the clergy, the Sangha, defined as the 'associated brotherhood of the monks'[1] formed an organic part of canonical Buddhism. The triple gems—the three sacred refuges—which every Buddhist had to invoke were, "I take refuge in the Buddha, I take refuge in the Dhama (Doctrine), I take refuge in the Sangha."

---

1. Ralph Pieris, *Sinhalese Social Organisation : The Kandyan Period* (Colombo, 1956), p. 307. Named by the Buddha as the 'Bhikkhu Sangha of the Four Quarters', the term Sangha has been defined by Nyanatiloka as 'herd', *Buddhist Dictionary and Manual of Buddhist Terms* (Colombo, 1956), p. 148; by Welhelm Geiger as 'community' (*Culture of Ceylon in Medieval Times*, ed. Heinz Bechert, Wiesbaden, 1960), p. 183; by Christian Humphreys as 'assembly' (*A Popular Dictionary of Buddhism*, London, 1962), p. 165; and by C.W. Nicholas and S. Paranavitana as 'National Church' in the Ceylonese context (*A Concise History of Ceylon*, Colombo, 1961), p. 109.

   Dr. Sukumar Dutt, emphasising on the actual as well as the ideal facets of Buddhism, maintains that the word Sangha has two meanings: 'an entire monk community' or the 'bond of association among monks'. While the former referred to the 'actual' Sangha, i.e., ' a body of persons' the latter connoted the 'ideal' Sangha, i.e., a confederation which makes them one body and which once was a historical reality. (*Early Buddhist Monachism*, Bombay, 1960, p. 59). This concept of the ideal Sangha, according to Dr. Dutt, is significant as it forebade the notion that Buddhism was only an

With the cardinal principle of Buddha's doctrine being
"seek not a refuge for any but for yourself", 'ancient'
Buddhism emerged as a 'technology' of wandering Bhikkhus
(recluses)[2] through whom the Dhamma—the essential of
Buddha's teachings—was to be transmitted, not only to an
initiated lay community but to humanity as such.[3]

During the first two hundred years of its inception, however, ancient Buddhism was transformed from its position
as a 'school' or a wandering sect to a settled order.[4] The
story of this transition, narrated incisively by Dr. Sukumar
Dutt, brings out the pertinent fact that before the advent of
Buddhism in Sri Lanka, the Bhikkhu community had already
become a self-governing organisation and every unit (Sangha) had become a 'body corporate'.[5] What brought about uniformity among these units was the Vinaya Pitaka—a detailed
code of behaviour governing the day-to-day life of the Bhikkhus.[6]

Thus, notwithstanding the highly individualistic character
of Buddhism, the 'wandering almsmen' gradually became
cenobitised, This tendency towards cenobitism and obedience
to certain codes of conduct was bound to lead to schisms[7] in

'organised missionary agency of a proselytising faith'. On the contrary, it signified that the sangha stood 'not only for a particular
society or body of persons, but for the great confederation of the
faithful' (*Buddhist Monks and Monasteries in India : Their History
and Contribution to Indian Culture*, London, 1962, p. 23).

2. Max Weber, *The Religions of India : The Sociology of Hinduism and
   Buddhism*, ed. and trans, Hans H. Gerth and Don T. Martindale
   (Illinois, 1958), p. 206.

3. For details refer to U. Thittila, 'The Fundamental Principles of
   Theravada Buddhism', in Kenneth Morgan, ed., *The Path of Buddha*
   (New York, 1957), p. 74. and Weber, n. 2, p. 216.

4. Weber, n. 2, p. 216.

5. Dutt, *Buddhist Monks and Monasteries in India*, n. 1, p. 52.

6. Ibid.. p. 80.

7. The convening of the First and Second Buddhist Councils in the
   fifth and the fourth century B.C. respectively was an attempt to
   save the Dhamma from corruption and disruption. The Third
   Council under the patronage of King Ashoka had, among other
   things, the task of expelling the heretic monks. L.H. Horace Perera
   and M. Ratnasabhapathy, *Ceylon and Indian History* (Colombo,
   1954), p. 45. However, it is significant to note that a "schism was

view of the non-authoritarian character of Buddhism.[8] And it is here that the king, with his traditional duty to save the association from internal or external disruption, could play an important role. Emperor Asoka's patronage of Buddhism in the third century B.C. is a significant landmark in this context; he was the first Buddhist king to use this convention not as an obligation but as 'service to the faith'.[9]

This 'service' of the emperor to Buddhism revolutionised the early Buddhist order; till then, the notion of establishing the Buddha Sasana was foreign to the teaching of the Buddha. As a logical corollary to this, the king had more effective powers over the Sangha as its temporal head than ever before. In the process, the foci of power in the Sangha were centralised in some monasteries with which the king dealt. Finally, the closer association of the state with the Sangha led to a gradual politicisation of early Buddhism. In analysing the evolution of the monastic system in Sri Lanka, one must bear in mind this legacy which the island inherited from Indian Buddhism.

Coupled with this legacy were the internal factors—the impact of the changing social structure of the country—which influenced the evolution, growth, functions and roles of the monastic order. An attempt will be made in this

---

an act recognised as constitutional and a 'division of sangha' (Sanghabheda) had to be allowed, provided it was grounded on honest differences", Dutt, *Buddhist Monks and Monasteries in India*, n. 1, p. 84.

8. Buddha himself said in the Mahavagga 'Now, look you Kalamas, do not be led by reports, or traditions, or hearsay. Be not led by the authority of religious texts, nor by mere logic or influence, nor by considering appearances, nor by delight in speculative opinions, nor by seeming possibilities, nor by the ideas. This is our teacher.' Humphreys, n. 1, p. 71. In other words, the Bhikkhus were bound neither by 'any vow of obedience to a higher supreme authority, nor by a crucial statement, nor by rituals'. Ibid. The obedience expected of the Bhikkhu was to the Dhamma, and to his seniors in the Sangha he simply owed a respectful submission. B. Ananda Maitreya Nayaka Thero, 'Buddhism in Theravada Countries', in Morgan, n. 3, p. 125.

9. Ibid., p. 80.

chapter to highlight the interaction between the social, political and economic systems and the monastic order in its historical context to underline the simultaneous and often cumulative processes of continuity and change therein.

HISTORICAL EVOLUTION Of THE BHIKKHU FRATERNITIES (NIKAYAS) BEFORE THE ADVENT OF THE WESTERN POWERS

In Sri Lanka, though the tradition of the Nikayas or fraternities is as old as the advent of Buddhism in the island, it has undergone several spells of discontinuities, necessitating the import of Bhikkhus from Theravada countries like Thailand and Burma. This is illustrated by a brief review of the historical antecedents of the Nikayas.[10]

10. During the past few years, several dissertations have been completed on the history and organisation of the Sangha in the post-Anuradhapura period. The pioneer studies in the field covering the Anuradhapura period have been E.W. Adikaram's *Early History of Buddhism in Ceylon* (published in Colombo in 1953 and covering the early period up to the 5th century A.D.) and Walpola Rahula's book entitled *History of Buddhism in Ceylon : The Anuradhapura Period : 3rd Century B.C. to 10th Century AD.* Initially a doctoral dissertation from London University, Dr. Rahula's work was published from Colombo in 1956.

The next contributor in chronological order was R.A.L.H. Gunawardhana who submitted his Ph.D. thesis in 1965 (University of London) on 'The History of Buddhist Sangha in Ceylon from the Reign of Sena I to the Invasion of Magha (800-1215 A.D.). This was followed by Yatadolawatta Dhammavisuddhi who analysed the organisation of the Sangha in his Ph.D. dissertation entitled 'The Buddhist Sangha in Ceylon (circa 1200-1400 A.D.)' and submitted to the University of London in 1970. The subsequent 300 years have formed the background of two other doctoral dissertations: Kotagama Wachissara's 'Valivata Saranankara and the Revival of Buddhism in Ceylon' (University of London 1951) and Kitisiri Malalagoda's 'Sociological Aspects of Revival and Change in Buddhism in Nineteenth Century Ceylon' (Oxford, 1970). Gunaratne Panabokke's doctoral thesis on 'The Evolution and History of the Buddhist Monastic Order with Special Reference to the Sangha in Ceylon' (Lancaster University, 1969), provides a historical perspective to the Sangha organisations up to the 18th century. Gombrich's study, *Traditional Buddhism in the Rural Highlands of Ceylon* (London, 1971), though having as its focus the interrelationship of canonical Buddhism and popular Buddhism, provides a

The term 'Nikaya' was earlier used to designate a division of the canon. Later it denoted a group or sect of monks[11]—"organisational grouping of the Sangha". Broadly speaking, it could be defined as "a body of monks with a head (Maha Nayaka) which holds independent Upasampada ceremonies for its novices, whether the line of pupillary succession has been renewed from abroad or there has merely been a fissure caused by a group of monks stating their autonomy".[12]

It may be noted that the contemporary Sangha has several features which have a long-drawn continuity. Thus, detailed injunctions regarding recruitment of young people as novices and their code of conduct as well as religious education and training during the samanera stage and later, are laid down in Buddha's writings as well as in subsequent commentaries. This is evident from similarities in details as regards the modalities of Upasampada (higher ordination ceremony) in the past and in the present day Sri Lanka.

The Upasampada is the primary act for the continuance of the monastic order. It bestows the status of a full-fledged Bhikkhu to a novice (samanera) who, after having been initiated in the rules and norms of the Buddhist scriptures by his preceptor for about a decade or so, is tested by an assembly of Bhikkhus and if declared fit, is ordained a Bhikkhu.[13] A single Bhikkhu can perform the lower ordination ceremony by which the layman enters the order as a novice. For the higher ordination, however, five Bhikkhus make the quorum. If such a quorum cannot be mustered for the Upasampada then the line of succession is broken.

It is necessary to note that apart from the quorum, the Upasampada ceremony must be carried out within a Sima. Defined in ordinary parlance as 'boundary', the term Sima, in this context, means a boundary demarcating a 'sacred' area

succinct account of the evolution of the Sangha too. All these dissertations except Gombrich's remain unpublished.

11. Pannabokke, n. 10, p. 203.
12. Gombrich, n. 10, pp. 309 and 343.
13. For details of the ordination ceremony see H.L. Seneviratne, 'The Sacred and the Profane in a Buddhist Rite', *Ceylon Studies Seminar*, 1969/70 series, University of Peradeniya, Mimeo, pp. 1-25.

within the precinct of which all the ecclesiastical acts including Upasampada are performed.[14] The boundary of the oldest Nikaya, the Maha vihara (the Great Monastery), for instance, was demarcated by Thera Mahinda by ploughing a furrow around the city of Anuradhapura for king Devanamapiyatissa (B.C. 247-207)—the first Sinhalese convert to Buddhism—who, after donating the royal park to Mahinda, wanted the whole city to come under the Sima.

The Buddhism which Thera Mahinda propagated was of the Theravada school and the Maha vihara was the first Buddhist monastery in the island. The Maha vihara was to continue as the bastion of the Theravada orthodoxy for about 1,000 years but it was in the initial 200 years that its glory was at its height during which it held an unrivalled position, with all the other monasteries paying allegiance to it.

The absence of authority in the cosmology of Buddhism coupled with the canonical justification of schism did not, however, facilitate the continuation of its monolithic position for long. Thus, by the fourth century A.D. the power and status of the Maha vihara was already challenged by the viharas founded by the dissident Bhikkhus with royal patronage. The dissensions within the Maha vihara leading to the emergence of Abhayagiri[15] and Jetavana

14. "Definitions of different types of boundaries and of different ways of making them constitute the subject matter of a substantial portion of Vinaya literature. One of these types which was fairly extensively used in Ceylon was the *Udakukkhepa Sima* or the 'boundary fixed by the throwing of water'. The chapter of monks, in this case, assembled on a raft or in a (temporary or permanent) building in the middle of a river (or a lake), and the boundary was fixed by one of the monks, of moderate strength, throwing out water in the four directions. The area inside the four furthermost points where water fell was considered the sima". Malalagoda, n. 10 pp. 234-5.

15. The Abhayagiri vihara was donated to a Maha vihara Bhikkhu named Mahatissa by King Vathagamini (B.C. 93-29) in appreciation of his services rendered during times of troubles in the kingdom. This act of personal donation was resented by the fellow monks at the Maha vihara, for, acceptance of personal gifts amounted to infringement of the Vinaya rules under which any donation needed to be made to the Sangha and not to a particular monk. Consequently, Mahatissa was charged with an offence of Vinaya—fre-

vihara[16] during this period aptly illustrate this. For the rest of
the Anuradhapura period the Sangha was mainly divided into
these three viharas. After the rule of Mahasena (A.D. 334-61)
'the Maha Vihara was Theravada, the Abhayagiri Mahayana,
and the Jetavana alternated."[17]

As regards the organisation of the viharas, it seems to conform to the democratic pattern of the Buddhist republics of
the era. The primacy of the monastery as the basic unit of
the monastic order coupled with considerable autonomy was
as much a feature of the Buddhist Sangha of the past as it is
of the contemporary Sangha. Referring to the organisation
of the Maha vihara, Dr. Rahula maintains that till the first
century A.D., "all the Bhikkhus in Ceylon, wherever they
lived, owed ecclesiastical allegiance to the Maha vihara at
Anuradhapura; and thus all monasteries were virtually affiliated to the Great Monastery, more or less as its branches."[18]
Various other studies on the subject also indicate that till the
tenth century or so, any organised form of hierarchical control of the monastic order had not developed in the island.
Only a sort of very loose federation existed in which certain

quenting the families of laymen—and was expelled. A dis-
ciple of Mahatissa who did not agree with the charge raised
objections, and he too was expelled from the order. The expelled
Bhikkhu left Maha vihara with a large number of his followers all
of whom made their new abode in the Abhayagiri vihara. Though
subsequently certain ideological differences developed between the
two viharas it seems that the Abhayagiri vihara owed its origin as
a separate organised unit to the 'Maha vihara's anger at its first
right of royal patronage'. Arnold L. Green, 'Sangha and King :
The Structure of Authority in Mediaeval Ceylon' (unpublished paper
read at a symposium on the problems in the sociology of Theravada
Buddhism, Honolulu, 21 August 1961), p. 7.

16. The Jetavana vihara came into being with the virtual demolition of
the Maha vihara by king Mahasena A.D. 334-61 who was initially
a Mahayanist but who subsequently adopted a mid-way course between the Theravadins and the Mahayanists. During the reign of
Mahasena's father, a group of Bhikkhus including one called
Sagala had left the Abhayagiri vihara, disturbed by the influence of
the Mahayana prevailing therein. After revolting against the Maha
vihara, Mahasena built the Jetavana vihara for a follower of
Sagala. Nicholas and Paranavitana, n. 10, pp. 111-12.

17. Gombrich, n. 10, p. 30.

18. Rahula, n. 10, p. 303. Also see Panabokke, n. 10, pp. 211-61.

temples owed allegiance to the premier centre of the sect to which they belonged.

Such a situation continued till the tenth century A.D. when Chola dynasty from South India defeated the Sinhalese Buddhist kings and plundered as well as destroyed many viharas. The efforts of the Sinhalese king Vijayabahu, (after reconquering the throne in A.D. 1065) to resuscitate the Sangha did not go far in the face of the almost continuous invasions from South India. It was only during the strong rule of Parakrambahu I (A.D.1155-83) that the earlier fraternities were unified.

Ironically, the unification did not connote the strengthening of the earlier Nikayas but the beginning of their end as identifiable sects.[19] Instead, between the twelfth and sixteenth centuries the old classification of the Bhikkhus into Gamavasin (village-dwelling) and Vanavasin (forest-dwelling) assumed a greater interdependence and distinctive significance. According to Dr. Dhamavisuddhi, "with the unification of all the three Nikayas, the Nikaya distinction ceased to exist, a situation which helped the two communities to develop into well-organised fraternities and ultimately to substitute for the Nikayas."[20]

The categorisation of the Bhikkhus as Gamavasins and Vanavasins was not a new distinction. In fact, the same division existed in Sri Lanka as early as the second century A.D.[21] The Vanavasins were those who chose the radical path of salvation as prescribed in the doctrines of the Buddha, and who lived in the forest reserves, spending their time in meditation. The Gamavasins, on the other hand, were those who

19. Referring to the Mahavamsa which records the attempts of Parakramabahu II (A.D. 1236-70) to import monks from South India and thereby establish harmony amongst the two fraternities. (Ubhayasasanam), Dr. Gombrich infers that "though the Abhayagiri and the Jetavana Nikayas had formally been extinguished some monks still held to Mahayana doctrine. This, however, is the last occasion on which we hear of them." Gombrich, n. 10,pp. 13-18.

20. Dhammairsuddhi, n. 10, pp. 77.

21. Apart from the distinction indicated in dwelling areas, the division also referred to a parallel distinction between the vocation of books (Ganthadhuras) and vocation of meditation (Vipassanadhuras).

lived in monasteries in the towns and villages and were engaged in learning and preaching.

Though renowned for their piety, integrity and determination, the forest-dwelling Bhikkhus had no particular social significance except that they personified the ultimate ideals of Buddhism for the lay devotee. At the social level it was the village and town-dwelling Bhikkhus who, as teachers and preachers to the laity, acquired far greater significance. "Living in society, they became, though in a special sense, part of society."[22]

A major development of the Parakramabahu era (A.D. 1156-83) was that the vocational distinction between the Gamavasin and Ganavasin communities became blurred. Some of the forest-dwelling Bhikkhus came to live conjointly with the Gamavasins in the village settlements. One result of this mixing together was that the Gamavasins, under the influence of the Vanavasins, paid more attention to the patipati (meditation or practice) as well. On the other hand, there were many learned Bhikkhus amongst the forest dwellers who could compare with any of their counterparts among the village dwellers in their mastery of the scriptures.[23]

If such changes brought the Vanavasin monks closer to society, it also obliged the Gamavasins to come to terms with the standards of piety and asceticism of the Vanavasins. Further, the Vanavasins not only formed part of the religious hierarchy which had evolved during this period but often held a dominant position in it.

Details of this hierarchy were spelt out in the second Katikavata[24] or rescript drawn by a Board of Elders, under the aegis of Parakramabahu II (A.D. 1236-1270). Under this, at the apex of the monastic system was the hierarch or the supreme pontiff called Mahasami or Mahimi, at times, referred to as Sangharaja. It is noteworthy that in most instances the Vanavasin monks held this position.

In the administration of his duties, the Mahimi was assisted

22. Malalagoda, n. 10, p. 16.
23. Dhammavisuddhi, n. 19, pp. 69-70.
24. For details see Panabokke, n. 10, pp. 341-5 and 374.5; and Nandsena Ratnapala, *The Katikivatas : Laws of the Buddhist Order of Ceylon from the 12th Century to the 18th Century* (critically edited, translated and annotated), (Munchen, 1971).

by a central organisation called Karaka Sabha (Executive Committee)[25] which consisted of the senior monks who held the
chief positions in the various Ayatanas and important pari-
venas.[26] Next in order to the Mahimi in the Sangha hierarchy
were the two Mahatheras,[27] who were the chief representatives
of the gamavasin and vanavasin communities respectively.
Given the traditional meaning of the term Mahathera as one
who has completed twenty years after higher ordination, one
might infer that though there were many Bhikkhus of the
Mahathera rank, these two were *primus inter pares* by virtue
of the fact that they were elected for this position by the entire
Sangha of the island. The first two held an office by that name
whereas the others held it as an epithet or a rank in keeping
with the ecclesiastical terminology.[28]

Next in the order of hierarchy came the heads of the eight
Ayatanas. The confirmation of these posts also required the
assent of all the monks and the ruler.[29] Below the Ayatana
chiefs were the heads of Pirivenas. Initially meaning the 'cell
of a monk' the term denoted in due course monastic educational centres, often named after the founder member; some of
the Pirivenas had as their head one who was also the chief of
an Ayatana.

A major feature of this hierarchical organisation was the
"power the monarchy exerted over the Sangha. In most of
the key posts, State approval was deemed necessary, a fact
which shows the over-dependence of the Sangha on the State
and also the control the State had over ecclesiastical
matters."[30] While there is no definitive data on how the

25. For details on the functions of the various office bearers in this
    structure, see Chapter III.
26. Dhammavisuddhi, n. 10, pp. 82-85. Also see Panabokke, n. 10,
    pp. 395-6. Ayatanas and Pirivenas were monastic colleges and centres
    of learning.
27. A Bhikkhu had to fulfil five conditions to be eligible for the posi-
    tion of the Mahathera. These were: (i) high moral character, (ii)
    deep knowledge of Tripitaka together with the commentaries
    (iii) competence in guiding the monks on ecclesiastical affairs, (iv)
    completion of at least 20 years in the order after the higher ordina-
    tion, and (v) acceptability of his position as such, by the supreme
    pontiff. Panabokke, n. 10, p. 397.
28. Dhammavisuddhi, n. 10, p. 82.
29. Panabokke, n. 10, pp. 396-7.
30. Ibid., p. 400.

hierarchical structure operated, the influence of the State over
the Sangha, however, has been apparent.

SANGHA AND STATE IN PRE-COLONIAL SRI LANKA[31]

The State's influence over the Sangha was a logical corollary of certain theological assumptions and historical traditions. However, what needs to be underlined in this context
is that such an influence was not a one-way process. The
pattern of relationship between the Sangha and the State was
characterized by mutuality and interdependence. The Sinhalese
kings needed the support of the Sangha as much as the Sangha
needed the support of the kingship.

As the dominant status group in the religious system, the
Bhikkhus "set the standard of legitimacy for all the religious
ideas held by the Sinhalese",[32] and evoked deference from
other groups. The Bhikkhus had to their credit several pio-
neering efforts in various fields. The Sinhalese script, for instance, derived as it was from Pali, was mainly shaped by
them. It was they who taught people the art of writing and
emerged also as painters and sculptors. Sinhalese architecture
revolved mainly around stupas and monasteries which were
the abode of the Bhikkhus. Besides being the centres for worship and meditation, the viharas were also the centres of
cultural activities. As virtually every village had a vihara, the
socio-cultural traditions were in the main transmitted by the
Bhikkhus.[33] This involvement in social activities was further
strengthened by their multiple roles as teachers and advisers
to the masses as much as to the nobility.

On the other hand, as royal patrons, the kings of Sri Lanka
assumed various functions with regard to the Sangha, namely,
maintenance of religious institutions by repairing or building
the viharas, interesting themselves in the education of the

31. As regards the rest of this section, I have heavily drawn upon my
    article 'Buddhism and State in Ceylon Before the Advent of the
    Portuguese', *Asian Studies*, Vol. 8, No. 1, April 1970, pp. 120-36.
32. Michael M. Ames, 'Magical Animism and Buddhism : A Structu-
    ral Analysis of the Sinhalese Religious System', *Journal of Asian
    Studies*, Vol. 23, No. 3, May 1964, pp. 21-22.
33. For details refer to Nicholas and Paranavitana, n. 1, pp. 116-21.

monks and getting Pali manuscripts on Buddhism from abroad. Further, they sent delegations to bring Bhikkhus from other Buddhist countries to restore higher ordination in the island. Finally, religious regulations relating to the doctrine and ritual were enforced by them. For this purpose, heretical elements within the order were expelled and meetings of the Bhikkhus were convened to formulate the Katikavatas, with the king putting the weight of his authority behind these disciplinary injunctions by promulgating them and thereby giving a new lease of life to the monastic order.

However, in the context of an almost continuous political fragmentation of the island, it was natural that at times the royal patronage could also be instrumental in creating or perpetuating the divisions. In fact, the emergence of Jetavana and to some extent Abhayagiri itself was an indication of the manner in which some rulers did try to strengthen one sect as a counterpoise to others. As against this, as has been mentioned already, there were many others who, apart from making attempts to 'purify' the Sangha, also took the initiative in unifying the monastic order.

If the task of resuscitation, unification and purification of the Sangha was performed by the ruler as the defender and promoter of the faith, as the interpreters of the Buddhist precepts the Bhikkhus legitimised his position as such. The doctrine of Karma, for instance, besides legitimising the State structure of Sinhalese society, provided a rationale for the authority of the ruler over the ruled. Besides, under the Mahayanist influence, the Bodhisattva and the emperor were identified by thirty-two marks on their bodies and both were deemed to be striving for similar penultimate objectives, i.e., Buddhahood. Kingship as such was 'divinely sanctioned'[34] and in such sanctions the popular traditions played a significant role particularly because they were supported to a considerable extent by the religious professionals. Besides, at times, apart from influencing the succession of the rulers, some of the Bhikkhus also acted as mediators in royal disputes.

The importance ascribed to Buddhism and Bhikkhus in the political system was not the consequence of conscious or con-

---

34. Pieris, n. 1, p. 11.

certed effort by either party but a reflection of a value system
in which religious ideas held precedence over the others.
Offers of kingdoms by certain rulers to the Buddha Sasana
were symbolic gestures to indicate that the State was run for
Buddhism. The kings thus not only endowed monasteries with
lavish grants in the form of paddy lands, forests and gardens
but also maintained a well-appointed department to administer
religious activities. Such endowments, usually referred to as
Buddhist temporalities, were governed by rules and regulations laid down by the king with the "approval of the
Sangha".

Theoretically, all land belonged to the king who, in turn,
distributed some of it among his nobility and the Hindu
temples as well as viharas. Once land was donated to a monastery, the economic obligations, primarily the obligation to
work for the king (Rajakariya) were also transferred to the
viharas. A tenant working on the vihara land (viharagama)
performed Rajakariya to the vihara. In times of peace, the
administration of the viharagama was subject to the 'appro-
ximate authority' of the king. In times of trouble, however,
the Bhikkhus themselves took over the temporalities' administration. Thus, some of the Bhikkhus assumed the role of
monastic landlords, participating in the feudal system.[35]

The bigger the landholdings of a particular vihara was, the
more affluent and powerful did it become. Land endowments
thus brought in a feudal element in Sinhalese Buddhism and
created a new division in the Sangha based on the relative
affluence of the various viharas.

The endowments served a two-fold purpose for the kingship
system: political as well as religious. The Sangha was termed
as 'Punyakheta' (merit field) and endowments to it symbolised
the process of sowing seeds of merit and reaping a good har-
vest in the next life. Further, as according to the Vinaya it
was the duty of the Bhikkhus to "side with the king", the
kings found in the Bhikkhus a powerful means of propaganda;

---

35. For details refer to Newton Gunasinghe, 'Buddhism and Econo-
    mic Growth with Special Reference to Ceylon' (unpublished
    Master's Thesis, Department of Anthropology and Sociology,
    Monash University, 1972), Chapter II.

using their influence over the masses, the Bhikkhus lent "support to the king who, in return, looked after their interests. It was a matter of mutual understanding though it was never explicitly stated."[36]

If the civil wars affected this arrangement to some extent, foreign invasions gave it a much more severe jolt as was evident from the state of many viharas during the frequent invasions from South India in the Polonnaruwa period (the eleventh to the sixteenth century A.D.). A further blow to it occurred with the advent of the European powers who not only challenged the local political authority but also the indigenous religion when they imported Christianity to the island.

BUDDHISM, THE PORTUGUESE AND THE DUTCH POWERS IN SRI LANKA (1505-1798)

The advent of the Europeans beginning with the Portuguese in 1505 created new conditions for the monastic system. Under the Portuguese, Roman Catholicism became the established religion in the maritime areas, and under the Dutch who displaced the Portuguese in 1656, Protestantism was given the prime position over all other religions including Roman Catholicism.

Both the Portuguese and the Dutch rule was patterned largely on the model of the traditional kinds except in the fields of religion and law (in which the Dutch left a legacy in the form of Roman Dutch law in the island), and education. Thus, in the littoral region of Sri Lanka which was under the control of the Portuguese and later the Dutch, the earlier administrative boundaries as well as the old administrative system were retained. Further, the traditional military system, based on the obligation of every citizen to fight for the king as and when required, was exploited by the new rulers to establish a local militia. Finally, the feudal economic system was kept virtually intact by the Portuguese and the Dutch as it was beneficial to them. They appropriated the royal villages for the treasury, collected customary dues from the villagers and distributed the temple lands and villages to their

36. Rahula, n. 10, pp. 75-76.

own soldiers and to the native Christians who were loyal to
them.

The retention of the traditional administrative-economic
system by the Portuguese and the Dutch facilitated their trade
policies. Absence of change in these fields ensured stability of
services necessary for the export of commercial commodities
such as cinnamon. However, both sets of rulers were committed not only to trade but also to the promotion of their
respective religions, and the activities of the priests and missionaries under their auspices had significant effects on the
Ceylonese social structure.

In their zeal to further the *Conquista Spiritual,* the Portuguese adopted remunerative as well as retributive measures.
Temptations of worldly gains were offered to the 'heathens'
first. The Sinhalese notables, for instance, were promised the
retention of their lands and privileges provided they embraced
Catholicism. In cases where such inducements were ineffective,
the use of terror and severe reprisals followed. The uncon-
verted 'heathens' were denied civil rights and were ineligible
for any office. Some of the more incorrigible were also dealt
with by the sword. Religious proselytism also brought in its
wake demolition of temples and monasteries accompanied by
plunder and arson.[37] In some cases the old centres of
Buddhist worship and preaching were converted into Catholic
churches almost overnight. Finally, lands ceded to the monasteries were confiscated and given to Christian orders as well as
to individuals loyal to the new conquerors.

Besides, convinced that education was the most effective
tool for religious proselytism, the Portuguese found ways and
means to spread it at all levels. However, unlike the Dutch,
the Portuguese did not make education a State subject but
delegated responsibility for it to the Church and extended
support through grants and endowments for the maintenance
of schools. The curriculum in these schools had a strong religious bias and education was imparted by the missionaries
themselves.[38] Thus, for the first time in the history of the

---

37. P.E. Pieris, *Ceylon and Portuguese* (Tellipallai, 1930), pp. 78-80; and
    T. Vimalananda, *Buddhism in Ceylon under the Christian Powers*
    (Colombo, 1963), pp. xx-xxx.
38. T. Ranjit Ruberu, *Education in Colonial Ceylon* (Colombo, 1963),
    pp. 18-29.

island, Buddhism had not only to give ground to a rival religion in the coastal region, but what is more, lost its monopoly over teaching which it had enjoyed for several centuries.

Though the Dutch adopted many policies similar to those
of their predecessors, their impact appears to have been much
less in effect. This seems to be due to the fact that the Dutch,
unlike the Portuguese, had trade as the main element in their
colonial policy. Consequently, trade considerations determined
the extent to which the Dutch religious legislation could be
implemented. Political expediency for economic benefits, for
instance, often imposed limits on the exercise of the coercive
authority of the Dutch in the religious sphere. The Dutch
Company was not prepared to antagonise the vihara chiefs
even within its own territory lest civil disturbances start and
the Sinhalese Buddhist king of Kandy take advantage of the
disorder. Further, despite their uneasy relationship with the
kings of Kandy (who, in spite of several incursions into their
territory by the western powers, retained their sovereignty in
the heartland of the island till 1815), they provided facilities
like ships to these kings from time to time to fetch Bhikkhus
from other countries to re-establish higher ordination.

As regards the impact of Catholicism and Protestantism on
the people in comparative terms, it seems that the former was
greater than the latter. Apart from the greater identification of
Church with State in Portuguese policies, the enthusiasm and
fanatical zeal of the Portuguese missionaries in contrast to the
tolerant spirit of the majority of the Dutch clergy was a significant factor in taking Catholicism to far-off villages. Besides,
the fact that the Dutch were unable to supplant Portuguese as
the language of preaching was another significant point to be
reckoned with. Further, notwithstanding the suppression of
Catholicism by the Dutch, the inflow of Catholic missionaries
from Goa provided it with a sort of continuity. Being Indians,
these missionaries could move about in the island undetected.
Many of them even adopted the Ceylonese way of life, though
with reservations, and were proficient in Sinhalese and Tamil.[39]

39. Edmund Pieris, 'Sinhalese Christian Literature of the 17th and
    18 th centuries', *Journal of Royal Asiatic Society* (Ceylon Branch),
    Vol. 35, No. 96, 1943, pp. 163-81 and 'Tamil Catholic Culture in
    Ceylon', *Tamil Culture*, Vol.2, Nos. 3 and 4, September 1953, pp.
    229-44.

Finally, Arasaratnam makes a pertinent point in maintaining
that 'the appeal of Catholicism lay in its close affinity in its
external observances and those of the religions it tried to
replace. Dutch Protestantism, with its lack of symbols in worship and its insistence on the Bible as the sole guide in religion
offered no attraction to the Catholic and much less to the
Buddhists and Hindus.'[40] Thus, despite the swelling of the
number of the converts or reconverts during the Dutch occupation, it was evident that in many cases the "religion of the
converts was described as sitting lightly on them."[41]

The comments of the Council of Priests at Galle in the
southern province are revealing in this context. Writing in
1760, the council of priests stated that most of the converts
were Christians to a limited extent. Every action in the lives
of even those professing Christianity was regulated by the
precepts and practices of Buddhism. "When a child is born,
they will consult the astrologers; when it is sick, they hang the
charms rounds its neck; and even after Baptism they disconti-
nue the use of its Christian name and a heathen name is given
to it as usual on the first occasion of its eating rice. They
will undertake no work without ascertaining a lucky day for
commencing. When they marry, it must be in the propitious
hour; and when they die, their graves are decorated with
leaves sacred to Buddha....The highest benediction they can
pronounce on their friends is, 'May you become Buddha.'[42]
The masses in general tended to regard the new forms of
beliefs and rituals as introduced by the missionaries as 'useful
supplements rather than as new substitutes', a tendency which
Nock has called *adhesion* in contradistinction to *conversion*".[43]

The conversion thus was a 'social mask' which was put on
because it paid dividends. This was particularly so in the case
of those Sinhalese notables who were ambitious politically and

---

40. Sinnapah Arasaratnam, *Dutch Power in Ceylon*, 1958-1687 (Amster-
    dam, 1958), p. 228.
41. Pieris, n. 1, p. 91.
42. Vimalananda, n. 37 pp. lxii-lxiii.
43. Nock defined conversion as a "turning point which implies a con-
    sciousness that a great change is involved, that the old was wrong
    and the new is right." A.D. Nock, *Conversion* (Oxford, 1965). p. 7
    in Malalagoda, n. 10, p. 36.

whose allegiance was sought for by the Portuguese and the
Dutch powers in order to secure mass acquiescence.

The Sangha in the Kandyan Kingdom

In traditional Sri Lanka, apart from the notables, the
Bhikkhus had also provided an important support base to
political authority. In the Portuguese and the Dutch-occupied
Ceylon littoral, while the allegiance of a segment of the nobility was sought and partially procured, the Bhikkhus were not
only ignored but had to withstand the hostile measures of the
non-Buddhist political authority. The political adversity and
its confrontation with the new religion affected the monastic
order in the maritime areas and the Bhikkhus began to take
refuge in the Kandyan kingdom. The kingdom thus became
virtually the successor to the previous Sinhalese kingdoms
ensuring a certain sense of continuity particularly in the field
of the Buddhist institutions, as its royal patron.

In this context, Kandyan rulers like Vimala Dharmasuriya I
(A.D. 1591-1604) and Vimala Dharmasuriya II (A.D. 1687-1707)
made special efforts to revive the Sasana by sending embassies
abroad to restore Upasampada, by promulgating rescripts
(Katikavatas), by making efforts to establish harmonious rela-
tionships between the various fraternities and at times by
purging the Sangha of undesirable elements. But in the context of the prevailing political instability due to the frequent
incursions from the Portuguese and the Dutch-occupied areas,
these attempts did not have any lasting effect. This is evident
from the fact that even when the kings sent embassies to the
Theravada countries[44] to restore higher ordination, it could
not be perpetuated for long as many fully ordained Bhikkhus
disrobed after some time. Some of them reverted to their
samanera status primarily for the purpose of looking after their
properties. The few who continued in the order did ordain
some of the laymen as their pupils but no ordination ceremony
was held. With the demise of these monks it again became

---

44. D.B. Jayatillaka, 'Sinhalese Embassies to Arakan', *Journal of
   Royal Asiatic Society* (Ceylon Branch), Vol. 35, No. 93, 1940 pp.
   1-6.

impossible for the novices (samaneras) to receive higher ordination or for a novice to join the order as a fully ordained
monk. And those who did join the order, did so without the
requisite prescribed rites.

Such developments gave rise to a new category of monks who
stood half way between the Bhikkhus and the laity. Termed
Ganinnanses, they retained their lay names and wore white,
not the saffron robes as was customary. Engaged most of
the time in secular activities, many of them were not even
celibates. In fact, most of the Buddhist clergy, in the late
sixteenth to the mid eighteenth century, belonged to this
category.[45]

Buddhist Revivalism in the Eighteenth Century

At the beginning of the eighteenth century, however, a
revivalist movement began to take shape within the monastic
order, largely due to the initiative of one single Bhikkhu—
Valivita Saranankara. Born in 1698, Saranankara succeeded in
initiating and leading a group of monks who came to be
known as Silvant Samagama (Fraternity of the Pious). These
monks laid great emphasis on piety and learning of the
scriptures. In recruiting new monks, familial considerations
were disregarded and great care was taken to ensure the
integrity and devotion of the candidate. As a reaction to the
then prevalent practice of holding property (which was contrary
to the Vinaya) the Samagama maintained the ancient Buddhist
ideal of poverty. Under the patronage of Narendra Sinha—
the last Sinhalese king of Kandy—the Samagama started a
monastic college which soon made its mark as one of the main
centres of learning.

Saranankara's repeated efforts to persuade the Kandyan
rulers to send a mission to Siam to bring fully ordained
Bhikkhus to re-establish Upasampada in the island were
successful when a party of 25 Siamese Bhikkhus led by Upali
Thera reached Kandy in 1753 and was warmly received
by the king. Upali Thera and his associates were provided
with a residence in Malwatta vihara (or Poyamalu—the main

45. For details on the Ganinnanses refer to Wachissara, n.10. pp. 120-47.

centre of the Gamavasins) and here they performed the first Upasampada ceremony in which the chief high priests of Malwatta and Asgiri viharas were the first two to be ordained. This was followed by another ordination at Asgiri vihara which was then the premier centre of the vanavasins. Soon after, the Siamese Bhikkhus toured the country and established Simas in other parts of the island as well. Thereafter there was a steady increase in the number of duly ordained monks who were well-instructed in the Buddhist scriptures as well as in the customs and ritual related to monastic life.[46]

In due course a formal and central organization of the Siam Nikaya came into being. Under this, at the apex was the Sangharaja (a title conferred on Saranankara by the king but discontinued after his death). Below him were the two monasteries of Asgiri and Malwatta (where the sima was consecrated first) with the others falling under the jurisdiction of either one or the other. At the head of these two monasteries was a Maha Nayaka (supreme chief monk) each, to be assisted by two Anu Nayakas (Deputy supreme chief monks) and a committee of Nayakas (chief monks) selected from the important monasteries within each chapter. The committee, called Karaka Sabha, exercised general supervision over the Bhikkus and looked into ecclesiastical disputes. Impious monks found guilty of criminal offences were disrobed formally by the Anu Nayakas before they were handed over to the secular authorities.[47]

More important than the power of expulsion were the exclusive powers of the Malwatta and Asgiri viharas with regard to the admission of the novices to higher ordination. According to the Vinaya regulations, the Upasampada ceremony could be performed within a sima anywhere by a chapter of Bhikkhus. However, by a royal decree of 1765, the Upasampada ceremony could be performed only at Malwatta and Asgiri viharas and Bhikkhus from other viharas all over the island were instructed to bring their novices to Kandy to be examined for higher ordination. "This indicated",

---

46. For a brief biography of Saranakara, see ibid., pp. 269-452; and Malalagoda, n. 10, pp. 81-94.
47. Ibid., pp. 94-96.

concludes Malalagoda, "further—and very vital—step in the
process of centralising the affairs of the Sasana and in the
growth of a strong and religious establishment." The decree
also implied that the religious establishment derived its
legitimacy not from the Vinaya regulations but from the secular political authority.

In his analysis of the nature of the Kandyan establishment,
a Ceylonese author discerns certain 'conspicuous' parallelisms
between the political and religious establishment. All political
authority emanated in theory from a specific centre; and so
apparently did all ecclesiastical authority. In the sphere of
politics, the king appointed the major chiefs and they appointed the lesser ones. In the realm of religious structure too,
the king appointed the chief monks and the latter in turn
appointed the incumbents of small temples. In both cases
the appointments were purely arbitrary as they were
to be guided by customary rules and regulations. Important
monasteries were endowed with land grants in much the
same manner as important chiefs were. The donations in
both cases were made by the king out of his own lands and
he thus exchanged his economic assets for non-economic
benefits of one sort or the other. The chiefs to whom land
was granted became recipients of the dues and services earlier
rendered to the crown by the tenants on them. The dues and
services were similarly transferred to the monasteries in the
case of temple lands. The Bhikkhus received the services
and dues attached to the lands as well as the obedience
and respect of the tenants not solely out of politico-legal
requirements. But what made their authority ultimately
effective was the coercive power of the monarch as their royal
patron.[48]

Some of the rulers exercised this authority in many
ways. Thus, when disputes regarding the incumbency of any
vihara arose, the king emerged as the final arbiter. Also, when
a monastery was newly built or an abandoned one was
restored and re-endowed, the king appointed an incumbent
at his discretion.[49]

48. Ibid., pp. 100-101.
49. Lorna Srimathi Dewaraja, *The Internal Politics of the Kandyan
    Kingdom*, 1707-1760 (Colombo, 1972), p. 130.

The overriding power of the political authority over the Sangha was also apparent in a decree promulgated by Kirti Siri Rajasinha soon after the founding of the Siam Nikaya under which no person outside the high caste (i.e., Goyigama caste) could be admitted to the monastic order. Such a fiat went against the traditions of Saranankara's Silvat Samagama which had had, amongst its prominent members, Bhikkhus belonging to the Goyigama as well as non-Goyigama castes. And yet, the Sangharaja agreed to the royal injunction abandoning the non-Goyigama members of the Samagama high and dry.[50]

It is necessary to note that such caste exclusiveness was not an innovation of this period. In fact even in the times of Vijayabahu II of Dambedeniya (A.D. 1232-1236), entrants to the monastic order had to be examined on their jati and gotra, i.e., caste. This injunction was specifically inscribed in the Dambadeni Katikavat which was promulgated by his successor Parakramabahu II (A.D. 1236-1270). The wide-spread observance of this clause had become evident during the Kandyan period (which could broadly be described as the period beginning with the reign of Vijayadharma Suriya I in 1592 and concluding with the end of the Kandyan monarchy in 1815). However, its legitimation by a royal writ and acquiescence in it by the Siam Nikaya leadership was most significant.

50. This caste exclusivity in regard to higher ordination of the monks was due to a royal writ issued by Kirti Siri Raja sinha. One popular explanation ascribed to this is that once some Bhikkhus, seeing the King, bowed to him. The king was shocked, for, it had been customary on the part of the kings to pay obeisance to the Sangha and not the other way round. On enquiry, the king discovered that these Bhikkhus came from the traditionally depressed castes. As such, it was stipulated that the low-caste-born were incapable of maintaining the decorum and dignity of monkhood. Consequently, the king convened an assembly of the Sangha including Sangha Raja and ordered that henceforth no person outside the Goyigama caste was to be admitted to the order. Thirty-two Bhikkhus belonging to the lower castes were banished to the Jaffna peninsula and monks of inferior castes were even prohibited from performing higher ordination. Wachissara, n. 10, p. 448. Also see Ratnapala, n. 24, pp. 199-259.

Since such caste exclusiveness was against the Vinaya,[51] a justification for protest movements was inherent in the situation. The success of such a movement necessitated (a) an adequate number of Bhikkhus willing to intiate low-caste individuals as novices; (b) an eagerness on the part of the low-caste ones to enter monastic life, and (c) non-regal patronage to enable these monks to go abroad, if necessary, for higher ordination and to sustain them thereafter. Such patronage was provided by the elites of the three emerging castes—the Karavas, the Duravas and the Salagamas whose socio-economic status was strengthened in the low country during the Portuguese and the Dutch occupation and who were in a position to challenge the Goyigama monopolies in several fields including religion.[52]

The immediate provocation for founding a dominantly non-Goyigama fraternity was the refusal of the Kandy authorities to grant Upasampada to those of non-Goyigama social origin. Consequently, during 1799-1818, five groups of Bhikkhus belonging to Karava, Durava and Salagama castes went to Burma and founded the Amarapura Nikaya.

Though the Amarapura Nikaya drew its members mainly from the Salagama, Karava and Durava castes, it was in no way limited to them. It had within its fold Bhikkhus belonging to castes below the ranks of these three in the castes hierarchy and also had some Goyigama monks who had originally belonged to the Siam fraternity and who had later transferred their allegiance to the Amampura Nikaya. Malalagoda maintains:

The Amarapura fraternity from its very beginning was not destined to have an ecclesiastical organisation even remotely resembling that of the Siyam fraternity. Whereas the Siyam fraternity was established...with the help of one

---

51. Buddha had preached against the prevailing Indian caste system as follows : "By birth one does not become an outcaste; By birth one does not become a Brahmin. By deed one becomes an outcaste and a Brahmin so". Dines Anderson and Helmer Smith, eds., *Sutta Vipata* p. 24, Vasala Sutta, verse 142 in Dewaraja n. 49, p. 121, footnote 14.

52. Malalagoda, n. 10, pp. 123-38.

group of Siamese monks...the Amarapura fraternity had its origins in five different groups of Ceylonese monks who went to Burma and returned with higher ordination at different times during the first two decades of the nineteenth century. Thus, even at the time of its enthusiastic beginning, the Amarapura fraternity had more the character of a loose federation of fraternities than that of a unified and monolithic fraternity to which the Siyam fraternity already approximated at the time of its establishment. In fact, although all the five groups of Ceylonese monks who returned from Burma came to be looked upon as belonging to one Amarapura fraternity not all of them had their higher ordination at the city of Amarapura in Burma. Even their Burmese preceptors did not belong to one clear and immediate line of pupillary succession.[53]

Though these groups had considerable interaction, they continued to retain their separate identities. They had different Simas for the performance of the higher ordination. "This helped them to maintain, and perpetuate different lines of pupillary succession. And the pupils of the founders (and, later on, of their successors) were almost invariably recruited within the rank of their own castes."[54]

Over the years, further 'segmentation' of the Amarapura Nikaya led to new sub-divisions, these being related either to caste differences or to personality clashes or to certain scriptural points such as delineation and legitimation of a Sima. The division of the Salagama Bhikkhus into Mulavamsa and Saddhamma vamsa sects, for instance, was the result of a

53. Ibid., pp. 217-18.
54. Ibid., pp. 218-19. Malalagoda further footnotes: "Even the practice of ordaining a close kinsman as one's chief pupil—a practice which was common in the Siyam fraternity especially in the Kandyan provinces—was not entirely uncommon in the Amarapura fraternity." For instance, the Chief pupil of Ambagahapitiye Nanavimala, Beratudave Dhammadhara, was his nephew; and the chief pupil of Beratudave, Ambagahapitiye Vimalasara, was in turn his nephew (and therefore Ambagahapitiye Nanavimala's grand-nephew).

difference of opinion on the validity of a Sima.[55]

The segmentation of the Amarapura Nikaya and the involvement of the Amarapura monks in such controversies disillusioned some of the Bhikkhus who had transferred their allegiance from the Siam Nikaya to the Amarapura Nikaya but who had found it equally strife-ridden. Their disenchantment with both prompted them to found a new fraternity which could aspire to the lofty ideals of Buddhism. The founder member of this fraternity, Ambagahawatte, had his higher ordination renewed at Ramanna province in Burma in 1862. As a result this fraternity was called the Ramanna Nikaya.[56]

55. Salagama monks of the coastal regions belonged to two major pupillary lines of succession of Ambagahapitiye Nanavimala who returned from Burma in 1803, and Kapugama Dhammakhanda who returned in 1809. Both had their different Simas at Balapitiya and at Gintota respectively for higher ordination. After a while both decided to have one *sima* at Balapitiya. For the purpose they decided to enlarge it. The basic structure of this Sima consisted of several pillars in the middle of a river over which a temporary hall was built. At this time when the Sima was enlarged in 1845, a bridge was built to approach it from the river bank. This bridge did not actually connect the bank to the building in the middle of the river; it stopped a few feet outside, as otherwise it would have intruded into a sacred area. From the bridge the monks approached the building over a plank which was taken away after the commencement of ecclesiastical acts.

One of the leading Bhikkhus of the Amarapura Nikaya, Lankagoda, Dhirananda, however, contended that though the bridge itself was not connected to the building, a part of it did intrude into the sacred area (demarcated by the water) thus rendering the boundary Samkara confused and therefore invalid. As such he refused to accept its legitimacy for ecclesiastical purposes. Such differences of opinion ultimately led to division. Ibid., pp. 230-46.

56. Writing the history of Ramanna Nikaya, Rev. Matale Sasanatilake maintains that the founding of the Ramanna Nikaya in 1864 could be regarded as the 'second beginning' of the order. During the reign of Vijaya Bahu, the first king of Polonnaruva, Bhikkhus from Ramanna had been invited to re-establish the Upasampada in Sri Lanka. Matale Sasanatilake, *Ramanna Vamsa* (Colombo, n.d.) pp. 1-5.

However, except for the continuity in terms of the place of origin, one does not discover any other linkage in the monastic order established by the monks from Ramanna in Sri Lanka in the beginnings of the Polannaruva period and subsequently in 1864.

Though the smallest amongst the three fraternities, the strength of the Ramanna Nikaya was not "in its numbers but in its radical spirit". As a small fraternity it was more manageable and more readily amenable to a close supervision by its leaders than its predecessors. Further, the 'reformism' of the Ramanna fraternity could be sustained for a longer period than that of the Amarapura Nikaya partly because alongside its religious idealism, it was not too seriously affected by caste issues. At the time the Ramanna fraternity had been founded, the major castes had already found representation in the various divisions of the Amarapura, and the new fraternity could therefore provide a focus for the "more religiously motivated—of whatever caste background".[57]

As parallel monastic orders of the non-Goyigama castes, the Amarapura and Ramanna Nikayas, were symbolic of the assertion on the part of the low-country Bhikkhus of their identity towards the Kandyan or the up-country Bhikkhus. Such a division of the clergy was rooted in socio-political situations. Thus, while the Siam Nikaya owed its founding to the king of Kandy, the establishment of the Amarapura Nikaya was the manifestation of protest against a royal writ, questioning for the first time "the right of secular authorities to regulate the affairs of the order". As a logical corollary to this, unlike the temples of the Siam Nikaya which enjoyed extensive royal endowments, the Amarapura Nikaya drew its sustenance from the rich non-Goyigama laity of the coastal areas who, during the colonial period, had acquired more power, affluence and status than they had formerly been given in the social hierarchy and were keen to register this change in the religious field. However, in terms of lay support, the Amarapura and Ramanna fraternities had neither the large membership of the Siam Nikaya nor its affluence. The lack of means turned out to be a blessing. The up-country Bhikkhus, having their temporal necessities served through royal

---

57. Malalagoda, n. 10, pp. 256-7. Subsequently, however, it seems that caste division affected this Nikaya too. At present, broadly speaking, there are two caste-bound major sections of this Nikaya, one belonging to Goyigama and another belonging to a lower caste called 'Padu'. (Based on interviews with some Bhikkhus).

endowments, did not have as much direct contact with the laity as the Bhikkhus of the new Nikayas. This led to not only greater involvement of the latter in 'parish' obligations, i.e., preaching, officiation at death ceremonies and so on, but also necessitated a sustained effort on their part to make themselves worthy of the patronage of their supporters.[58]

On the other hand, the Bhikkhus in the Kandyan highlands, partly because of their relative insulation from the coastal areas which became the hub of activities during the western colonial era, and because of the fear that any change in the *status quo* posed a threat to their vested interests, remained largely conservative and traditional. Against this, the Siam Nikaya monks in the coastal areas as well as the Amarapura and the Ramanna Nikaya Bhikkhus, exposed as they were closely and directly than the Kandyan Bhikkhus to the religious and educational thrusts of the missionaries as well as to the socio-economic changes, could survive only by reacting to these developments. It is not surprising that in the religious controversies with the missionaries during the British period the coastal monks were in the forefront.

A discussion of these religious controversies, signifying the beginnings of the Buddhist revivalism in the nineteenth century, however, needs to have as its setting a brief review of the British policy towards Buddhism during this period.

BRITISH POLICY TOWARDS BUDDHISM (1796-1948)

As is well known, the beginnings of the British rule in Sri Lanka in 1795 is traceable to Anglo-French rivalry in Europe. Soon after the end of the revolution, Republican France, then at war with Britain, took over Holland and with it, control over Ceylon littoral, then under the Dutch. As the British Government did not want the strategic port of Trincomalee in eastern Ceylon (formerly part of Dutch-occupied Sri Lanka) to fall into the hands of an unfriendly power, the East India Company moved its forces to Sri Lanka and by 1796 had taken over the Ceylon littoral, till then under the Dutch.

---

58. Ibid., pp. 144-52.

In 1815, the internal dissension among the Sinhalese chiefs as well as clergy and the King of Kandy helped the take-over of the kingdom of Kandy by the British. Soon after, the Kandyan aristocracy signed a convention with the British, agreeing to the accession of the kingdom to the British Government. In return, according to article 5 of the convention, Buddhism was declared "inviolable and its Rites, Ministers and Place of worship"[59] were to be maintained and protected by the successor government.

During the early decades of its rule (A.D. 1815-1839) the British Government, though with 'obvious lack of enthusiasm', sought to play the same role in relation to Buddhism which the Kandyan kings had played. At moments of crises or when a radical social change was envisaged, the government always made it clear that such measures did not affect the monastic institutions.[60] Thus, in spite of the radical nature of socio-economic reforms which followed the Colebrook-Cameroon Commission Report of 1832[61], certain privileges of the Buddhist viharas were maintained. The temple lands, for instance, were exempted from the operation of the ordinance that abolished Rajakariya or compulsory labour in the island. Tenants of temple lands were to continue the traditional service to the vihara for the land they held.

Further, as in the past, the government continued to give a monthly allowance for the support of Bhikkhus and also a substantial grant for the performance of various traditional Buddhist festivals (for example, the Kandy Perahera); the custodianship of the Temple of the Tooth in Kandy was assumed by the British administration and last but not least, warrants of appointment to the incumbents of important

59. For details of the cession of the kingdom to the British see Colvin R. de Silva, *Ceylon under the British Occupation* 1795-1833 (Colombo, 1953), Vol. 2, impression 3.
60. For an excellent exposition of the British policy towards Buddhism see K.M. de Silva, *Social Policy and Missionary Organisation in Ceylon* 1840-1855 (London, 1965). For the text of the convention see ibid., p. 64.
61. For a detailed exposition of these recommendations and their impact on the social structure of Sri Lanka refer to G.C. Mendis, *The Colebrook Cameron Papers* (Colombo, 1956), Vol. 2.

positions in the various viharas as well as to their lay administrators continued to be issued by the government.

During 1838-1853, however, the propriety of a Christian government being the patron of the 'heathen religion' was questioned by Christian missionaries and by Sir James Stephen (the Under-Secretary of State in the Colonial Office during 1840-1847). This led to a virtual reversal of the earlier policy of the British towards Buddhism.

The basic issue before the policy makers in Colombo as well as in London was whether a suitable body or central organisation could be brought into being to take over the functions exercised so far by the Crown in this respect. Amongst the proposals considered were: (*a*) the 1846 ordinance of Earl Grey (Secretary of State) providing, for a council of monks and chiefs to which the powers of the government in relation to Buddhism were to be transferred; and (*b*) Governor Campbell's ordinance of 1846 providing for the appointment of a committee of sixteen persons (six of whom were to be Bhikkhus), to which the custodianship of the Tooth relic as well as all the "ecclesiastical authority vested in the Government by the Kandyan Convention was to be transferred".[62]

The opponents of the idea of such a Council or a committee like Frederick Rogers (Assistant Secretary of State), argued that this would give the Buddhist religion a "most dangerous force and unity and to the Sangha a dangerous organisation". Extremists like Stephen, objected to the principle of delegating authority held so far by the Crown to a central organisation and maintained that it implied continuance of some sort of a link between Buddhism and the State and was, therefore, not warranted. Under the circumstances, it was suggested, the Buddhists ought to be left on their own to make any kind of arrangement amongst themselves, and all that was necessary for the government to do would be to enact "a Law to recognise, or perhaps, to establish this right."[63]

The protagonists of the proposals did not seem to realise that they were trying to give overnight a central organisation

62. Silva, n. 60, pp. 86-93 and 108.
63. Ibid., p. 66.

to Buddhism which the Sinhalese rulers had failed to evolve over the centuries and had preferred to leave it to tradition. Thus, the Buddhist viharas, though having varying ranges of power, depending on their respective status and affluence, were fairly independent of each other. It was the king at the apex of this loose structure who had compensated to some extent for what the religious hierarchical structure did not have, i.e., a coercive authority.

The extent to which the traditional religious and bureaucratic elites valued the connection of Buddhism with the political authority was evident from the record of a conference convened by Governor Torrington in 1847 to discuss the issue. In this conference, the Bhikkhus took the position that "the Queen is the head of our religion, and that we wish it to be; that is what you promised and what you are bound to do."[64]

Explanaing the reasons for this insistence, Sir James Emerson Tennent (Colonial Secretary 1845-50) rightly maintained that it was not "*protection* which they look to us for...it is not our *management* they want....But what they really want under the semblance of interference and appearance of control is really our identification with their religion and the prestige of the Government's name as associated with their appointments and patronage".[65]

That the British Government was not in a mood to oblige the Buddhist clergy on this point was obvious from the process toward 'disestablishment' of Buddhism which was initiated with the official transfer of the tooth relic to a committee of Sinhalese notables and Bhikkhus and the approval of a grant to the committee for the management of religious rites. The Pakington-Anderson[66] despatch of 1852 on Buddhism, apart from continuing these arrangements, also spelt out the steps to be taken regarding the appointment of monks as the incumbent of the vihara and the administration of temporalities.

64. Ibid., p. 65.
65. Ibid., p. 104.
66. Sir George Anderson was the Governor of Ceylon during 1850-55. Pakington was Secretary of State during this period.

The despatch brought an end to the possibility of a central organisation for the Buddhists by stipulating that each temple was to be treated and administered as a separate unit. While retaining the individualistic tradition of Ceylonese Buddhism, the declaration thus deprived the constraints of a coercive and corrective authority in ecclesiastical affairs. The secular rights vested in the Sangha and exercised by the temple incumbent were to be protected by the government as a purely 'temporal function of sovereignty itself'. Thus, though divesting itself of the obligation to revive and unify the Buddhist Sangha, the government continued to exercise its legal authority over the secular affairs of the Sangha.

As regards the Sacred Tooth relic, it was handed over to the committee which had held it earlier but with a warning that the committee would be held responsible for all the property of the temple and that government reserved to itself the right acquiring back the possession of the temple if the relic was used for any purpose other than religious. Clearly then, the British government reserved the right to be the final authority of the 'national palladium'. Similarly, unlike the earlier practice of using warrants of appointment, the government issued, after the election of the incumbent of the temple, a certificate of a purely declaratory form, recognising the validity of his election and thereby giving him a legal status to discharge the responsibility of maintaining and administering the temple properties.[67] In a dispute for an incumbency, however, the British court had the final authority.

The Pakington-Anderson despatch which provided the guidelines for the British policy towards Buddhism in broad essentials for almost a century neither provided for a complete severance of the State's connection with Buddhism nor preserved the spirit of the Kandyan convention.[68] In any event,

67. Silva, n. 60, pp. 125-9.
68. The state of mind of the Buddhist clergy was ably summed up by some of the senior monks in a petition submitted to King Edward VII in 1904 in which they maintained that "the official connection of the British Government should either cease absolutely, not only in name but in reality as well, and the Buddhist religion should be left perfectly unfettered to work out its own salvation, or its temporal affairs should be placed in the hands of officers like the Government Agents. The present state of

Britain itself was going through an era of reforms in its own political system. The controversy among colonial administrators can be partially ascribed to differences at home over the broader issue of the role of the State in religious affairs. This explains why the colonial administrators did not resist in their efforts to reform the Sangha. Such a dichotomous nature of the British policy was also reflected in its approach towards the administrative procedures for the Buddhist temporalities.

British Policy Towards the Temporalities Administration

In accordance with article 5 of the Kandyan convention, the British undertaking to maintain and preserve the Buddhist 'Rites, Ministers and Places of Worships' was also extended to the landed property of the Buddhist temples. In 1918, Governor Brownrigg declared that the revenues appropriated in support of various 'Religious Establishments' were not to be diverted from the purpose to which the former government had allotted them. In another proclamation of the same year, it was declared that temporalities would be exempted from taxation (as was the traditional practice). A proclamation of 1819, however, prohibited any new donations (except the Crown grants) to the temples without licence from the Governor himself. Finally, as mentioned already, notwithstanding the abolition of Rajakariya in 1832, temporalities continued to enjoy traditional compulsory services from the tenants.

Since the immunities enjoyed by the temporalities were part of the privileges granted under the Kandyan convention, they came under attack once the question of the State's association with indigeneous religions was raised. Antagonists of the entrenched position of temple lands found in the 1840s indirect but substantial support from the colonial officials in their movement due to an emergent economic factor. With the dramatic success of the coffee

affairs is best calculated to slowly undermine and ruin Buddhism than to foster its growth." This memorial was signed by the senior monks of some of the most important chapters like Malwatta and Asgiri, Ceylon, *Ceylon Correspondence Relating to the Buddhist Temporalities Ordinance IV of* 1907 (Colombo, 1907), p. 8.

plantations in the hilly Kandyan areas, the bulk of the temporalities, consisting of virgin forests and hence of little economic value earlier, became properties of great commerical value almost overnight. Since many of the civil servants were themselves coffee planters they were "more than ordinarily alive to the need to make land available for plantation agriculture."[69]

Thanks to the religious and economic considerations, the process of registration of temple lands which was going on at a snail's pace since 1819 gathered momentum in the 1850s. In 1856, an ordinance was promulgated to provide for the settlement of claims of exemption from taxation of temple lands and for due registration of all lands belonging to such temples.

The temple land commissioners completed operations on the ordinance in 1865. In this process several cases where the incumbents "failed to register their claims in time the land was confiscated".[70] This ordinance adversely affected the temple lands. Out of 12,778 Amunams (one Amunam equal to about five bushels) of field, the Commission rejected the temple's claims in 8,553. In the Highlands (including gardens, chenas and forests) while 27,979 Amunams were registered,

69. K.M. de Silva, 'The Development of British Policy on Temple Lands in Ceylon, 1840-55', *Journal of the Ceylon Branch of the Royal Asiatic Society*, New Series, Vol. 8, part 2, pp. 314-17. In 1940, the Colonial Secretary of the Ceylon Government, Philip Anstruther, in a confidential memorandum stated: "Vast quantities of waste lands are possessed by temples... These lands are of extremely little value to their possessors but are well suited to the cultivation of coffee and sugar, and indeed nearly the whole of one of the finest provinces, Saffragam, is thus locked up and rendered useless: if they could be alienated they could be speedily sold to the great advantage of the public and in my opinion the power so conferred upon the Governor to authorise the alienation of Temple Lands does not exceed the powers exercised by the Kings of Kandy and therefore can be considered no invasion of the rights of the temples, or departure from the intention of the donors." Ansthruther, it might be mentioned, was also Governor Mackenzie's son-in-law and had an economic stake in plantation agriculture.

70. Buddhist Committee of Enquiry, *The Betrayal of Buddhism* (Balangoda, 1956), pp. 6-7

40,316 Amunams were rejected.[71] In other words, in the case of forest lands the confiscated land was proportionately much more.

Besides land registration, Ordinance No. 6 of 1840 according to which a vihara tenant could commute his services for money, also affected the vihara administration adversely. At times, the rate of commutations fixed was very low. Further, there were instances when tenants "sold rights and left, mortgaged and leased their holdings to outsiders who very often demurred either to pay the rents or to perform the services." Such practices, as and when they occurred, did upset a settled order and its chain of obligations.[72]

It is also noteworthy that while the Temple Lands Registration Ordinance had given temples and viharas an absolute right to property which did not exist before, it did not provide for any checks on the misappropriation of the revenues of temporalities. Under the circumstances, abuses regarding temple property increased in scandalous proportions, leading to the appointment of a commission in 1876. Meanwhile, another official proposal to confiscate the temporalities was mooted but this move was thwarted by the timely intervention of Colonel Olcott who got the matter raised before the House of Commons in 1862.[73]

The correspondence and discussion on the question of administering the temporalities once more highlighted the question of giving a 'sound working Constitution' or a 'central organisation' to the Buddhists. The issue was however, ruled out by the British authorities for fear that such an

---

71. Ceylon, *Report of the Commission on Tenure af Lands of Viharagam Deualagam and Nindagam* (Colombo, 1956), Appendix A.

72. Ceylon, *Correspondence*, n. 68 p. 6. Also see Ceylon, *Buddhist Temporalities, Interim and Final Reports, of a Commission appointed to enquire into the Working of Buddhist Temporality Ordinance No. 8 of 1905*, XXIV-1920 (Colombo, 1920), p. 13. "Further, it became possible' to sell a tenant's rights for services due and large acreages of land today have been sold in that manner and form part of estates. Most strange of all it became possible to build Christian Churches on land dedicated to temples." *Betrayal of* ,*Buddhism*, n. 70, p. 7.

73. C.D.S. Siriwardene, *Tax Exemption and Religious Bodies* (Colombo, 1955), p. 7.

organisation might provide the nucleus of 'a new and possibly formidable power'.[74]

In 1889 the Temporalities Ordinance was promulgated. Under the ordinance the legal title to temple endowments was vested in lay trustees committing to them the administration and management of these endowments. The trustees were elected by the District Committees consisting of one member from each sub-district elected by the resident priest and male householders of full age professing Buddhism.

As regards the effectiveness of the lay trustees under the Temporalities Ordinance of 1889, it was maintained by another Commission on temporalities in 1919 that if, in 1876, the corruption and fraud were reported to have been commited by the priests, in 1919 it was the trustees and committees which were charged with misappropriating the temple revenues. The trustees paid no heed to the temple incumbents as they were not 'under them' but 'under the committees'. Consequently, the priests, "lost in prestige and local influence".[75]

According to the Commissioners, the earlier policy of 'localising' and not centralising control over temples was not desirable. It, therefore, proposed the establishment of a Buddhist Temporalities Council, composed of elected members—priests as well as laymen—as representatives of District Councils along with a number of ex-officio members. This body was to administer the major temples, supervise the work of District Councils and carry on the auditing of the accounts of the temples.

The reccommendations of the Commission were partly incorporated in the Buddhist Temporalaties Ordinance of 1931. They did not provide for a Buddhist Temporalities Council on an elective basis but for a public trustee—a government official —who exercised supervisory power over the temples. However, only certain important temples were brought under the supervision of the public trustees; the number of temples not brought under his direct control remained far in excess of the number of temples which were to be regulated by the Ordinance. As regards the management of properties, it was vested

74. Ceylon, *Correspondence*, n. 68, pp. 12-14.
75. Ceylon, *Buddhist Temporalities Reports*, n. 72, pp. 5-15, and 22-26.

in a person or persons as trustees who were to be nominated by the Viharadhipati (principal Bhikkhu of the temple). However, the Viharadhipati was also entitled to nominate himself as trustee,[76] and this was done in many cases of disputed successions in the civil courts and thereby lowering the image of the Bhikkhus in the public eye. Thus, it was not so much the religious policies of the British Government as its legal, economic and educational measures which affected the traditional religious structures in many ways.

As regards their educational policies, it needs to be added that when the British took over the island, Christian missionaries were already well entrenched in the field of education. Moreover, British regulations for State assistance provided patronage to the missionary schools. According to the School Commission of 1861, for instance, one of the conditions for obtaining state assistance was the compulsory teaching of "Bible and the leading tracts of Christianity".[77]

As late as 1865, only Protestant mission schools received government aid.[78] During the latter part of the nineteenth century, however, the government "added a number of vernacular schools for non-Christians, provided grant-in-aid to all private and mission schools giving secular education, and advocated a principle of religious neutrality for all government schools."[79] However, the Christian missionary schools had had almost a century's official backing. Also, as corporations, they were able to organise their educational institutions more effectively.

76. H.W. Tambish, 'Buddhist Ecclesiastical Law', *Journal of the Ceylon Branch of the Royal Asiatic Society*, New Series, Vol. 8, Part 1, pp. 95-96.
77. Buddhist Committee of Enquiry, n. 70, p. 49.
78. It needs to be noted that the move towards religious tolerance in Britain itself (though not towards religious secularisation so much, had its impact on the colonial educational policies. In fact, till 1871 even the Roman Catholic schools in Britain were under heavy educational disabilities. For details, see. R.C.K. Ensor, *England* 1870-1914 (London, 1936).
79. Michael M. Ames, 'The Impact of Western Education on Religion and Society in Ceylon', *Pacific Affairs*, Vol. 40, Nos. 1-2, Spring and Summer 1967, p. 27.

The first Buddhist educational organisation to receive Government grant was the Vidyodaya Pirivena (a monastic college) in 1873; the Buddhist lay schools did not get any grant till 1879. By 1880 only three Buddhist (both temple and lay-managed) schools were able to receive Government grants as against 811 State-aided mission schools. By 1900 their number had increased from 3 to 120 as against 1100 missionary schools (virtually all of whom were State aided) and 500 government schools. Notwithstanding this acceleration in number the late inception of the Buddhist schools and the absence of any central Buddhist organisation to sustain and co-ordinate their activities were potential hindrances. As such, they were not in a position to pose a challenge to the dominant position of the missionary schools either in terms of resources or opportunities.

Despite the avowed neutrality of the British government in educational matters in the late nineteenth century, both in the government schools as well as missionary schools, the emphasis continued to be on Christianity; Christianity continued to be looked upon as the 'government religion'. Profession of Christianity together with knowledge of English became the major criteria for securing government employment.

With English as the official language, no one could aspire for an elitist status in the colonial society without knowing the language. Knowledge of English coupled with an emulation of the colonial customs, traditions, dress and manners symbolised identification with the dominant mores of political authority. As the harbingers of colonial culture, the Christian missionaries provided facilities for such an emulation in their schools. Westernisation and Christianisation were its logical corollaries. In due course reaction to this had to set in in the attitude of the rising middle class[80] which, in the process of finding a place in the sun, was exposed most to such an emulative process.

80. For details about the growth of this class refer Michael Roberts, 'Reformism, Nationalism and Protest in British Ceylon, The Roots and Ingredients of Leadership', Mimeo. Paper read at the School of Oriental and African Studies, University of London, 1974.

The emerging entrepreneurial-professional class thus found in the schools a Christianity-saturated ethos. The atmosphere at home continued, however, to be that of the traditional Buddhist society. In many cases, the divergence of home culture and school culture led to the development of a split personality. Notwithstanding the attempts to coalesce the two, reaction in favour of one came up specially when protagonists of one culture tried to be arrogantly militant.

BUDDHIST REVIVALISM OF THE NINETEENTH CENTURY

The militancy of Christian missionaries, the Buddhist literary resurgence which gave a spurt to the emergence of literature extolling traditional Buddhist Sri Lanka, and the rise of the Ceylonese middle class with the impact of cultural upbringing, were the major causes of the Buddhist revival which gained momentum in the 1860s; stray but overt manifestation of this protest, however, could be discerned as early as 1828 in the composition of parodies against Christian tracts.[81] The major purpose of such a religious revival was to resuscitate the old faiths through new liberal influence and to give the younger generation a modern education which would impart to them a sense of pride in their traditional culture.[82]

Beginning with the public debates of some of the Bhikkhus with the Christian missionaries regarding the relative merits of the two religions, the revivalist movement gained momentum, employing in the process the same methods which the missionaries had used for the propagation of Christianity, i.e., the use of public media and preaching.[83]

The pioneer of this movement in its initial phase was Miguettuwatte Gunananda, a militant monk of Kotehena temple who started a society for the propagation of Buddhism in

81. Ananda Guruge, ed., *Return to Righteousness : A Collection of Speeches, Essays and Letters of Anagarika Dharmapala* (Colombo, 1965), p. xxx.
82. Visakha Kumari Jayawardena, *The Rise of the Labour Movement in Ceylon* (Durham, 1972), p. 43. Alongside Buddhism, Hinduism and Islam also had their revivalist phase during this period in reaction to militant christianity. Ibid., pp. 39-42.
83. Malalagoda, n. 10, pp. 293-393.

1862 as a rival organisation to the Society for the Propagation of the Gospel which was active in Sri Lanka since 1840.
He also acquired a printing press. Along with some other
Bhikkhus he issued pamphlets replying to the polemical tracts
of the missionaries and made significant contribution in the
religious controversies of the 1860s and 1870s. With the founding of Vidyodaya Pirivena at Colombo in 1873 and Vidyalankara Pirivena at Kelaniya, a few milesa way from Colombo,
the promotion of Buddhist centres of learning was also accelerated.

With the arrival of Col. Olcott in 1880, the second phase
of the movement began. Olcott and Madame Blavatsky embraced Buddhism after they reached the island and formed
the Colombo Buddhists Theosophical Society. Soon after,
Olcott launched the National Fund scheme for the establishment of Buddhist schools, complied a Buddhist catechism, designed a Buddhist flag and laid the foundations of a Buddhist
education movement.

Contacts with the masses were made in more than one
way. Journals in Sinhalese were started, tracts were published,
semi-religious organisations were initiated, religious fraternities
promoted and Buddhist schools all over the island were open-
ed. The model of these schools however conformed to that of
the Christian missionary school. "In so far as political and
economic dominance was Christian, there was motivation for
the cathexis of the Victorian Protestant ethical ideas into the
culture of elite Buddhist....Alongside the cathexis of norms
there was an adoption of institutional 'forms' of Chrisanity-
Young Men's (Women's) Buddhist Associations, Buddhist
army chaplains, Sunday school for Buddhists... Since traditional Buddhism lacked any formal modern organisational appa-
ratus, the existent protestant models were adopted by the
Buddhists. Thus Contemporary Buddhism could conveniently
be called Protestant Buddhism."[84]

In the establishment of schools, in publishing tracts and
in conducting other literary activities, some of the Bhikkhus

84. Gananath Obeysekere, 'Religious Symbolism and Political Change
    in Ceylon', *Modern Ceylon Studies* Vol. 1, No. 1, 1970, p. 46. Also
    see Gunasinghe, Chapter I, n. 36.

were closely associated with lay leaders. Gunananda Thera was in close touch with Col Olcott and Ven. Sri Sumangala Thera the first Principal of Vidyodya Pirivena was also the vice-president of the Theosophical Society in Great Britain.

In Anagarika Dharampala, earlier known as Don David Hevavitharna, the Budhhist laity found the most ardent and fiery champion of the Sinhalese nationalism. Influenced considerably by the first phase of the Buddhist revivalist movement and latter by Theosophy, he tried to inculcate among the Sinhalese people a sense of nationalism. His 'Banas' (religious preaching) were as much a scathing critique of western culture as an exhortation of the Sinhalese culture. It was for the sake of 'mammon', contended Dharampala, that the European races came to Ceylon. He claimed that the contribution of the 'white Brahmins', interested in making money, was "drunkeness, poverty, increase of crime and increasing insanity".[85] He emphasised that there was no need to be afraid of the white masters. "Be proud of your civilisation, your language, stand erect before the conquerors....Be yourselves and not cheap imitation to barbarians...." In a message to the Buddhist boys in 1921 Dharampala chalked out an economic plan for independent Ceylon. "Learn industries, learn weaving, learn arts and crafts, learn agriculture, learn medical sciences.... To be independent we must produce our own rice, our own cloth, our building materials, our own medicines and then will come independence."[86]

Finally, Dharampala, with the blessings of the clergy, started a campaign against alcohol. The temperance movement had a dual purpose. To reiterate Buddhist advice against alcohol was to assert anew the validity and relevance of Buddhist values after years of acquiescence to the values of the foreign ruler. On the political plane it represented a move to attack an important source of British revenue.[87]

85. Guruge, n. 81, pp. lxxxi-lxxiv.
86. Anagarika Dharmapala, 'A Message to the Buddhist Boys of Ceylon', *Mahabodhi and the UBM*, Vol. 29, No. 18, October 1921, p. 351.
87. Howard W. Wriggins, *Ceylon : Dilemmas of a New Nation* (Princeton, 1960), pp. 80-81.

The Buddhist revivalist movement brought in its wake national renaissance. The nationalism of the era had racial and religious overtones as well as a cultural bias in favour of indigenous values. It was derived "from feelings of inferiority in the reluctant acquisition of western technology and thought combined with feelings of superiority in their own religiosity and philosophically grounded way of life."[88]

The religious controversies vindicated the importance of the indigenous religion—the religion of the masses—over the religion of the colonial rulers. Also, the religious resurgence resulted in political discontent. The Buddhists, aware of their weakness compared to the Christian missionaries and conscious of their lack of political power, made the Legislative Council the target of their criticism. The Buddhist journals complained that the only Sinhalese representative in the Legislature (till 1888) was a Christian who "misrepresented rather than represented the Buddhists".[89]

As in the case of several colonies, religious revivalism of nineteenth century Sri Lanka seemed to be a precursor of its nationalist movement. In the process, it had underlined the catalytic role of some of the Bhikkhus. However, in comparison to its role in the eighteenth century, the revivalist movement of the nineteenth century, embedded as it was in a colonial setting, had many more challenges with which to cope. Thus, while Saranankara and his group had royal backing for the Buddhist revivalist movement, the nineteenth century Bhikkhus had to rest content with the support of the laity and to compete with the proselytising zeal of various brands of Christianity. Besides, if the eighteenth century revivalist movement had the kingdom of Kandy as its centre, the nineteenth century movement had its base in the urban areas of Sri Lanka littoral, but its impact was wider. Finally, if the main task of Saranankara had been the resuscitation of the monastic order, the major concern of some of the Bhikkhus a century later was its purification as was evident from the founding of the Ramanna Nikaya.

88. Karl Jaspers, 'End of Colonialism', in Harry Eckstein and David E. Apter, eds., *Comparative Politics : A Reader* (London, 1963), p. 608.
89. Jayawardena, n. 82, p. 61.

The British Administration in Ceylon watched the Buddhist revivalist movement with anxiety and concern and kept a watch on the activists—both national as well as foreign—lest its rising strength posed a challenge to its authority. However, the movement did not retain its initial momentum for long; the exile of Dharampala to India deprived Sri Lanka of one of its fiery leaders of the era.

It appears that this second phase of the nationalist movement in Sri Lanka continued till the first two decades of the twentieth century. During this period a significant interrelationship came to be established between the labour movement and the Buddhist revivalist movement. In fact, they had many leaders in common. The situation changed in the 1920s with the decline of the 'radicals' in nationalist politics. Instead, during the third phase of the island's nationalist movement the leadership was taken over by the 'moderates' in politics who, believing in the "inevitability of gradualness", agitated initially for a greater share in the decision-making process and ultimately for self-government. For this purpose the lofty halls of the State Council, and not the streets, became the political arena for the majority of the Ceylonese elite.

Unlike India where the moderate politics of the first decade of the twentieth century moved towards mass politics under the leadership of Gandhi, Sri Lanka politics did not take a radical turn. The small size of the country's elite (because of which both the Sinhalese, the Tamil and the Burgher elite found a place under the sun), the coalescence of economic interests between the Ceylonese middle class and the British entreprenurial class (in view of the overriding significance of its export-oriented plantation agriculture and its major mineral industries like graphite and gems, in its overall economic structure),[90] the relatively high economic standard of the 'common' man, and last but not the least, the success of the democratically elected State Council in promulgating some significant welfare measures in the fields of education and health during 30s and 40s, seem to be some of the factors

90. For a comparative analysis of the economic dimensions of Ceylonese nationalism *vis-a-vis* Indian and Malayan nationalism, see Roberts, n. 80.

responsible for the emergence of the constitutional and 'middle path' political culture of the colony.

In this setting, the attitudes of the low-country and up-country Bhikkhus towards the British rule present some significant variations. In view of their rather insulated position, the upper echelon of the up-country Bhikkhus, tended to be *status quo* oriented (as it preserved their social status and protected their economic position) and seemed to share the moderate constitutionalist stand of the indigenous colonial elite, most of whom belonged to the low-country. As against this were a small group of highly volatile and articulate low-country Bhikkhus, who associated themselves closely with the militant oppositional politics of the low-country and Marxist leadership which strove for radical socio-economic changes and demanded complete independence. Thus, during 1946-47, while some of the low-country Bhikkhus issued a declaration of independence, some Bhikkhus from the up country openly affirmed their allegiance to the crown.[91]

CONCLUSION

In pre-colonial Ceylon a close relationship existed between the religious and political systems which was characterized by interdependence and mutuality of interests. The colonial period was not only a point of entry for new and western religious forms and institutions but also involved an apparent secularisation of authority particularly during the British era. In traditional Sri Lanka, the legitimacy of the government had depended upon religious myths and populist sanctions; the legitimacy of the colonial regime relied on traditional as well as non-traditional sources. The sources of colonial power were derived as much from within as from without; its military might, its superiority as whites and aliens who received the patronage of at least one of the Ceylonese kings immediately after its arrival in the island, were some of the external factors. Within the island, the colonial authority utilized traditional loyalties whenever possible and mobilised the support of a segment of notables willing to be part of the new order.

91. For further details see Chapter IV.

This resource mobilisation within the country could only be at the cost of those who, in traditional Sri Lanka, had had an elitist status but had refused to bow to an alien authority by accepting a colonial religion and acquiesce with its political power. Consequently, it was a very limited and select group at the centre which, identifying itself with colonial policy and practice, won the favour of the alien power and could be termed as colonial elite.

While the colonial rule enhanced the position of a certain segment of the Buddhist laity, it eroded the authority of the Buddist monks in more than one way. The Portuguese-Dutch patronage of Christianity robbed the Buddhist clergy of its position as the harbinger of the dominant religion in the island. In traditional Sri Lanka, the monks played the role of 'bridge' elites in transmitting Sinhalese Buddhist culture at the local and national levels. The Sinhalese Buddhist values dominated the ethos of the national as well as ths local political systems. Buddhism played a dominant role in cities as well as in villages. With the advent of the Portuguese and the Dutch, the influence of the Buddhist clergy was eroded in the maritime areas to some extent but in the Kandyan kingdom as well as at the village level its influence continued. Even during the British period, at the village community level the influence of the Bhikkhu over the laity continued in varying degrees though the ambivalence of British religious policy and practice kept it insulated at the centre.

This differentiation can be explained in terms of the lack of balance in the processes of change and transition that could be found between the central level and the local level— the national political system and local political system. Most of the changes introduced by the colonial powers were focused on the central institutions. The introduction of a unitary system of administration, the regularisation of taxation, the establishment of modern court procedure, provision of modern education to select native elites and the introduction of market economy with its concomitants, did have an overall impact on political institutions and orientations. However, what is significant in this context is that though the common factor in these changes was towards the promotion of systemic change in the society as a whole, the colonial authority thought it prudent to introduce these within a relatively unchanged social setting at the local level.

This was brought about through the two-fold policy of either maintaining the *status quo* or through a policy of ambivalence. In the village, for instance, the traditional position of Headman was kept intact. This earned the British the allegiance of the village chief. The other significant village elite—the Buddhist monk—was either ignored or left undisturbed. However, the economic, educational and legal policies of the British affected not as much the structure of the Sangha as its functions. Deprived of its linkages with the State authority, which had proved to be the only corrective in the past, the Buddhist clergy went its own way. Absence of a central organisation was never felt so much as during the British period for, notwithstanding the lack of central organisation in the past, the powers of the ruler as the temporal head of the church vested in him considerable power to resuscitate the Sangha. The propagation of an ambivalent and so-called secular policy on the part of the British could only be at the cost of the Buddhist institutions.

In the low country areas where the direction of change was much more varied and its thrust much more severe, the Christian missionaries were too pronounced in their activities. This dominance was resented by the various segments of the people for different reasons. The Buddhist clergy, sustained by the rich laity of the area and being in close touch with them, was more enlightened than its counterparts in the Kandyan region for they had to be more assertive to maintain that Buddhism was superior to Christianity. This required knowledge of the Sinhalese scripture, as much as the tenets of Christianity. The importance ascribed to oriental learning by some of the whites, the eulogisation of Buddhist culture by Westerners like Olcott and Madam Blovatsky, were the external factors helping Buddhist revival in which the Bhikkhus played a significant role.

The success of the Bhikkhus in religious controversies with the Christian clergy was one thing, acquiring State patronage was another. Also, the missionaries had kept themselves entrenched too long to be thrown out of educational field. Nor was the clergy prepared at this juncture to go as far as to accept the curriculm of missionary schools in its 'pansala', i.e. temple schools and pirivenas.

The educational system of the past had enabled the Bhikkhus to fulfil the role of communication elites; during the colonial era the situation had changed altogether. However, it was still evident that a combination of Buddhist clergy and influential urbanised laity could pose a challenge to colonial authority. In this, it was the laity who had to take the lead and initiative. Traditionally, the monk 'advised' and advice had to be sought before given. Besides, the monks could prove to be most effective in a situation when there was an onslaught on colonial authority and a demand for complete independence was made. The elitist character of the nationalist movement did not facilitate such a trend; the colonial elite still had faith in the benevolence of the British rule and the British colonial policy as such continued to be oriented towards measures under which the unification of the Sangha was well nigh impossible. In fact, some of its legislation, particularly those pertaining to the Buddhist temporalities, had been in effect contributory to further fragmentation of the various Nikayas which had come into being during this period.

And yet, a significant fact in this context was that inspite of multiplicity in the monastic order, the structural hierarchy of all these divisions followed a closely similar pattern. An analysis of the hierarchical structure of the various Nikayas brings out that similarity in organisation.

Chapter III

CONTEMPORARY SANGHA : ORGANISATION AND ROLES

INTRODUCTION

Composed of nearly 15,000-18,000 Bhikkhus,[1] the monastic order of the island is divided into three Nikayas or fraternities. The oldest of them—the Siam Nikaya—is the largest with about 11,000-12,000 Bhikkhus belonging to this sect. Next in numerical terms is the Amarapura Nikaya, having about 3,000 Bhikkhus, to be followed by Ramanna Nikaya to which belong the rest—about 2,000 Bhikkhus.

1. Bechert gives this figure in 'Buddhismus, Staat und Gesellschaft in den Landern des Theravadh'—Bd. I, Allgemeines und Ceylon, Frankfurt, 1966 referred in Hans-Dieter Evers, 'Kinship and Property Rights in a Buddhist Monastery in Central Ceylon', *American Anthropologist*, Vol. 69, No. 6, December 1967, p. 704. During my interviews with several monks in 1967-68 this approximation was corroborated.

   However, H.L. Seneviratne's comment needs to be noted in this context. "No accurate statistics", he maintains, "are available as to the numerical composition of the Sangha. The gross statistics are however available. By the Ordinance No. 19 of 1931 of the Government of Ceylon, all Buddhist monks were required to register themselves at the office of the registrar-general. These records show that there are, at the time these were consulted, (June 1969) 31, 370 monks in Ceylon. Of these some would have died and some would have given up robes". H.L. Seneviratne, 'The Sacred and the Profane in a Buddhist Rite', *Ceylon Studies Seminar*, 69/70 Series, No. 7, University of Peradeniya, Mimeo, ootnote 1.

Except the Ramanna Nikaya, the other two fraternities are divided in various chapters, sects and divisions.[2] Such a tradition of Nikaya-fragmentation is, however, as much the characteristic of contemporary Sangha as of the fraternities of the past. In fact, soon after Buddha's death it was divided into 18 sects in India and even in Sri Lanka, except for the first two centuries, the Sangha did not exist as a monolith.

Despite such fragmentation, however, there is a striking identity in the pattern of nomenclature, organisation, function and the hierarchical structure of various chapters and divisions of the present day Sangha. This appears to have been due to the common allegiance to the Theravada doctrines by all these units, and consequently, a common allegiance to and an almost uniform emphasis on certain areas of monastic activities —monastic discipline, ecclesiastical matters and so on.

In view of such similarities, the organisation of one chapter/ sect of Siam and Amarapura Nikaya is presented as a case study in this chapter along with that of the Ramanna Nikaya (which has no such divisions) in a comparative framework. Further, because of the historical importance of the vihara as the basic unit of the order, its internal dynamics are analysed in some detail to focus the perception of the functions and roles of the Bhikkhus by themselves as much as by the non-Bhikkhus, in the social system of Sri Lanka.

CONTEMPORARY NIKAYA ORGANISATION IN A HISTORICAL CONTEXT

It appears that contemporary Nikaya organisations are much more elaborate in many ways than their counterparts in the past. To begin with, as has been discussed already, even when the Maha vihara was in the pinnacle of authority, when other monasteries operated more or less as its branches, the structure was loose and submission to it was voluntary.

2. The term sect is used to connote divisions based on some canonical point, e.g., the division between Mulavamsika and Saddhammavamsika in Amarapura Nikaya. For details see Chapter II, footnote 55. The term 'division' has been used to denote those split-away groups in the case of which the cause for the division was non-canonical. The term chapter more or less connotes branches but with a definite identity.

During the 12th and 13th centuries, when the hierarchical structure of the Sangha was spelt out in some detail in verious Katikavatas,[3] one does not get much evidence to question the autonomy of the vihara *in effect* in the total set-up which can be tabled as follows :

Table 1

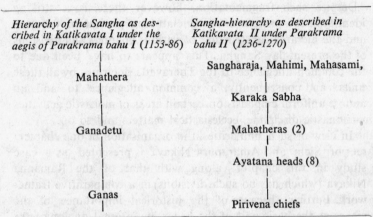

Hierarchy of the Sangha as described in Katikavata I under the aegis of Parakrama bahu I (1153-86)	Sangha-hierarchy as described in Katikavata II under Parakrama bahu II (1236-1270)
	Sangharaja, Mahimi, Mahasami,
Mahathera	
	Karaka Sabha
Ganadetu	Mahatheras (2)
	Ayatana heads (8)
Ganas	
	Pirivena chiefs

As can be seen, the religious hierarchy in the first Katikavata was much simpler. Under this, the Mahathera being at the apex of the Buddhist hierarchy, was vested with the highest ecclesiastical authority over all the monasteries. The monestries were sub-divided under groupleader called Ganadetu (leader of the Ganas, i.e., a group of fraternity of monks living in one communion or a large congregation of monks

3. Katikavata is a set of rules prepared for the guidance of Bhikkhus. The first Katikavata was promulgated by Parakramabahu (1153-86) in the form of an inscription and the second, called Dambadeni Katikavata came into being under the aegis of Parakramabahu II (1236-70). The third and fourth Katikavatas were prepared during the reign of the Kandyan King Kirti Sri Rajasinha (1747-82). His successor, Rajadhi Rajasinha (1782-98) promulgated the fifth and the last Katikavata. For further details see Nandsena Ratnapala, *The Katikavatas : Laws of the Buddhist Order of Ceylon from the 12th Century to the 18th Century* (critically edited, translated and annotated (Munchen, 1971).

living in several monasteries). Ganadetu had supervisory control over the Bhikkhus in the group.

As against this, the hierarchical structure, promulgated almost a century later, was not only more elaborate but also laid a special emphasis on learning. Thus, a great deal of importance was given to the chiefs of monastic colleges and centres of learning (Aytanas and Pirivenas) in the hierarchy in which the supreme pontiff, referred to as Mahasami, Mahimi or Sangharaja was vested with the jurisdiction over all matters concerning the Sangha in the entire island. Appointments of the Bhikkhus to officiate at the higher ordination ceremony as well as appointment to the incumbencies of minor monastic educational establishments (Pirivenas) came directly under his control. The Mahasami also convened assemblies to discuss matters concerning the Sangha as a whole, i.e., discussions on the drafting of a rescript or issues dealing with the unification and purification of the Sasana.

In order to assist the Mahimi in his functions, a central organisation called Karaka Sabha (Executive Committee) was created which, in functional terms, seemed to represent the Sangha as a whole. Comprising the heads of monastic centres of learning, members of the Karaka Sabha sat in the assemblies mentioned above. The Karaka Sabha's assent was also necessary for legitimising appointments in various Ayatanas as well as for the incumbencies of major Pirivenas. The presence of such a body thus, if necessary, could act as a check against the over-riding powers of the Mahimi.

Next in order to the Mahimi in the Sangha hierarchy were two Maha sthaviras or Maha theras who were elected to this position by the unanimous consent of the Bhikkhus of the entire island and formally invested by the king. Whenever the office of Mahimi fall vacant, one of the two Maha theras was elected by the entire Sangha to the vacancy thereby preventing other Bhikkhus from contesting this high position and avoiding the possibility of open competition for the office. Next in rank were the heads of the Ayatanas to be followed by the chiefs of the Pirivenas. It is significant that every

Bhikkhu was attached to one of the eight Ayatanas.[4]

It is noteworthy that in spite of Buddha's injunctions that the only teacher for a Bhikkhu was the Dhamma and that to his seniors he owed only a respectful submission, the criteria of 'seniority' had become a qualification for assumption of higher positions in the ecclesiastical hierarchy. Thus, according to Katikavata II, Maha sthaviraship (continuance in the monastic order for 20 years after higher ordination entitled Bhikkhus this title) as one of the qualifications for becoming the Mahimi or one of his deputies.

Some of these assumptions seem to prevail in the organisational set-up of the chapters/divisions/sects of the various Nikayas of contemporary Sangha many of whom have their own Katikavatas or constitutions (Sasana Vyvastha). These spell out in minute details an explanation of the various terms used therein, the mode of organisation of the various bodies and their functions and last but not the least, the mode of election, tenure, power and functions of the major office bearers.

NIKAYA ORGANISATION—RAMANNA NIKAYA[5]

As, amongst the three Nikayas, the most recent one, the Ramanna Nikaya, presents a highly elaborate and detailed hierarchical structure, it is described first. It might be noted that its constitution had been revised from time to time taking note of the needs and exigencies of the times and has had, amongst its patrons, late D.S. Senanayake and his son Dudley

---

4. Ibid. Also see Gunaratne Panabookke, *The Evolution and History of the Buddhist Monastic Order with Special Reference to the Sangha in Ceylon* (Ph. D. Thesis, Lancaster University, 1969), pp. 341-5, and 374-5 and 395-7. Yatadolawatta Dhammavisuddhi, *The Buddhist Sangha in Ceylon (Circa 1200-1400)* (Ph. D. Thesis, University of London, 1970), pp. 82-85.

5. The organization of Ramanna Nikaya, as has been described in this section, is based on (a) my interview with Rev. Matale Sasanatilake, Vice-President, Sri Lanka Vidyalaya and member Ramanna Palaka Sabha in 1967; (b) Matale Sasanatilake, *Ramanna Vamsa* (Ramanna Chronicles) Colombo, 1964 and (c) *Sri Lanka Ramanna Nikaya Palaka Maha Sangha Vyavastha Sangrahaya* set of rules and constitution of Ramanna Nikaya (Colombo, n.d.).

Senanayake, the leaders of the United National Party who seemed to have been fairly active in such re-organisations.

In one respect, the evolution of Ramanna Nikaya hierarchy reminds one of the era of the Buddha and the first Buddhist Council. During the Maha Nayakaship of its founder member, Ambagahawatte, there was virtually no organisation. The Maha Nayaka carried on various functions of the Ramanna Nikaya with the help of some of his close associates. Soon after his death in 1886, however, the senior Bhikkhus of the fraternity decided to convene a meeting of all the Bhikkhus (Sangha Sabha). A Karaka Sabha (Executive Committee), comprising of ten senior Bhikkhus (Maha sthavira) was formed and a President with a life tenure was elected. Simultaneously, the post of Sanna Lekhakachariya (Registrar-General) whose major function was to issue certificates to the newly ordained monks as well as to maintain an up-to-date register of the Bhikkhus of the Nikaya was also created.

Initially, the routine jobs of a secretary were performed by Sanna Lekhakachariya. In due course, howerer, these two positions were separated and the office of Maha Lekhaka (Chief Secretary) was created. Gradually, the Nikaya hierarchy was constitutionalised at provincial level too and many new positions at the provincial as well as at central level were created through amendments of the original constitution from time to time.

As in the case of all the Nikayas, sects and divisions, at the base of the hierarchical structure are the viharas (temples) owing allegiance to a particular Nikaya, chapter, sect or division. The temple has, amongst its incumbents, the chief monk (Viharadhipati), other Bhikkhus and samaneras (novices). These temples are divided into various divisions. In the beginning, Ramanna Nikaya had 10 divisions but with more viharas coming into being, the number of divisions was increased from 10 to 13. After a while 7 more were added to it and now the number of divisions is 25 as is evident from Table 2.

Divisional Organisation

All the fully ordained monks in a division form a body called Pradeshika Sangha Sabha. The Sangha elects from amongst its members a smaller body entitled Pradeshika Karaka Sabha. The tenure of the Karaka Sabha is five years.

Table 2

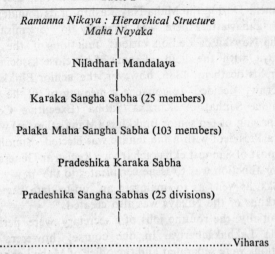

Ramanna Nikaya : Hierarchical Structure
Maha Nayaka
|
Niladhari Mandalaya
|
Karaka Sangha Sabha (25 members)
|
Palaka Maha Sangha Sabha (103 members)
|
Pradeshika Karaka Sabha
|
Pradeshika Sangha Sabhas (25 divisions)
|
....Viharas

The Karaka Sabha appoints a committee from amongst its members called Pradeshika Sangha Sabhave Karaka Sabha. This committee comprises the President (Sabhapati), Vice-President (Upa-Sabhapati), Secretary and few others.[6]

The major functions of the Pradeshika Sangha Sabha are as follows:

(a) Framing of the rules necessary for the convening of the meeting of all the Bhikkhus of the division.

(b) In the event of the demise of the chief monk of a vihara, making arrangements for the election of his successor and sending the name of the new chief monk to the Palaka Maha Sangha Sabha (central legislative body).

6. "Pradeshika Sangha Sabha could be compared to the provincial Legislative Assembly, Karaka Sabha to its Executive Committee and Sangha Sabhave Karaka Sabha to its working committee". Interview with Rev. Sasanatilake, n. 5.

(c) Selection of members to Palaka Sangha Sabha and filling of vacancies therein as per rules in the constitution.

(d) Compilation of the register of the Bhikkhus and Samaneras in the division.

(e) Holding religious examinations for the novices seeking higher ordination.

(f) Dispatch of annual reports on the activities of the Divisional Sangha Sabha to the Palaka Sangha Sabha.

(g) Furnishing any other information required by the Palaka Sangha Sabha regarding the division.

Palaka Maha Sangha Sabha (PMSS) : Organisation and Functions

Palaka Maha Sabha comprises three members each from every division two of whom look after the general interests of the division and the third, called Anuvijjaka (holding a sort of high court judge position) brings forward the ecclesiastical matters of his division before the Sabha; ten additional members irrespective of their divisional affiliations; thirteen life members who primarily look after the ordination procedures and five senior members. The PMSS meets once in six months and its functions include : (a) formation of committees to make arrangements for the selection of the members of the PMSS; (b) looking after the matters related to various temples which are brought to it; (c) framing of laws for the Nikaya; and (d) discussion on any scriptural point on which a doubt is raised.

The working committee of the PMSS is called Karaka Sangha Sabha composed of 25 members (one each from every division) and it meets once in six months. Planning for the PMSS activities is done in this committee.

Except for the Nayakas (i.e., Maha Nayaka, Anu Nayaka and Adhikarana Nayaka), Sanna Lekhaka (Registrar-General) and 13 members of the PMSS who have a life tenure, all the other persons hold office for five years.

Niladhari Mandalaya (NM)

Apart from its 75 elected members the PMSS has several

ex-officio members who comprise Niladhari Mandalaya (committee of officials). This seems to be the most high powered body of the Nikaya. Every member of the Mandalaya has clearly assinged duties. Members of the Mandalaya are elected by the elective unit (i.e., 75 members elected from 25 divisions).

Members of the NM include the Maha Nayaka, the most high ranking official in the Sangha hierarchy. After the demise of the Maha Nayaka but before his funeral, the Karaka Sangha Sabha proposes the name of his successor (he should be a member of this Sabha). The succeeding Maha Nayaka, however, is deemed to be confirmed only after six months from the date of appointment. The time lag is with a view to meet any dispute regarding his suitability for the post of Maha Nayakaship.

Other members of the Mandalaya are Annu Nayaka (Deputy Chief who acts on behalf of the Maha Nayaka as and when necessary); Adhikarana Nayaka (who acts as attorney general); Adhikarana Lekhaka (Judicial Secretary); Adhikaran Up-lekhaka (Judicial Deputy Secretary); Sanna Lekhaka (Registrar-General, who keeps the complete record of the monks ordinated, dead and disrobed); Maha Lekhaka (Chief Secretary); Up-Maha Lekhaka (Deputy Secretary); Sabhapati (President—who presides in all the meetings) and ten Upadhayaya (who are in charge of Upasampada). The functions of all these officials are spelt out in great detail in the Nikaya constitution.

Judicial Organisation

Incorporated within this framework is a parallel structure consisting of judicial organisation of Bhikkhus which operate as ecclesiastical courts. The highest court of appeal is called Agganu Vijjaka Mandalaya (AVM). Members who have served in the Palaka Sabha for five years are eligible for this office. Consisting of six members, the AVM is elected by the Palaka Sabha for five years.

Next to this court comes the Jyeshtha Anuvijjaka Mandalaya. It serves as an intermediary body between the divisional units and the central legislative body. The members are also appointed by Palaka Sabha with a five year tenure.

This is followed by the Pradeshika Anuvijjaka Mandalaya. This comprises all the divisional Anuvijjakas in the Palaka Maha Sangha Sabha.

Most of the cases deal with the disputes regarding succession in vihara. Generally, the cases are brought by provincial Sangha Sabha to the Anuvijjaka Mandalaya. In cases where either party to the dispute does not find the decision satisfactory, the matter is taken to the higher bodies. However, the decisions of the highest judicial body, i.e., AVM, are not legally binding and many cases do come before the secular courts of law.

Siam Nikaya : Organisation of its Chapters and Sects

Siam Nikaya is divided into two chapters, i.e., Malwatta and Asgiri chapters which owe their inception to the beginnings of this fraternity. The third chapter, Kalyani Samagri Dharma Maha Sangha Shabha, has been divided into Kotte and Kelaniya branches (Parshwaya) both of which have become autonomous and independent of one another. Apart from this, two divisions, Uva Siam Nikaya and Arannika Nikaya have branched off from Malwatta chapter during the last few decades.[7]

The establishment of the Kalyani Samagri Dharma Maha Sangha Sabha brings out the points of clashes between low-country and up-country Bhikkhus in its historical context. In 1850s the chief high priest of Kotte temple, Rev. Maligaspe Dhama Kirtisri Mangala, raised certain controversial issues with the Maha Nayaka of Malwatta in respect of the concept of Sanghika Dana (alms to be given to the Sangha) and Buddhist calendar year. These issues remained unresolved. In 1855 Rev. Maligaspe, supported by certain other vihara chiefs of low-country, decided to grant Upasampada within the low country because of the problems of travel from those areas to Kandy and requested the Malwatta Maha Nayaka to send five Bhikkhus to officiate. Refusing to comply to this request, the

7. For a brief historical exposition of these chapters see Ceylon, *Buddha Sasana Commission Vartava* (Buddha Sasana Commission Report), sessional paper 18 of 1959 (Colombo, 1959), pp. 24-34.

Malwatta Maha Nayaka expressed his unwillingness to grant his sanction to Upsampada in any other place expcept in Kandy. This was not acceptable to Maligaspe who decided to go ahead with the Upasampada ceremony of the Bhikkhus in May 1956 at Kotte. Certain others—a bigger number—made their headquarters at Kelaniya.[8]

Reacting to the Kotte chief's action, the Maha Nayaka of Malwatta, together with the Maha Nayaka of Asgiri wrote a letter to the Siam Nikaya Bhikkhus, condemning the Upasampada ceremony and asking them to cease all contacts with the Kotte chief and his supporters till a final injunction was issued. Soon after, Maligaspe thero was divested of his position as the Nayaka of Malwatta fraternity in Colombo district and another Bhikkhu, loyal to Kandy, was made the Nayaka.[9] However, the new chapter which already had fairly large endowments as well as the support of some of the lay leaders, had come to stay.

As regards the organisation of the various chapters and divisions of Siam Nikaya, though it is not as elaborate as that of Ramanna Nikaya, it follows more or less the same pattern. As such, only a brief description of the hierarchy of Kotte Sri Kalyani Samagri Dharma Maha Sangha Sabha is presented. This is as follows:

As evident from the table, at the lowest rung of this chapter are all Bhikkhus. Their viharas are, by and large, concentrated in five localities of western, southern, sabaragamuva province and central province (Kotte, Bentara, Galgoda, Arugoda and Ratmalana). Each division has a provincial chief (Pradeshika Nayaka). Consisting of about 1,000 Bhikkhus, the Kalyani Samagri Dharma Sabha Bhikkhus get together at Kotte (near

8. For details refer to Kitsiri Malalagoda, *Sociological Aspects of Revival and Change in Buddhism in Nineteenth Century Ceylon* (Ph. D. Thesis, Oxford, 1970), pp. 190-209.

9. Ibid.

10. Data regarding the organisation of this division is based on my interview with the late Dr. K. Wachissara in 1967, correspondence with M. Ariyawamsa Thero Maha Nayaka on 13 September 1967 and Abugama Lankananda Thera, *Jayawardana Pura Kotte Sri Kalyani Samagri Dharma Maha Sangha Sabha* (Colombo, n.d.)

Colombo) and through secret ballot, elect five members from
each division.

Table 3

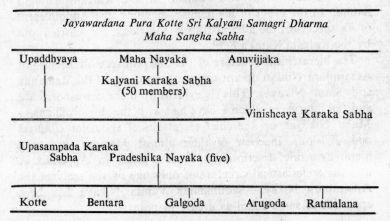

*Jayawardana Pura Kotte Sri Kalyani Samagri Dharma
Maha Sangha Sabha*

Upaddhyaya   Maha Nayaka   Anuvijjaka

Kalyani Karaka Sabha
(50 members)

Vinishcaya Karaka Sabha

Upasampada Karaka
Sabha   Pradeshika Nayaka (five)

Kotte   Bentara   Galgoda   Arugoda   Ratmalana

Kalyani Karaka Sabha: Organisation and Functions

These twenty five elected members, along with 25 members
appointed by the Maha Nayaka (who form the Upasampada
Karaka Sabha) form the Karaka Sabha. The tenure of elected
members is five years; some of the appointed ones, however,
have a life tenure.

The Kalyani Karaka Sabha appoints the divisional chiefs
(Pradeshika Nayakas), Maha Nayaka, and his two deputies—
Anu Nayakas. If there is more than one name proposed for
any of these offices then voting by secret ballot takes place.

Another body appointed by the Maha Nayaka, and forming
an integral part of the Karaka Sabha is Upasampada Karaka
Sabha. It consists of five Upaddhyaya Bhikkhus and 20
Karmavaggacariyan. Except the Upaddhyayas who are the
senior Bhikkhus officiating at the ordination ceremonies and
having a life tenure, the rest are elected for five years.

Out of the fifty member Karaka Sabha, another committee,
comprising ten members and elected from and by Karaka
Sabhiks themselves, is formed to look after judicial matters.
This is called Vinishcaya Karaka Sabha. Its tenure is for five
years and its president is called Anu Vijjaka. As both the

Vinishcaya Sabha and Kalyani Karaka Sabha have a five year tenure, till their term ends the administrative powers vest in the Upasampada Karaka Sabha. However, in normal times, the Maha Nayaka is the chief official of the Kalyani Samagri Sabha. In the event of his demise, pending the appointment of his successor, the administrative functions are carried out by the Kalyani Karaka Sabha.

The hierarchical structure of the different sects/divisions[11] of Amarapura Nikaya do not deviate from those of the Ramanna and Siam Nikayas. This is evident from the correspondence and the interviews which I have had with the high officials— Maha Nikayas or the chief secretaries of about ten chapters and divisions. In view of their almost identical structural hierarchy a brief description of those is given in Appendix A and the ecclesiastical structure of only one of the sects of the Amarapura Nikaya—Saddhamma Vamsa Nikaya has been spelt out in some detail as a case in point.

Amarapura Saddhamma Vamsa Nikaya[12]

The beginning of Saddhamma Vamsa Nikaya is an appropriate example of the process of segmentation of the Amarapura Nikaya. As has been mentioned earlier, in the beginning of the nineteenth century, several groups of the Salagama, Karava and later Durava Bhikkhus from the low-country went to Burma and started the new fraternity. Amongst them were two belonging to Salagama castle—led by Ambagahapitiye Nanavimala and Kapugama Dhammakkhanda who worked closely together

11. In 1970s attempts were made by the Maha Nayakas of some of the Amarapura sects to unify the Nikaya. Accordingly, by unanimous consent, Rev. Balangoda Ananda Maitreya Thero was designated as the Maha Nayaka of the order as a whole. However, this seems to be a symbolic and not an effective effort towards unification of Amarapura fraternity.

12. Information under this section is based on (a) reply to my questionnaire by Kosgoda Dhammavamsa Maha Nayaka dated 16 March, 1967 and my subsequent interviews with him on 2 October, 1967; (b) *Amarapura Saddhamma Vamsa Maha Nikaya Vyvavastha Sangrahaya* (Sinhalese Manuscript). Details regarding the historical inception of the Nikaya are provided in detail in Malalagoda, n. 8, pp. 230-46.

though they had different pupillary successions and different Simas for higher ordination. Although the Nanavimala line had its main temple at Valitara and its sima at Balapitiya (both in southern province), the pupils of Dhammakkhanda had their main temple at Dadalla (southern province) and the Sima at the river Gin at Gintota (southern province).

With the founder of the Dadalla line giving up his robes and embracing Christianity in 1816, some of the Salagama lay elite (who had provided patronage to these chapters of Amarapura) took the initiative and succeeded in unifying these two groups. The unity however proved to be short-lived. Lankagoda Dhirananda, the chief pupil of the then Maha Nayaka Bopagoda Sumana, questioned the validity of the new Sima of the unified salagama fraternity[13] in 1851-1852. The controversy resulted in Lankagoda forming a separate sect. While the larger group of the Salagama Bhikkhus called themselves Mulavamsa Nikaya (original lineage of the fraternity as majority of them had derived their pupillary succession from Nanavimala. the founder of the earliest group of Amarapura Nikaya), the splinter group named itself Amarapura Saddhamma Vamsa Nikaya after Lankagoda's title of Saddhammavamsapala which was also held before him, by Kapugama Dhammakkhanda, (the founder of Dadalla line of monks) who had received it from the king of Burma after his ordination in 1807.

It can be seen from the Table 4 that all the viharas belonging to the ASN are divided into seven divisions, i.e., Matara, Galle Kalutara, Walitara Kosgoda, Colombo, Madhyama Palatha (up-country) and Sabaragamuva. The divisions falling within the precincts of southern and western provinces, however, do not conform to the districts or provincial boundary but only connote a particular district or province where the ASN has a certain number of temples. The members, which these divisions send to the Karaka Sabha, indicate the relative strength of the sect in the area. Thus, while Matara, Colombo and Kosgoda divisional Sangha Sabha send four members each to the Central Karaka Sabha, Sabaragamuva and Central province divisional Sangha Sabhas send only one each. The other two divisions send three members each to the central Karaka Sabha.

---

13. For details of this controversy see, n. 55 of Chapter II.

The organisation of the ASN can be tabled as follows:

Table 4

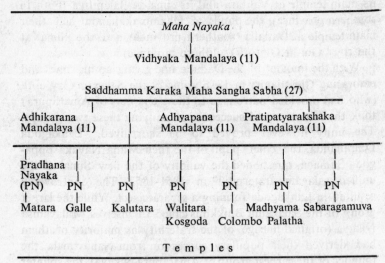

```
                              Maha Nayaka
                                   |
                         Vidhyaka Mandalaya (11)
                                   |
                 Saddhamma Karaka Maha Sangha Sabha (27)

Adhikarana          |        Adhyapana      Pratipatyarakshaka
Mandalaya (11)      |        Mandalaya (11)  Mandalaya (11)

  |      |      |      |      |      |      |      |
Pradhana |      |      |      |      |      |      |
Nayaka   |      |      |      |      |      |      |
(PN)    PN     PN     PN     PN     PN     PN
  |      |      |      |      |      |      |
Matara  Galle  Kalutara  Walitara  |   Madhyama Sabaragamuva
                       Kosgoda Colombo Palatha

                         T e m p l e s
```

Bhikkhus of the 7 divisions have their respective Sangha Sabhas. The regional Sabhas have their respective Karaka Sabha which is elected by Sangha Sabhas through show of hands. Every Karaka Sabha has 11 members including Nayaka, Anu Nayaka, Adhikarana Nayaka, Lekam (Secretary) and seven other members. The Nayakas, Anu Nayakas, Adhikarana Nayakas and Lekam are elected by the Central Karaka Sabha with the consent of the divisional Karaka Sabhas and have a life tenure. The other seven members are elected by the divisional Sangha Sabha for five years.

Saddhamma Karaka Maha Sangha Sabha (SKMSS): Organisation and Functions

The SKMSS consists of 27 members. These include 20 members representing the seven divisions (in proportion to the respective strength of the temples as mentioned above), Maha Nayaka and six others appointed by him. The other office bearers of the Sabha, apart from Maha Nayaka (who is its president) are Anu Nayaka, Adhikarana Nayaka, Secretary

(Lekam) and two joint secretaries. Maha Nayaka and Anu Nayaka have a life tenure. The rest of the members have a five year term. The tenure of Karaka Sabha itself is five years and its duration can be extended for two more years.

Karaka Sabha should meet at least once in six months. Its functions are manifold. It is empowered to settle ecclesiastical disputes as well as discuss matters related to the Buddhist doctrines. However, its functions are in the main conducted by three committees or Mandalayas, each comprising eleven members. These sub-committees are Adhikarana (judicial) Mandalaya, Adhyapana (Teaching) Mandalaya and Pratipatya-rakshaka Mandalaya which looks after matters related to the issues dealing with Vinaya, disciplinary action with regard to the novices, the delineation of consecrated boundary—Sima, Upasampada, etc. Each of these sub-committees has a secretary.

Apart from the judicial sub-committee, the Karaka Sabha also appoints a higher judicial body called Maha Sanghadhi-karana Mandalaya comprising eleven members. This is the highest court of appeal.

Finally, the Karaka Sabha appoints from its members an executive committee called Vidhayaka Mandalaya. This is the body of high officials including the Maha Nayaka, the chief judicial officer (Pradhana Adhikarana Nayaka), two joint secretaries (Samalekhadhikarana), educational secretary (Katayutu Philibanda Lekhaka), secretary in charge of Vinaya rules (Pratipatyarakshaka Lekhaka), the Anu Nayakas and two others. The Maha Nayaka is the chairman of the body and the two joint secretaries are the secretaries of this committee.

Though an advisory body, every proposal coming before the Karaka Sabha needs to be perused by the executive committee. It is the responsibility of the executive committee to fix a date for the Upasampada ceremony, enquire into the various matters pertaining to the divisional Sabhas, recommend the names for the offices of Nayakas and Upaddhayas (i.e., those who have completed 20 years of higher ordination and are entitled to perform the Upasampada ceremony) and to suggest the names of persons deserving honorary titles, for the consideration of the Karaka Sabha. Finally, if any matter deserves immediate action, the committee has the power to take action on it with-out bringing it before the Karaka Sabha. However, it should present a report of this to the Karaka Sabha in its next meeting and have it confirmed. The committee must meet at least once in three months. Five members form the quorum. Comprising of the high officials of the various bodies, the Vidhayaka Mandalaya in effect is the most powerful body despite its advisory character. However, it is the Maha Nayaka who wields the real and, at, times over-riding powers.

Powers of the Maha Nayaka

As has already been mentioned, the Maha Nayaka is the president of the central Karaka Sabha as well as of the Vidhayaka Mandalaya and has the power to nominate six members of the Karaka Sabha. If any provincial Sangha Sabha fails to select its representatives before the specified date then the Maha Nayaka has also the power to nominate representatives from that division. Further, the venue, date and time of the meetings of the Karaka Sabha is fixed by him and no decision of the Sabha is valid unless confirmed by him. Not only this, if the Vidhayaka Mandalaya decides that a particular decision of the Karaka Sabha is not conducive to the interest of the Nikaya, the Maha Nayaka should ask the Karaka Sabha to reconsider it. However, if the Sabha fails to take a decision in three meetings, the Maha Nayaka has the power to dismiss both the bodies and make arrangements for a new Karaka Sabha as well as Vidhayaka Mandalaya not later than three months of the dissolution. Even in normal times, all the important documents are kept under his custody and the venue of the central office of the Nikaya is decided according to his wish and convenience.

This brief description of the ecclesiastical structure of the various fraternities bears out some general points. The elaborate nature of several of the provisions indicates almost a degree of professional care in the drafting of rules and regulations. The constitutions or Katikavatas in some cases embody rules even for relatively minor procedures. Further, the hierarchy has, by and large, a similar nomenclature; the Pradeshika (provincial or divisional) committees at the division level and the Vidhayaka or Niladhari Mandalaya headed by the Maha Nayaka at the apex. In most of them, high officials such as the Maha Nayaka, have a life tenure and the elected members by and large have a five year tenure.

The areas to which virtually all of them pay special attention are the education of the novices, ecclesiastical disputes and matters relating to the interpretation of Buddhist scriptures. Elaborate arrangements to look after these subjects—either through committees or Sabhas—are provided for in the constitution. And in all the fraternities, the Maha Nayaka seems to be the most powerful official in the entire set-up.

We have noted the specific, elaborate and systematic character of these hierarchies. The point to explore now is: How effective is the hierarchical structure in practice? How seriously do the lower rungs of the hierarchy take the mandate from the Maha Nayaka? To a great extent it depends upon the charisma of the Maha Nayaka but there have been several occasions when the elaborate hierarchical structure has proved ineffective despite the Maha Nayaka's efforts.

There have been cases, for instance, where a particular Bhikkhu, when not elected to the higher position in an area, has decided to form a new division; there have been others (particularly disputes regarding the incumbency of a particular vihara) in which the decision of the Maha Nayaka has been over-ruled, the matter taken to the court and the decision of the ecclesiastical court (Adhikarana Mandalaya) done away with. Last but not least, on many political issues, the directive of the Maha Nayaka has gone unheeded by many as will be discussed in some detail in the fourth chapter.

It appears. thus, that a new form of dualism has come into being in the Sangha. In monastic and religious matters, the ecclesiastical hierarchy is still fairly effective. In political and social activities, the Bhikkhus join associations which have no connection with the Nikaya organisation; in fact they cut across them.

The Nikaya structure on paper, thus, shows tremendous potential for organisation; in effect however, except on a few religious matters such as Upasampada ceremonies, the viharas seem to have functioned as autonomous and independent units. The tradition of the Nikaya-evolution, coupled with the customary practices pertaining to the bases of the clergy-recruitment and pupillary succession have not facilitated the emergence of a centralised organisation either. A unified hierarchical structure of the Sangha was drawn in various Katikavatas from time to time, but though neatly drawn on paper, it appeared to be tenuous in effect. Finally, the British policy towards Buddhism and the ecclesiastical laws of Sri Lanka as they were codified during the British rule also played an important role in this patterning. In legal terms, every vihara was viewed as a separate, autonomous and independent unit.

The ecclesiastical structure of the various fraternities thus had only the powers of voluntary arbitration; the verdict of their Sangha Sabhas or the Adhikarana Sabhas had no legal validity on several issues dealing with temple property and succession to the vihara. A brief description of the internal dynamics of a vihara (the grass-root unit in the Nikaya hierarchy)—the mode of its organization, the ordination lineage, the status of the various pupils in the temple in relation to the chief high priest and the forms of succession for the chief incumbency of the vihara bring into bold relief the extent of autonomy which a vihara has *vis-a-vis* the Nikaya hierarchy.

INTERNAL DYNAMICS OF A VIHARA

As has been mentioned already, a vihara has as its incumbents, the chief high priest (Viharadhipati) and resident monks for most of whom the high priest is the preceptor. By and large, boys around 11-12 years of age join the order as novices. Higher ordination is performed not before they are 20 years old.

Here, one needs to ask a question, answer to which facilitate an understanding of the psyche of the Bhikkhu and thereby his attitude and behaviour towards polity and society to some extent: how and why does one join the Buddhist order?

"Why did you become a monk ?" Answer to this question, when asked in oral interviews and in questionnaire were striking for their apparent uniformity and diverse motivations which lay behind it. The open-endedness of the question facilitated this to a great extent. My respondents included persons of varying age and position. Some of them were

learned and eminent senior Bhikkhus many of whom held a
high position (often Maha Nayaka or Karaka Sabhika) in
the Nikaya hierarchy. Most of them were in 50-70 years
age group. Others were young undergraduates of Vidyalankara university mostly in the 20-30 age group. Answers of
my respondents—42 in all[14]—could be classified as follows:

Table 5

Number of Respondents (Total 42)
Causes for Joining the Monastic Order

(a) Respondent's own wish	...	28
(b) Parent's wish	...	7
(c) Parent's and teachers's wish	...	3
(d) No answer	...	4
Total	...	42

Let me elucidate category (a) through my two respondents
of whom one was a 70-year old Bhikkhu and another, a 22-
year old undergraduate. "As a child", said the former, "I
saw a Bhikkhu arriving. The white cloth was spread for him
to walk on it and the people around us said 'sadhu, sadhu'.
Then he sat on a chair and everyone paid obeisance to him.
His serenity and the reverence shown by everyone towards

14. During my field visit to Sri Lanka (1967-68), I collected some of
my data through questionnaires. A large questionnaire, dealing with
the attitude of the Bhikkhus and the laity towards various social,
economic and political questions, had one section on the internal
organisation of the temple. Data for this questionnaire was collected through oral interviews and I did not ask all the questions to
all my respondents because they belonged to various strata and
occupational groups. The second questionnaire, focussing on the
hierarchical structure of the various Nikayas, was sent by post to
the Maha Nayakas of various chapters and sects. This also included a question as to why the person concerned became a monk. The
third questionnaire was addressed to the undergraduate Bhikkhus
of the Vidyalankara University. Data was collected on a random
sampling basis. In the case of the last questionnaire, I went to the
library along with a faculty Bhikkhu member and circulated the
questionnaire to the Bhikkhus studying in the library. All of them
readily filled the questionnaire in a couple of hours and handed
them back to me.

him left a deep imprint on my mind. I wanted to be like him. Next day I talked to my brothers who told this to my father. My parents discussed this and said that I might have been a Bhikkhu in my previous life. They made arrangements for my joining the order...." The young undergraduate's answer was almost similar to the old thero: "As a young boy, I used to go to the temple. My association with the Bhikkhu and his image in my mind stirred some sort of inner feeling within me. I wanted to feel like him and be like him so I sought permission from my parents to be a monk."

Answers of others in category (a) reflected some sort of escapism from lay life; others had a romantic attitude towards Buddhism and 'social service'.[15] Many liked the Bhikkhus and wanted to be like them. Finally, there were some who frankly admitted that they 'just joined the order' but began to like it later on.

Category (b) and (c) raises the question why parents should initiate their own children to lead the life of a Bhikkhu. Behind such a decision of the parents lie plethora of motivations: religious, social, economic and customary. Perhaps the most significant one is derived from the religious traditions of the society. This is the belief that entry of a son in the monastic order is a highly meritorious act which leads on to the attainment of salvation. Besides the consideration

---

The second questionnaire, by and large, had middle aged and old Bhikkhus as my respondents. They were 14 in all. The undergraduates at the University numbered 28. As such, the total number of my sample was 42. While the first questionnaire was in English, the other two were in Sinhalese. The questionnaires are reproduced as Appendices B, C and D.

15. Answers to the question connoting escapism for instance were : "wanted emancipation from the suffering"; "I saw the trials of a layman's life. I wanted to reject it and be emancipated"; "I liked it as a child because I thought through monkhood one could be emancipated from worldly sufferings." Others referred to their association with the village priests and their liking for him. Some maintained that they decided to join the order because they wanted to "understand Buddhism better.". They desired to do "religious and social services", and lead "esteemed independent life which the ascetics led in the past" and so on.

of merit-accumulation, astrological beliefs of the Sinhalese also affect such a decision. In the rural surroundings, immediately after the child's birth, his horoscope is prepared to forecast his fortune. Sometimes the astrologer (often a Bhikkhu) may foretell that there is an unavoidable death-omen in the life of the child and the only way to avoid it is to make him a monk. Or the sooth-sayer may predict that the boy is not destined to lead a successful layman's life. This prompts the parents to take such a decision and maintain that if the child is going to be an unsuccessful householder, he should be made a successful monk.[16]

In some cases, pious parents who are poor but have a big family, decide to make one of their child a Bhikkhu. This would leave them with one mouth less to feed in the (not-too-happy) life of this world and accumulation of merit in the world to come.[17] Further, they can envisage him as a member of a highly respected order, having a secure and definite position in Sinhalese society.

Another consideration is the economic advantage which may be derived from membership of the vihara itself. In the case of some of the temples with large temple-holdings, it is specified that a member of the initial donor family should be the chief incumbent.[18] In such cases, the child, joining the order, has not only the esteem but also the affluence. In many others even though such a specification is not made in

16. Based on an unpublished article 'The Contemporary Ceylonese Sangha', of Rev. P. Vajiragnana, Department of Philosophy, University of Ceylon, Peradeniya.

17. Ibid.

18. e.g., in the case of Kobbekaduva vihara, the lands belonging to this Vihara were given on specific instructions that the property was to remain in the 'religious descent'. (Sasana Paramparawa). In course of time religious descent came to be connected with the familial descent of the Kobbekaduva family. Testifying before the Buddhist Temporalities Commission in September 1876 one member of this family declared "our family possesses the Kobbekaduva Vihara. The incumbency must always be held by a member of my family and for that purpose some member becomes a priest and is specially educated for the office." Ceylon *Report of the Commission appointed to enquire into the Administration of the Buddhist Temporalities* (Sessional Paper 17 of 1876), p. 5 in Malalagoda, n. 8, pp. 71-72.

the original deed of dedication, the chief incumbents of viharas with large temple properties, do wish the property to be inherited by a member in their family line. Often a boy who is a close relative (usually a nephew), is sought as the successor and the parents accede to this.

The motivations for joining the monastic order are thus complex, and the categorization as those presented in Table 1 need not be quite exclusive of one another. A young boy, attracted by the dignity of the Bhikkhu and the honour bestowed on the young novices by his seniors, may like to be one of them. The parents, because of the reasons mentioned above, may be interested in the child becoming a Bhikkhu and may make direct or indirect suggestions to him regarding the social advantages of being a Bhikkhu. Almost simultaneously, one of the Bhikkhu may find the boy a suitable successor and may persuade the parents to give him to the Sangha. Moreover, in cases where familial concerns assume primacy, there may even be an understanding between the chief high priest and the parents that in the event of his demise their son would succeed him as the chief incumbent.

It is necessary to note that the office of high chief priest is customary. Further, according to the Buddhist Temporalities Ordinance (No. 19) of 1931, a Buddhist temple or a vihara is "not a juristic person. It is not like the deity of a Hindu Temple. It is not a corporation. It has no legal personality".[19] According to Section 20 of the 1931 Ordinance, (as has been mentioned earlier) all property relating to the vihara or any place of Buddhist worship will vest in the trustee. Section 4 of the same ordinance, however, allows the chief monk of a temple to appoint himself as the trustee—the 'controlling' Viharadhipati[20]—and this is what is done in many cases. Thus, though in theory the temple property is sanghika—belonging to the whole order, "the actual control and factual ownership of the temple and the

---

19. For details see, T.B. Dissanayake and A.B. Colin de Soysa, *Kandyan Law and Buddhist Ecclesiastical Law* (Colombo, 1963), pp. 251-2.

20. Ibid. Also see H.W. Tambiah, 'Buddhist Ecclesiastical Law', *Journal of the Ceylon Branch of the Royal Asiatic Society*, New Series, Vol. 8, part 1, pp. 95-107.

temple land lie with the chief monk, who usually is also the trustee in the case of important temples".[21] It is in this context that the property rights of the Viharadhipati become important and so does the question of succession.

Succession to headship of a temple is regulated by two sets of legal norms, the one drawing sustenance from the canons and the other running counter to them. They are termed as Sisyanu Sisya Paramparawa and Sivuru Paramparawa respectively.[22] "The former, strictly speaking, is the succession by a priest to temple property by right of its tutor, as the eldest and the most qualified pupil; whereas the latter is only by right of having been robed and intended for succession to the property by the living incumbent, and such often are near relatives of the incumbent priest".[23] The Sivuru Paramparawa, however, is not very common. It is the Sisayanu Sisya Paramparawa that is accepted as the general rule of succession.

As regards the Sisyanu Sisya Paramparawa, the earliest reference to it is in a 10th century stone inscription[24] and it is part of the customary law. Generally, the rule of pupillary succession presupposes handing over of rights of temple property from senior pupil to senior pupil in an unbroken line. A senior pupil is defined as one who has received the higher ordination first and who has therefore spent more 'rainy seasons' in the vihara of his preceptor than his co-pupils.[25] By and large this rule prevails in pupillary succession except in cases where the chief incumbent decides to appoint or nominate one of his pupils. Such a pupil, even though a junior one, then succeeds to the exclusion of the senior pupils.[26]

21. Evers, n. 1, p. 706.
22. For details on the pupillary succession, apart from Dissanayake, n. 19, and Tambiah, n. 20; also see George William Woodehouse, *Sissiyanu Sissia Paramparawa and other Laws Relating to Buddhist Priests in Ceylon* (Tellippalli, 1916).
23. Dissanayake and de Soysa, n. 19, pp. 282-3.
24. Buddhannahala Pillar Inscription, *Epigraphica Zeylanica*, vol. 1, 1904-12, pp. 191-200 in Hans-Dieter Evers, *Monks, Priests and Peasants : A Study of Buddhism and Social Structure in Central Ceylon* (Leiden, E.J. Brill, 1972), p. 16.
25. Evers, n. 21, p, 706.
26. Dissanayake and de Soysa, n. 19, p. 285.

The Sivuru Paramparawa has legitimacy *vis-ā-vis* certain
monasteries only as far as succession is concerned. In effect,
however, particularly in the cases of viharas in Central
Sri Lanka with large land holdings, family considerations
count a great deal. In his empirical study of the succession
patterns of the various senior monks living at the Malwatta
Vihara (each of whom own fairly large holdings) Dr Evers
concludes that "It is statistically normal for chief monks to
ordain relatives as pupils with a claim to temple property
and non-relatives as pupils without property rights."[27] This
is partly corroborated by the answers to my questionnaire
distributed to 28 undergraduate Bhikkhus of the Vidyalankara University in Table 6 in 1968.[28]

Table 6[29]

Degree of kinship relation between the chief incumbents and the respondents		
(a) Not related and not the senior most pupil	...	14
(b) Not related but the senior most pupil	...	8
(c) Related and the senior most pupil	...	5
(d) Related but not the senior most pupil	...	1
Total	...	28

It is noteworthy that out of the eight falling in category
(b) i.e., those who were not related by the senior most pupils,
three were the only pupils of their respective teachers.

An enquiry into the sources of the financial assistance for
their university education revealed that the family ties of the
Bhikkhus were close. About one quarter were supported
by the family. In the case of about one half of them, the
vihara looked after their material needs while in the university and in the case of about 25 per cent, the financial
responsibilities were shared by the teachers and the parents.

It might also be added that a Bhikkhu, if he is the only

27. Evers, n. 21, p. 707.
28. For details on the questionnaire and the respondents see footnote
    14.
29. Ibid.

Table 7 [30]

	Sources of financial support of the respondents at the University	
(a)	Preceptor	...	12
(b)	Home (parents and brothers)	...	7
(c)	Parents and teacher	...	7
(d)	No particular person	...	2
	Total	...	28

child, has a right to inherit his father's property in preference to collateral heirs. The rule that a Bhikkhu taking the
robe, renounces all wealth is not universal. He may take
gifts, accept bequests and inherit from the mother and from
brothers and sisters. And after his death this private property
is not to be inherited by his pupil but is to revert to his
next of kin.[31]

The analysis of the basis and modes of non-recruitment
as well as his legal status thus presents a picture which is
more than a deviation from the early image of the monk and
monkhood. In most of the cases a Bhikkhu does not become
a Bhikkhu; he is made to be one. His act of renouncing to
the world is not the rational decision of an adult but is
often the romantic decision (if it is his decision at all) of a
twelve year old boy. The process of renunciation has un-
doubtedly some of the traditional significance; in most of
the cases the teacher seems to put great emphasis on the
mode of the samanera's public behaviour; how he should
walk, how he should talk; his sleeping, eating and study hours
are property defined and he is expected to have a poise,
dignity and decorum which clearly distinguishes his behaviour
from that of his lay peers.

In many other respects, however, the traditional image of
the Bhikkhu gets distorted. The succession patterns underlining the caste and family linkages, coupled with the legal
status of the Bhikkhus (as the controlling Viharadhipati and

30. Ibid.
31. For details see Dissanayake and de Soysa, n. 19, pp. 150, 180 and
297.

as the inheritor of his close relatives' property), legitimised as they have been through customary practices and modern legal system, tend to be some of the factors for such a distortion.

Behind such legacies of the past lie the interaction of the religious system with the social, economic and political systems, the responses of the religious professional elite to the demands of these systems and the delineation of his functions and roles therein.

BHIKKHUS IN SRI LANKA : FUNCTIONS AND ROLES

As should be obvious from the preceding pages, the functions and roles of the Bhikkhu community in Sri Lanka have been diverse and manifold. As a temple priest he performs several rituals but it is his role as friend, philosopher and guide (particularly in rural areas) which is most apparent. His service is sought on several issues and in very many cases, adhered to. In the case of the vihara having property, he may assume, in effect, the role of a landlord. As one who thus has power, affluence and status, his roles in politics have been, at times, critical in the monarchical past as much as in the democratic set-up of the present.

The societal roles of the monk are closely related to his status and 'category'. If he is a either a 'Tapasa'[32] Bhikkhu or a hermit monk (following the old tradition of Gamvasin) he evokes reverence and esteem and symbolises the high ideals of Buddhism. There are two kinds of hermitages in Sri Lanka—island and forest. An exemplary instance of the former is Pogasduwa Island and hermitage near Galle in the south of Sri Lanka. Most of the monks in the hermitage have donned the robes on their own conviction and are

---

32. 'Tapasa' means mortification of flesh. In his article Nur Yalman refers to the presence of some of these Bhikkhus who appear to be a "modern version of the ancient Pamsulikas who wore rag-robes and emphasised strict observance of monastic regulations." Michael Ames, 'Ideological and Social Change in Ceylon', *Human Organisation*, Vol. 22, No. 1, Spring 1963, p. 52, footnote 22. For details on the Tapasa monks see Nur Yalman, 'Ascetic Buddhist Monks of Ceylon', *Ethnology*, Vol. 1, No. 3, 1962, pp. 315-28.

highly educated. They devote their time to meditation and to other religious activities. Some of the forest hermitages, apart from putting considerable emphasis on meditation are also active in the dissemination of knowledge regarding Buddhism throughout the world, through their publications. Apart from the hermitage monks, there are learned Bhikkhus in Colombo and elsewhere too. For example, the Revs. Narada, Piyadassi and Vinita are engaged in similar pursuits. They have contributed much to the propagation of Dhamma abroad, through their writings and visits. In the local context, Bhikkhus like the late Rev. Polwatte Buddhadatte and Henepitigedara Gnanaseeha attempted to elucidate the Buddhist concepts for the modern laity through their works.[33]

In the past, dissemination of knowledge of Buddhism was done through Pirivenas and several other higher educational monastic (Ayatanas or Mulas) colleges which formed part of the structural complex of the Buddhist monastery. Even at present, there are several Pirivenas in which the laity and the Bhikkhus are educated. The Sunday or the Poya day (day connoting quarters of the moon) schools in the temples are another institution through which the Bhikkhu performs his role as an educator as well as a missionary. The Pirivenas are more than often, located in the viharas.

Besides, both the Vihara and the Devala (temples enshrining gods) officials perform three types of ritual activities: (a) the regular rituals performed by the Bhikkhus at the vihara (Buddha Pujava—worship of the Buddha) three times a day; (b) the annual temple festivals, and (c) other ritual activities in which the ritual specialist of the temple are involved but which are not specifically related to the vihara like Pirith chanting in the Dayaka's houses or participation of the Bhikkhus in the rites of passages etc.[34]

33. P. Vajiragnana, n. 16. Also see *Indian Express*, 21 October 1968, referring to the opening of a new hermitage at Mitirigala.
34. Evers, n. 24., pp. 48-71. See also Ganannath Obeyesekere, *Land Tenure in Village Ceylon : A Sociological and Historical Study* Cambridge, 1967); 'The Buddhist Pantheon in Ceylon and its Extensions', in M. Nash, ed., *Anthropological Studies in Theravada Buddhism* (New Haven, 1966), pp. 1-26.

In viharas having more than one Bhikkhu, the senior most amongst them is expected to look after their daily necessities and if he has some novices under him, he performs the requisite functions of a preceptor and a teacher. If the chief high priest also happens to be the trustee (controlling Viharadhipati) then his functions, legally specified as they are, includes: (a) the repair and furnishing of the vihara; (b) the maintenance of the resident Bhikkhus and the ministerial officers attached to it; (c) the performance of religious worship and such customary ceremonies as were hitherto maintained in connection with the temple; (d) promotion of education; (e) customary hospitality to other Bhikkhus; (f) payment of such share of expenses as shall be incurred in carrying out the provision of the ordination; and (g) remuneration of trustee and the payment of expenses incurred by them in carrying out the provisions of this ordinance. As regards the temple property, his powers and functions regarding its administration, the mortgage, sale or alienation of the immovable property belonging to the temple, leasing of the land holdings etc., are spelt out in fairly great details in the Buddhhist Temporalities Ordinance No. 19 of 1931.[35]

Notwithstanding the critical canonical approach towards the division of society into classes, the historical context of the administration of temple endowments has resulted in a class-ridden Bhikkhu community. Historically speaking, though there was no uniform pattern regarding the grant of endowments to the monasteries, the general practice was to dedicate it to the body of Bhikkhus as a whole or to a group of Bhikkhus living in a particular vihara. In due course, however, the practice of dedicating property to a particular Bhikkhu came into vogue, and the earliest dates from the first century A.D. when, as has already been mentioned, King Vatthagamini dedicated a vihara to a particular Bhikkhu, who as a consequence, incurred the wrath of the Maha vihara monks.

There are temples which can be termed as poor. Having no permanent source of sustenance, their daily necessities are looked after by the Buddhist benefactors—the Dayakas. Above them are the middle range viharas which have some temple holdings

35. Tambiah, n. 20, pp. 102-7.

but which cannot be termed as affluent. Barring a few cases, the viharas pertaining to Ramanna and Amarapura Nikaya belong to one or other of the two category because right from their inception the source of their sustenance was endowments from the Buddhist laity which could not compete with the huge endowments which a segment of the Bhikkhus in the Siam Nikaya had acquired from the royalty.

The Bhikkhu community in Siam Nikaya in fact has from the very poor to very rich and (excepting a few cases) the incumbency of the viharas having large landholdings is vested in the upper echelons—the Karaka Sabhika—of the various chapters of the Nikaya. There have been cases in which the income from these landholdings have been invested in real-estate, money-lending or companies.[36]

A reference has been made to the analysis of the inter-relationship of caste, kinship and ordination lineage made by Dr Evers in respect of Malwatta vihara. It needs to be reiterated that all chief priests of the major monasteries in Central Sri Lanka—the former Kandyan Kingdom—belong to the Goyigama caste; many belong to the Radala sub-caste of the Kandyan aristocracy. Together with the temple lords (Basnayke nilame) of the Devales, almost all of whom are radalas, and landlords, they have perpetuated the feudal system of the past in more than one way. Controlling large tracts of land and accumulating considerable funds, they have tremendous potential for influence over many Bhikkhus and temple tenants many of whom even today, do traditional services (Rajkaria) for them.[37] As regards the democratic politics of independent Sri Lanka, it is as yet to affect their economic position and change the *status quo*. Attempts have been made by the State in this direction but these have been thwarted so far by the monastic landlords as will be discussed later.

36. e.g. : 'In the village of Terutenne, the priest of one of the temples had a considerable amount of cash always available from the sale of produce of lands.. He had always been a shrewd money lender.' Yalman, n. 32, p. 318. Also see Nur Yalman, 'The Flexibility of Caste Principles in a Kandyan Community', in E.R. Leach, ed., *Aspects of Caste in South India, Ceylon and North-West Pakistan* (Cambridge, 1960), p. 81.
37. Evers, n. 24, pp. 12-22 and 94-97.

CONCLUSION

In the evolution of the monastic order in Sri Lanka, discontinuities are as marked as continuities. To begin with, the Gramvasin and Vanavasin traditions in the Sangha seem to have survived the onslaughts of time and exist even today. Further if some of the continuities in the contemporary Sangha can be discerned in the use of suttas, jatakas and litturgical texts in certain rituals e.g., the format of the Upasampada ceremony, the observance of lent (vassa), the recitation of Patimokkha, which have been handed down from the classical past, there are others which, deriving their legitimacy and strength in a purely indigenous context, have an indigenous flavour. The blend of myths, legends and history, emphasising the Sinhalese Buddhist inheritance of its society and polity is an important instance in this respect.

Besides, partly as a result of changed socio-economic conditions, other changes have also taken place in the monastic systems which are contrary to Nikaya regulations. If caste and kinship considerations as the basis of Bhikkhu-recruitment is one, the owning of private property by the Bhikkhu as well as the handling of money is another. Caste has also been one of the factors in the fragmentation of the Sangha. Coupled with the tradition of monastic landlordism it has brought in class division too. However, the caste-class divisions do not always converge; in cases, they cut across each other. To illustrate, most of the affluent viharas in the island have as their chief monk a Bhikkhu of Goyigama caste but the chiefs of all the temples belonging to the high caste are not affluent. A Siam Nikaya Vihara may belong to the category of a poor temple, while a non-Goyigama dominated Amarapura vihara may be fairly rich.

In contemporary Sri Lanka, some of the viharas may not have had the power and influence commensurate to their affluence in comparison to the others who may not have affluence but more esteem, status and influence in the socio-political life of the area. In this context, the up-country low-country division of the Sinhalese Buddhists assumes certain significance. By and large, it was the low-country Bhikkhus who, irrespective of the Nikaya differences, had been more directly involved in the socio-political issues. They were more radical and forward-looking than the upper echelons of the up-country Bhikkhus who had been more traditional and conservative.

Historical compulsions seem to have wrought this division. For one thing, the low-country monks were opposed to the colonial thrust for 450 years whereas the up-country clergy lived in relative isolation till a century ago. As such, the low country clergy had to cope with the socio-economic changes consequent to the colonial rule and contain, to the extent possible, the manifold thrusts of an alien, often aggressive, religion. Moreover, being more dependent on the endowments of the laity than the up-country clergy, its low-country counterpart had to be involved with the day to day problems of the laity than afford to live in seclusion.

In sum, an analysis of the role of the Sangha in the contemporary politics of Sri Lanka necessitates taking stock of the pertinent fact that the Sangha in Ceylon is not a monolith but a congery of various units, divided on caste, class and ideological basis and at times cutting across these divisions too.

It must be added that such divisions did not stop at the chapter or sect level, but permeated at the vihara level—the micro-unit of the order—which very often found itself involved in the vortex of controversies affecting the Sangha as a whole. To illustrate, the chief high priest of a vihara with landholdings may have a certain amount of direct influence over the tenants; another Bhikkhu resident in the same vihara may be more pious and learned thereby evoking greater esteem of the laity (some of whom may be tenants of the temporalities) and consequently, having greater influence. It is in this context that the effects of the methods of Bhikkhu recruitment also needs to be examined. Most of the Bhikkhus have not *chosen* to be monks; they have *become* Bhikkhus. With this background, the urge on the part of some of them to remedy the socio-political maladies (as they perceived them) and thereby become harbingers of change, seemed logical, especially, amongst some of those who, with a deep sense of history and having the realisation of the importance of the common destiny of the Sangha and State did have ambitions to convert their potential into actual power.

With the withdrawal of the British power, it was hoped by a segment of the Buddhist laity and the clergy that the Ceylonese leadership would try to restore the traditional continuity in Sangha-State relationship which had snapped during the colonial era. The response of political leadership to such depended as much upon the intensity as varied manifestation of such demands by the Bhikkhus as on the dynamics of the party system as it evolved since 1948.

Chapter IV

PARTY SYSTEM AND RELIGIOUS ISSUES :
THE INTERACTION

INTRODUCTION

In the preceding chapter an attempt has been made to analyse
the historical process which resulted in Buddhism acquiring
its 'transformative capabilities'[1] to emerge as a focal point of
social sanctions in secular affairs. To discern the continuity of
this process in the contemporary era, an overview is necessary
of the trends in civic culture which occurred in Sri Lanka as a
consequence of ever increasing political socialisation.

Specifically, Buddhism's 'transformative capabilities' have
to be related to the compulsions inherent in the political system which evolved with the endowment of restricted franchise
by the Colonial Government. This was followed by its enlarge-
ment in 1931 when universal adult franchise was introduced
in the island but its potential as a source of effective political
power was laid bare only in 1947 with the creation of a State
structure appropriate to the parliamentary form of Government.

In this context, a pertinent point of which note needs to be
taken is the observation of Max Weber in respect of the
growth of the party system in the UK that adult franchise
was a catalytic agent.[2] Experience in Sri Lanka bears out the

1. S.N. Eisenstadt, 'The Protestant Ethic Thesis', in Ronald Robertson, ed., *Sociology of Religion* (London 1965), pp. 293-314.
2. Max Weber, 'Politics as a Vocation', in H.H. Gerth and C.
   Wright Mills, eds., *Max Weber, Essays in Sociology* (New York,
   1958), pp. 77-128.

importance of the ballot box in the evolution of the party system but it emphasises at the same time the significant fact that franchise becomes active as a catalyst only when an institutional context is provided for it to become a critical element as a sequential power factor in society. Thus, in Sri Lanka it was more than two decades after its introduction, that adult franchise began to exercise its influence, firstly, in fostering the growth of parties and, secondly, in the development of the party system as such in its present form.

Broadly speaking, therefore, the emergence of Buddhism as a political factor in the competitive ethos of the parliamentary system not only conditioned but was also conditioned by the nature of political parties, their avowed goals whether they be self-promotional or social or both,[3] as well as the situational pressures obtaining in a democratic system. Such pressures, as historical experience shows, may result in the gradual watering down of the radical ideology of one party or may tend to loosen the conservatism of another. Likewise the attitudinal correlation between religion and parties tend to be influenced by electoral demands. Such a correlation is intelligible in Sri Lanka in the context of the distinctive features of its electoral traditions which set it apart from other similar societies. Briefly, therefore, it is necessary to trace the growth of the party system in the country and its dominant characteristics.

3. For an emphasis on the social roles of the parties see Sigmund Neuman, ed., *Modern Political Parties : Approaches to Comparative Politics* (Chicago, 1956), p. 2 and Gabriel Almond and P.G.Bingham Powell, Jr.,*Comparative Politics : A Developmental Approach* (Boston, 1966), pp. 114-27, Pareto, Mosca and Robert Michels, however, discerned in the party a vehicle for the perpetuation of the oligarchic role within a democratic framework and thereby underlined the self-promotional roles of its small coterie. For details see Vilfredo Pareto, *The Mind and Society*, ed., by Arthur Livingstone (New York, 1935); Gaetano Mosca, *The Ruling Class*, trans. by Hannah D. Kaan, ed. and revised with an Introduction by Arthur Livingston (New York, 1939); Robert Michels, *Political Parties* (New York, 1959); Authors like Apter and Eldersveld, however, believe that the parties perform both social and self-promotional functions. Harry Eckstein and David Apter, eds., *Comparative Politics* (New York, 1963), and S.J. Eldersveld, *Political Parties : A Behavioural Analysis* (Chicago, 1964).

THE PARTY SYSTEM : EVOLUTION AND GROWTH

The crystallisation of political impulses in the form of organised grouping began in Sri Lanka soon after the introduction of restricted franchise in 1910 when the Ceylon Reform League came into being in 1916 and was subsequently reorganised as the Ceylon National Congress in 1919. The Congress soon, however, suffered a split when a section of up-country Sinhalese broke away from it in 1924 to form the Kandyan National Assembly. Other interest conglomerations that emerged were the European Association in 1927 and Ceylon Muslim League as well as All Ceylon Moors' Association.[4]

The restrictive character of the franchise[5] and the marginal nature of influence on the administration which the elected representatives were in a position to wield endowed them with more prestige than power. As a consequence, the groups tended to be highly personalised congeries of 'notables' competing with each other for the privilege of the advisory role in the governance of the country.

The introduction of universal adult franchise in 1931 did bring in a fair measure of mass involvement in the electoral process despite the reservations of national leaders who, as the Donoughmore Commission recorded, "proposed to work full responsible government with an electorate from which the greater proportion of the people were excluded", [6] on the plea

---

4. Calvin A. Woodwards, *The Growth of a Party System in Ceylon* (Rhode Island, 1969), pp. 21-39.

5. The beginnings of universal adult franchise can be traced to the reforms of 1910 according to which 4 members were to be elected on a restricted franchise in a Legislative Council of 21. The reforms of 1920 provided the elected representatives with a bare majority ; in the 37 member council, 19 were elected. With the promulgation of the Order in Council of 1923, the number of elected representatives rose from 19 to 34 in a council of 47. The Donoughmore Commission recommended the formation of a State Council with 3 officers of the state, not more than 8 nominated state officers and 50 elected members. For details refer to Sir Charles Jeffries, *Ceylon The Path to Independence* (London, 1962) pp. 33-57.

6. Ceylon, *Report of Special Commission on the Constitution* (London, 1928), pp. 13-17 and 80-90.

that the masses in the country were not as yet "sufficiently mature to be given franchise rights."[7] This view was not shared by the Commission which recommended the formation of State Council on the basis of adult franchise.[8]

With a turnout of 56 per cent of the electorate in the first election under adult franchise, it cannot be said that the reservations of the Ceylonese leaders were well-founded. Even so, the broad-basing of the electorate did not result in any significant change in the character of political groupings which continued to accrete round personalities and were, often communal in character. Thus the Sinhala Maha Sabha, founded by SWRD Bandaranaike in 1934 claimed to represent the

7. Except the leaders of the left Labour Party, most of the colonial elites, while favouring the extension of franchise, opposed the universal adult franchise. So far, the unofficial members of the legislative council were elected on the basis of a limited franchise with sex, property and literacy being the requisite qualification. Women, for instance, had no voting rights. While having a broad consensus on giving women the right to vote, the majority of national leaders insisted on the continuity of a literacy test. They argued that the illiterate mass had not yet attained the level of political sophistication to enable them to use their vote in a discrete fashion. The proposal of universal adult franchise, at this stage was immature and might lead to political nepotism and corruption. Ibid. However, behind these objections lay also the fears of the minority group leaders (particularly the Ceylon Tamils) that the introduction of the universal franchise might lead to the domination of the minority by the majority community. For details on the attitude of the leaders of various communities towards extension of franchise rights and towards universal adult franchise see Karunasena Hewawasan Jayasinghe, *The Extension of the Franchise in Ceylon with Some Consideration of their Political and Social Consequences* (unpublished Ph. D. Thesis, London School of Economics and Political Science, University of London, 1965), pp. 93-192.

8. Ibid. It may be added that the commission was set up by L.S. Amery, Secretary of State for the Colonies. The victory of the Labour party in the elections leading to the change of the government and the fact that one member of the Commission (Dr. Drummond Shiels, who became the Parliamentary under secretary of state under the Labour Government) held an important portfolio in the new government, facilitated a speedy acceptance of the Commission's recommendations by the colonial office, with certain modifications. For details, see Jeffries, n. 5, pp. 33-60.

Sinhalese and the All Ceylon Tamil Congress emerged in 1944 as the spokesman of Tamil interests with G.G. Ponnambalam as its leading light.

The principal factor inhibiting the growth of parties in the accepted stereotype of the term in a parliamentary democracy was the absence of the accountability principle which establishes the functional nexus between the electorate and those competing for its favour. This was implicit in the provisions of Donoughmore Constitution under which ministers were responsible only to the Governor and not as a group to the legislature. Thus, by ignoring the twin principles of collective responsibility and the responsibility of the executive to the legislature, the Donoughmore Constitution encouraged 'individualism in political activity and behaviour'[9] and militated against the emergence of the party system.[10] The apparent unimportance of the party system during this period was also evident in the manner in which the break-up of election results were given; these were on communal and not on party basis.[11]

An exception to this pattern of political mobilisation were the left parties like the Trotskyite Lanka Sama Samaja Party (LSSP) which had come into being in December 1935 and Communist Party (1943) which, unlike the communal groups and 'notable parties', had organization as well as ideology and which attempted to mobilise popular support horizontally, cutting across vertical solidarities. However, internal schism

9. A.J. Wilson, 'Ceylon Cabinet Ministers 1947-1960 : Their Political Economic and Social Background', *Ceylon Economist*, Vol. 5, No.1, March 1960, p. 5.

10. Ivor Jennings went even a step further and argued that if there had been parties, the Donoughmore Constitution would not have worked at all. It was designed to suit a legislature without political parties and therefore it actively discouraged them. W.I. Jennings, 'Ceylon General Elections of 1947', *University of Ceylon Review*, Vol. 6, No. 3, July 1948, p. 134. I.D.S. Weerawardena, *Government and Politics in Ceylon* 1931-1946 (Colombo, 1951), p. 140.

11. See Table 1.

and ideological feuds[12] resulted in left fragementation and deprived it of an impact which otherwise it might have made on the political system.

A decisive change, setting the pace for the development of political parties in 1945, was the provisions of a new constitution, based on the recommendations of the Soulbury Commission which introduced the cabinet system on the

Table I

Composition of the State Council

C o m m u n i t y		1931	1936
Elected			
Sinhalese Low Country	...	28	31
Sinhalese Kandyans	...	10	8
Ceylon Tamils	...	3	8
Indian Tamils	...	2	2
Europeans	...	2	1
Moors	...	1	—
Total		46*	50
Nominated			
Burghers	...	2	1
Muslims	...	1	2
Indians	...	1	1
Europeans	...	4	4
Total		8	8

Jeffries, n. 5, pp. 68 and 76.

Because of the boycott of the Tamils as a protest to the abolition of communal electorates, four seats in Jaffna remained vacant in 1931 elections.

12. The most serious split in the LSSP occurred in 1939 when majority of its members decided to pass a motion of no confidence in the Third International and expelled the Stalinist minority led by S.A. Wickramasinghe and Pieter Keuneman. The expelled leaders founded the United Socialist Party in 1940 which was dissolved in 1943 and the Ceylon Communist Party was set up. In 1945 leadership competition led to another split within the LSSP and its splinter group formed Bolshevik Leninist party under the leadership of Colin R. de Silva. For details refer to Leslie Goonewardene, *A Short History of the Lanka Sama Samaja Party* (Colombo, 1960), pp. 1-34 and Pieter Keuneman, *25 Years of the Ceylon Communist Party* (Colombo, 1968), pp. 1-12.

British pattern. With the introduction of the cabinet system and that of the principle of collective responsibility in the new constitution, the working of the constitution on party lines became necessary. It was in this context that the United National Party (UNP), including majority of the former members of the State Council, was formed under the leadership of D.S. Senanayake. Two political groups—Ceylon National Congress and Sinhala Maha Sabha provided the nucleus for it. Apart from the UNP, other parties entering the election arena were the Labour Party, the first left political party of the island founded by A.E. Goonesinha, the LSSP, led by N.M. Perera, the Bolshevik Leninist Party and the Communist Party, Lanka Swaraj Party, the Tamil Congress and Ceylon Indian Congress representing the interests of the persons of Indian origin in Ceylon.[13]

In the initial years of the working of the new system, the electorate was badly splintered with a multiplicity of parties and independents contesting the elections. Even so, the UNP emerged as the dominant party— a position which it retained through two General elections of 1947 and 1952.

The election of 1956 provided to be an eventful one. The Sri Lanka Freedom Party (SLFP), which had splintered from the UNP brought before the electorate issues which were of fundamental importance to the future of Buddhism and of the Sinhala language. This was the beginning of a process which eventually resulted in the polarisation of the Sinhalese electorate and the emergence of the two—major party system with the two major parties—the SLFP and the UNP—having an almost equally strong support base and virtually all the minor parties and groups aligning themselves with one of the major two.

Underlying this evolution lay several factors such as the emergence of the SLFP as a 'Movement' party during 1955-56, a fairly consistent electoral alliance pattern between the major and minor parties and some of the provisions of

13. For details refer to W.I. Jennings, *The Constitution of Ceylon* (Bombay, 1953), pp. 28-30 and S. Namasivayam, *The Legislatures of Ceylon* (London, 1951), pp. 19-31.

electoral laws.[14]

Innovations in election procedure discouraged the proliferation of parties and fostered the conglomerative trend towards the emergence of the two-major party system. The
first of these innovations was made in 1956 when the electoral
law was amended to provide for the allotment of symbols to
parties and not to individual contestants as was the practice till
then. This was followed by another amendment in 1959 under
which the Election Commission was empowered to 'recognise' parties for the allotment of symbols on the basis of
criteria stipulated in the amended Act. It was specified that to
be eligible for the symbol, parties had to have been in existence
for at least five years prior to the date of application or, at least,
two of its members ought to have been members of Parliament.[15]
The requirements of parties to claim a symbol were made
more stringent in further amendments introduced in 1964.[16]

If changes in electoral laws provided the institutional compulsions for the emergence of a pattern of major parties, a high
degree of maturity of the electorate provided the political
impulse for the coalitional trends in the party system.
Consistently in successive elections, the electorate (exclud-
ing in the Tamil populated regions) made its verdict un-
mistakably clear that it did not take the minor parties seriously unless they were the electoral allies of one or the other
major parties.

A consequence of these factors was that by July 1960, the
UNP and the SLFP had emerged as the two major contenders
for powers sharing between them 71.2 per cent of the total
votes polled.[17] In terms of seats, except in the Tamil domina-

14. Ceylon, *Report of the Sixth Parliamentary General Elections of
Ceylon*, 22 March 1965, Sessional Paper xx of 1966 (Colombo,
1966), p. 6.

15. Ceylon Daily News, *Parliament of Ceylon*, 1960 (Colombo 1960),
p. 14. Also see, Ceylon, *Report on the Parliamentary General
Elections*, March 19 and July 20, 1920, Sessional Paper 11 of 1962
(Colombo, 1962).

16. For details see Ceylon, *Report on the Sixth Parliamentary General
Election*, n. 14, pp. 7-8, and Ceylon, *Report on the Seventh Parliamentary General Election in Ceylon*, 27 May 1970, Sessional paper
7 of 1971 (Colombo, 1971), pp. 8-9.

17. Ceylon, *Report on the Sixth Parliamentary General Election*, n. 14,
Table VI.

ted northern and eastern provinces, the two major parties and their allies divided virtually all the seats between them in 1965 and 1970 elections and had shared between them more than 80 per cent of the votes polled.[18]

A word needs to be added about the Tamil parties in the north and the eastern provinces which, despite their regional character, seemed to be gradually yielding to the competitive two major parly system of the island, not so much through electoral adjustments as through their bargaining position in the event of the formation of a coalition government. The interaction of the Sinhalese-Tamil parties however had a set-back during 1956-64 when communalisation of politics in the wake of the Sinhalese Buddhist upsurge of 1956 alienated the dominant minority community. Consequently, amongst the Tamil parties, the Federal Party (which had broken away from Tamil Congress in 1949) emerged strongest in the northern and eastern provinces in the election of 1956 and continued to hold a dominant position in subsequent elections. The Tamil parties played an oppositional-agitational role during the next five years till 1965 when they decided to join hands with the UNP in the formation of a coalition government.[19]

Coalitional Patterns of Party Politics[20]

If the emergence of the two major party system compelled

18. Ibid. Also see Ceylon, *Report on the Seventh Parliamentary General Election in Ceylon*, n. 16, Table VII.
19. The Federal Party, however, decided to walk out of the government in 1968 on certain aspects of the language policy of the Senanayake Government. For details refer to Urmila Phadnis, 'Federal Party in Ceylon : Towards Power or Wilderness', *Economic and Political Weekly*, Vol. 4, No. 20, 17 May 1969, pp. 839-43.
20. For details on various points referred in this section see (1) my paper entitled 'Politics of Coalition Governments in Ceylon', in a seminar on *Politics of Coalition Governments in India*, organised by the Indian Institute of Advanced Study, Simla, 13-20 October, 1970; and subsequently reproduced (without footnotes) in *Tribune*, Vol. 17, Nos.1-3, 30 June 1971, pp. 26-28, and Vol. 17, No. 4, 14 July 1971, pp. 12-13. (2) 'Trends in Ceylon Politics', *India Quarterly*, Vol. 27, No. 2, April-June 1971, pp. 122-39, and (3), 'The UF Government in Ceylon : Challenges and Responses', *World Today*, Vol. 27, No. 6, June 1971, pp. 267-76.

an alliance pattern at the hustings, it was only logical that it
should lead on to coalitional forms of government. Thus of
the seven parliamentary elections which the island has had
since 1947, three resulted in the formation of a coalition
government and the fourth, a United Front government which
has governed the country since 1970. Of the rest, in one
(March 1960) the governing party—the UNP, was voted out
of power almost immediately after elections primarily because
it had failed to obtain a coalitional consensus; in another,
the ruling party—the SLFP—hanging on to a precariously
slender majority for $3\frac{1}{2}$ years (1960-64) had to negotiate with
one of the left parties in opposition (LSSP) for the formation
of a coalition government.

Coalition governments thus appear to be in tradition of the
politics of Sri Lanka. However, unlike India, they symbolise
aggregation and not fragmentation of its politics. The coalitional patterns in the island, while representing the diversities
of its pluralist society, has proved to be fairly stable and has a
certain continuity. If the credit for such a stability can be
ascribed to the existence of two mojor parties, one of which
has been the pivot of every coalition, the measure of continuity
can be discerned in a system in which neither of the major
parties has survived more than two elections as the ruling
party. The two term cycle of the UNP and the SLFP as parties
in governance and opposition alternatively has facilitated the
widening of inter-party consensus areas and the blurring of
differences. At times, it has been dictated by the expediency of
the scarce resources of society, at others, continuity in 'ruling'
has demanded it. Such compulsions and demands have, more
than often, led to a shift, if not a reversal, of the party's
earlier stand on various issues, whether political, economic or
religious. A perusal of the religious policies of the two major
parties—the UNP and the SLFP—as well as the left parties
like the CP and the LSSP and the regional parties like the
FP facilitates an understanding of the factors which propel a
party to either change its policy or give a new emphasis to it
or provide a special emphasis, thereby underlining the importance of the issue which it did not have earlier.

THE UNP : RELIGIOUS POLICIES AND PERFORMANCE

Imbued with the secular-liberalist traditions of the UK, the founders of the UNP did not seem to be too concerned about defining a policy towards either religion or culture. This is evident from the fact that the election manifesto of the UNP in 1947 and its other publications during 1947-50 hardly referred to the subject. The only reference to religion was a statement by D.S. Senanayake in early 1947, emphasising that religion was essentially a personal matter and that the UNP stood for the individual's rights to freedom of worship.[21]

If religion was mentioned on the political agenda at all during this period, it was only as a reaction to the 'anti-religious' policies of the left. One of the UNP slogans in the 1947 elections, and even earlier, was "Don't give vote to the Marxists because if you do, your religion, whatever it is, will be destroyed".[22] By implication, thus, the UNP as the first ruling party of the island, adopted an attitude which was reassuring to all the religious groups that it had no 'favourites' amongst them.

Such a secular approach, however, did not appear to be without a bias. A section of opinion began to feel that in the wake of colonial rule, a tiny segment belonging to the minority racial and religious communities, had succeeded in getting too many privileges. To illustrate, the best educational institutions which were in the hands of the missionaries continued to be financed largely by the government grants. English education continued to be the pass word for power and status and Sinhalese remained a vernacular language. Christians as a group and Ceylon Tamils, about 10 per cent of the total population, held official positions not commensurate to their number. In the ruling UNP, the influence of Christians, especially Roman Catholics, was dominant. These facts, when added up, led to the inevitable conclusion: that the Sinhalese

---

21. *UNP Newssheet* issued before the beginning of the UNP Journal, date not given. Available in the UNP Office.
22. *UNP*, Vol. 1, No. 29, 26 September 1947, p. 2. While the title page refers to it as the party organ of UNP, the title on every page is 'UNP Journal' from Vol. 1, No. 31, 10 October 1947. In the earlier issues the inside pages do not have page number.

Buddhist majority was in a markedly inferior position compared to other religious and racial minority groups and that its religion, language and culture were relegated a secondary place. Consequently, the government's attitude of maintaining the *status quo* (this is what its secularism implied) favoured this segment only. What was needed in this context was a special attention to Buddhism as the religion of the 'backward' majority community and thereby restore it to its 'rightful place'.

In December 1950, a delegation of high ranking Buddhist monks met Premier D.S. Senanayake requesting state protection and support for Buddhism. A devout Buddhist and one of the foremost patrons of the Ramanna Nikaya, the Prime Minister had all along believed that religion was a personal matter and the State should adopt a secular attitude towards it. "The Buddha", replied the Premier, "has pointed out the path of development and no state aid can take man there."[23]

Such an attitude, however, did not satisfy the Buddhist groups like the All Ceylon Buddhist Congress (ACBC). Having operated (under different names)[24] since 1918, the ACBC had amongst its leaders, several renowned Buddhists and one of its major objectives was the promotion of Buddhism and safeguarding the interests of Buddhists.

On 25 April 1951 the leader of the ACBC, Dr. G.P. Malalasekera, who had been its president since 1939, wrote a letter to the Prime Minister, in which he stressed "the disappointment, almost resentment, growing among the Buddhists with regard to the present position of Buddhism in Ceylon. When all relevant facts are taken into consideration, the conviction is inescapable that the present government, as

23. *Ceylon Daily News*, 5 December 1950.
24. Founded in 1918 by some of the well known Buddhist leaders, including C.A. Hewawitarane, F.R. Senanayake and D.B. Jayatilake, the organisation had its origins in the Young Men's Buddhist Association (YMBA) and was initially known as the All Ceylon Congress of the YMBAs. Around 1924 it renamed itself as the All Ceylon Congress of Buddhist Associations. In 1940, it was redesignated as All Ceylon Buddhist Congress. All Ceylon Buddhist Congress, *Presidential Address of Sir Lalita Rajapaksa*, 30 December 1961 (Colombo 1962), pp. 2-3.

successor to previous governments, is legally and morally bound to protect and maintain Buddhism and Buddhist institutions. The Buddhists feel, however, that our present rulers have shown a marked reluctance to acknowledge this fact." In a memorandum attached to the letter, he alleged that Buddhism had been neglected. It was maintained that though it might be politically inexpedient for government to extend to Buddhism the patronage that had been extended to it by the Sinhalese rulers of the old, the government could at least provide a sound and workable constitution for the Buddhists for the management of their affairs and, till the formulation of the constitution, could establish a Buddha Sasana Department to look after Buddhist interests.[25]

Subsequently, on 30 July 1951 a delegation of the ACBC met the Premier and requested that a commission be appointed to enquire into the state of Budbhism in the island. During the talk with the Premier, Dr. Malalasekera recounted the damage' done to Buddhism under alien rule and the various 'disabilities' Buddhists had been subjected to. After independence, Buddhists, he felt, needed to be given every facility to rehabilitate themselves.

Agreeing with this view, Senanayake asked the deputation to submit names for the commission. At a subsequent meeting, however, the Prime Minister told the deputation that he had doubts whether such a commission could be appointed without violating paras (c) and (d) of section 29 of the Soulbury Constitution.[26] He also asked the deputation

---

25. All Ceylon Buddhist Congress, *Buddhism and the State Resolutions and Memorandum of the All Ceylon Buddhist Congress* (Colombo, 1951), pp. 1-3.

26. Clauses (c) and (d) of section 29 are as follows :

(1) Subject to the provisions of this order, Parliament shall have power to make laws for the peace, order and general government of the island. (2) No such law shall :

(a) prohibit or restrict the free exercise of any religion; or

(b) make persons of any community or religion liable to disabilities or restriction to which persons of other communities or religions are not made liable; or

(c) confer on persons of any community or religion any privilege or advantage which is not conferred on persons of other communities or religions ; or,

whether the Buddhists wanted a fourth Refuge in government in addition to the three : Buddha, Dhamma and Sangha.[27]

As a devout Buddhist who had taken active interest in the restoration of the cultural monuments and ancient cities cf the country like Anuradhapura, and as a powerful popular leader, it was possible for Senanayake to ride rough shod over the proposals of the ACBC delegation who, in their turn, probably not doubting his sincerity as a Buddhist, felt that he was too dominated by the Catholics and its clergy in such matters.

Under the circumstances, it came as a surprise when, only a few months later, in the fourth annual conference of the UNP held at Kandy, the Prime Minister announced his government's intention to appoint such a commission. This decision was ratified by the UNP. In a resolution, the party emphasised the need for "spiritual values for the well being of society" and reaffirmed "its desire to protect and assist all religions in their struggle against the forces of irreligion". The last part of the sentence was an obvious dig at the left parties. Further, while approving the appointment of a commission to investigate and make recommendations on all matters to the well-being and progress of Buddhism, the UNP also recommended to the government that due attention should be given to "similar requests by other Religious Bodies".[28]

The context of the appointment of a commission on Buddhism (in Senanayake's speech) was perhaps as significant as the commitment. It seemed to be a promise reluctantly wrung from him. Declaring that the government would give all possible assistance to "ensure the flourishing state of this great religion" and would appoint a commission 'at no distant date' to report on how it could be done, Senanayake continued : "But to reduce this sublime creed to

---

(d) alter the constitution of any religious body except with the concent of the governing authority of that body.

27. Based on Interviews with Dr. Malalesekhera and L.C. Caldeira, Secretary ACBC. Also see Buddha Jatika Balavegaya, *Catholic Action* (Colombo, 1953), p. 126.

28. United National Party, *Fourth Anniversary Celebrations*. Kandy 29 and 30 September 1951 (Colombo, 1951), p. 42.

the level of a state authority, to reduce the members of our illustrious Sangha to the position of minor state officials, to supervise and control religion through the medium of a state department, is something I, for a moment, cannot countenance. To label Buddhism as a state religion or to label Lanka as a Buddhist State does not advance the interests of either the religion or the country. A religion that has flourished in this country for twenty centuries and more, is too deeply enshrined in the hearts of our people to need any artificial aid for its maintenance and protection."[29]

The announcement was apparently intended to satisfy certain sections within the party[30] as well as to take the wind out of the sails of the newly emergent Sri Lanka Freedom Party which had almost similar resolution as one of the six, and the non-ratification of which had led to Mr. Bandaranaike's breaking away from the UNP and founding the new party. The non-challent remark of the SLFP leader on this was revealing; "the best way to give the slip", commented Bandaranaike, "is to appoint a Commission. I, as a former Minister, know it best".[31]

In August 1952, it was reported that the Prime Minister has decided not to appoint the Buddhist Sasana Commission "in view of the attitude of the Sangha who do not wish to participate in such a commission". Lest such a news might create some flutter, the Prime Minister made a statement soon after that no decision was yet being taken regarding the appointment of the commission. According to him, however, it was true that the Sangha was opposed to the appointment of such a commission.[32] The 'Sangha' in this context however seemed to mean the Maha Nayakas of some of

29. *UNP Journal*, Vol. 5, No. 19, 5 October 1951, p. 2.
30. Two party branches—Matara UNP branch and Kolonna Korale branch had initiated the resolution on religion. United National Party, n. 28, p. 42.
31. Bandaranaike took to national dress after his return from Oxford in 1925. In 1931 he attended the dinner in Queen's House as well as the State Council opening, in national dress made of home-grown cotton and home spun as well as home woven cloth. S.W. R.D. Bandaranaike, *Speeches and Writings* (Colombo, 1963) p. 305.
32. *Ceylon Daily News*, 1 and 2 August 1952.

the chapters. The idea of an official Buddhist Commission was shelved on the pretext of the reluctance of the 'Sangha' but in reality it seemed to be because of a fear that the appointment of such a commission might lead to religious tension.[33]

In the election of 1952, religion did not merit a place in the UNP manifesto. The issue, however, was raised again in the context of the celebrations of Buddha Jayanti which was to be celebrated in 1956. For the Sinhalese Buddhists, Buddha Jayanti had an added significance. The full moon day of May 1956 was not simply the date of the birth and passing away of Buddha 2500 years ago but was also the day when Prince Vijaya, the legendary ancestor of the Sinhalese had stepped into the island. The Sinhalese chronicle had dramatically described this event and also the declaration of the Buddha that it was in Sri Lanka that Buddhism was destined to flourish in all its pristine purity. Buddha Jayanti thus, symbolised a nationalist mystique round race and religion.

The Buddhist activism had an impetus from official as well as unofficial sources. The ACBC had already gone ahead in appointing a commission in 1953 to look into the condition of Buddhism. The other Buddhist organisations were busy planning their programme for the Jayanti celebrations. At this stage, UNP Government had also begun to think of the ways in which the State could be involved in the Jayanti celebrations without compromising its secular policy. This, however, was not easy. It was not a question of the State providing assistance for Jayanti celebrations; it was the extent to which it could identify itself with it and yet avoid being described as a Buddhist government. What role the State should play in Buddha Jayanti celebrations was an issue which was bound to evoke varied responses.

In the 1953 annual conference of the UNP, the outgoing Premier Dudley Senanayake, (who was a devout Buddhist) proposed that the government should take appropriate steps for the celebration of Buddha Jayanti. The proposal

33. Howard W. Wriggins, *Ceylon : Dilemmas of a New Nation* (Princeton, 1960), p. 195.

was carried in the conference. Acting on the UNP resolution on the subject, the Home Minister, A. Ratnayake wrote a letter to Premier Kotelawala, suggesting the appointment of a Council of Buddhist clergy to chalk out the programme for Jayanti, the simultaneous appointment of a Council of Buddhist laity for its implementation and lastly the provision of funds "from various sources to give effect to such a programme."[34] Acting on the proposal, the Prime Minister appointed a Cabinet sub-committee to report on all matters connected with Buddha Jayanti.

After eliciting the opinion of various Buddhist associations and of some of the prominent monks, the Cabinet subcommittee recommended a series of activities which were to be undertaken in connection with the Buddha Jayanti. The committee's report was a suave elucidation of the UNP's stand. "The Government", declared the committee, "while guaranteeing freedom of worship to all religions and maintaining its policy of religious tolerance, should, as occasion arise, assist the activities of all religions." The Buddha, argued the committee further, did not belong to a parochial religious group but to humanity as a whole. As such, the 25th century of such a leader must be celebrated by the State to bring out its cultural-religious dimension. Besides, promptly added the committee, Buddhism was a national asset and the Government had always done everything to protect and safeguard this religion.[35]

The sub-committee report caused serious debate within the cabinet.[36] It qualified its report with the proviso that similar facilities should be provided for other religions and recommended that a semi-official organisation should be set up to look after the Jayanti celebrations. The dividing line of its non-official character, however, seemed to be dubious as it was to be formed under the official auspices, enjoying the State patronage.

The Buddha Jayanti celebrations were officially inaugurat-

34. Lanka Bauddha Mandalaya, *An Event of Dual Significance* (Colombo, n.d.), pp. 6-7.
35. Ibid.
36. *Times of Ceylon*, 24 March 1955.

ed in October 1954 with the appointment of the Buddhist Council as suggesed by the Cabinet report. The venue of this event was the Independence Hall in Colombo. Over 2,500 saffron robed monks assembled at the Hall (decorated in traditional fashion of a 'Pirit Mandalaya') and recited Pirit for about an hour and after which the Prime Minister announced the appointment of a Buddhist Council entitled as Lanka Bauddha Mandalaya (LBM). The Mandalaya, consisting of a Lay Council and a Sangha Council was to make representation to the Government on matters pertaining to the Jayanti and to assume responsibity for it.

The Mandalaya had an executive council consisting of four cabinet ministers and the leader of the opposition, S.W.R.D. Bandaranaike. A senior government official acted as its secretary. Its ambitious programme included the translation of Tripitaka, the compilation of Sinhalese Encyclopaedia, the publication of Buddhist literature, restoration of Dalada Maligawa and other monuments. The Council had under it 17 committees. The Committee for Religious Affairs, Sangha Affairs, Buddhist Literature, Tripitaka translation and Vidyalankara Sangamaya had some of the eminent senior monks as chairmen and secretaries.[37]

The appointment of Lanka Baudha Mandalaya met with critical comments from the press. The opposition parties maintained that by this act the government was giving too much importance to a particular religion and thereby contravening the spirit of article 29 of the Ceylonese Constitution.[38]

During the debate on the supplementary demands for

37. Lanka Bauddha Mandalaya, n. 34, pp. 16-24. Also see *Jayanti*, Vol. 1, No. 1, May 1955, pp. 6-8, and Vol. 1, No. 6, October 1955, pp. 27 and 32. A paper submitted to the delegates of the Bandung Conference, outlined the programme of the Kotelawala Government during the Jayanti Year. *Ceylon Daily News*, 21 April 1955.

38. See the editorials of *Times of Ceylon*, 6 October and 2 December 1954; *Ceylon Daily News*, 17 December 1954 ; *Ceylon Observer*, 17, and 19 June and a spate of letters on this subject. See in particular a letter by Senator S. Nadesan in *Ceylon Daily News*, 20 September 1954.

grants for the LBM, some of the opposition leaders declared that while they were in favour of celebrating Buddhist Jayanti on a grand scale and endorsed the ambitious programme, they were strongly against the way it was being done. They objected the UNP Coordinating the work of the Councils through LBM. They maintained that most of its work should have been initiated by people, not by the State. Instead, the whole State machinery was being used right from the village level onwards for making preparations for the Jayanti "to be celebrated as a purely govermental event."

Left leaders like Dr. N.M. Perera also stated that there was a strong feeling that the UNP Government was "utilising a sacred event for its own partisan purposes" and that "poltical kudos" were being sought to be obtained from this event.[39] One of the SLFP members wondered whether the government was not intending to convert Buddha Jayanti into an "election Jayanti" (Chandaya Jayanti).

The inaugural ceremony of the LBM itself became an occasion for protest. While the message of the Governor General was being read in the meeting, some monks from the audience shouted "we do not want a message from a Christian Governor-General." They also objected to the message being read in English. Some of them even questioned the propriety of the Prime Minister presiding over such a function instead of a Bhikkhu. In the pandemonium that prevailed, the monks asked how they were to respect a Premier who had participated in such a 'barbaric ritual' of roasting the calf and eating its flesh. Questions were also raised as to why representatives from eminent Buddhist organisations like the Mahabodhi Society and Buddhist Theosophical Society were not invited.[40]

Notwithstanding such opposition, it must be noted that the inception of the LBM was symbolic of the official recognition and State patronage which was being given to the religion of the majority for the first time since independence.

39. Ceylon, *Parliamentary Debates* (House of Representatives), Vol. 20, No. 6, April 1955, cols. 4005-19.
40. *Ceylon Daily News*, 1 November 1954. Also see United National Party, *General Election 1956, Manifesto of the United National Party* (Colombo, 1956), pp. 6-7.

The irony of the situation, however, was that it was being done under a government whose credibility was suspect as the defender of Buddhism and whose image was not that of a party reflecting the hopes, fears and aspirations of the 'common man' belonging to the majority community.

There were signs of a coming avalanche. The Buddhist Commission report prepared under the auspices of the ACBC was entitled Betrayal of Buddhism. Notwithstanding the statements of the UNP leaders as well as a clause in the UNP election manifesto that the report, when submitted, would receive the full support of the government,[41] the sponsors of the report decided to submit it to the Sangha and not to the government, thereby demonstrating a lack of faith in it.

The defeat of the UNP in the 1956 elections was a manifestation of this lack of faith of the average Sinhalese in the policies of the party not only in religious sphere but also in economic and social spheres.[42] It took the UNP leadership some time to take stock of the reasons for its loss of support and to adapt itself to the new situations and precedents which were established under the long regime of the MEP headed by S.W.R.D. Bandaranaike. This is clear from the fact that almost two years after the elections when a fairly elaborate draft of the party's policy statement was approved by the party conference there was not a single reference to what it proposed to do in regard to the Buddhist clergy or even Buddhist grievances, except such vague pronouncements as the need for the "spread of spiritual values" and "religious education and upbringing".[43]

The party manifesto issued during the 1960 elections, however, revealed, a shift of emphasis. For one thing, if its two clauses guaranteeing freedom of religion to all and promising active work for "the preservation of Ceylon's cultural and spiritual values" were a reiteration of the earlier general approach of the UNP

---

41. *Ceylon Observer*, 5 February 1956.
42. For an analysis of the various factors leading to the defeat of the UNP see Wriggins, n. 33 pp. 326-69, and I.D.S. Weerawardana, *Ceylon General Elections* (Colombo, 1960).
43. United National Party, *Progress through Stability : United National Party Manifesto* (Colombo, n.d.), p. 21.

on the subject, the grant to the Nikayas a "corporate status by legislation" by their consent was, for the first time, a specific promise. Further, in the background of the rather controversial recommendations of the Buddha Sasana Commission,[44] appointed under the MEP regime regarding the role of State in unifying and purifying the Sangha, the UNP promised the "establishment of a 'Sasana Mandalaya, consisting of representatives of the Sangha and the laity to work for the welfare of both without the infringement of the autonomy of Nikayas".[45] However, in March 1960, when the UNP was sworn to office, neither its leaders' message to the nation nor the Governor-General's address made any reference to religion.

The party was out of power in a few months and it was only in 1963 that it presented an exhaustive statement of policy on religion at its annual conference. In a 35-page document entitled 'What We Believe In' the statement on religion covered three pages. "We would like to say at the outset" stated the party pamphlet, "that our party has the highest regard for Religion...The long years of servitude have left their mark, and the claim of Buddhists that the wrongs done to them should be righted, and that the place Buddhism occupied when we were free and Kings ruled according to Dhasa Raja Dharma (Ten Buddhist Principles) should be restored is a just one".[46]

"Some suggest", continued the document, "that Buddhism should be made the State Religion. If by making Buddhism the State Religion it means that the Government of the day can appoint and transfer Mahanayake Theras and Viharadhipatis; control religious ceremonies in Temples and manage the Sangha as a State Department, our Party cannot agree to the Buddha Sasana being made subservient to the State. If, however, it means that the State will aid the Sasana, that the Sangha will be helped to re-organise itself, and the directives of

44. For details on the Buddha Sasana Commission see Chapter VI.
45. Ceylon Daily News, *Parliaments of Ceylon* 1960 (Colombo, 1960), p. 198.
46. United National Party, *What We Believe* (Colombo, 1963), p. 9.

State Policy should be based on the principles of the Buddha
Dharma, we hereby pledge ourselves to adopt such a policy. In
practice, since independence, Buddhism has gradually been
recognised by the State as its official religion and Buddhist ceremonies are performed at the chief State functions".[47]

This was the first time that the UNP had officially committed itself to the restoration of Buddhism to its rightful place in
the State. It further added that it was not necessary to discuss
religious organisations other than the Buddhist Sangha, "for
they have no problem similar to these of the Buddhists . . ."[48]

By 1963 thus the religious policy of the UNP in effect did
not appear different from that of the SLFP. This is borne out
by a comparison of the manifestoes of both for the 1965
elections. Both talked of restoration of Buddhism to its rightful place. Both promised to make the Poya days weekly
holidays. Both promised to safeguard the rights of those
belonging to other faiths and ensured them the freedom of
worship.

The bipartisan approach on religious issues between the
UNP and the SLFP can be seen from the fact that though it
was the SLFP manifesto which pledged itself to set up a
Buddhist University at Anuradhapura "exclusively for the
education and training of Bhikkhus",[49] the implementation of
this pledge was made by the UNP during its tenure of office.
And it was in 1968, when the UNP was in power that Poya
day was made a weekly holiday in lieu of the Sunday. However,
when the UF Government decided to revert to the pre-1968
position in this respect, the UNP thought it prudent not to
make political capital out of it in view of its practical implications.

It might be mentioned that both the UNP as well as the
SLFP had vied with each other equal ardour even earlier to
strive for the propagation of Buddhism abroad. Thus, if in the
Sixth Great Buddhist Council[50] (convened by the Burmese
Prime Minister U Nu in May 1954 at Rangoon) Dudley

47. Ibid., p. 10.
48. Ibid.
49. *Parliament of Ceylon*, n. 45, pp. 167-8, and 173.
50. Donald Eugene Smith, *Religion and Politics in Burma* (Princeton,
    1965), p. 157.

Senanayake headed the delegation, the Pan Asian celebrations of the completion of 2500 years of Buddhism in 1957 had an equally strong enthusiast in S.W.R.D. Bandaranaike. Besides, both the parties had been sending missions of Bhikkhus abroad to propagate the Damma.[51] Also, official patronage was provided for the formation of the world Buddhist Sangha Council in 1966.[52]

By 1970 this bipartisan approach on religious issues appeared to have been further crystallised, the reference to religion in the UNP manifesto in 1970 for instance could as well be a substitute for the para in the SLFP manifesto. Both reiterated their pledge to restore Buddhism its rightful place in the affairs of the country and at the same time protect the rights of those who professed other faiths. Further, the provisions according Buddhism a 'foremost place' in the Constitution of Sri Lanka, promulgated in 1972 during the UF regime, had the approval of the UNP.

Finally, it may be added that in the process of the implementation of religious policies, the ruling party lost no time in 'infiltrating' its supporters in the institutional structures which had been created earlier, instead of demolishing them. A case in point is the Sasanaraksha Samitis' structure which, as will be discussed later, had come into being during the MEP regime.

The change of the party in power in 1965 and its aftermath indicated that politics had crept into some of these Samitis and they were being turned into the support base of the SLFP.[53] The easiest way for the UNP Government to neutralise the SLFP support in the Samitis was to inundate the institution of Sasanarakasha Samitis with the pro-UNP elements which it did. In 1964, for instance, there were 4,050 Samitis; in 1965-1966, 3,705 new Samitis

---

51. *Ceylon Daily News*, 17 June 1967 and *Times of Ceylon*, 11, April 1967.
52. For details see World Buddhist Sangha Conference, *Sangha Souvenir* (Colombo, 1966), and World Buddhist Sangha Council, *Constitution* (Colombo, n.d.).
53. Information based on the interviews with various officials of the Ministry of Cultural Affairs.

were registered by the department, leading to a total of 7,755 out of which nearly 40 per cent had been established under the UNP regime.[54]

Since 1947 thus, the UNP had moved a long way and had adopted by early 60s a policy which was almost identical to that of the SLFP. The compulsion of its fostering its image as the Sinhalese Buddhist party was one major factor in this process. Further, in terms of political costs and gains, it was not only expedient but also beneficial to adopt a bipartisan approach on religious issues.

THE SLFP : RELIGIOUS POLICIES AND PERFORMANCE

Unlike the UNP, the religious policies of which had been by and large, a response or reaction to the SLFP, the latter showed a firm initiative in this area and in fact succeeded in capitalising it to a great extent in the elections of 1956.

The revival of the 'value of religious ideas'[55] in the march of progress being one of the major points of the Sinhala Maha Sabha's programme, it was essy for S.W.R.D. Bandaranaike to underline it when he formed the SLFP. Partly, it was the response of a politician to the then existing political situation, partly it was the inner conviction of a man who, born and bred in an Anglicised family and after having had the best English education, decided to embrace Buddhism as early as 1931. He discarded the western dress for the indigenous one, taught himself Sinhalese and had founded the Sinhala Mahasabha which in some of the essentials of its religious programme reminded one of the Hindu Mahasabha of India.

Soon after the formation of the UNP, although D.S. Senanayake was elected as its leader, Bandaranaike, as the leader of the largest single group within the UNP was considered as his successor. Within a few years of the UNP rule, Bandaranaike felt that his position was assailed from within and that D.S. Senanayake was wanting to keep the succession line

54. Ceylon, *Administrative Report of the Director of Cultural Affairs for the Financial Year* 1966-67 (Colombo, 1968), p. 33.
55. Bandaranaike, n. 31, p. 305.

within the family. As a Minister of Local Government, Bandaranaike had known the temper as well as the moods of Ceylonese rural population and the role of Buddhism in its work-a-day life. Consequently, he sought to mobilise his personal following by reviving Sinhala Mahasabha and by projecting himself as the leader of the Buddhist revivalist movement.

In some of his speeches, Bandaranaike was even alleged to have said that Buddhism should be a State religion. Such statements were met with his denial[56] but there was no doubt that the emphasis he put on the propagation of national religion and national language was one which did not find favour with Senanyake.

In June 1951, the annual session of the Sinhala Mahasabha adopted six resolutions, one of which demanded State assistance for the revival of Buddhism particularly by setting up a department. In accordance with the earlier practice, the resolutions were sent to the UNP for its approval and for further action. The UNP reacted strongly on the resolution on Buddhism and pointed out that such a step would amount to giving State assistance at the cost of other religions.[57] The resolutions were not approved by the UNP and Bandaranaike, declaring this as a vote of no-confidence in his policies, joined the opposition bench soon after.

Explaining the reasons for his joining the opposition, Bandaranaike maintained in one of his parlimentary speeches that he did not want Buddhism to be made the State religion with all its legal implications but he did ask the government to do 'certain just things' for the vast majority of the Sinhalese whose religion, linked as it was with their lives, had suffered more than any other religion under foreign rule.[58]

56. Winburn T. Thomas, 'Ceylon Christians faced by Crises', *Christian Century*, Vol. 68, 1951, pp. 58-60. Quoted in Donald E. Smith, *South Asian Politics and Religion* (Princeton, 1966), p. 456. Also see *UNP*, Vol. 5, No. 11, 10 August 1951, p. 1, and ibid., Vol. 5, no. 24, 23 November 1951, p. 1.

57. *UNP*, Vol. 5, No. 5, 29 June 1951, p. 8; also see *Ceylon Daily News* 11 June 1951 and 6 August 1951.

58. S.W.R.D. Bandaranaike, *Towards a New Era : Select Speeches of SWRD Bandaranaike Made in the Legislature of Ceylon*, 1931-1959 (Colombo, 1961), p. 693.

Speaking at the inaugural meeting of the SLFP, Bandaranaike, emphasising on the revival of spiritual values, maintained that all necessary help for this should come from the government as well as from the public, "whatever religion it may be".[59]

On the surface, Bandaranaike's statement took cognisance of all religions. In effect, however, it happened to be the religion of the majority community which had not been meted the 'just, and 'fair' treatment in the colonial past. The conclusion thus, was obvious: the State should assist all the religions but initially it must find ways and means of mitigating the disabilities which the foreign dominance had caused to a vast number of the majority community of island. In the Buddha Jayanti decade, this had a further emotive appeal and D.S. Senanayake was quick in discerning its potential. He adopted a part of Bandaranaike's thesis in a resolution at Kandy in 1951 as has been mentioned already.

Bandaranaike's SLFP which was not even a year old, was not in a position to be very categorical on religious questions at this stage. This was evident from the reference to religion in its 1952 manifesto. "We realise", ran the SLFP manifesto, "the value, particularly today, of all religious to help mankind to deal satisfactorily with the manifold and fundamental problems that face him in the new age. In accordance with this view, we are of the opinion that all steps necessary both by the public and the Government be taken to revive and assist religion and make it a living force amongst our people."[60] Neither the type of assistance which the SLFP expected the State to provide was spelt out nor the earlier demand for establishing a Department of Religious Affairs mentioned.

This was understandable. Contesting the election soon after its inception, the SLFP had to evolve an all round election strategy in the context of which promises in socio-economic affairs needed to be underlined. It is, however, noteworthy that neither in its first annual conference in December 1952, nor in its second conference held a year

59. Bandaranaike, n. 31, p. 147.
60. Sri Lanka Freedom Party, *Manifesto and Constitution of the Sri Lanka Freedom Party* 1951 (Wellampitiya, 1951), p. 9.

later, was any resolution on religion mooted.[61] Bandaranaike's presidential address in 1953 conference was a mere reiteration of his election pledge on religion: giving the spiritual values their proper place "in our lives" and revival of "our national cultures".[62]

In fact, even on the eve of elections of 1956, the SLFP leader did not wish to go all the way with one of his party colleagues, C.R. Beligammana, who had moved in the House of Representatives that Buddhism be made the State religion. "In view of the fact", began the motion, "that the majority of the citizens of Ceylon are Buddhists, this House is of the opinion that immediate action should be taken by the Government to make Buddhism the State religion of Ceylon without prejudice to other religions".[63]

Commenting editorially on the motion, a Ceylonese paper stated that so far as Bandaranaike was concerned he had once publicly stated that while he was in favour of special assistance to Buddhism, he was not asking for Buddhism to be made the State religion. "We hope" continued the editorial, that "he will clarify his position and take the opportunity to clear himself of this particular suspicion of reckless opportunism of proxy".[64]

Bandaranaike disowned the motion soon after the publication of the editorial. Reiterating his party's stand on religion as stated in the 1952 election manifesto, he added: "This continues to be our policy. Our view is that while recognising the position of Buddhism as the faith of a large majority of the people and therefore, being prepared to give all our assistance to Buddhism, we are of the opinion that there should be freedom of conscience and worship and that just assistance may be given to other faiths as well."[65]

The reference to religion in the 1955 manifesto of the SLFP was an elaboration of the above mentioned statement of Bandaranaike. While recounting the significance of Buddhism

---

61. For details of the various resolutions of the SLFP see *Times of Ceylon*, 29 December 1952 and *Times of Ceylon*, 12 December 1953.
62. Ibid., 12 December 1953.
63. *Morning Times*, 30 January 1956.
64. Ibid.
65. Ibid.

as "woven in our culture, our way of life and our very thoughts and actions" and reviewing the injustices meted to it during colonial era, the manifesto maintained that "in rebuilding our people in this new era of freedom, it is very essential to remedy the injustices done to Buddhism to take the fullest advantage of their religion and culture." This did not mean that Buddhism should be made the state religion. All that was necessary to be done to achieve these objects, concluded the manifesto, must be done "without injustice to other religions".[66]

The SLFP had made a common front with Philip Goonewardane's Viplavakari Lanka Sama Samaj Party and Eksath Bhasa Peramuna (political front of monks and laity who were protagonists of Sinhalese as the official language only). Designated as the Mahajana Eksath Peramuna (MEP-People's United Front) it issued a separate manifesto. While 'generally approving' the recommendations of the Buddhist Commission report, the manifesto assured the fullest freedom of worship and conscience to all and assured non-Buddhists continued religious tolerance. It is noteworthy that the phrase 'generally approving' did not find place in the Sinhalese version of the MEP manifesto.[67]

The election ended in a spectacular victory for the MEP and the ceremonial opening of the third parliament on 20 April 1956, marking the advent of the Bandaranaike era, gave an inkling of the main political currents of the next decade.

The ceremony began, not with the fanfare of Western trumpets as before, but with the playing of Magul Bera (ceremonial drumming) in traditional style. A glimpse of the tenor of the style of politics of the ruling coalition was further reflected in majority of the MPs donning spotless white national dress in place of the Western suit.

The gathering also gave some idea of the prospective political alignment; for the first time the left parties' leaders attended the inaugural ceremony, thereby showing their tacit approval of the policies of the new regime with which they had concluded a no-contest pact. Some of the left leaders who had earlier broken away from the LSSP had already become a constituent unit of Bandaranaike's People's Front. Last but not least, for

66. Weerawardana, n. 42, pp. 57-58.
67. Ibid., p. 67.

the first time in the history of Sri Lanka, the Governor-General's speech was read first, not in English, but in Sinhalese.[68]

Heading a government which was a coalition of various groups and whose support he had succeeded in mobilising the socialist-Sinhalese-Buddhist sense of grievances, and fully aware of the loosely organised base of his party, Bandaranaike lost no time in projecting the image of his party as the party of the 'common man'. Speaking in Sinhala in the annual session of the All Ceylon Village Committees, Bandaranaike declared the political change of 1956 as a "peaceful revolution by the votes of the people".

Amongst various factors which, according to him, "contributed to this result, the chief was an urge on the part of the masses to overthrow a regime which...paid little attention to the needs of the mass of the people and to which independence meant little more than merely a change of rulers......What happened in 1956 was a victory for the people, a victory for progress as against reaction".[69] Elsewhere, referring to the tribute paid to him as a 'Diyasena' (mythological hero who will redeem the State of Buddhism 2500 years after Buddha's death), Bandaranaike declared that he was merely a servant of the people (mahajana sewak).[70]

The 'Diyasena' title and the responses of the SLFP leader was an apt illustration of the amalgam of the traditional base with contemporary populist norms of a democratic polity. Such a political manipulation of cultural idiom in Buddhist terms, besides being a hallmark of Bandaranaike era, also set the pattern for the future. Any party aspiring to acquire and exercise political power since 1956 had to project a Sinhalese Buddhist image.

In May 1956, the MEP set up the Department of Cultural Affairs, the formation of which was in fact the implementation of one of a long drawn proposals on which Bandaranaike had clashed with the UNP. The formation of the Department brought the government into limelight as the patron of

---

68. *Ceylon Daily News*, 21 April 1956. Also see B.M. 'A People's Government : Social and Political Trends in Ceylon', *World Today*, Vol. 12, No. 7, July 1956, pp. 281-91.
69. Ceylon, *The Government and the People* (Colombo, 1959), pp. 144-7.
70. *Morning Times*, 27 April 1956.

indigeneous culture during the Jayanti Year.   Its first Director
was N.Q. Dias who had already shown imagination, initiative
and drive in organising the Buddhist government servants and
had played a significant behind-the-scene role, in the Buddhist
upsurge.[71]

The three major taks with which the department was entrusted were promotion of fine arts and crafts, literary
activities and religious activities. In this respect, the department, besides initiating innovatory measures, also performed
certain traditional practices such as making arrangements for
the funerals of the Mahanayakas and presenting Acts of
Appointment to the Chief high priests. Finally, since 1956,
though Buddhist religious ceremonies like Pirith chanting were
not formally incorporated, they became, as it were, an essential part of any State function and were organised by the
department.

An analysis of the personnel, resources and functions of the
department indicates that many traditions set during the
Bandaranaike era were continued under the Senanayake regime.
Thus since its inception, the department has had a Buddhist
minister in charge of the portfolio of Cultural Affairs.[72] Further,
in terms of the fund allocation to the triple services, i.e., promotion of religion, art and literature, religious activities claimed the lion's share. And amongst the religious grants of
various communities, the amount allocated for Buddhist activities was larger than the grants[73] allotted for the religious
activities of Hindus, Muslims and Christians.

71. The work of N.Q. Dias are discussed in Chapter V.
72. In 1960, though it was felt that education and cultural affairs could
most profitably be entrusted to one man, in view of Badiuddin
Mahmud (who was considered to be the most appropriate MP to
hold the education portfolio in view of his varied experience in
the education field) holding the education portfolio it was felt that
the major burden of the department's activities was related to
Buddhism. It was, therefore, decided that the portfolio should go
to a Buddhist. The religious susceptibilities of the majority community were thus taken into consideration in the allocation of
portfolios. Based on interviews with Dr. A.W.P. Guruge and
Mr. Maithripala Senanayake.
73. In 1957, for instance, the amount spent on religious activities was
Rs. 583,631 as against Rs. 317, 297 and Rs. 79, 975 spent on pro-

Soon after its inception, the Department organised the Dhamma schools on the pattern of Christian Sunday Schools and initiated the formation of Sasanaraksha Samitis (Protection of Buddhist Religious Societies) with an all-island network. First, a request was made to the incumbent of every temple to form a Sasanaraksha society. Thereafter the societies in each Divisional Revenue Officer's division were co-ordinated by forming a Council (Samiti) called the Provincial Councils for the protection of 'Sasana' (Pradeshika Sasanaraksha Samitis). These regional council's comprising of the

motion of arts and literary activities. In 1958, the expenditure on religious activities increased to Rs. 7,41,474 at the cost of the other two areas which together accounted for Rs. 2,37,220. Later pattern of expenditure by the department showed more or less similar trend. For details refer to the Administrative Reports of the Director of Cultural Affairs, published annually since 1958.

The promotion of religious activities was performed by the department with the assistance of the Buddhist, Hindu and Islamic Affairs Advisory Committee. These committees were set up with a view to help select suitable programmes which would then be aided by the department. However, an important difference was that Buddhist programmes were frequently aided directly by the department while the other two religions were usually aided through grants made to the Councils of those religions.

Donald Eugene Smith in *South Asian Politics and Religion*, n. 56, p. 473, is partly correct in maintaining that the grants to the Islam and Hindu institutions were made to the institutions of those religions. According to various official reports, it was on the recommendation of the two advisory committees that grants were given by the department. Some reports, however, also maintain that these committees themselves were given a grant for promoting religious activities and imparting religious instruction. The figures of the latter period seem to indicate that perhaps a bloc grant was made for various religions and the money was allocated to the various institutions on the recommendation of these Advisory Councils.

As regards the Christians, no such Committee was formed because the Christian clergy did not favour the formation of such committees. However, during 1959-60, on an application from the Archbishop of Colombo, the department paid, for the first time, a subsidy of Rs. 10,000 for Catholic religious publications.

For details of the break-up of grants for Buddhist, Islamic and Christian religious activities see the Annual Administrative Reports of the Department of Cultural Affairs.

members of the temple societies (maximum number of four from each temple), president of the local government bodies and the MP (if Buddhist), operated under the department of Cultural Affairs and it was stipulated that the temple societies should comply with the circulars issued by the department on the advice of the regional councils.[74]

The objects of the temple societies were multifarious—to strengthen the relationship between the laity and the monks, to organise special ceremonies on Poya days, to improve existing Dhamma schools and open new ones, to work for the prevention of crimes and prohibition of liquor and to uphold Buddhist tradition.[75] The regional council, apart from co-ordinating the functions of the temple societies within its area was also entrusted with the task of developing the Buddhist Association in government as well as in assisted schools and to establish meditation centres.[76]

With about 4,000 temple societies at the base, several regional councils in the middle and the Department of Cultural Affairs at the apex, this innovation was in fact the culmination of the Samiti movement of 1952-53 of which the first director of Cultural Affairs N.Q. Dias, himself was the precurser. Though the functions of this hierarchy was purely religious, the organisation, under close supervision could always be developed along political lines particularly in view of the presence of the elected representatives of local as well as central political institutions in its deliberations.

Apart from the department of Cultural Affairs, another significant measure which was welcomed by virtually all the Buddhists was the creation of two Buddhist universities. It is wrongly assumed that the two old Pirivenas—Vidyodaya and Vidyalankara[77] were elevated to the status of universities in

---

74. Information from the Administrative Reports of the Department of Cultural Affairs, 1956-59.
75. *Ceylon Daily News*, 30 August 1957.
76. Ceylon, Department of Cultural Affairs, *Viharastha Sasanarakshaka Samiti Saha Pradeshika Sasanarakshaka Mandalaya* (Temple Societies for the Promotion of Buddhism and Regional Boards for the Promotion of Buddhism (Colombo, 1959), pp. 1-6; also see *Ceylon Daily News*, 30 August 1957.
77. It is significant that even government announcements erred on this point.

this scheme. What in fact happened was that while the old Pirivenas remained as they were, virtually all their staff members were absorbed in the new universities and the pirivenas were affiliated to them. The new universities gave special concessions to the Buddhist monks in admission and had Sinhalese as the medium of instruction.

Although the Cultural Affairs Department and the new universities were established without much difficulty, the promise of the MEP to implement the Buddhist Commission report proved difficult to fulfil. This was primarily because the SLFP government, in its enthusiasm for "restoring Buddhism its proper place" wanted to play the role of the ancient Sinhalese kings as the purifier and unifier of the Sasana. This was not easy even under the monarchies of the ancient days; it was more than formidable a task under a democratic parliamentary set-up.

The details of the SLFP's attempt to reorganise the Sangha and the causes of its failure in this task are discussed in detail in Chapter VI. Suffice it to say here that the SLFP decided to probe deep into the recommendations of the Buddhist Commission report by appointing a Buddha Sasana Commission; that the mode of its appointment was vociferously questioned by some of the prelates of the Malwatta and Asgiri Nikaya on the plea that such an official commission was an impingement of the traditional autonomy of the Nikayas, that its recommendations met with serious disapproval by a large number of Bhikkhus, some of whom saw, in the proposals, the high hand of the State attempting to control the Sangha. Sensing the mood of the clergy, the SLFP government decided to shelve the Sasana Commissions's recommendations in 1963 after which virtually nothing was heard about its implementation.

The only recommendation of the Commission which the SLFP Government failed miserably to implement dealt with the ban on the appointment of Bhikkhus for salaried positions. Such a decision raised a hue and cry, particularly from those Bhikkhus who had already been holding remunerative positions in various educational institutions and had been the

supporters of the Sirimavo Government. Realising the extent
of this opposition, the government decided to beat a retreat
and revoked the earlier official order imposing restrictions on
the appointment of Bhikkhus.[78]

Another issue on which the Government's decision was
revoked related to the proposal to permit free tapping of toddy
from coconut trees. Initiated by the Trotskyite leader, Dr.
N.M. Perera (who had joined the treasury benches along
with two of his colleagues in June 1964) who was the new
Finance Minister under the SLFP-LSSP coalition government,
the proposal drew heavy criticism from the Buddhist leaders.
In the course of presenting the budget (which incorporated
the proposal) the Minister had explained that it had been
proposed in order to put an end to the traffic in illicit liquor
which, apart from causing serious loss of revenue to the
government, was also a menace to the health of the people.

The Buddhist monks and certain pressure groups, however,
alleged that in a country where temperance had always been
advocated as a Buddhist virtue, "the Marxists in keeping with
their policy of undermining religion were seeking to corrupt
people through toddy proposals". Sensing the Buddhist
anxiety, the SLFP first postponed consideration of the issue
and then finally decided to drop it. In a letter to the High
Prelate of the Malwatta Chapter, the Prime Minister Mrs.
Bandaranaike intimated that the Government had decided
to abandon the proposal "in deference to the wishes of the
Maha Sangha".[79]

The opposstion to the proposal was not only a censure of
the government; it was a reiteration of lack of faith and
confidence on the part of a large segment of Buddhists in the
policies of the left parties, like the LSSP, towards religious
issues. And the opposition lost no time in mobilising and
articulating this sense of grievance.

In the course of gradually mounting opposition in which
the coalition government's decision to partly nationalise the
press also played an important role the UF government decided
to adopt another course of action to assuage and assure

---

78. For details see Chapter VI.
79. A. Jeyaratnam Wilson, 'Buddhism in Ceylon Politics', in Smith,
    n. 56, pp. 525-7.

Buddhists, When the Parliament met after a sudden prorogation on 20 November, the Governor-General's address envisaged legislation to guarantee Buddhism its proper place as the religion of the majority.[80]

The announcement, however, was received with suspicion and scepticism. One of the organisation of the Buddhist Bhikkhus—the Maha Sangha Peramuna—called it a 'fraudulent cunning' on the part of the government and its Marxist allies,[81] and in an editorial the *Ceylon Observer* called it the "most blatant political stunt that has been so far pulled by this Government."[82]

The SLFP paid a heavy price for its association with the LSSP. A score of the SLFP members crossed the floor and the government was defeated by one vote in December 1964. In the elections which followed, the SLFP's links with the LSSP as well as some of the policies of the coalition government came under heavy attack by a large number of Bhikkhus. As will be discussed in the next chapter, this did influence the outcome of the 1965 elections to some extent.

The SLFP thus had to wait till 1970 when it was back in power to honour its pledge regarding Buddhism. This was done in the Constitution of 1972 and with the approval of the major opposition party—the UNP.

It is evident that the SLFP took initiative on formulating religious policies which eventually assumed a bipartisan approach as a consequence of the competitive nature of electoral politics. As such, on issues which were by and large non-controversial, both the SLFP and UNP found themselves following similar policies. On issues which proved controversial, like the Sasana Commission, the SLFP moved towards the UNP view. On the other hand, on issues like toddy, the SLFP decided that discretion was the better part of valour. This was not only politically expedient but was also a mark of the SLFP prudence. Toddy proposal was initiated not by the SLFP but by the LSSP leadership. Besides, it was not a 'critical' issue in its overall policies and programme.

80. Ibid.
81. *Ceylon Daily News*, 20 November 1964.
82. Editorial, *Ceylon Observer*, 24 November 1964.

Finally, it was politically better to shelve or rescind such issues rather than alienate the Buddhist clergy because even as late as 1965, it was obvious that, divided as they were on the side of both the parties, the Bhikkhus maintained a precarious balance. If this was disturbed by any measure, it could go against the political interest of either of them. As against the UNP and the SLFP, the left parties had a dilemma of a different sort. If their ideology necessitated them to adopt an approach different from that of the UNP or the SLFP, their minor party position in a two major party system compelled them to drop their doctrinaire stand on religion.

RELIGIOUS POLICIES OF THE LEFT PARTIES WITH SPECIAL REFERENCE TO THE LSSP AND THE CP

If on the left continuum, one discerns at one end parties like Mahajana Eksath Peramuna led by Philip Gunawardena, assuming strong Sinhalese Buddhist overtones, the LSSP (R) headed by Edmund Samarakkody as well as the Communist Party of Ceylon (Peking Wing) led by Shanmughathasan continued with a doctrinaire Marxist approach. In the middle is the LSSP. Beginning its political career with an approach towards religion which was essentially non-religious, the party, along with the CP adopted an overt secular approach during the 50s. By the middle of the sixties however, the party leadership appeared to find ways and means to present its image as a dominantly Sinhalese Buddhist one without deviating from its traditional approach in its documents. And it is not without significance that the new constitution of 1972, assuring a 'foremost' place to the religion of majority, was drafted under the aegis of an LSSP minister, Colvin R. de Silva.

The various phases of the LSSP's attitude towards religion, illustrates the major variations amongst the left approaches towards the issue. In the process, it indicates that such shifts were partly in response to the aspirations of the majority community (which provide its major support base) and partly the consequence of its minor party status in a coalitional polity.

To begin with, in the thirties and the forties virtually, all the left parties and groups viewed religion either as inimical or as one of the spheres which needed to be 'reformed' in view of the dominantly land-owning character of the upper echelon of the Buddhist clergy. It is however significant to note that the LSSP leadership of the thirties and the forties representing the voice of dissent in an otherwise complacent indigenous leadership, had some of the most politically vociferous and articulate Bhikkhus as its ardent allies. It is also noteworthy that one of the founder members of the CP as well as its first president happened to be a Buddhist monk— Udakandawela Sri Saranankara Thero.

The participation of the segment of the Buddhist clergy with the left movement was significant in more than one way. While endorsing the Marxian view of society, it ventured to emphasise the congruity between communism and Buddhism—the traditional religion of the masses. The anomaly of this exercise was, however, pointed out, time and again, by the UNP leadership and it harped on the theme that believing in the Marxian axiom of religion being the 'opium of society' the Marxist parties, if came to power, were bound to destroy the religion of all and sundry.[83]

The UNP allegations were answered in the LSSP mainfesto of 1952. (The 1947 manifesto did not refer to the issue). "All the clap-trap about religion", continued the mainfesto, "is only so much deceit. The LSSP's whole long record shows that its guarantee of religious freedom to all faiths and persuasions is real and solid, and that, besides, unlike the UNP, it refuses to prostitute religious feeling towards political ends."[84]

Elsewhere, while addressing at one of the Buddhist Pirivenas, the LSSP leader, Dr. N.M. Perera stated that Buddhism

---

83. e.g., an article of Colvin R. de Silva, 'A Ceylonese in Soviet Russia', (Ceylon Daily News, 29 April 1932) was reproduced in full by the UNP as part of its political propaganda. In this article Dr. de Silva had concluded : "While destroying the traditional religion of Russia, the Bolshevists have erected a new religion to take its place. That religion, which is the religion of every Russian youth, is no other than communism".

84. Lanka Sama Samaja Party, Election Manifesto (Colombo, 1952).

depended for its progress on the farmers and workers of the
island who had always sustained it and had supported its
Bhikkhus which enabled it to survive despite western colonial onslaughts. Dr. Perera argued further that the re-estab-
lishment of a sturdy, independent, economically sound
peasantry and working class must necessarily react on
Buddhism bringing about a renaissance in religion. Samasa-
majism thus, was synonymous with religious revival. The
LSSP was thus, not opposed to religion. However, unlike the
UNP, it did not want to use it as "the stalking buffalo of
politics".[85]

The 1952 manifesto along with Dr. Perera's statement
seemed to underline three points. Firstly, that Marxism was
not anti-thetical to Buddhism. Secondly the LSSP was not
irreligious or a—religious. It, however, did not want to make
political capital out of religious issues and adopted a secular
approach. Finally the party stood firmly on the principle
"that every person must be free to practise his religion without interference by those who hold different or contrary
views".[86]

Recapitulating the LSSP's stand, the party secretary,
Leslie Goonawardene wrote that his party had always considered "religion to be a private matter. The duty of the state
in this connection is to guarantee the right of every one to
practise his religion without hindrance from others. The
propaganda carried on by our enemies. . . , that the LSSP is
against religion and would destroy religious liberty once it
came into power is belied by not only the pronouncements
but also the actions of the party over the past 23 years. Such
fairy tales stand exposed today as the crude propaganda of
those who wish to protect, not religion, but capitalist
property..."[87]

Soon after, in its election manifesto of July 1960, the
LSSP reiterated its secular approach towards religion—
promising freedom of religious beliefs, worship and organisa-

85. Ceylon Observer, 11 November 1952,
86. Lanka Sama Samaja Party, Parliamentary General Elections 1956 :
    Manifesto of the LSSP (Colombo, n.d.), p. 4.
87. Leslie Goonawardene, What We Stand For (Maradana, 1959), p. 9.

tion and assuring that in all State schools, religious instruction would be provided to children according to the wishes of the parents.[88]

In the wake of the revival of Sinhalese Buddhist militancy, such a secular approach did not seem very popular with the majority community. Further, initially, the LSSP had its support-base amongst the plantation workers most of whom were Tamil Hindus as well as in the working class of the urban areas. With the disfranchisement of most of these labourers and their political allegiance being drawn more and more in communal terms, the LSSP did not appear to draw any political benefits from its secular approach. With the Tamil provinces becoming the virtual political monopoly of the Tamil parties and with the Tamil estate labourers, expressing their political aspirations in communal terms (as was evident from the political ascendancy of the Ceylon Workers' Congress led by a Tamil Hindu) the LSSP base needed to be more responsive to the Sinhalese Buddhist ethos of rural Sri Lanka. This necessitated a second look at its religious policies.

The formation of the tri-party United Left Front of LSSP, CP and MEP appeared to arrest this process; religion was not even mentioned in the United Left Front agreement signed by the three parties in August 1963.[89] However, before the ULF could even complete a year, the LSSP had decided to accept Premier Bandaranaike's offer to form a coalition government.

As a minor partner in the coalition, the LSSP leaders now apparently had no choice but to fall into the pattern set by the dominantly Sinhalese Buddhist SLFP Government. The first manifestation of this was a symbolic gesture; soon after being sworn-in, the LSSP ministers went to Dalada Maligawa in Kandy. Clad in white and carrying trays of Jasmine flowers, the Ministers paid their obeisance in traditional style to Buddha and later called on the two Maha Nayaka theras of the Malwatta and Asgiri chapters of Siam Nikaya.[90]

88. Lanka Sama Samaja Party, *Election Manifesto of the Lanka Sama Samaja Party, July 1960* (Maradana, 1960).

89. For the text of the agreement see, *United Left Front Agreement* (Colombo, 1963).

90. *World Buddhism*, Vol. 13, no. 5, December 1964, p. 17.

The critical reaction of the press and that of a section of Bhikkhus on the coalition government as well as their out-burst on the free toddy tapping proposal of Perera was similar in certain respects to the criticism levelled against the MEP after its Finance Minister had introduced the Paddy Land Bill. The criticism rallied round two points: (a) that the 'infiltration of Marxist parties' would spell the doom of Bandaranaike's SLFP, and (b) that with their basic philoso-phy being anti-religious, the Marxists would adopt measures which would destroy democracy and religion. The proposed legislation of the coalition on the takeover of the press and the free tapping of toddy provided ample ammunition in the armoury of the non-Marxists who discerned in such measures the beginning of what they feared as the end of democratic and religious freedoms.

Though the SLFP leader Mrs Bandaranaike stated time and again that the Trotskyites had accepted her policies and that the support of the LSSP was a manifestation of the desire on her part to mobilise the 'progressive forces' with-out in any way, deviating from the 'middle path' policies of her late husband, the anti-coalitionist groups continued to be sceptical of the wisdom of such a move. "How can we accept", stated one Bhikkhu, "that Buddhism will be restored to its rightful place or be made a state religion by men who had never practiced a religion, never contributed anything to foster any religion and never can adduce any evidence to prove their good faith"?[91]

The LSSP leaders on the other hand, while maintaining that they adhered to Marxism, attempted to impress upon the people that Marxism was not against Buddhism.[92] How-ever, certain statements of the LSSP leaders did not appear to be too reassuring. "It is meaningless", stated Vivienne Gunawardene, the LSSP Junior Minister for Local Govern-ment and Home Affairs, "for a lot of people suffering from poverty, unemployment, disease, hunger, house (sic) and land-lessness and like problems to sacrifice their lives for the cause

91. Ceylon Observer, 22 November 1964.
92. Ceylon Daily News, 9 October 1962.

of religion. Without improving their social and living conditions it was futile to preach religions".[93]

The electoral realities were such, however, that they
compelled the LSSP to soft-pedal its stance on religious
issues and decided to identify itself completely with the SLFP in
electoral contests. Thus, if Mrs. Bandaranaike had taken her
first step in ensuring a long drawn alliance with the LSSP
and had initially paid the price for it, the LSSP had also
decided to identify completely with the SLFP policies in electoral contests. As a consequence both the LSSP and the CP
decided for the first time in the electoral history of Sri Lanka
that they would not come out with their own independent
election manifestoes in 1965. One of the party newspapers
declared that both of them had endorsed the programmes
issued by the SLFP.[94]

On religion, the SLFP's "programme for the future",
reiterated its assurance of freedom of worship to those
belonging to other religions but stressed the 'rightful
place' which would be provided to Buddhism. Further, it
promised a review of the entire system of public holidays with a view to making all Poya days holidays (full
moon days had already been declared public holidays),
greater assistance to Sunday Dhamma Schools, propagation of
Buddhism abroad and "in compliance with the wishes of the
Maha Sangha", the establishment of a Buddhist university at
Anuradhapura, exclusively for the educational training of
Bhikkhus. The SLFP also promised to expand the activities of the department of Cultural Affairs to "provide
Buddhist sermons, Buddhist discussions, the theatre and
literature for religious and moral development". The last
promise of the SLFP's future programme was, in a way, a
negation of the LSSP's view on toddy tapping. "The SLFP",
the manifesto stated, "will also launch a campaign to fight the
Kasippu menace and to educate people on the evils of
drinking".[95]

93. Ibid., 6 July 1964.
94. Ceylon Daily News, *Parliament of Ceylon*, 1965 (Colombo, 1965)
    p. 175.
95. Ibid., p. 173.

After having been in opposition for three years, the three-party team—the SLFP, the LSSP and the CP—agreed on a common programme on 5 June 1968 "to carry forward the progressive advance began in 1965" and to establish in Sri Lanka a "Socialist democracy". It was on the basis of this common programme that the 1970 elections were contested by them as the United Left Front with the LSSP and the CP winning the largest number of seats ever.

The traditional obeisance of the LSSP and CP at the temple of Buddha which had made many raise their eyebrows in 1964 ministry appeared to be part of the accepted 'routine' in 1970. The minor party status of the LSSP and the CP in terms of the implementation of religious policies seemed to be tacitly accepted. After about four decades of politica l experience, the LSSP and the CP leadership seemed to realise that if the parliamentary framework was to be accepted as the path towards socialist democracy, the left parties, in the setting of the two major-party system of the island and in the context of an increasing communalisation of its politics, had to join hands firmly with one of the major parties or go into political wilderness.

RELIGIOUS POLICIES OF THE REGIONAL PARTIES : THE FEDERAL PARTY (FP) [96]

In their tussle for power in the heavily Tamil populated north and eastern provinces, the Tamil parties of the island have vied with each other to represent the 'community'.[97] However, it is more in linguistic terms and in a regional context that the communal character of the parties manifested

96. In writing this section I have drawn heavily on one of my articles entitled "Federal Party in Ceylon Politics", n. 19, pp. 839-43.
97. Community denotes "a people who share a common sense of identity and think of themselves as constituting a unique and sepa-rate group, usually on the basis of a distinctive language, religion, social organisation or ancestral origin. The related term 'com-munalism' refers to an attitude which emphasizes the primacy and exclusiveness of the communal group and demands the solidarity of members of the community in political and social action". Robert N. Kearney, *Communalism and Language in the Politics of Ceylon* (Durham, 1967), pp. 4-5.

itself. Unlike the Sinhalese who seemed to have put almost an equal emphasis on promotion of Buddhist 'religion' and Sinhalese 'language', the Tamil cry predominantly has been for parity for Tamil with Sinhala. This is partly due to the fact that the top Tamil leadership has been, by and large, Christian, and partly due to the promulgation of Sinhala as the official language in 1956. The cry of "religion in danger" would have *ipso facto* meant a cry for Christianity as much as for Hinduism; in the context of the colonial legacy it would have drawn more antagonism from the majority community which had perceived in 'Catholic Action',[98] a serious menace to its religion and culture, finally, and in the context of the Hindu-Christian Tamil community, appeal to religion would not have proved to be as emotive an issue as language.

With a much larger share of appointments in the public services than was warranted by the Tamil population, the displacement of English by Sinhala as the official language had not only an economic implication for the Tamils but had emotive undertones too. The Tamil language was the fountain-spring of cultural identity of the community. If it could be provided parity with Sinhala, both the economic as well as the cultural interests of the minority community could be ensured.

It is not surprising, therefore, that all the Tamil parties vociferously concentrated on the demand for parity of Tamil with the official language. The Reasonable Use of Tamil Act, promulgated two years after the declaration of Sinhala as the official language, had accorded a special position for Tamil in the northern and eastern provinces but in the wake of

---

98. For the Buddhist viewpoints on the activities of Catholics, see The Buddhist Committee of Enquiry, *The Betrayal of Buddhism* (Balangoda, Dharma Vijaya Press, 1956), and Bauddha Jatika Balavegaya, *Catholic Action* (Colombo, 1963). For a refutation of the above mentioned publications see, *Catholic Union of Ceylon, Education in Ceylon according to the Buddhist Commission Report: A Commentary* (Colombo, 1957); *The Church, The State and Catholic Action* (Colombo, n.d.), and *Catholic Action According to Balavegaya* (Colombo, n.d.). Also see Sir Kanthiah Vaithianathan, *Catholic Action and Thiruketheeswaram* (Colombo, 1964), and Christian John, *What is Catholic Action ?* (Colombo, 1964).

communal tensions which erupted in riots, the promulgation
of the enabling legislation on the Act was shelved till 1966.

Meanwhile, the Federal Party, demanding parity of the two
languages and grant of greater regional autonomy in a
federal set-up continued to be entrenched in the Tamil
areas[99] as was evident from its electoral victories. From 1956
to 1970 it continued to win about two-thirds of the total
seats in the northern province and nearly half in the eastern
province[100] with its only rival—the Tamil Congress (TC)—
lagging behind with one to three seats during this period.

In March 1960, with the election ending in plurality the
political manoeuvrability of the FP seemed to be high. It,
however, refused to collaborate with either the UNP or the
SLFP, presumably, because the UNP's volte-face on language
issue was still fresh and the effects of the SLFP's language
policy, still raw. Another reason could be that in the heavily
charged communal atmosphere of 1960, neither the UNP nor
the SLFP was prepared to accept the FP's terms for overt
support.

The FP thus continued to be in opposition till 1965 when
the election results endowed it once again the position of
a balancer. It decided to throw its weight with the UNP
which had won the maximum number of seats, and on its
own terms. These terms, incorporated in a secret pact,

99. For a succinct account regarding the attitude of Tamil parties on
    the language question see Kearney, n. 97.

100.   Table 2

Seats won by the FP in Northern and Eastern Provinces
During 1956-1970

Year	Total number of seats, northern and eastern provinces	Seats won by the FP
1956	16	10
March 1960	24	15
July 1960	24	16
1965	24	14
1970	24	13

Ceylon, *Report on the Seventh Parliamentary General Election*, n. 16.
p. 55, and Ceylon Daily News, *Parliament of Ceylon* 1956 (Colombo,
1956), p. 86.

envisaged the implementation of the Reasonable Use of Tamil Act, formation of District Councils with a view to giving greater power to the provinces, reprieve for those Tamil Civil servants who had failed to gain proficiency in Sinhala within a scheduled time. By 1968, the FP had, however, decided to withdraw from the coalition on the plea that though the Senanayake Government had fulfilled its promise with regard to the promulgation of the enabling legislation for the Reasonable Use of Tamil Act, it had not put its heart in its implementation. Besides, due to the pressure of the Sinhalese Buddhist opinion, the FP alleged, it had shelved the District Councils Bill providing greater autonomy at the district level. Further, the FP's demand for the establishment of a Tamil University in Jaffna, though accepted in principle, had not been put through.[101]

The immediate cause for precipitating the crisis in the UNP-FP relationship was related to a temple called Koneswaram in Fort Frederick area at Trincomalee (Eastern Province). In early 1968 the FP Minister for Local Self Government Tiruchelvam decided to appoint a committee to enquire into the question of declaring Koneswaram temple as a sacred area for the Hindus. The committee was appointed. Meanwhile a Bhikkhu brought to the notice of the UNP leader that Koneswaram temple was an ancient place of Buddhist worship. As such, he questioned its handing over to a community which was neither Sinhalese nor Buddhist.

The Prime Minister wrote to the Minister of Local Government asking him to direct the Commission to stop all activities in this matter for the time being. He also maintained that the Minister should have consulted him before because the area in which the temple was situated was a strategic area under army control.

In his reply Tiruchelvam maintained that at no time had Senanayake even hinted that the temple could not be declared as a sacred area as (being within the military area) it might have repercussions on the security of the State. In fact, Tiruchelvam emphasized that his decision to appoint the committee was a sequel to a note sent to him by the Premier on

101. The Jaffna University came into being in 1974.

the subject with the comment "for necessary action". However, in view of the hesitant attitude of the Premier with regard to his various promises to the FP the time had come when the Tamil party could not acquiesce with such inactivity any longer. It therefore had decided on an amiable parting of ways. Consequently, the FP decided to quit the government and act as an independent group, supporting the government on issues which would not adversely affect the Tamil-speaking people.

The political behaviour of the FP thus dramatised the constraints of a communal party which had to justify its major party position in a regional context and almost simultaneously withstand the pressures in the national context where it was a minor partner in power. The advent of the UF in power in 1970 and its firm attitude on language question made the job of the FP relatively easier. Collaboration involved delicate balancing. Confrontation—either covert or overt maintained the differentiation. This was evident from its protests and walk—outs from the parliament during the debate on the new constitution. In May 1971, during the discussions on the basic resolution, providing Buddhism its "rightful place" (the word 'rightful' was later substituted by 'foremost'), the FP, for instance, put forward another resolution seeking to make the island a secular State which would protect and foster Buddhism, Hinduism and Islam, the three main religions of the island.[102]

Moving the FP resolution, V. Dharmalingam said that to give Buddhism the pride of place was against secularism and democracy. "Is Buddhism the only religion in the country? Are there no other religions in the island ?" he asked.[103]

Because of the overwhelming majority of the UF the substitute resolution of the FP was rejected by voice vote but it did reveal the mood of the FP which, right from the beginning had favoured a secular approach towards religion by the State and had decided to express its vote of no-confidence in the new constitution, specially on the clauses dealing with fundamental rights. It had dramatised this by staging a walk-

102. *Patriot* 16 May 1971.
103. Ibid.

out, on the plea that some of its provisions in effect, accorded the status of second class citizens to the members of the minority community. Subsequently, the FP forming the nucleus of Tamil United Front continued to oppose the constitution on the plea that it discriminated against the religious and linguistic rights of the Tamil community.[104]

CONCLUSION

The patterns of religious policies of the various parties in Sri Lanka have been determined to a considerable extent by the emerging contours of the electoral and party system itself. Thus, if the electoral laws have, in effect, discouraged the growth of mushroom parties, the no-contest pacts have facilitated the major party-polarisation during elections. At times, the electoral alliances have also led to the formation of coalition governments, though this has not always been the case.

With the UNP and the SLFP emerging as the major parties, the 'established' minor parties have played the role of balancer. In the process, both the major and the minor parties have tended to come to terms with each other. If such an alliance has led to intra-party conflicts they have also tended to be a source for resource mobilisation. Thus, if the LSSP-SLFP coalition of 1964 led to an accretion of strength for the LSSP it also witnessed the walk-out of its more radical segment which opposed such a coalition. As regards the SLFP, the coalition was a manifestation on the part of Mrs. Bandaranaike to withstand the right wing pressure within. The action of the SLFP leader perhaps precipitated the 'purge' of the party and paved the way for a more stable and durable alliance with the left parties as was evident from the formation of the UF.

Apart from bringing out the intricacies of the internal power structure of the various parties, the coalition governments in Sri Lanka have tended to be catalysts. The containment of conflict within a coalition with partners having divergent objectives has necessitated the widening of 'consensus

104. *Patriot,* 26 December 1974.

areas' and has led to several concessions from the various partners. This has been more hazardous for the minor parties who needed to emphasize their distinct identity in ideological or communal terms more than the major parties. The political behaviour of the LSSP and the FP have also been indicative of the fact that in the Ceylonese ethos, it is more difficult for a regional party to wrest its demands from a party which, by and large, represents the majority community.

And yet, taking the cue from other countries, what is surprising in the Ceylonese context is not the withering of coalition governments but their capability to control and contain intra-coalitional conflicts. Also, the fact of the two major parties taking turns in power has further facilitated certain continuity in policy implementation and has consequently led to the widening of consensus areas. This is evident from the fact of the UNP fulfilling the SLFP's promise of establishing a separate university for the Bhikkhus as well as promulgating the enabling legislation for the Reasonable Use of Tamil Act legislated under SWRD Bandaranaike. The UF, on the other hand, has honoured in 1974 the UNP pledge for the formation of the Tamil University at Jaffna.

The emergence of such an approach to cultural policies seems to be due to the fact that religious issues, though important, have not been 'critical' in the overall programme of any party in Sri Lanka where, ultimately, economic factors dominate political life. However, what seems to be significant in this context is the extent to which religious attitudes and gestures have been given a special meaning in the 'image building' of the party, particularly after 1956. Since then, the leaderships of different parties have vied with each other to 'appear' more Buddhist than the other.

The ritualisation of politics in Sri Lanka with a special emphasis on certain external Buddhistic traits thus seemed to have come to stay as was evident from the leaders of all parties paying their obeisance to Buddha soon after they had been sworn in as ministers. If such postures on the part of left leadership evoked perhaps a sense of dismay among some (who perceived some sort of 'political hypocrisy' in such actions), they evoked a sense of suspicion in the minds of others. However, there is no doubt that most of them continued to be critical towards such gestures and waited till such gestures had been translated into something concrete.

This was natural in view of the gradually increasing political socialisation of an electorate which had been made more than aware of its voting power and demanded the translation of promises into performance. Further, thanks to the almost even electoral strength of the two major parties in the context of which each vote mattered, the support of every group— religious, cultural, economic and political—needed to be sought.

Where did the Buddhist monks fit into this picture ? How did the political parties view their potential as 'vote banks'? What role did they play in the evolution of the Sinhalese Buddhist ethos since 1956 ? How did they react to the ballot box politics of the island ? Answers to these questions need an appraisal of the political behaviour of the Bhikkhus in the nine elections which, spread over a span of four decades, marked the beginning of universal adult franchise in the island.

Chapter V

THE SAFFRON-ROBED AND BALLOT-BOX POLITICS

INTRODUCTION

In traditional societies, religion tends to be a mass phenomenon; politics, the prerogative of the privileged few. In
transitional Societies, specially with a democratic political
system, religion and religious groups have often served
channels for the masses to become politicised. The effectiveness of religious organisations, as agents of political
socialisation, depends on several factors, economic as well as
political, such as urbanisation, means of communication, mass
media, literacy, and, last but not the least, the nature of
suffrage.

In countries developing as well as developed, the dynamics
of electoral politics may have its short-term repercussions
as well as long term implications. The conversion of a
traditionally elitist politics into a 'polyarchy'[1] may be considered to be its long range consequence. Its short-term
impact, however, seems to be a greater degree of politicisation
of the intermediary links of the society.

Such intermediary links tend to be, among others, traditional elites—religious, political and economic. The princes

---

1 Polyarchy is defined as a system in which opportunities for public
  contestation are available to the great bulk of the population. For
  details see Robert A. Dahl, *Polyarchy—Participation and Opposition* (London, 1971).

and zamindars in India and the Bhikkhus in Sri Lanka happen to be a critical segment of intermediary elites in this respect.

What have been the strategies of those who wield political levers and party leadership to mobilise the popular influence of the Bhikkhus in their favour ? What has been the attitude of the Bhikkhus themselves towards the politics of the ballot-box? What has been their role in various elections ? How have the politically active Bhikkhus mobilised their power ? What have been their strategies and styles of operation during elections ? What impact has such participation had on the structure of the Sangha ? Has it led to new divisions cutting across chapteral lines and leading to greater mobilisation? Or, can it be simply viewed as a new type of division respond-ing to the democratic pressures and pulls without imparting either more popular deference or a new dynamism to the Sangha as a whole? Answers to these questions may be found in an appraisal of the Bhikkhus' attitude towards the ballot-box politics and the patterns of their participation in various elections since 1931.

BHIKKHUS AND THE ELECTIONS OF 1931 AND 1936

The grant of universal adult franchise in Sri Lanka changed the face of 1931 election altogether. Earlier, property and literary qualifications more or less limited the scope for political mobilisation to a segment of people in which the proportion of urban electorate was much larger than commensurate with its proportion of the total popula-tion. Universal suffrage not only led to a phenomenal increase in the size of the electorate[2] but also implied the necessity for the mobilisation of political resources of support at the rural level.

In the election of 1931, the leading elite's ambitions to attain power and influence colonial policy through the State Council led to their evolving varying types of contact-strategies with a view to eliciting the support of traditional

---

2. Before 1931 about 200,000 males had voting rights. In 1931 their number shot up to 1,577,932 and in 1936 to 2,451,323.

rural elites like village headmen and Bhikkhus. As regards the Bhikkhu, at places, candidates approached him as *Dayka* (patron—person who looks after the material needs of the Sangha) if he belonged to the area or through an important *Dayka* of the temple. In certain constituencies where contest was real, the political leaders in Colombo persuaded the principals of some of the Pirivenas to send the young Bhikkhus belonging to the constituency, to help in the campaign.[3]

Support from the clergy took divese forms. In certain cases advice to the laity was given by the High Priest, when sought. In others' meetings were held in the vihara and the candidate was introduced by the vihara priest to the people. At times, in conversation, the Bhikkhu expressed his viewpoint supporting a candidate. In many cases the monks attended election meetings which were often presided by one of the senior Bhikkhus of the area. It might be mentioned that in the villages of Ceylon of 1930s and 1940s it was customary on the part of a Bhikkhu to hold the chair in any village meeting in view of his elevated position in the social hierarchy. However, there is no doubt that this customary practice in election meetings often went in favour of the candidate for whom the meeting was held. Some of the Bhikkhus also addressed such meetings.

During the elections of 1931 and 1936 such activities of the Bhikkhus were covert, sporadic and limited. As many political leaders were the influential men of the area, people voted for them thereby confirming their dominant position in the rural society. Elections were, thus, more personalised[4] than politicised during this period.

The situation remained more or less the same in the election of 1936 despite the emergence of the leftist Lanka Sama Samaja Party (LSSP). In view of its inception hardly a year before the general election, it did not make much head-

3. Based on interviews with I. Karannagoda (former Senator), Rev. Dr. Ananda, Maithripala Senanayake, M.P., Rev. M. Vipulasara and Rev. P. Soratha. Also see speech of Rev. Palannoruwa Wimaladharma Nayaka Thero, President of the All Ceylon Congress of Bhikkhus in 1946. *Ceylon Daily News*, 18 February 1946.
4. Ibid.

way and the two LSSP leaders won the seats more as individuals who had played a significant role in the malaria eradication campaign of 1930s rather than as leaders of a left party.

As regards the role of the Buddhist clergy, in the elections of 1931 and 1936, it seems that notwithstanding their diffused performance, their influence was exploited successfully at least in some constituencies. In Kalutara constituency in the Western Province, for instance, the local contestant was a Christian. Some influential families of the area desiring to oppose him, invited an outsider who was a Goyigama Buddhist and made religion a major issue. The Buddhist candidate won. Another extreme case, reported by an English daily, was the defeat of S.A. Wickrmasinghe, a Buddhist who contested on the LSSP ticket. Through Sir D.B. Jayatillake's influence with the clergy in the area, a Christian won the election.[5] However, the number of Bhikkhus involved in activities associated with election was limited. The majority of them were neutral and presumably disinterested in elections.

While the role of the monks was limited and sporadic the slogans of 'religion and race' were the 'greatest forces' in deciding contests in both the elections. Thus, barring exceptional cases, a non-Buddhist had no chance in a straight fight against a Buddhist in a Buddhist constituency.[6] "The discovery", lamented a Ceylonese Daily, "made in the first general election was that religion was the winning ticket. Only the more perspicacious and less scrupulous had employed it....In the general election of 1936 the religious argument was widely used....Those who regarded their good record of

5. Editorial. 'Religion and Politics' *Times of Ceylon* (Colombo), 20 February 1946 and Editorial 'Bhikkhus and Politics', *Times of Ceylon*, 4 April 1946.
6. T.W. Roberts, *Problems of Public Life in India and Ceylon* (Colombo, n.d.), p. 1. According to a perceptive left leader "Although universal franchiee had existed from 1931, elections did not proceed on party lines, and political issues were hardly raised. Voters used to vote on caste, religious or personal considerations." Leslie Goonewardene, *A Short History of Lanka Sama Samaja Party* (Colombo, 1960), p. 5.

service as a passport to the Council, Mr. E.W. Perera, for instance, were defeated, simply because they did not profess the same faith as the voters. To such an extent was religious prejudice exploited that yellow, the colour of the sacred-Sangha, was ruled out as a colour for candidates."[7] The introduction of the religious element in the 1936 election was also deplored by Governor Edward Stubbs in the opening address to the State Council on 20 March 1936.[8]

From Donoughmore to Soulbury Commission

The State Council, elected in 1936, happened to have the longest tenure because of the Second World War. Meanwhile, another Commission for constitutional reforms was appointed in 1943 under the chairmanship of Lord Soulbury which submitted its report in 1945. It recommended a Legislature with two houses—the House of Representatives of 101 representatives (95 elected members and 6 nominated members) and the Senate consisting of 30 members. The Soulbury Constitution was accepted by the State Council in late 1945. The State Council was dissolved in July 1947 and preparations for general election under the provisions of the Soulbury Constitution were made.

The election of 1947 marked the emergence of a group of young, highly articulate Bhikkhus supporting the left parties like the LSSP and the CP. They mostly belonged to the Pirivenas in Colombo or in adjacent areas and both students and teachers participated in the campaign. Bhikkhus like Rev.

---

7. Editorial, 'Religion and Politics' *Times of Ceylon*, 20 February 1946 : Owing to the inability of the illiterate voters to read the names of the candidates on the ballot papers, colours were allotted to the candidates and ballot boxes corresponding to these colours were provided. A voter had to take his ballot paper and deposit it in secret in the ballot box bearing the colour of candidates of his or her choice. This led to grave abuse, with voters bringing back the ballot paper and selling it to the highest bidder among the agents of candidates. In the election of 1947, therefore, a new system of voting by symbols was introduced. Ceylon Daily News, *Parliament of Ceylon 1947* (Colombo, 1947), p. 9.

8. Cited in Editorial, 'Bhikkhus and Politics', *Times of Ceylon*, 4 April 1946.

Naravila Dhammaratana, Udakandawela Saranankara, Kala-
lalle Anandasagara, Bambarende Siriseevali and Walpola
Rahula[9] were some of the leaders of this group. These left-
inclined monks had certain points in common; virtually all of
them had been to India; they had been influenced by the
Indian nationalist movement and were closely associated with
some of its eminent socialist leaders. They had been connected
in some way or the other with the Vidyalankara Pirivena so
much so that they came to be known as the 'Vidyalankara
group'. They believed that the Buddhist clergy had an important role to play in the nationalist movement of Sri Lanka.
But the movement did not develop the kind of a momentum
which would have accommodated the radical views held by
these monks.

Should Monks Participate in Politics? The Debate

The initial provocation for these Bhikkhus to participate
in politics came from a statement of D.S. Senanayake, the
leader of the State Council, who in a speech at Matale in
January 1946, expressed his distress that the monks should be
thronging the galleries of the State Council. This was followed
up by the statement of another member of the State Council,
Mr. R.G. Senanayake that Bhikkhus should not participate in
politics and that they should not support any candidate in
the forthcoming elections and should in fact stay away from
it.[10]

9. Rev. Udakandawela Saranankara, Walpola Rahula, Naravila Dhammaratna studied in Calcutta;Bambardene Siriseevali studied in Kashi
   Vidyaneeth, Varanasi. Based on interviews with Rev. Siriseevali and
   Rev Rahula. Udakandawela Saranankara Thero was involved in the
   Indian national movement, while studying. In 1931 he was imprisoned and later sent back to Ceylon. He was forbidden to enter
   Bengal. Finding no national party in Ceylon, he contacted the LSSP
   leaders. He also issued a pamphlet stating why Sama Samajism was
   needed in Ceylon. The pamphlet was a critique of colonial administration and a plea for socialist change. Special correspondent,
   'Monks at Hustings', *Ceylon Observer*, 16 July 1962. For a profile
   of Rev. Rahula see D.B. Dhanapala, *Eminent Indians* (Bombay,
   1943), pp. 179-80.
10. *Ceylon Daily News*, 17 and 21 January 1946.

The reply to this advice of Senanayake came in the form of a declaration issued by K. Pannasara (Principal, Vidyalan-kara Pirivena). Entitled 'Bhikkhus and Politics' the declaration asserted that politics embraced all fields of human activities directed towards public welfare. As such, it was nothing but fitting for the Bhikkhus to identify themselves with activities conducive to public welfare—whether they were labelled as politics or something else. "We believe" continued the declaration, "that it is incumbent on the Bhikkhus not only to further the efforts directed towards the welfare of the country, but also to oppose such measures as are detrimental to the common good."[11] The Vidyalankara group lost no time in convening a meeting under the auspices of All Ceylon Congress of Monks (a non-political organisation of the monks initiated in 1920s) in which similar views were expressed.

This was the first time that the question of defining the role of Bhikkhus in the politics of Sri Lanka was raised and debated. The 'Vidyalankare Bhikkhus' alleged that political leaders like D.S. Senanayake and R.G. Senanayake adopted double standards. While they did not hesitate in exploiting the influence of the Bhikkhus for their political ends during the elections, they later preached that the clergy should abstain from politics.[12] They further maintained that a lay leader like D.S. Senanayake had no right to pass an injunction on what the Bhikkhus should or should not do. Such questions, they assert-ed, should be decided by the Bhikkhus themselves.[13]

In order to counteract the arguments of the Ceylonese press which seemed to be almost uniformly against the

11. *Bhikkhus and Politics : Declaration of the Vidyalankara Pirivena.* I am very grateful to Rev. N. Pannakara for giving me a copy of the declaration as well as permitting me to peruse his personal collection of press cuttings on the controversy during 1946-47. For the text of the declaration see Appendix E.
12. *Ceylon Daily News*, 18 February 1946.
13. In a speech, Rev. Rahula commented that R.G. Senanayake had gone from temple to temple requesting the Bhikkhus and other religious leaders to work for him and owed at least 13,000 votes to the monks. *Times of Ceylon*, 28 January 1946 and 20 February 1946.

Bhikkhus' participating in politics, the Vidyalankara Bhikkhus started their own weekly in Sinhalese entitled 'Kalaya'.[14] Their main theme was that 'politics' was not merely the government and administration but combined all social activities; that nowhere had the Vinaya banned participation of Bhikkhus in politics; that Marxism was not an anathema to Buddhism; that the UNP, as the party of 'capitalists' was trying to exploit the workers and that as citizens of this island the progressive Bhikkhus had to assert themselves.[15] In the annual Old Boys' meeting of Vidyalankara Pirivena, the protagonists of Bhikkhus' participation in politics resolved that in a predominantly Buddhist country like Sri Lanka any attempt to restrict the activities of the Sangha or to do away with the leadership of the Bhikkhus was fraught with danger to the religion itself.[16]

The Bhikkhus also found amongst their supporters lay leaders like Dr. A.P. de Soyza and W. Dahanayake, a member of the State Council, who initiated a motion in the State Council "proclaiming the Council's pleasure in the movement among members of the Sangha to participate in politics upon the basis of a forward programme and policy."[17]

The protagonists of Bhikkhus' participation in politics were not only severely castigated in the Ceylonese press and by

14. The first issue of *Kalaya*, was published on 14 March 1946 and the last in March 1947. Published in Sinhalese, the weekly gives a fairly clear picture of the militancy of its leaders.
15. Several articles by Rev. Rahula, Naravila Dhammaratna, K. Pannassara, B. Siriseevali in *Kalaya* are replete with these ideas. Apart from *Kalaya* Bhikkhu Rahula wrote a book entitled *Bhikkhuyuge Urumaya* (The Heritage of Bhikkhus) which was a revised and expanded version of his speech in Kandy on 9 March 1946. In this book, quoting from primary sources, he showed how, from the beginning, the monks played a significant role in the polity and society of Ceylon. The book was also an indictment of the imperialist policies of the British which according to him led to the degeneration of the Buddhist Sangha. The book seems to have been amongst the best seller of 1946, for the entire edition was sold out within three months of its publication and another was brought out in 1948.
16. *Times of Ceylon*, 20 and 23 March 1946.
17. Editorial, 'Priest Ridden Politics', *Times of Ceylon*, 28 February 1946.

certain lay Buddhist organisations but their stand was also deplored by some senior Bhikkhus.[18] The chief high priest of Malwatta chapter went to the extent of issuing an injunction asking monks to keep away from politics and warned that Bhikkhus participating in political activities e.g., membership in village committees, urban and municipal councils, would be expelled from the order.[19] The Maha Nayaka of Ramanna Nikaya also advised the monks of his chapter neither to enter in any political organisation nor to take sides in a political contest.[20]

Amongst the lay organisations, the official organ of the Maha Bodhi Society (founded by Anagarika Dharmapala) joined the dailies in censuring the Vidyalankara monks. Another Buddhist organisation, which convened a special conference of the Bhikkhus and laity to discuss the issue of Bhikkhus' participation in politics was the All-Ceylon Buddhist Congress (ACBC). An association of Buddhist laity and monks, the ACBC was founded in 1929 with a view to promoting and fostering the interest of Buddhists and Buddhism in Ceylon and had an enthusiastic chairman in Dr. G.P. Malalasekhera.

The special conference which was convened by the ACBC in April 1946 at Kelaniya (near Colombo) and was attended by the priests of virtually all sects resolved that in no circumstances should a monk seek election to or be a member of the State Council, Parliament, Senate and Municipal Council, Urban Council, Village Committee or any such other institution, or any political organisation. The monk should not seek registration as a voter or exercise the rights of a voter in respect of any of the political institutions mentioned above nor should he associate himself with any election in respect of these institutions.[21]

The 'Young Turks' of the Sangha, however, did not relent. They formed an organisation called *Lanka Eksath Bhikkhu*

18. For the text of the views of these priests refer to *Peramuna* (Sinhalese, Colombo), 8 February 1946.
19. For the text of this injunction see *Ceylon Daily News*, 7 March 1946.
20. *Silumina* (Sinhalese, Colombo), 10 March 1946.
21. For the text of resolutions and summary of proceedings see *Ceylon Daily News*, 2 April 1946.

Mandalaya (Ceylon Union of Bhikkhus) and held a meeting on 29 June 1946 in Colombo to (*a*) censure the method adopted by certain parties obstructing the religious and national liberties and rights of both monks and laymen, (*b*) protect the civil and political rights of the Sangha, and (*c*) to declare the future policy to be followed by the Sangha for the furtherance of Buddhism.[22]

In this meeting which was presided by Polwatta Buddhadatta Thero—a senior Bhikkhu of Amarapura Nikaya and a renowned scholar in Pali—the resolutions of the ACBC came under heavy attack. The Bhikkhus resolved that they had no faith in "the present leaders of the country who, for their personal gains", had handed over the country to the imperialists. The Congress, it was maintained, would fight to the last for complete freedom and would not be "satisfied with Dominion Status, like Mr. D.S. Senanayake".[23] The Union of Bhikkhus made it clear that while none of their members wanted to enter the State Council, or any other political organisation, their aim was to "overthrow those leaders who were exploiting the masses to serve their own ends, and to purify political life." The Sangha, they resolved, should take part in politics and protect the people and religion. The Bhikkhus also proposed to appoint a tribunal with a view to reforming the Sangha.[24]

In a meeting on 2 March 1947 the Ceylon Union of Bhikkhus announced its programme. It rejected the Soulbury Constitution and called upon the people to work for complete independence. Its socio-economic programme included the nationalisation of all transport services, mines and estates; control of foreign investments, support for the free education bill scheme, introduction of complete prohibition.[25] The LEBM also adopted resolutions protesting against the official attempts to introduce repressive and discriminatory legislation with a view to depriving the Bhikkhus of their civic rights and

---

22. *Times of Ceylon*, 28 June 1946, and *Ceylon Daily News*, 1 July 1946.
23. *Ceylon Daily News*, 9 September 1946.
24. Ibid., 1 July and 9 September 1946.
25. *Times of Ceylon*, 3 March 1947. Also see *Kalaya*, Vol. 1, No. 50, 6 March 1947, pp. 1-4.

called upon the monks to be ready for such an eventuality.

Finally, it requested the Maha Nayakas of Malwatta and Asgiri chapters to give a lead in maintaining the independence and self-respect in the Sangha by insisting on the deletion of a degrading clause in the Instrument of Appointment (conferred on them aswell as on other Nayakas. which enjoined them to be loyal and obedient to the Imperial Government as well as bound them to act as 'spies' of the British Government.[26] They also signified their approval to the declaration made on 6 January 1947 at Sri Kalyani Raja Maha Vihara at Kelaniya in which "the Sangha of Sri Lanka, the Guardian of the Life, and Liberty, and Sponsors of the well-being and Happiness of the people of this island", not satisfied with the provisions of Ceylon Independence Act, claimed its right to be a "Free and Independent Sovereign State".[27]

The inception and growth of the LEBM was significant. For the first time a group of Bhikkhus had raised their voice not only against the colonial rulers but also against the country's elite co-operating with them. Coming in closer touch with the Socialist leaders of India, they found themselves nearer to the leftist leaders in their own country rather than to those in power. Their allegation was that if the British had deprived them of their tradition and foisted on them an alien culture, the leaders, believing in the benevolence of the British rule, had betrayed the national cause. Indigenous interests thus had joined hands with the imperialist power and had not looked after the well-being of the masses.

26. Ibid. The Instrument of Appointment contained the following clause: "You are therefore hereby directed and enjoined diligently to obey and execute all such orders as you may receive from us; or the Government Agent, and fully to discover and make known to us or the constituted authorities of Government, all things which may come to your knowledge affecting the public interests and all treasons or traitorous conspiracies which you may hear of against His Majesty's Government." Ceylon, *Correspondence Relating to the Buddhist Temporalities Ordinance*, IV-1907 (Colombo, 1907), p. 14.

27. For the text of this declaration refer to (anonymous), *Dharma Vijaya* (Triumph of Righteousness) or *The Revolt in the Temple* (Colombo, 1953), pp. 157-8.

The militant monks resented a policy which meant the preservation and maintenance of a social order wherein seniority was an important criteria in determining the structural hierarchy of the various Nikayas. Under the circumstances, the angry young monks were bound to be closer to the political personalities and groups which stood against the *status quo* and demanded radical changes in Sri Lanka's political system. Sama Samajist monks argued that Sama Samajism and Buddhism were not anti-thetical as both aimed at an egalitarian society.[28]

The movement of the LEBM can be seen as a movement of the young against the old; a confrontation of the incumbents of rich temples against those of the poor ones. Most of the Bhikkhus participating in LEBM, though occupying prestigious positions in the various Pirivenas did not seem to belong either to rich families or rich temples. Even when belonging to the Siam Nikaya they resented the domination of the up-country Bhikkhus many of whom, according to them, were neither learned nor pious.

The learned Bhikkhus belonging to the Malwatta and Asgiri chapters, they maintained, were often from the low-country but were not given positions in the Karaka Sabha (Executive Council) of the Malwatta and Asgiri chapters of the Siam Nikaya. Nayakaship (title of High Priest), they alleged, was given to Bhikkhus not for their piety or learning but were 'sold' for extraneous considerations. As such, the high echelon of the Sangha had forfeited the confidence of the young 'progressive' Bhikkhus. In their attempt to safeguard their vested interest, the High Priests stood for *status quo* and did not want to antagonise either the rich political leaders or the

---

28. Musing over the events of 1947 two decades later, Rev. Dr. Rahula, who was one of the pioneers of the LEBM told the author: "We initiated the movement with a view to help the suffering masses, for us it was based on compassion. It is the legitimate right of the Bhikkhus to protect the rights of the toiling masses." See also a series of articles entitled 'Marxism or Buddhism'? by Rev. Yakkaduwa Sri Prannarama in *Kalaya* Vol. 1, Nos. 34, 35 and 36; 7, 14 and 21 November 1946.

imperialist powers.[29]

The LEBM was, by and large, an urban phenomenon. In the rural areas its impact was felt only to the extent that the students from Pirivenas like Vidyalankara, imbibed with some of the socialist ideas, were in a position to influence the vicinity of their villages. However, it appears that those who had the potential often did not go back to the villages. Colombo and the adjoining areas seemed to be more fertile for dissemination of such ideas.

In the absence of any other alternative, the first political organisation of the Bhikkhus, the LEBM found itself closely associated with the left parties like the LSSP and the CP which were then anything but religious. In fact, one is struck by the similarities in the programmes of the LEBM and the LSSP. It was the economic aspect and not the cultural aspect of Celyonese life which the political manifesto of the LEBM emphasized. The question of resuscitating the Sangh was not a priority item on the political agenda of the LEBM; economic amelioration of the masses and the defeat of the 'capitalist' parties assumed higher priorities.

A few months before the elections of 1947, the LEBM announced that it had decided not to put up any candidate but to support those who had honest policies and were "faithful to the country, people and religion". It was also made clear that the LEBM would oppose "imperialist political parties who do not work with a view to achieve independence."[30]

The obvious target of the LEBM was the UNP. Its members supported the left candidates in general and the LSSP candidates in particular. In Kelaniya and Mirigama in the western provinces, for instance, the LEBM put its weight in favour of the LSSP candidate against J.R. Jayawardane and D.S. Senanayake respectively. D.S. Senanayake frankly opposed

---

29. Based on interviews with Rev. Dr. Ananda, Rev. Siriseevali, T.B. Subasinghe, Rev. P. Soratha, Rev. Hawanpola Ratnassara. The notable exception to this was the Kelania Raja Maha Vihara, an old temple with several endowments.

30. *Kalaya*, Vol. 1, No. 38, 12 December 1946, p. 1.

the participation of the Bhikkhus in elections, but he did not refrain from seeking the support of Rev. Henepitigedera Gnanaseeha, a revered monk and a powerful speaker of Ratnapura.[31]

The activities of the Bhikkhus were countered effectively by the UNP in many ways. To begin with, the UNP declared that it stood for religious tolerance—the major tenet of Buddhism. "Religion", said D.S. Senanayake, was "essentially a personal and individual matter, the conviction of our innermost being. We as a party believe and stand by the individual's fundamental right to freedom of worship. In this we uphold the tradition of the past. Didn't Rajasinha the Second ...allow full freedom to his Portuguese prisoners to practise their Christian form of worship...?"[32] Quoting some of the speeches of the LSSP leaders the UNP speakers argued that the LSSP was an anti-religious party.[33] As such, if a left government was formed there would be no religion. UNP leaders like J.R. Jayawardane also refuted the theme that Marxism and Buddhism were not anti-thetical; Marxism believed in matter, Buddhism in spirit.[34]

The main burden of the UNP propaganda was that the left parties would destroy religion.[35] The UNP carried on an extensive poster propaganda against its antagonists. Huge posters were displayed all over showing the Buddhist temples, mosques and churches in flame under the sickle of the LSSP with the caption 'Save Buddhism from the flame of Marxism', 'Save Islam from the flame of Marxism', 'Save Hinduism from the flame of Marxism'. The party castigated activist monks as

---

31. Based on interviews with Rev. H. Gnanavas, Lecturer in Vidyodaya University. Rev. Gnanaseeha had himself told this to Rev. Gnanavas.

32. UNP (News sheet), p. 1. Available in the beginning in the bound volume of the UNP journal in the UNP office, the sheet bears no date. Perhaps it was issued just before the launching of the UNP Journal in February-March 1947.

33. See for instance UNP, Communism Suppresses Religion—What Dr. Colvin R. de Silva Saw in Russia (Colombo, n.d.), pp. 1-5.

34. UNP (Colombo), Vol. 1, No. 15, 20 June 1947, p. 2. J.R. Jayawardane expounded this in a monograph entitled Buddhism and Marxism (Colombo, n.d.)

35. Leslie Goonewardane, n. 6, p. 34.

'political bhikkhus' or 'Sama Samaja Bhikkhus' and tried to denigrate them.

In the background of the rural Buddhist ethos of 1947, people watched the activities of the LEBM with curiosity but not with much favour. Nor did the enthusiasm of the 'Young Turks' continue for long. The LEBM virtually became defunct once the 1947 election was over. Its leadership lost its initiative, and the group broke up.

One of its leaders went abroad for studies, another disrobed and became an LSSP activist; a few others continued to put their energy and force behind the Communist party. The incumbency dispute of a certain temple created dissension amongst some of its activists and divided them. However, the performance of the LEBM during 1946-47 did give an indication of the political potential of the clergy in a democratic set-up. The cultural elite, however, could be more effective if the cultural policies of the State were questioned.

During 1947-52 a segment of the articulate Buddhist lay leadership and Bhikkhus had begun to wonder whether in this 'little bit of England' (as Sri Lanka was called by many in terms of the cultural orientations of its western educated ruling elite), the indigenous culture and religion had any place at all. However, the scepticism of this segment needed yet to be mobilised in political articulation. The timing of the next election in 1952 seemed to be too early for such a mobilisation for several reasons.

The 'father of the nation', D.S. Senanayake, who died in 1951, had commanded popular deference as a Buddhist. His assurance to appoint a Buddhist Commission in the Kandy Conference of the UNP in 1951[36] had assuaged the Buddhist sense of grievance and had also given them a measure of assurance of the Buddhist sympathies of the ruling party. Besides, during this period, this segment of the Buddhist leadership did not discern any political alternative to the UNP in terms of its Sinhalese Buddhist credentials for, as regards the left parties, their secular radicalism could not be reconciled with the Sinhalese-Buddhist overtones of groups like the All-Ceylon Buddhist Congress. As regard the SLFP, it had

36. For details see Chapter IV.

appeared on the political scene only a few months before the
elections.

RELIGION AND RELIGIOUS ISSUES IN THE ELECTION OF 1952

In such a setting, religious issues were relegated to a peripheral position, if at all, in the 1952 election. In fact, several
parties ignored the subject altogether in their respective manifestoes. The UNP manifesto, for instance, which was, in the
main, a statement of its achievements during the past $4\frac{1}{2}$ years
did not even mention it. Nor did the left parties dwell on the
issue. Bandaranaike's SLFP had a paragraph emphasising the
need for the revival of spiritual values and the role of the State
as well as the people therein.[37] However, in its manifesto it
made no specific mention of Buddhism, nor of the disabilities
it had suffered under foreign dominance. Further, except
in a few constituencies, religion did not seem to be a very
important issue in the election campaign either.

The support mobilisation of the religious groups by the
UNP, however, did take place but in an indirect fashion. Thus,
in a pastoral letter, the Archbishop of Colombo, Thomas
Cooray, declared that no Catholic, with even an atom of conscience could vote for a candidate who subscribed to a political creed banned by the Church—be it communism or otherwise.[38] This indirectly supported the UNP and the letter was
much publicised.

The statement of the Maha Nayakas of Malwatta and
Asgiri issued by the Matara branch of the UNP had similar
overtones. Linking the destiny of the Sinhalese Buddhists
with that of the elections, the Maha Nayakas maintained that
though it was not proper to think of religion in respect to
political questions, votes should not be cast for political parties
which were against religion or which encouraged or supported
anti-religious trends; if they assumed political power, the national religion would be destroyed. The Matara branch of the
UNP had an explanatory postscript appended to this state-

---

37. Sri Lanka Freedom Party, *Manifesto and Constitution of the Sri
   Lanka Freedom Party* (Wellampitiya, 1951), p. 9.
38. *Ceylon Observer*, 11 May 1952.

ment that "parties which were against the religion" were to
the CP and the LSSP. The clause "parties which encouraged or
supported them" referred to the SLFP and the Republican
Party.[39]

Notwithstanding the similarity in both the statements, there
was one major difference. The statement of the Maha Nayakas was not much publicised. The pastoral letter on the other
hand gained wide publicity through press and other communication media. Also, the Archbishop's letter carried a great
deal of weight among the Catholics. The same could not be
said of the Maha Nayakas' statement in respect of either
the clergy or the Buddhist laity.

The Bhikkhus were divided. If the UNP enjoyed the
support of some Bhikkhus, there were others who were keen
campaigners against it. However, it is noteworthy that the
Bhikkhus supported one or the other party candidate not as
a group but as individuals.[40] The LEBM was not active in
the 1952 elections. Also, there did not seem to be either ideological or political cohesiveness amongst the Bhikkhus at this
juncture to encourage them to form a group, though the SLFP
did have some of the Bhikkhus like Rev. Mapitigama Buddharakhita and Talpavila Seelawamsa as its founder members.

Notwithstanding the victory of the UNP and the contribution of D.S. Senanayake in the propagation of Buddhism, a
feeling continued among a segment of English educated Buddhist elite, that all was not well with Buddhism. The resignation of Dudley Senanayake in 1953 and the succession to premiership of Sir John Kotelawala, who was widely considered to
be highly westernized, caused a great deal of anxiety and concern among this section of elite regarding the future of Buddhism in the island.

39. UNP (Matara Branch), *Buddha Sasanaya Ruka Gama, Yayi Maha
    Nayaka Semi Tada Vary Avavada Karati* (Protect Buddha Sasana—
    Advice of the Maha Nayakas (Matara, 1952).
40. I.D.S. Weerawardane, 'The General Elections in Ceylon, 1952',
    Ceylon Historical Journal, Vol. 2, Nos. 1 and 2, July and October
    1952 (Special Supplement), p. 129.

The Years of Buddhist Activism : 1952-56

The beginning of Kotelawala's regime marked the beginning of activities for the Buddha Jayanti. By 1954 Buddhist activism could be seen at different levels and under the guidance of different groups. The Jayanti, however, seems to have given them a common purpose, at least for the time being. This was a multi-stream movement. At places the streams coalesced; at others they flowed side by side. All this created an image of the spectacular Jayanti in the mass mind.

The Buddhist activism had impetus from official as well as unofficial sources. The UNP had launched its Jayanti programme under the auspices of Lanka Buddha Mandalaya and the ACBC had already decided to appoint a commission in 1953 to enquire into the state of Buddhism. Meanwhile, a quiet Buddhist movement was being initiated by a government servant, N.Q. Dias, the beginnings of which can be traced to the early months of 1952 at Ratnapura where Dias was the Government Agent. Dias found that Catholics were not only well entrenched in government positions but were also well organised under the Church. He realised that the unorganised state of Buddhism and the absence of an effective linkage between the Government—Buddhist interests was largely responsible for this. As such, he sponsored a Government Buddhist Society with a view to safeguarding material as well as spiritual interests of the Buddhists.[41]

Soon after, Dias came in close touch with the Rev. Henepitigedera Gnanaseeha Thero, one of the most revered and popular preachers in the area. In view of his past experiences

41. The first public effort of N.Q. Dias was referred to in the *World Fellowship of Buddhists*, No. 11, June 1952, p. 2. N.Q. Dias, *Rajya Sewakayange Bauddha Katayutu Ha Ehi Prativipaka* (Buddhist activities of the Government Servants and their consequences) (Colombo, 1965). This pamphlet is very significant for it throws light on the way a movement, started in a humble manner, caught on primarily because it was able to aggregate feelings of frustration and disillusionment of the Sinhalese *vis-à-vis* their traditions and culture.

with the UNP leadership,[42] the Thero had begun to doubt its credibility as the promoter of Buddhist interests and presumably Dias, himself a government servant, had shared the Bhikkhu's scepticism in this respect. After prolonged discussions on the state of Buddhism, both seemed to have arrived at the same conclusion that what was not being done by the State had to be accomplished through unofficial collective efforts.

It was said of this team : "Quintus Dias had the official status and finance. Gnanaseeha Thero had his personal popularity'.[43] The collaboration of both led to the launching of Bauddha Sasana Samiti in virtually every village of Sabaragamuva. These societies were expected to look after the needs of Bhikkhus, the management of Dhamma schools and the education of its members in respect of their rights as citizens. Another prominent Bhikkhu of Ratnapura who joined actively in this venture was Rev. Balangoda Ananda Maitreya Thero.

Soon, these societies spread virtually all over the country and their number exceeded 3,500. In order to co-ordinate the activities of these societies and to take the message of their utility in areas where such societies were not operating, it was deemed necessary to start a paper. A printing press called Dharma Vijaya Press was established in the Pirivena of Rev. Ananda Maitreya Thero and the weekly Dharma Vijaya was started. In a short time, its circulation went up to about 27,000. Meanwhile, inspired by similar reasons, some Bhikkhus and laity had also started a fortnightly in English at Colombo called Buddha Jayanti. This was also printed in the Dharma Vijaya Press.

42. Gnanaseeha Thero had bitter experience too. In the elections of 1947, on an assurance from D.S. Senanayake for the establishment of a Buddhist University in his area, Gnanaseeha Thero had actively supported his candidates. The post-election period seemed to indicate that the 'Father of the Nation' had much bigger things to do than bother himself with matters concerning Gnanaseeha's plans for the propagation of Buddhism. Rev. Gnanaseeha Thero was disappointed in D.S Senanayake's attitude and found his successors no better in this respect. The indifference of the UNP towards the Sangha, he felt, was too obvious to be ignored.

43. Dias, n. 41, pp. 1-4. Also see Muditha, 'Secret Face of Politics', *Ceylon Observer*, 28 September 1962.

These journals emphasised such issues as the question of upgrading Buddhist schools, the problem of the nursing sisters in the hospitals, and the significance of Sinhalese as the official language. The journal also provoked questions as to whether Sri Lanka was really independent and whether the Sinhalese were the real rulers of the country. Generally speaking, the main thrust of the publications was to suggest that the fault lay with the government, as the biggest patron and as the final arbiter. It was inevitable that the Dharma Vijaya and Buddha Jayanti soon acquired a political orientation.[44]

By 1954, Dias had come back to Colombo as Registrar-General and found in L.H. Mettananda, Principal of Ananda College (one of the foremost Buddhist schools) an equal enthusiast. At this stage it was deemed necessary to organise the Sangha too. Consequently, Sangha Sabhas (Associations of Bhikkhus) began to be established in various electorates and a paper called Sangha Samaggi was started. By 1954 there were as many as 72 Sangha Sabhas. The members of the Government and Local Government Servants Buddhist Societies, with Dias as chairman, facilitated the formation of such organisations. Each of these Sabhas encouraged austere and dedicated living on the part of its members. Members from all sects participated in its activities although its leadership was usually said to be from low-country sects.

By the end of 1954, its leading members decided to have a central organisation incorporating all the 72 Sabhas. Accordingly, Sri Lanka Maha Sangha Sabha (SLMSS) came into

44. The *Buddha Jayanti*, for instance, started a series entitled 'Pages from Ceylon History' quoting in extenso official documents to show the influence of the missionaries on the government's religious policy during the nineteenth century. Apart from this, on an average at least, one out of its three editorials raised political issues. Containing a great deal of factual data, the editorials did not mince words in reprimanding the government for its favouritism to Catholics and for its indifferent treatment towards Buddhists and Buddhist organisations. An emotive appeal ran through its many editorials: Let Buddhists try to find reasons for the degeneration of Buddhism; Let the national religion be given its proper place; Let the Government respresent the aspirations of the majority community in its cultural policies.

being, with its constitution ratified on 4 December 1954 at
Ananda College in Colombo. It was Ananda College which
became the hub of Bhikkhus' activities. Amongst those drawn
in the SLMSS were Rev. Baddegama Wimalawamsa Thero,
Principal of Sri Lanka Vidyalaya (a leading Pirivena in
Colombo), Rev. Henepitigedera Gnanseeha Thero (Ratnapura),
Kelepitimulla Sanghapala Thero (Sri Lanka Vidyalaya), Hene-
pitigedera Piyananda Thero (Vice-Principal, Sri Lanka Vidya-
laya), Kotagama Wachissara thero (a teacher in Ananda
College), Hawanpola Ratnasara Thero (Vidyalankara Pirivena)
and W. Ananda Thero (Vidyalankara Pirivena), Medagoda
Sumantissa Thero (Principal, Sunetra Devi Pirivena), Attuduwa
Gunaratna Thero (Ratnapura) and Devamottawe Amarawamsa
Thero (Tilakaratnaramaya temple, Colombo).[45] The major
architects of the EBP thus, were, by and large, Colombo-based
Bhikkhus who were politically active and some of whom had
ample economic resources.

The Buddhist Committee of Enquiry

The presence of voluntary Buddhist organisations like the
Sangha Sabha, the Buddha Sasana Samiti and Government
Buddhists Associations all over the country greatly facilitated
the work of the Buddhist Committee which had already come
into being. N.Q. Dias's associations provided an organized
itinerary for the committee's visits,[46] and the various journals

45. The information in this para is taken from the files (in nSihalese)
of the Sri Lanka Maha Sabha available with Rev. Talpavila
Seelavamsa. The author is very grateful to Rev. Talpavila Seelavamsa for providing access to these papers.

Initially, the name of the Sabha suggested was "Sri Lanka Eksath
Bhikkhu Bala Mandalaya" (All Ceylon United Monks' Organisation). The Karaka Sabha (Executive Council) which framed the
constitution of this changed it to Sri Lanka Maha Sangha Sabha.
(Constitution of the Sri Lanka Maha Sangha Sabha
(Sinhalese) available with Rev. Medagoda Sumanatissa, Principal
of Sunetra Devi Pirivena, Pepiliyana. Rev. Sumanatissa took
great pains in arranging the material on the subject, available with
him and in Sinhalese. I am grateful to him for making them
available to me.
46. Based on interviews with government officials and Bhikkhus.

mentioned above gave it ample publicity.

Composed of fourteen members—seven monks representing the major sects, and seven laymen—the Committee had articulate lay leaders[47] as well as Bhikkhus on its panel, who were acclaimed scholars and were revered for their piety and integrity. Four out of seven Bhikkhus were the vice-presidents of some of the best Pirivenas of the country; the fifth, Rev. Madihe Pannaseeha Thero, held a high position in a reputed Colombo Pirivena (Vajiraramaya). The other two members were Nayakas (chiefs) from the two major chapters—Malwatta and Asgiri—of the up-country Siam Nikaya. Nikayawise, four belonged to Siam Nikaya, two to Amarapura and one to Ramannya Nikaya.

The inclusion of the two chief priests (Nayakas) in the Committee was opposed by the Maha Nayakas of the Malwatta and Asgiri chapters. Not only did they announce their dissociation with the Committee on the plea that the laity had no business to indulge in the appointment of such a Committee but they also put pressure on the two member-Nayakas to withdraw from it. Both the members, however, refused to oblige their respective chief priests on the plea that they were participating in their individual capacity.[48]

As regards the government, the appointment of the Buddhist Committee evoked comments from two of its Buddhist members. "The Buddhist Commission", declared J.R. Jayawardane, Minister of Food and Agriculture, "is a body appointed by the people, for the people and therefore it is an august body". "Its report, continued" the Minister, "would

---

47. Besides articulate lay leaders like Mettananda, Malalasekhara and P. de S. Kularatne, it had among its member Dr. T. Vimalananda a university don who had been engaged in a study of the impact of the British colonial policy on Buddhism; C.D.S. Siriwardane (a leading advocate and a law lecturer in the University of Ceylon, Colombo), who had spent long hours amongst the dusty materials of the Ceylonese archives and museum to construct the legal implication of missionary activities on Buddhism and D.C. Wijewardane, one of the patrons of Kelaniya Vihara who had already anonymously written a book entitled *The Revolt in the Temple*.

48. *Times of Ceylon*, 8 October 1954.

be published after its submission by the propaganda Council of the Buddhist Council. The Minister of Home Affairs, A. Ratnaike, who was looking after the Jayanti celebrations, went a step further and declared that although the Committee was not a body appointed by the Government, its proposals "when submitted to the government and the Buddhist Council will receive my full support as proposals coming from Buddhist leaders of the country." The report was, however, submitted to the Sangha but not to the government.

It took the Committee a year to go round the country, record the evidence of about 1,800 laymen and 700 Bhikkhus and submit its report to the Sangha at a mass meeting held at Ananda College in February 1956. About 3,000 Bhikkhus and a vast gathering of laity were present in the meeting.[49] Initially published in Sinhalese, its abridged version in English entitled "Betrayal of Buddhism" appeared thereafter. Apart from being an indictment of the colonial rule, it preserved a "case of Buddhist action, a set of objectives and a concrete programme."[50] While the report's narrative of the past had provided the emotional thrust of Sinhalese grievances, its recommendations reckoned with the changing world of the twentieth century.

The value of the report, to quote a perceptive Ceylonese scholar, "lay not so much in the correctness of the diagnosis, the soundness of the remedies or the methods proposed for the restoration of Buddhism as on its appeal to the sentiments of a large section of Buddhism whose imagination it captured."[51] Perhaps no other document in contemporary Sri Lanka had put forward such a forceful critique of the activities of the Catholics as well as of colonial powers and stirred the sentiments of the majority community as the report of the Buddhist Committee. More than this, perhaps no other non-religious document was studied so religiously and quoted so copiously during the elections by such a large body of Bhikkhus as the "Betrayal of Buddhism".

49. *Ceylon Observer*, 5 February 1956.
50. For an excellent analysis of the report see, G.C. Mendis, *Ceylon Today and Yesterday—Main Currents of Ceylon History* (Colombo, 1963), second revd. edn., p. 145.
51. Ibid.

The emergence of the Eksath Bhikkhu Peramuna(EBP-United Front of the Bhikkhus) in February 1956 before the elections was largerly responsible for this upsurge of sentiment. The EBP was a coalition of two monk organisations—Sri Lanka Maha Sangha Sabha (SLMSS) and Samastha Lanka Bhikkhu Sammelanaya (SLBS—All-Ceylon Congress of Bhikkhus).

Most of the members of the SLBS belonged to the old LEBM which was reorganised in 1954 and had Telpavila Seelawamsa and Mapitigama Buddharakkhita Theros as its joint secretaries. Rev. Buddharakkhita, the Viharadhipati of Kelaniya Raja Maha Vihara had already been a political figure in the elections of 1947 and 1952 at Kelaniya and Rev. Tal-pavila Seelawamsa, Principal of Lanka Loka Pirivena at Kolonnawa (near Colombo), had been politically active since 1947. Both of them had also been close associates of Bandara-naike.[52]

The EBP was an organisation of these two associations with both maintaining their separate identities. All the letters issued by the EBP for instance were signed by five Bhikkhus— the three secretaries of the SLMSS signing on the left and the two secretaries of the SLBS on the right. The leadership and the majority of the member-ship of the EBP was from the Amarapura and Ramanna Nikayas. And though Siam Nikaya as a chapter kept aloof from its activities, Siam Nikaya Bhikkhus from Vidyalankara Pirivena, from the wealthy temple of Kelaniya and from its Kotte chapter in the low country were active in its delibera-tions.

Of the two organisations, the SLMSS appears to have been more vocal and articulate than the SLBS during 1955. Soon after its inception it wrote letters to the Premier and Governor-General seeking confirmation of certain information, or, where necessary, protesting against official action. For instance, it pro-tested against the proposal for the establishment of a Catholic Centre for Southeast Asia with its head office in Colombo. It maintained that the Catholic religious institutions shoula not be exempted from taxation. It also sent a resolution duly

52. For a brief history of the evolution of the EBP see L.H. Mettananda's letter in *Ceylon Daily News*, 4 September 1956.

adopted by the EBP to the Prime Minister that Sinhala should be made the official language. In a telegram dated 3 December 1955 to him, the Sabha also protested against the transfer of the Permanent Secretary to the Ministry of Educa tion, Jinadasa Samarakkody and declared that in this transfer the Sabha "strongly suspected the Catholic pressure". In his reply Premier Kotelawala denied the charge[53] but the issue which evoked the comments of the Sabha made its attitude towards the government clear.

"No Elections before Jayanti", Says the Clergy

The SLMSS had also begun to suspect the hands of Catholic Action in the timing of the dissolution of Parliament as early as September 1955 and had sent a telegram to the Premier enquiring whether it was true that the Roman Catholic Church was pressing the Government to hold a snap general election before the Buddha Jayanti. The Premier merely acknowledged the letter,[54] and did not deem it neces- sary to issue an explanatory statement as desired by the EBP.

The Government's decision to hold the election almost a year before the scheduled date i.e., 1957 and on the eve of Jayanti Year (May 1956-May 1957) meant, according to the critics, the virtual disruption of the Buddhist fervour which was being built around Jayanti celebrations. "There is a possibility", maintained the SLMSS in a circular to all its branches, "that the original enthusiasm amongst Buddhists regarding the Jayanti will be lost owing to the differences that might arise amongst the Buddhists themselves as a result of a general election."[55] It was also said in political quarters that the real reason behind the Premier's decision to dissolve the Parliament was that his admirers were perturbed over the developing organisations of the Sangha and wanted to 'nip' it before it got 'set'.[56]

---

53. Files at Rev. Talpavila Seelawamsa's Pirivena.
54. Text of the telegram available in Talpavilla Seelawamsa's files.
55. Text of the letter of the EBP available in the EBP files at Sunetra Devi Pirivena.
56. Sangha Campaigns, *Ceylon Observer*, 17 July 1962.

EBP's Election Manifesto : Dasa Panatha

In a meeting held at Colombo Town Hall, the Bhikkhus urged the Government not to drag the country into elections on the eve of Buddha Jayanti but the Prime Minister remained adamant. In the absence of any favourable response from the Government, the EBP gave a call to the Bhikkhus to observe a day's fast as a protest. While the fast was on the Betrayal of Buddhism was to be read by them to the masses and the danger which awaited the Buddhists was to be explained to them. The Bhikkhus were also to persuade the MPs of their respective areas to hold as many meetings as possible against the holding of elections on the eve of Jayanti.[57]

The call went round and several demonstrations as well as satyagrahas were organised by the clergy all over the country denouncing the elections as an action of 'Mara' (Satan) from whom Buddhism was to be safeguarded. In the capital, about 250 Bhikkhus staged a fast at the doors of the Parliament and then held a protest meeting.[58] In the organisation of such a protest movement, the leading Bhikkhus of the EBP along with some of the prominent members of the ACBC played a significant role.

The ACBC now seemed to be clear in its opposition to the UNP regime. So had been the EBP from the beginning. But it was now faced with the issue of supporting a political party. Moreover, a leader had to be found. Rev. Gnanaseeha Thero assumed this responsibility and contacted Dudley Senanayake who, after resigning from premiership, had expressed his desire to remain out of politics. Dudley Senanayake politely refused the offer, but is alleged to have suggested the name of S.W.R.D. Bandaranaike.[59]

Some Bhikkhus contacted Bandaranaike soon after. While agreeing with their 10-point programme called Dasa Panatha (Ten Principles) as, according to him they fell in line with

57. Files at Sunetra Devi Pirivena.
58. I.D.S, Weerawardana, *Ceylon General Elections* (Colombo, 1960), p. 145.
59. Muditha, 'Secret Face of Politics', *Ceylon Obeserver* 20 September 1962.

the SLFP manifesto, Bandaranaike made it clear that he was
not in favour of a Buddhist theocracy. While agreeing to grant
Buddhism its due place, he was not for Buddhism being made
the state religion.[60]

It is difficult to say who propounded the idea of Dasa
Panatha which virtually served the purpose of being an election
manifesto of the EBP. Whoever its author, there is no doubt
that it was an ingenious idea which reckoned with certain
limitations of the EBP. The EBP had neither a politically
trained nor politically disciplined cadre as that of a political
party. Besides, traditionally, the clergy's image was that of
an objective and dispassionate adviser. In order to draw the
best from the 'ideal' image of the clergy it had to keep up the
garb of giving impartial advice to the people and yet get them
round the party or person it had in view. What it did in
this context was to provide a check list against which devout
Buddhists were to test the candidates and decide accordingly.

These points fell into three categories: to live a dedicated
Buddhist life; to make Sinhala only the official language and
to implement the Buddhist Commission report. In other words,
the candidate to be supported had to be pious and firm
Buddhists having faith in democratic socialism and the ability
"to remove the anti-democratic acts and institutions of the
UNP government". It expected the party or candidate supported by the electorate to manage public affairs in such a way
that would give opportunity of "felicitous living to all" and
would find ways and means to facilitate a more equitable
distribution of wealth among the people. The only party
which appeared to incorporate the tenor and content of
Dasa Panatha was the SLFP; Bandaranaike was not its
author but was alleged to have given final touches to some
of its points.[61]

Election Strategy of the EBP in 1956

The election strategy of the EBP showed the zeal and single-

---

60. Based on interviews with Maithripala Senanayake (SLFP) a close
    associate of Mr. Bandaranaike.
61. Ibid.

mindedness of its organisers. It harnessed its resources at
various levels. The local sangha sabhas were politically activised with the Bhikkhus from Colombo going to various areas
and keeping up the momentum. Besides, the clergy—young
as well as old—was assigned such jobs as it could handle.
The young novices (samaneras) in the Pirivenas at Colombo,
for instance, did the odd jobs like writing election cards and
drawing posters. The older monks addressed election meetings. The young Bhikkhus from Colombo mobilised the rural
Bhikkhus in the election campaign.

The campaign of the clergy made the best use of face-to-
face contacts. While going from house to house they also
distributed election literature. Apart from the Betrayal of
Buddhism pamphlets touching on economic questions such
as the removal of rice subsidy (leading to a sharp rise in the
price of rice—the staple food of Sri Lanka) and that of the
midday meal for the school children were published. Another
EBP pamphlet entitled "Enemies of Buddhism" denounced
the Lake House press (one of the two major newspaper
combines and strongly pro-UNP) as Christian dominated and
anti-Buddhist.

Reiterating the arguments of the Buddhist Committee of
Enquiry, the EBP members denounced the UNP as a party
which had done very little for the common man, his religion
and his culture. While canvassing in the rural areas, the
Bhikkhus, for instance, proclaimed "A vote for the UNP is
a vote for the Catholics, a vote for the MEP is a vote for
the Buddhists". They maintained that most of the UNP
members knew nothing about Buddhism. They imitated the
west and emulated an alien culture. That they had no
regard for the Buddhist susceptibilities, was clear from the
fact that despite the public protest, they held the elections
during the Jayanti year.

A poster which was widely displayed demonstrated the EBP's
election strategy. It depicted the Buddha under the tree at one
end of the poster. The rest of the poster depicted Sir John
Kotelawala on an elephant (the UNP election symbol) along
with a girl friend, holding a spear pointed at the statue. In
the background were persons drinking and dancing, waving
newspapers and holding dollars. In the foreground was a

cart with a dead calf reminding the Buddhists of the act of
irreverance committed once by the Prime Minister when he
cut a barbecued calf. 'In this year of Buddha Jayanti' ran the
caption of the poster, 'rescue your country, your race and
your religion from danger of evil'. In the traditional
Ceylonese lore, depicted in many temples, Mara—the
mythical deity of evil—riding on the elephant attacks Buddha
but is thrown on the ground. The poster was an attempt
on the part of the clergy to apply traditional lore in contemporary politics.

The EBP campaign thus could be summed in
triple 'antis'—it was anti-west, anti-catholic and anti-UNP.
In constituencies where there was no MEP candidate
(MEP had set up 60 candidates and had signed no contest
agreement with the CP and the LSSP, thereby agreeing
to support their candidates in certain constituencies in return
for the same support for its candidates by these parties) the
EBP supported the anti-UNP candidates.[62] Virtually every
election meeting was addressed by a prominent Bhikkhu with
some of the popular and more vociferous ones moving on
from one meeting to another, from electorate to electorate.
Bandaranaike claimed that he had the support of 12,000
monks. This was probably an exaggerated figure; perceptive
observers put it around 3,000.[63]

The campaign of the EBP alarmed Premier Kotelawala
who attempted to repudiate its claim that the Sangha was
with the MEP. In several of his speeches he denounced the
politically active monks as the ones 'masquerading in yellow
robes'. Besides, he also sought the support of some of the
senior Bhikkhus who addressed the UNP meetings and
praised the UNP's role in propagating and promoting Buddhism. The Premier also succeeded in persuading the acting
High Priest of Ramannya Nikaya and the High Priests of
Kotte, Malwatta and Asgiri chapters of Siam Nikaya to issue
statements asking the Bhikkhus to refrain from participating

62. Howard W. Wriggins, *Ceylon : Dilemmas of a New Nation*
    (Princeton, 1960) pp. 354-7.
63. Ibid., p. 347.

in election activities and to remain neutral.[64] The Principal of Vidyodaya and Vidyalankara Pirivenas were also persuaded to issue similar statements. These were ignored because the disciplinary powers of these heads were limited and each individual Bhikkhu was canonically free to act according to his conscience. The appeals of the senior Bhikkhus and the performance of the pro-UNP ones was, however, no match for the activities of the EBP.

The election results were spectacular even for the leader of the MEP. Out of 60 seats which it contested in a house of 101 (including 6 nominated members) the MEP won 51. The victory of the MEP could not, however, be exclusively ascribed to the support of the Buddhist clergy but to a combination of a number of factors. The image of Sir John Kotelawala as a "playboy of the West"; the exit of the two Senanayakes—R.G. Senanayake and Dudley Senanayake—from the UNP; the United Front of opposition forces and the no-contest pact amongst them; the switchover of the UNP on the language question which not only left Buddhists bewildered and unsure of its political sincerity but also alienated the Tamils; the decade-long dominance of the UNP and lastly the intensification of the Buddhist movement were some of the factors which turned table, against the UNP, reducing its strength in the House of Representatives from 54 to 8.

How effective was the clergy's support for the victory of the MEP is a moot question. A random sample survey of about fifty elites including monks, bureaucrats, political leaders and educationists provided an indirect answer to the question : very few Bhikkhus had participated in earlier elections. In 1956, the number of monks involved in one way or other ran to about 3,000-4,000—about a fourth of the clergy. The major contribution of the EBP was its role in the support mobilisation of the Buddhists and in providing a country-wide Bhikkhu cadre to a party with very little organisation and projecting its image as the party of the common man.

64. *Times of Ceylon*, 24 and 26 March 1956 and *Ceylon Daily News*, 26 March 1956.

The EBP's efforts in this direction could not have been very successful in the case of left parties in view of their secular, almost irreligious, attitude. In the context of the SLFP, however, which projected itself as a middle party and had taken a definite stand on Buddhism and the language question, the Bhikkhus' appeal carried a great deal of credibility. Lastly, to the common Sinhalese Buddhist, the campaign of the clergy symbolised a community interest; unlike the politicians, the saffron-robed monks, it was believed at this stage, could not be self-seekers. If they were opposing the party of the Senanayakes then something was certainly wrong with that party. The demand for Buddhist rivival and the language movement thus provided the nucleus for an articulation of the majority community's sense of grievances and no sector could have worked on this sense of grievance as effectively as the Bhikkhus.

Elections of 1960

The image of the politicaly active Bhikkhus suffered a serious set-back when Bandaranaike was assassinated by a Bhikkhu in September 1959 and the complicity of one of his old-time associates, Buddharakkhita, came to be known. Public opinion ran high against the Bhikkhus' participation in politics and the elections of 1960 thus found the politically active Bhikkhus in a subdued mood. Their isolation was all the more because of the declarations of parties like the Mahajana Eksath Peramuna (MEP) and the SLFP that while accepting the advice and support of the Bhikkhus, they would not involve them in election campaigns.[65] Also, much before this, one of the EBP General Secretaries, Talpavila Seelawamsa, had declared that his group would refrain from participation in the election.[66] Its internal dissensions[67] coupled with the fact that one of its leading members was

---

65. *Ceylon Daily News*, 23 January 1960.
66. Ibid., 28 December 1959.
67. On the question of Paddy Land Act a group of Bhikkhus led by Medagoda Sumanatissa Thero had broken away from it. For details see Chapter VI.

involved in the conspiracy for Bandaranaike's assassination[68] had in any case affected it adversely and it had virtually become moribund. Meanwhile, the Maha Nayaka of Malwatta had said in an interview that participation of Bhikkhus in elections would be a defiance of his injunctions.[69] Finally, authorities of Vidyodaya and Vidayalankara universities had also directed the Bhikkhu students and teachers to refrain from election campaign.[70]

BHIKKHUS AND 1965 ELECTIONS : THE SETTING

By 1965 the period of Bhikhu—reticence over electiene-ring had virtually come to an end. Meanwhile, the attempt of the SLFP Government to implement certain recommendations of the Buddha Sasana Commission relating to the salaried position of the Bhikkhus as well as the reorganisation and unification of various Bhikkhu chapters had provoked a heated controversy in the clergy. Many Bhikkhus, who were supporters of the SLFP, had become its critics. Moreover, the Government's abortive efforts to impose a greater control on Buddhist temporalities antagonised a number of the party's supporters among the Bhikkhus.[71]

In this context, the SLFP-LSSP coalition brought about new alignments amongst the Bhikkhus. Some of the old SLFP stalwarts turned against its alliance with the left parties and openly voiced their opposition to such an alliance.

Among the Bhikkhus, the new Maha Nayaka of Malwatta chapter, Amunugama Rajaguru Sri Vipassi Thero was one

---

68. For details see Donald E. Smith, ed., 'The Political Monks and Monastic Reform' in *South Asian Politics and Religion* (Princeton, 1969), pp. 489-509. Ceylon, *Report to His Excellency the Governor-General By The Commission Appointed in terms of the Commissions of Enquiry into and Report on Certain Matters Connected with the Assassination of the Late Prime Minister Solomon West Ridgeway Dias Bandaranaike* (Colombo, 1965), Sessional Paper III, 1965.

69. *Times of Ceylon*, 7 December 1959.

70. Ibid., 10 March 1960.

71. For details on the Bhikkhus' response to these issues see Chapter VI.

of the most articulate in questioning the claims of the LSSP
leadership to be Buddhist. It is noteworthy in this context
as late as April 1964 the Thero had advised the Bhikkhus
to be loyal to the Government and not interfere in politics.[72]
However, soon after the coalition-formation the temper of
his statements had changed. Notwithstanding the Prime
Minister's statement that, as long as she was in power,
Buddhism was safe,[73] the Thero viewed such assurances with
scepticism.[74]

Leading Bhikkhus in the Buddhist organisations like the
Bauddha Jatika Balavegaya.[75] All-Ceylon Bhikkhu Congress
(whose leading lights like Talpavila Seelawamsa Thero had
earlier supported Mrs. Bandaranaike) not only voiced the
misgivings of the Malwatta Maha Nayaka but also decided
to mobilise their protest against the infiltration of 'anti-
religious', 'anti-democratic' Marxists in the Government.[76]

Reacting to this move, the pro-coalitionist Bhikkhus held
meetings under the auspices of All Ceylon Bhikkhu Congress
and resolved that the new government should coalesce
with the other 'progressive' forces to help solve the economic
problem of the country.[77]

The partisan attitude of the Bhikkhus had thus come into
open on the question of coalition formation. A number of
other issues deepened the division among the pro-SLFP
Bhikkhus. These were the budget proposal on toddy tapping and the move to take over the press by the Government.
These alienated some of the Bhikkhus like Kalukondayawe
Pannasekera Thero, the Vice-Chancellor of Vidyodaya University, who had been a leading figure in the prohibition
campaign[78] and a prominent member of the All-Ceylon
Buddhist Congress. So far the Thero had been non-partisan.

72. *Ceylon Observer*, 1 April 1964 and 16 May 1964.
73. Ibid., 9 May 1964. Also see *World Buddhism*, Vol. 12, No. 12, July
    1964, p. 13,
74. Ibid., 24 May 1964 and *Ceylon Daily News*, 23 May 1964.
75. *Ceylon Observer*, 9 June 1964.
76. Ibid., 14 June 1964 and *Ceylon Daily News*, 15 June 1964.
77. Ibid., 28 June 1964. Also see *World Buddhism*, Vol. 12, No, 12, July
    1964, p. 13.
78. *Ceylon Daily News*, 1 August 1964. *Ceylon Observer*, 13 August
    1964, and *Times of Ceylon*, 16 October 1964.

There is no doubt that the toddy proposal led to a further erosion of the credibility of the coalition government. Several Bhikkhu and lay organisations,—old as well as new—joined hands[79] and formed a 'Maha Sangha Sabha' to launch an island-wide campaign against the proposed Bills.[80] In November 1964, after an infructuous meeting with the Government officials, the Maha Nayakas of various chapters issued a circular asking the Bhikkhus to participate in a meeting to oppose the free toddy tapping proposal and the press take-over bill. Several public meetings and rallies were organised[81] and a deputation comprising the senior Bhikkhus of the various chapters met the Premier.[82] Though the government decided to drop the free toddy tapping proposal 'in deference to the wishes of the Sangha', it was obvious that the proposal had been fairly costly to the SLFP in political terms.

It was in this setting that the axe fell on the coalition government when the Minister of Lands and the Leader of the House, C.P. de Silva crossed the floor leading to the Government's defeat by one vote on the Throne Speech on 3 December 1964. Almost immediately a press release was issued by several Bhikkhu organisations congratulating these 'heroic MPs' and ensuring them their full coopera-tion.[83]

That the major party in opposition—the UNP—along-with a few others had had its share in the Bhikkhu mobili-sation against the government was evident from the fact that the meeting convened by the clergy on 28 November had, amongst its speakers, leaders of the UNP, Jatika Vim-ukti Peramuna (JVP) and Mahajana Eksath Peramuna (MEP).

---

79. *Ceylon Daily News*, 27 August 1964.
80. Ibid., 30 September 1964 and 13 October 1964.
81. Ibid., 16 and 18 November 1964.
82. *Ceylon Observer*, 4 November 1964.
83. The statement was issued by (1) The All-Ceylon Maha Sangha Sabha, (2) Sinhala Jatika Sangamaya, (3) Sri Lanka Maha Bhikkhu Association, (4) Bentota Bhikkhu Bala Mandalaya, (5) Sabaragamuwa Tri Nikaya Maha Sangha Sabha, (6) Dakshina Lanka Maha Sangha Sabha, and (7) Lanka Maha Mahinda Bhikkhu Sangamaya. *Ceylon Daily News*, 4 December 1964, and *Times of Ceylon*, 4 December 1964.

Also in a statement, Dudley Senanayake expressed his party's gratefulness to the Maha Sangha and to the Buddhist laity who had responded to the "call of the country in its hour of peril when an endeavour was made to crush their freedom and impose an iron dictatorship".[84]

Bhikkhu Organisations in 1965 Poll

The March 1965 elections once again brought a large number of Bhikkhus on various platforms. The Bhikkhus spear-heading the coalition government were Talpavila Seelawamsa and Dewamottawe Amarawamsa (who had earlier supported the SLFP), Malewana Gnanissara, Medagoda Dhammajothi, H. Vajirabuddhi, Meetiyagoda Gunaratne Theros. All of them had, either a Bhikkhu organisation already which they dominated or had created such organisations. As has been mentioned elsewhere, Rev. Seelawamsa was the leading figure in the Sinhala Jatika Sangamaya. Malewana Gnanissara was the president of Sri Lanka Bhikkhu Sangamaya which was later reorganised and re-designated as Tri Nikaya Maha Sangha Sabha. Medagoda Dhammajothi Thero was the president of the newly formed Maha Sangha Sabha and Meetiyagoda Gunaratne was the initiator of the newly created Maha Sangha Peramuna. Along with these Colombo based Bhikkhus, the Maha Nayaka of Malwatta chapter was one of the most vocal critics of the coalition.

As against this, the Bhikkhus supporting the coalition had formed Sri Lanka Eksath Bhikkhu Mandalaya which included amongst its office bearers, teachers of the Vidyodaya and Vidyalankara universities and some colleges as well as some old SLFP stalwarts like Henepitigedera Gnaneseeha, Medagoda Sumantissa Thero and Nattandiya Pannakara Theros.

The pattern of support mobilisation from both the sides was the same. Pamphlets were issued, meetings were held,

---

84. *Siyarata*, Vol. 17, No. 34, 11 December 1964, p. 1. For details refer to A. Jeyaratnam Wilson, 'Buddhism in Politics', in Smith, n. 68, pp. 524-8.

rallies were organised and statements made. By and
large the arguments of both the sides in their campaign were
somewhat similar. It was maintained that the Bhikkhus'
tasks were not restricted to the temples only; they also needed to enlighten people on socio-political questions and give
them the right advice.[85]

Such an 'advice' then took a partisan turn depending
upon the political preference of the Bhikkhus. The anti-
coalitionists for instance emphasised on the theme that the
SLFP of 1965 was not the SLFP of 1956 but was dominantly
influenced and virtually controlled by the Marxists. A vote
for a Marxist was therefore a vote against Buddhism for, if
the Marxists came to power Buddhism would be destroyed.
Consequently, the election was a battle in which the Buddha
Dhamma and Buddha Sasana needed to be saved from the
Marxists.[86] "Are we going to bring back the anti-Sinhalese politicians of the coalition and let them ruin our cherished religion,
our nation and the freedom we have enjoyed"? So ran the text
of the statement issued by the Maha Sangha Mandalaya.[87]
Speaking in the same vein in many speeches, the Maha Nayaka
of Malwatta maintained that if irreligious elements came to
power, those who encourage them would prosper and the
rest would be slaves for ever. "We have no desire", continued the Maha Nayaka "to introduce into this country
traditions and conventions of the so-called pure Buddhism
supposed to be prevalent in China..."[88]

It is further alleged that the Communist countries were
pouring in money and carrying out a well-organised campaign to create disharmony in the Sangha;[89] that the Buddhist rights of freedom of worship were being circumvented
by the Marxists.[90] Earlier, one of the Bhikkhu organisations
had also issued an appeal to all opposition parties to sink
their differences and to operate as a united front to save the
nation from "the inhuman dictatorial forces rising to destroy

85. *Ceylon Daily News*, 3 March 1965.
86. Ibid., 23 February 1965 and *Ceylon Observer*, 16 February 1965.
87. *Ceylon Observer*, 20 December 1964.
88. Ibid., 14 March 1965.
89. *Ceylon Daily News*, 15 February 1965.
90. Ibid., 27 February 1965.

religion, language and democracy".[91]

A resolution adopted at a meeting of the Bhikkhus on 13 February 1965 summed up the standpoint of the anti-coalitionists: "The vast gathering of Maha Sangha of the three Nikaya", continued the resolution, "assembled at the Kandy Esplanade call upon all incumbents of the viharas throughout the country and other members of the Sangha to advise peacefully and calmly all laity attached to the respective viharas and elsewhere not to vote for the Marxists, materialists and anti-religious parties, or any other party aligned with such forces in the coming general election and to advise the people to support a fully democratic party pledged to protect democracy, religion nation and country."[92]

The pro-coalitionist Bhikkhus did try to counteract such a campaign by highlighting the performance of the SLFP and the 'progressive' measures of the ruling coalition. However, the grievances articulated by the Bhikkhus as well as their scepticism of the Buddhist claims of the coalition seemed to be making a greater impact. Moreover, the Lake House press gave them support which exaggerated their strength. However, it was for the first time that the UNP had such a large group of articulate Bhikkhu supporters.

It is noteworthy that most of the anti-coalitionist Bhikkhu groups worked independently during the elections. No organisation like the EBP was formed. Further, these Bhikkhus were essentially reactive to some of the governmental measures and did not put forward a concrete programme of the Dasa Panth a type either. Their major target seemed to be the ruling coalition and their stance was not positive but mainly anti-Marxist.

In the 1965 elections, the Bhikkhus adopted the same strategies they had followed earlier. However, what needs to be underlined in this election was the appearance of the high echelons of the Malwatta and Asgiri chapters whose open denunciation of the Bandaranaike Government clearly benefited the UNP. 1965 could thus be termed as the

91. *Ceylon Observer*, 20 December 1964.
92. Ibid., 14 February 1965.

point when the Bhikkhus' participation in electoral politics had turned full circle. Political polarisation of the Bhikkhu community had reached its high water mark as both the major parties were supported by a conglomeration of Bhikkhu groups who, whatever their nomenclature, could be easily identified in their political alignments.

BHIKKHUS AND 1970 ELECTIONS

In comparison to the 1965 elections, the Bhikkhus, by and large, seemed to be in a subdued mood in 1970. The earlier Bhikkhu groups campaigning on partisan lines, however. did appear on the scene as usual and in a set pattern.

Meanwhile, a segment of clergy had expressed its concern at the minority Tamil parties playing the role of king-maker in case the election ended in a plurality. As such, a statement was issued in Kandy on 7 May 1970 by the high priests of all the three Nikayas appealing to the leaders of both the parties to agree to form a coalition in such an eventuality.[93] The appeal was, however, politely rejected by the UNP leader Dudley Senanayake on the plea that such a grouping would entail "reconciling profound divergencies in economic policy and ways of life. The differences would be so fundamental that there could be no effective government."[94] As regards the United Front leader, Mrs Bandaranaike, her rejection was indirect; she contended that the UNP had reversed many 'desirable steps' towards a Buddhist socialist revolution and as and when the implementation was sought, the objectives were vitiated.[95]

Prepared for a close fight, both the UNP and the United Front had their Bhikkhu organisations ready to campaign during elections. On the side of the UF the most organised group was Sri Lanka Eksath Bhikkhu Bala Mandalaya (SLEBBM—Sri Lanka United Bhikkhu Organisation) with its headquarters in one of the Pirivena at Colombo. The UNP was supported by Maha Sangha Peramuna headed by Rev.

93. For the text of the Appeal see *Ceylon Daily New.*, 18 May 1970.
94. For the text of Dudley Senanayake's reply, see Ibid.
95. For the text of Mrs Bandaranaike's reply see *Sun*, 24 May 1970.

Meetiyagoda Gunaratne and Tri Nikaya Bhikkhu Maha Bala Mandalaya (TNBMBM) with Rev. Malewana Gnanissara and Rev. Devamottawe Amarawamsa as its main organisers. Both the organisations had their headquarters in Colombo.

In organisation and ideological terms these 'Mandalayas' reveal an interesting pattern. The antecedents of SLEBBM could be traced to the EBM from which some of its leading members had broken away in 1958 on the temporalities issue[96] and had re-designated themselves as Sri Lanka Sangha Samvidhanaya (Sri Lanka Organisation of Monks) in 1961. The ideological tenor of this group was amply clear in its statements during 1958-61 when it maintained that the Sangha must lead in social and cultural affairs and that its organisation should be on the pattern prevalent in socialist countries.[97] It had openly supported the UF in 1965 elections. In the application form for enrolling Bhikkhu members in 1969, it had spelt out the objective of the Mandalaya thus: "to form a UF government headed by SLFP on a socialist basis" and "to revive the nation, country, language and religion..."[98]

The SLEBBM did not seem to have a detailed constitutional framework; its publications mentioned three presidents and five secretaries whose names kept changing from time to time. However, it was maintained by one of its office bearers that the Mandalaya had several branch organisations all over the country.[99]

As with the SLEBBM, the pro-UNP TNBMBM had also a history of change in nomenclature. It began in 1959 as Sri Lanka Maha Bhikkhu Sangamaya (All-Ceylon Congress of Bhikkhus) with Rev. Gnanissara as its president, Rev. Narawila Dhammaratna as its vice president, Rev. Seelananda as its secretary and a 21-member executive council. As most of its membership was initially drawn from Siam Nikaya Bhikkhus, it was decided to broadbase it before 1965 elections

---

96. *Times of Ceylon*, 29 April 1959. Initially it was designated as Lanka Sangha Sabha. Subsequently its name was changed.

97. *Ceylon Observer*, 12 July 1961.

98. The files in Medagoda Sumanatissa Thero's Pirivena contain a letter dated 10 April 1965 from Mrs. Bandaranaike, thanking the secretary for all the help given to the SLFP during election time.

99. Application form available in the files, n. 98.

and redesignate it as Tri Nikaya Maha Sangha Sabha with
Rev. Gnanissara as the president and Devamottawe Amara-
mamsa as its secretary. The publications as well as the speeches
of these Bhikkhus indicated their anti-Marxist views in no
uncertain terms.[100]

Unlike the SLEBBM and TNBMBM, the Maha Sangha
Peramuna headed by Meetiyagoda Gunaratne appears to
have been of a recent origin and the creation of a young
Bhikkhu who had neither the social status nor the economic resources of the leadership of the other pro-UNP
and pro-SLFP Bhikkhu groups. Rev. Gnanissara was an
Ayurvedic physician with a successful practice in Colombo
and Rev. Amarawamsa as well as Sumanatissa Theros held
eminent positions in the Colombo-based Pirivenas. Rev.
Gunaratne had neither the academic eminence nor an endowed (as for instance the high priestship of a vihara) status but
was a powerful speaker. The support he had given to the
UNP in 1965 helped him to get a house in the heart of the
capital from where he carried on his activities.

The election campaign of the Bhikkhus ran pretty close
to the line of the respective party with which each was
aligned. The SLEBBM for instance condemned the January
8 firing in which a Bhikkhu had been shot; criticised the
Government for victimising the pro-SLFP government servants,
censured the Government plans for family planning as a secret
scheme to stop the growth of the Sinhalese nation, decried the
pace of implementation of the Sirimavo-Shastri Pact, which,
if expedited, would have created job opportunities for the
Sinhalese. It further declared that the Government policies
helped only the rich, that it had sold the country to the World
Bank and that the loans received from the Western countries
were not used for development but for the purchase of luxury
goods for the privileged few.[101]

The Bhikkhu protagonistis of the UNP on the other hand
eulogised the performance of the party, particularly in the
agricultural field and maintained that Mrs Bandaranaike was

100. Based on the interviews with Rev. Malewana Gnanissara in 1967.
     For details on the Organisation's inception and ideological tenor
     see Chapter VIII.
101. Sri Lanka Eksath Bhikkhu Bala Mandalaya, *Prakashanaya*
     (Colombo, 1970).

not following the policies of her late husband but was a puppet
in the hands of the Marxists. The pronouncements from the
UF platforms to change the Poya holidays came under heavy
censure from them and so did the proposed People's Committee. Further, the promise of the United Front to restore the cut
in rice ration and give every one two measures of rice if it won,
was ridiculed by them as political gimmickry.[102]

As regards the style of campaign of these organisations,
they were more or less similar to those in the earlier elections.
Election propaganda material in the form of posters and leaf-
lets was published and Bhikkhu rallies were organised by
them. Besides, they addressed meetings and issued statements.

An interesting episode in this election was a news item in
some newspaper referring to the Maha Nayaka of Malwatta's
support to the coalition. Apart from a denial that the statement, as appeared in the press, presented a twisted version of
his statement, the Maha Nayaka, it is alleged, was persuaded
to make a further statement which ran as follows: "I am
deeply distressed at this last minute by the futile effort to gain
political benefit by attributing a false statement to me... I
believe that a socialist dictatorship fashioned according to
the Marxist philosophy will not guarantee democratic freedoms
and protect national and religious interests".[103] The statement,
it is noteworthy, was reported on the radio every hour. Such
publicity, in the context of the highly politically mature electorate of the island, could not cut much ice.

In the earlier elections the three R's—rice, race and
religion—seemed to have been critical variables. By 1970,

102. For details see *Ceylon Observer*, 5 May 1970, and *Ceylon Daily
     News*, 7 May 1970. Also see Malewana Gnanissara and Devamot-
     tawe Amarawamsa, *Kokad Hari-Hath Havula? Tun Havula*? (Which
     is right? Six party front or the Three party front?) (Colombo,
     n.d.). Malewana Gnanissara, *Halsairu Deka Denna Keseda?* (How
     can the two measures of rice be given?) (Colombo, n.d.). Besides,
     during 1970 elections, the Maha Sangha Peramana published a
     series of articles which could also be used as posters. They more
     or less covered similar grounds with titles such as 'Will this be the
     Victory of Mara or of Dhamma', 'Mahaveli Project', 'Democracy
     or Dictatorship'? By and large, many articles tended to be a
     eulogisation of the UNP regime.
103. For the text see *Daily Mirror*, 27 May 1970.

however, the issues of 'race and religion did not seem to evoke the same emotive response because most of the Sinhalese Buddhist demands had already been met. Besides, the polarisation of the politically active Bhikkhus into both camps had somewhat neutralised their influence in swinging the choice of the voter one way or the other.

In the election, it was not the cultural but economic issues in the main, which were decisive. The rising cost of living and increasing unemployment had alienated the UNP from the common man. It was also felt that its policies had not succeeded in reducing the gap between the rich and poor; even its agricultural policies had given virtually no relief to the small landholders or landless.[104] As against this, the United Front's promise to bring down the cost of living as well as its undertaking to solve (or at least reduce the unemployment problem) coupled with its pledge to restore the cut in rice ration, were some of the factors facilitating its victory.

From 1947 to 1970 thus, much water had flowed in the Kelaniya. The 'novelty' of the Bhikkhu participation in the electoral politics had ebbed and they had merely existed as pressure groups, a segment of which needed to be cultivated to counterpoise those on the other side. Increasing participation and consequent polarisation of the Bhikkhus in the politics of ballot box, thus, had neutralised their political weight to a considerable extent.

104. Analysing the causes the National government's defeat, Balasuriya rightly maintained that the UNP did not succeed in "harmonising satisfactorily the different and almost contradictory objectives of the country's development: economic growth with social justice and employment; freedom with equality, openness to the West with fidelity to our culture; foreign aid with economic self-reliance and self—respect; softness on capital with a concern for the underprivileged", Fr. Tissa Balasuriya (OMI), 'Toward a Ceylonese Socialist Democracy"? Ceylon Observer Sunday Maganize, 26 June 1970. Besides, the Catholic votes, which by and large, went to the UNP earlier were divided in this election. For an analysis leading to this change see Ashoka, 'The Catholic Vote I and II', Ceylon Daily News, 29 and 30 June 1969 and Urmila Phadnis, 'Political Profile of a Religious Minority in Ceylon : Negombo—A Case Study', in M.. Rajan, ed·, Studies in Politics—National and International (Delhi, 1971), pp. 270-97.

This did not mean that the major political parties could ignore them; as interest groups, they needed to be kept in good humour lest their united efforts in the favour of one major party might upset this equilibrium. And this task was performed by the UNP as well as the SLFP with great finesse.

The correspondence between the president of the Buddha Raksha Balamandalaya[105] and the UNP leader, Dudley Senanayake is revealing in this respect. In his letter, the president of the Balamandalaya, making a plea to keep Bhikkhus out of politics, requested the UNP's co-operation in this respect. In his reply, the Prime Minister wrote that while his party was willing to approve the objective of the Balamandalaya on a policy level, the desired result could not be achieved without enlisting the co-operation of other parties. "If the UNP alone is to take an independent decision so as not to seek the services of Bhikkhus in politics, such a *decision may cause irreparable loss to the party itself*. The Balamandalaya should make an earnest attempt to secure the support of other parties to achieve the desired result. Under such circumstances the UNP will guarantee the maximum co-operation in promoting the ideals of Balamandalaya."[106]

In the context of the political traditions of the island, it was apparent that this ideal, however desirable, could not be a reality. The Bhikkhus had stepped into electoral politics and they were going to stay there.

CONCLUSIONS

An over-view of the Bhikkhus' participation in electoral processes over the past four decades highlights some interesting features regarding their attitude towards politics, organisations, strategies and styles. Till 1960 the politically active Bhikkhu organisations like the LEBM and the EBP had emerged as anti-establishment groups. Critical as they were of UNP policies and roles, they challenged its political

---

105. The Mandalaya had in fact made an appeal to all the political parties to refrain from using the Bhikkhus in electoral politics. *Daily Mirror*, 5 October 1966. Italics mine.

106. *Ceylon Daily News*, 20 December 1966.

authority through the ballot-box. Both decried the Western influence and Catholic domination over the socio-political life of the country and made UNP leaders responsible for the perpetuation of an alien culture at the cost of indigenous traditions. Both had certain common members. However, EBP had a wider span and had several branch organisations. The LEBM, on the other hand, had limited membership. Because of this, while LEBM's activities were limited to certain constituencies, EBP activised the clergy in virtually all the Sinhalese constituencies.

LEBM's emergence could be ascribed to the efforts of the monks of a particular Pirivena. In the EBP, low country Bhikkhus from various chapters—Ramannya Nikaya, Amarapura Nikaya and Kotte chapter of Siam Nikaya—seemed to dominate its activities. One could, thus, trace to the EBP the emergence of Bhikkhus as a political force and the beginning of a process of power adjustment between less favoured low country chapters and more favoured up-country ones. This was the first time when the clergy had successfully sought political support to remedy the regional imbalance in terms of redistribution of status by the political power.

The Bhikkhu organisations had certain unique structural characteristics. Every Buddhist temple, specially a temple with a Pirivena, had the requisite institutional structure of a voluntary organisation. It had space and office facilities. It could provide services and goods. It had a ready membership and a leader. In many cases, the idealistic ascetic life which a monk was supposed to lead might not have been followed by many but was followed by some who developed the qualities of leadership—discipline, single-mindedness and organisational capability. Congeries of such temples provided, therefore, the readymade structure to develop themselves into a full-fledged organisation. However, the highly personalised character of the temples, and the predominantly individual character of the clergy coupled with the tradition of autonomy of the viharas inhibited the growth of an organisation of viharas, except for limited purposes. The EBP itself was an example in this context. Its constituent groups chose to retain their group identity with care as seen by the five signatures appended on each of its communications.

Structurally, the Bhikkhu groups seemed to belong to the category of a non-associational group, its distinguishing characteristics being "intermittent pattern of articulation, the absence of an organised procedure for establishing the nature and means of articulation and the lack of continuity in internal structure."[107] Only a few had a constitution and though people talked of 'branches' they seemed to be informal in character, too diffuse in structure and often ineffective in operation. Structural amorphousness as well as change in nomenclature characterised most of the clergy organisations. This seemed to be a source of strength as well as weakness. While amorphous character deprived them of the strength of organised associations, the diffuse nature of the clergy group enabled the monks to create different groups having one common, and therefore limited, goal. Such groups permitted wide alignments of various sorts at different points of time. The effectiveness of the group depended as much on the leaders as on the issue but there is no doubt that given an issue concerning Buddhism and Buddhist culture (e.g., the ones raised in 1956 and 1965) the clergy had tremendous potential to articulate the demands on its own behalf as well as on behalf of the Buddhist community.

The style of this articulation and the extent of its manifested during the elections was a clear admixture of the use of traditional symbols with modern means. The slogans used by the Bhikkhus included not only a comparison of the party of capitalist and party of the common man but also the allegory of *Mara* (Satan). The Bhikkhus used informal face-to-face contacts and also distributed election literature. They preached a political bana (sermon) when they could. Earlier, the tactic of exploiting the fear complex of rural Buddhists was to extract a promise of support by getting them to swear by touching a Buddha statute or the end of the robe. In other words, as opinion leaders of rural Ceylon, they did have the potential to influence the choice of the voter.

In 1956, apart from influencing the Buddhist laity, the process of temple-to-temple campaigning accelerated the poli-

---

107. Gabriel A. Almond and G. Bingham Powell, *Comparative Politics : A Developmental Approach* (Boston, 1966), pp. 73-97.

tical socialisation of the clergy itself. This is evident from the fact that their number increased with every election.

The end of Jayanti saw the emergence of the Bhikkhus as a prime political force. Apart from facilitating a further broad-basing of the political structure in 1956 elections, the Bhikkhn associations cut into the strength of the political parties in diverse ways. To the UNP the cost was in terms of seats, to the LSSP in terms of credit. As part of the no-contest agreement, it was the leftist party workers who did the job of the 'organisation' of the meetings. But in effect, they remained merely the curtain raisers. The Bhikkhus assumed the main actor role. Finally, the emergence of a centrist SLFP, providing a clear alternative to the 'rightist' and 'leftist' parties was ample inducement for the clergy to lend support to it.

The secular policy of the UNP might have been rationally ideal in a pluralist society but past circumstances had been such that it was too ideal to be real. Once religion was harnessed in the service of politics it followed that the redress of the majority community's sense of grievance could be made only by providing more state patronage to the religion of the Sinhalese. In this setting, it also meant enunciation of cultural policies in an effective and assertive manner. And this was done with great aplomb by both the UNP and the SLFP during 1956-1970 period.

The elections of 1956 had laid to rest the controversy regarding the appropriateness of monk's participation in politics. The involvement of the Bhikkhus in the political process was tacitly accepted by the political parties as a settled fact and was harnessed to the full as was evident in the elections of 1965 and 1970. However, the elections of 1965 had also drawn in a large number of the high echelons of the Kandyan Bhikkhus openly in the political arena.

No doubt, the political activities of the Bhikkhus in electoral politics did pay its dividends but in the context of the two major party system, this depended upon their being on the winning side. Further, such an involvement affected their traditional non-partisan image to a great extent. The 'advice' of the Bhikkhus in 1956 made greater impact on the Buddhists than it did in 1970. Politics might have brought them certain mundane privileges, but only at the cost of diminution of their charisma which tradition had endowed on them. Nor did it lead to a new dynamism in the Sangha as such.

However, in the developing political traditions of post-independent island, the Bhikkhus could not remain isolated from the mainstream of political life. They had been drawn into the political orbit and had to be the satellite of one or the other party. Besides, in the ethos of patronage politics, the politically ambitious ones amongst them needed parties as much for status and resources as the parties needed them for support mobilisation and aggregation.

Chapter VI

BHIKKHU ORGANISATIONS, STATE AUTHORITY AND SANGHA REFORMS

INTRODUCTION

In the post-independence politics of Sri Lanka, besides influencing electoral politics, the Bhikkhus have also been active in the process of initiating, formulating and implementing public policies on several issues. In such situations they have formed special organisations to articulate their views and influence governmental policies and decisions.

These aspects of their political behaviour need to be analysed in the context of the studies on pressure and interest groups. Precursors of such studies have been Arthur Bentley and David Truman.[1] The major point of these and related studies was the emphasis on groups as the focal point of politics. Some of the follow-up studies underlined the processes of public policies on a particular issue featuring specialised or organised groups and their role therein. Some of the pluralists have also assumed, in this exercise, a theory of decision-making which was built around the idea that the government was passive, a *tabula rasa* on which the interest groups wrote their wishes, with the Government merely reflecting the respective strength of the various groups. Yet others provided the Government a position of a referee between various contenders

---

1. Arthur F. Bentley, *The Process of Government* (Evanston, 1949), and David B. Truman, *The Governmental Process* (New York, 1951).

"with no power or will of its own". Yet another view was to ascribe a much more active role for the government and a dominant position, with the groups contending to influence the government to extract a decision in their favour.[2]

Subjected to various criticisms,[3] the major contribution of the pluralists, however, has been their emphasis (at times overdone) on the role of the informal segments of politics like interest groups, associations, social elites.

In the process of underlining their role, several authors have also ventured to provide a range of nomenclature (pressure groups, interest groups, lobbies)[4] for such organisations as well as a number of typologies. Almond and Powell, for instance, make a four-fold category of interest groups, viz., (a) anomic interest groups which are more or less spontaneous penetrations into the political system from the society e.g. riot, demonstrations, (b) institutional interest groups which are found within such organisations such as political parties, legislatures, armies, bureaucracies and churches (c) associational interest groups, and (d) non-associational interest groups.[5]

However, while the role of associational interest groups

2. Stephen L. Wasby, *Political Science—The Discipline and its Dimensions* (Calcutta, 1970), pp. 113-16. Also see John Dearlove, *The Politics of Policy in Local Government : The Making and Maintenance of Public Policy in the Royal Borough of Kensington and Chelsea* (Cambridge, 1973).

3. For some of the major points of these criticisms see Robert E. Dowse and John A. Hughes, *Political Sociology* (London, 1972), pp. 379-97. For a succinct bibliography on the subject see Ibid., pp. 398-9. Also see Joseph La Palombara, "The Utility and Limitations of Interest Group Theory in Non-American Field Situtions", in Harry Eckstein and David E. Apter, *Comparative Politics—A Reader* (New York, 1963), pp. 421-30.

4. For a discussion on nomenclature of various groups, see Graham Wootton, *Interest Groups* (New Jersey, 1970), pp. 1-5. Also see S.K. Finer, *Anonymous Empire* (London, 1969), edn. 2; Francis G. Castles, *Pressure Groups and Political Culture* (London, 1967), pp. 1-8.

5. Gabriel A. Almond and G. Bingham Powell, *Comparative Politics: A Developmental Approach* (Boston, 1966), pp. 73-97. Also see Maurice Duverger, *Party Politics and Pressure Groups—A Comparative Introduction*, trans. by Robert Wagoner (London, 1972), pp. 103-58.

(such as trade unions and business associations) have been the themes of some of the studies,[6] the dynamics of non-associational interest groups in the govermental policies and decisions have merited scant attention.[7] In this context, the organisation and roles of Bhikkhu organisations, which, as we have briefly stated in Chapter V, falls into the category of non-associational interest groups provide an insight into the linkage patterns between the professional religious elite and political elite in the decision-making process.

At this stage, certain propositions regarding the structures of the Bhikkhu pressure groups (which are briefly spelt out earlier) are recapitulated and further tested in the following chapters. These are as follows:

(1) The 'non-associational interest groups' of the Bhikkhus are highly personalised in nature and *ad hoc* in character.

(2) Such groups articulate their interets intermittently through an individual/collective leadership.

(3) Issues which have evoked interest from such groups can be divided into the following three categories:

   (a) Those which have posed a direct threat to their present power and status, e.g., Paddy Land Act of 1958 and the land legislation of 1972 as well as legislation dealing with the structural reorganisation of the Sangha as a whole.

   (b) Those which have affected their socio-eeonomic status indirectly, e.g., legislation regarding the official language and education.

   (c) Those which concern them as Buddhists as well as members of Pan-Buddhist community but affect them

6. Harry Eckstein, *Pressure Groups Politics—The Case of British Medical Association* (London, 1960); Stanley A. Kochanek, *Business and Politics in India* (Berkeley, 1974); Bruce H. Millen, *The Labor in Developing Countries* (Washington, D.C., 1963); and Robert N. Kearney, *Trade Unions and Politic. in Ceylon* (New Delhi, 1971).

7. As exceptions, mention needs to be made of Myron Weiner's, *The Politics of Scarcity* (Bombay, 1963), the thrust of which has been the interaction of pressure groups and public opinion in India and Rajni Kothari's edited volume *Caste in Indian Politics* (Delhi, 1973).

only remotely, e.g., legislation regarding the political status of the 'Stateless' in Sri Lanka as well as governmental policies on the position of Buddhists in Tibet and Vietnam.

(4) Depending on the issue concerned, alignment-patterns of most of these groups keep changing.

(5) If tradition has imparted a certain degree of legitimacy to such activities of the Bhikkhu organisations, the demands of democratic politics have necessitated a re-construction of their strategies and styles which emerge as a conglomeration of tradition and modernity.

Alongside such specific propositions in respect of structures, strategies and styles of the non-associational interest groups of the Bhikkhus, certain general propositions on the role of interest groups in public policies have also been put forward, taking the above mentioned groups as case studies. These are as follows:

(1) In a democratic system, the stronger the emphasis on social welfare values by the state (e.g. greater planning, direction and regulation of social activities), the greater the impetus for organisations of interested social groups to emerge as pressure groups.

(2) The more pluralistic and differentiated the governmental structures involved, the greater are the opportunities for success of the pressure groups through influence by special clientele relationship with the decision-makers, using various means for the mobilisation of public opinion.

(3) The greater the importance of a particular issue as per-ceived by the leaders of pressure groups, the more inten-sive are the efforts to influence the decision-making process.

(4) The more favourable the 'objective of contextual situa-tion' (as measured by public opinion, political parties and other pressure groups involved) of an issue, the more effective are the tactics of the pressure groups in attempting to influence the course of direction in their favour.

These propositions need to be examined in the context of the political process in the system. Does one see a proliferation of Bhikkhu pressure groups since the country attained independent Statehood ? Through what channels of access do they opt for to influence Governmental policies ? What strategies do they adopt to achieve their objectives ? And finally, in what way have their strategies and tactics been functional and/or dysfunctional in the processes of modernisation of a third world State like Sri Lanka ?

In this chapter an attempt is made to answer these questions by describing the Bhikkhus' initiative and/or response on two issues affecting their interests directly, namely the legislative policies and processes regarding the administration and control of Buddhist temporalities (monastic land) and legislation on the reform as well as unification of the Sangha.

BUDDHIST MONKS AND MONASTIC REFORMS

If the State legislation on Buddhist temporalities led to the formation of new Bhikkhu organisations, proposed legislation for the reform and unification of the Sangha gave a new lease of life to the higher executive bodies (Karaka Sabhas) of some of the chapters to operate as pressure groups.

The governmental tasks of Sangha-reform and its unification was more than hazardous in view of the nature of the Sangha itself which was never a monolith but a complex conglomeration of several units, some of which with a very small membership and others like Malwatta and Asgiri, with fairly large membership and extensive land-holdings. Further, despite the elective principle of the Sangha hierarchy, the Chief High Priests of fairly prosperous viharas in the upcountry also happened to be the members of the Karaka Sabha (Executive Council) in these chapters. As such, apart from affluence, their official status in the hierarchical structure of such chapters also tended to be a source of their power. Such power, however, was not total; the structures of the councils of a particular Nikaya or chapter could always be questioned in the law courts and defaulters could afford to ignore the commands of the Karaka Sabha but there is no doubt that for certain ecclesiastical purposes, the members of the Karaka

Sabha wielded considerable authority. The larger the membership of the chapter, the greater was the authority. And till
such authority was questioned as such, the Karaka Sabha's
decisions were deemed to be binding on the members of the
sect, division or the chapter.

Under the circumstances, any effort to bring all the Buddhist monks under one organisational set-up ran the risk of
either the loss of power or its curtailment for those who were
already office bearers in the traditional set-up. The office-
bearers of the smaller sects or chapters in this context had
much less to lose than the dignitaries of the bigger ones.

Apart from the class and caste differences, the upcountry-
low country classification of the Bhikkhus was also significant
in this respect. The low-country Bhikkhus had been more
articulate, active and forward-looking than most of the up-
country high priests.[8] As such, it was natural that the Chief
High Priests of the up-country region, who had already set for
themselves a niche in the Sangha hierarchy, preferred the
status quo and resented State intervention.

It is in this setting that a brief analytical description of the
Sangha-State interaction in the enunciation of policies and
proposals regarding monastic reforms is made.

It is significant to note that the initiative for monastic reforms was taken by certain Buddhist lay leaders who maintained that before the British occupation of the island, as
Buddhism was the State religion, the Sangha's power to maintain discipline within had the backing of the ruler. The State
authority thus tended to be a vigilant supervisory authority
over the ecclesiastical and temporal affairs of the Sangha.
British policies towards the monastic organisations, however,
had led to its disintegration and deprived the Bhikkhu community the legitimacy of decision making which it had con-
ventionally enjoyed under the Sinhalese royalty.

Under the circumstances, the first step by the Sangha for
monastic reforms necessitated the formulation of a constitution
(as the Roman Catholic Church had) with a single governing
body of its own choice. Such a constitution, with the sanctions
of the State, would enable the various Nikayas to function

8. These points have been detailed in Chapter II.

more effectively to disseminate and propagate the Dhamma. It would enable the Sangha to maintain better discipline amongst the Bhikkhus.[9]

These views were further strengthened by several resolutions of the All-Ceylon Buddhist Congress (ACBC—an organisation in which the Buddhist lay leaders dominated) which had demanded as early as 1946, the introduction of suitable legislation for the enforcement of the decisions of the Sangha Sabhas of the respective Nikayas.

In 1950, a delegation of Bhikkhus met Prime Minister D.S. Senanayake requesting State support and protection for Buddhism. Almost at the same time, the ACBC sent a detailed memorandum entitled "Buddhism and the State" to the Prime Minister which, after expressing its regret at the scant attention paid to the promotion of Buddhism even after independence, requested State initiative in the formulation of an "autonomous, sound and workable constitution". Meanwhile, till the promulgation of such a constitution, it was requested that the government should establish a Buddha Sasana[10] Department to look after the Buddhist interests.[11]

In the enclosed letter to the memorandum, the President of the ACBC, Dr G.P. Malalasekhera also maintained that the first step in the resuscitation of the Buddhist institutions was

9. C.D.S. Siriwardane, 'Buddhist Reorganisation in Ceylon', in Donald Eugene Smith, ed., *South Asian Politics and Religion* (Princeton, 1966), pp. 531-46.

10. 'Sasana', as used in the canonical texts means 'instruction' or 'order'. Later, the term also came to mean a continuous succession of Buddhist institutions since the Fifth Century B.C. In effect, the phrase "establishment of Sasana" means the establishment of a customary tradition of monastic ordination. Heinz Bechert, 'Thereavada Buddhist Sangha: Some General Observations on Historical and Political Factors in its Development', *Journal of Asian Studies*, Vol. 29, no. 4, August 1970, p. 762, footnote 3.

11. All Ceylon Buddhist Congress, *Buddhism and the State: Resolutions and Memorandum of the All Ceylon Buddhist Congress* (Colombo, 1951).

the reorganisation of the Sangha. In view of its disruption and disintegration during the British period, such a reorganisation, however, could not be brought about 'except by active Government interference. Such requests, however, were not heeded to by the Prime Minister for reasons mentioned already and were shelved by his son who succeeded him.'[12]

In September 1954, the Mahabodhi Society of Ceylon (an organisation dominated by the laity) also raised the issue of the appointment of a Buddha Sasana Council with a view to plan, initiate, co-ordinate and execute schemes within and outside the island for the propagation of Dhamma, including the Buddhist education at Pirivenas as well as at primary, secondary and university level. Other functions of the Council included the preparation and publication of books as well as the adjudication of disputes pertaining to the monastic institutions. Finally, the memorandum maintained that the functions of the Buddha Sasana Council should be free of State control except within the narrowest possible confines and should be strictly limited to the provision of funds and such financial control as may be necessary.[13]

In 1956, an outline for Sangha reform and the role of the Government therein was presented in the report of the Buddhist Committee of Enquiry. Apart from recommending measures for the education and discipline within the Nikayas, the Committee also noted that during the British period, the withdrawal of the State patronage to Buddhism in 1850s and the absence of a central organisation, which was promised, but never provided for by the British Governors, had led to the disruption and disintegration of the monastic organisations. In order to remedy such a situation, the Government should establish a Buddha Sasana Council, comprising the representatives of the Sangha and laity. "to which may be entrusted all the prerogatives of the Buddhist kings as regards

---

12. Ibid., 2. For reasons which prompted the UNP leaders to adopt such an approach see Chapter IV.
13. *Guardian*, 13 September 1954.

the Buddhist religion, assumed by the British Crown in 1815".[14]

Appointment of the Buddha Sasana Commission

The implementation of the recommendation of the Buddhist Committee of Enquiry was one of the election promises of the People's United Front (Mahajan Eksath Peramuna) led by Bandaranaike. Soon after assuming power in 1956, the MEP began to take steps to fulfil its promise. In July 1956 the Cultural Affairs Ministry announced that a commission to enquire into the affairs of the Bhikkhu order would be appointed shortly.[15]

The announcement had the unanimous approval of the Chief High Priests (Maha Nayakas) of the Amarapura Nikaya with whom Prime Minister Bandaranaike himself had conferred in October 1956.[16] It, however, met with a strong opposition from the Chief High Priests of Malwatta and Asgiri chapters.

In October 1956, the Minister of Cultural Affairs P.G.B. Kalugalle met the High Priests at Malwatta and Asgiri at Kandy. He maintained that he was prepared to appoint the Maha Nayakas of Malwatta and Asgiri as well as other representatives of the chapters to serve on the Commission so that they would have enough members to submit a dissenting report if they so wished. If this was not acceptable to them, the government was prepared to accept any report submitted by the two chapters which could be considered along with the recommendations of the official Commission. The Maha Nayakas did not agree to this proposal. Finally, the Minister's query whether the Maha Nayakas would allow eminent members of the two chapters to join the commission to function in their individual capacity was also rejected by them. In fact, the High Priests told the Minister curtly that as soon as the appointment of the Commission was gazetted, they would start

---

14. *The Betrayal of Buddhism: An Abridged Version of the Report of the Buddhist Committee of Enquiry* (Balangoda, 1956), pp. a 41 and 115-19.
15. *Times of Ceylon*, 18 July 1956.
16. *Morning Times*, 17 October 1956.

a country-wide campaign against the establishment of the proposed Council.[17]

In a 25-point memorandum submitted to the Prime Minister in January 1957, the two Maha Nayakas stated the reasons for opposing the appointment of the Commission. They maintained that there was no need for such a Sasana Council as their respective chapters already had their own Sasana Councils (Karaka Sabhas) which had managed the affairs of the Sangha over the past two centuries. They felt that instead of attempting to unify and reform the Sangha, the State should first ensure a revival of Buddhist activities such as the introduction of prohibition, banning of racing, gambling, making Buddhism a compulsory subject in the schools, making four Poya days instead of Sundays a weekly holiday, publication of Buddhist catechism and provision for the translation of the Tripitatka into Sinhalese.

Behind the resentment of any sort of State interference lay the Maha Nayakas' cynicism of the sincerity of the future politicians to be their torch-bearers. "Supposing that we having faith in your Government", continued the memorandum, "acceded to your Government's request to enforce laws for the control of our religious affairs or agreed to the appointment of a commission to investigate such matters, in what manner would we be able to resist the demands of some future Government which had no love for our religion, if that Government too, at the request of various persons, decided to appoint a commission to enquire into religious affairs ? If we, in any way, keep the door open to such things, our religion would in the future become the playground of the country's politicians."[18]

Apart from opposing the appointment of the Sasana Commission, the High Prelates had already tried to strengthen their hands by inviting the Chief High Priests of Kotte, Kelaniya and Uva sects of the Siam Nikaya, asking them to sink their minor differences and emerge as a unified order. They also invited the members of the entire Siam Nikaya to participate in the discussions on the proposed Sangha Council on

17. *Ceylon Daily News*, 7 January 1957.
18. *Times of Ceylon*, 21 January 1957.

22 September 1956. Nothing, however, came out of this.

The antagonism of the two Maha Nayakas was natural in view of the fact that under any scheme of Sangha reform, there was a distinct possibility of the leadership of the other two Nikayas, i.e., Amarapura and Ramanna improving their power and status *vis-à-vis* the ecclesiastical leadership of these two chapters. Besides, it was obvious that once the issue of Sangha reform was acceded, the question of temporalities was bound to come within the purview of the Council. This again would have affected the Chief High Priests of the temples with big landholdings, many of whom were the Karaka Sabhiks of the Malwatta and Asgiri chapters.

Though the ACBC, in view of the stout opposition from the Maha Nayakas of the two chapters, suggested the postponement of the appointment of such a Commission,[19] the Government was under pressure from the militant Bhikkhus as well as from a segment of the Buddhist leaders, some of whom had gone to the extent of dubbing the Maha Nayakas as 'reactionaries' who had put their weight in the favour of the UNP and who wanted to obstruct such reforms with a view to protecting their land and wealth. The Government, they insisted, should honour its election pledge and appoint the Commission.[20]

Accordingly, in March 1957, the Government appointed the Buddha Sasana Commission comprising 10 Bhikkhus and 5 lay leaders. Two members each were from Ramanna and Amarapura Nikaya and six from Siam sect. In a communique issued by the Director of Cultural Affairs, it was maintained that the names of the members of the Sangha representing the Ramanna and Amarapura Nikayas were submitted to the Ministry as the nominees of the Nikayas. In view of the refusal of the Malwatta and Asgiri chapters to submit their nominees, the Government itself had decided to

19. *Ceylon Daily News*, 4 Febuary 1957.
20. E.g. see the statements of the EBP, *Times of Ceylon*, 23 January 1954; and memoranda of several Bhikkhus, Ibid., 29 January 1954; *Ceylon Daily News*, 18 August 1956, and *Times of Ceylon*, 23 January 1957. Also see various statements of T.B. Illangaratne for a scathing attack on the High Prelates. *Ceylon Observer*, 29 January 1957, and *Times of Ceylon*, 4 February 1954.

nominate members from the Siam Nikaya. Out of the six persons nominated by the Government two belonged to the Vidyodaya and Vidyalankara Pirivenas and the other two were from the Eksath Bhikkhu Peramuna (EBP-United Bhikkhu Front).

As regards the terms of reference, the Commission was required to inquire into the proposals of the Buddhist Committee of Enquiry for the establishment of a Buddha Sasana Council for the purpose of promoting the welfare of the Budddha Sasana and the constitution of ecclesiastical courts having exclusive jurisdiction in matters relating to the Sangha. The Commission was also to suggest measures which could be adopted for the efficient management and supervision of Buddhist temporalities, for providing facilities for the training as well as education of the Bhikkhus and for preventing persons who had not been duly ordained, as Bhikkhus, but had pretended to be so. Besides, the Commission was to explore as to whether the Buddhist places of worship could be registered under the control of the Sasana Council or under any such body appointed for the protection of Buddha Sasana.[21]

In a joint communication to the Governor-General, the Karaka Sabha of the Malwatta and Asgiri chapters maintained that, as the Sasana Commission was 'unrepresented by members of the Sangha formally and not officially nominated by our Siamese Sect', it had no "right or power to examine, investigate into or report on any matter relating to the viharas and monasteries managed and controlled by our sect or about the lands and properties attached to them or concerning the reforms of the methods and rules and regulations governing their management."[22] Soon after, the executive committees of the Malwatta and Asgiri chapters issued an injunction calling upon all the Siam Nikaya members of the Sasana Commission to resign from it before 31 March 1957.

The injunction, however, was ignored by the Siam Nikaya members of the Commission. This was not unusual. Even in

---

21. *Morning Times*, 15 November 1956. The terms of reference were announced much before the appointment of the Commission members.

22. *Morning Times*, 13 March 1957.

the past, particularly during the elections of 1956, for instance, the directive of the Maha Nayakas, dissuading Bhikkhus from participating in electoral politics, had been ignored. Besides, as part of the post-election Buddhist renaissance, it was strongly felt by many that a central organisation of the Bhikkhus and laity was needed for the resuscitation of the Buddhist Sangha and Dhamma. In such an ethos, the insistence of the High Prelates for the maintenance of the *status quo* was looked upon with hostility and misgivings. The Maha Nayakas thus had no option but to watch and wait for the recommendation of the Sasana Commission.

Affer visiting some of the Buddhist countries and eliciting public opinion through questionnaires and memoranda, the Commission submitted its report in July 1959. It was released as a Sessional Paper in November 1959.

Recommendations of the Commission

Dealing with the problems pertaining to the clergy in their historical perspective, the Report concluded that recommendations regarding temporalities, ecclesiastical courts and Buddha Sasana Council should be promulgated through legislative enactments to give them constitutional sanction.

The Buddha Sasana Council, born out of an ordinance or act, was to be the highest body entrusted with manifold functions. These included safeguarding of rights of the Buddhist clergy and the laity; advising the government on all matters relating to Buddhism; undertaking functions which were earlier performed by the kings of Ceylon but were not being performed by the Government now; bringing about the unification of the Buddhist order ; organising religious rituals in keeping with modern times; encouraging research in Buddhism and organising monk education as well as religious education of the laity ; training men and women for leadership in Buddhist work ; assisting Buddhist associations in carrying out their activities ; looking after the revenues from temples; renovating and maintaining the temples and viharas; receiving contributions and raising funds for Buddhist activities; developing Buddhist arts and culture, and providing any other facility necessary for the protection and furtherance of Buddha Sasana.[23]

The organisation of the Sasana Council was spelt out in great detail in the Report. The Sasana Council was to include (a) Uttara Sangha Sabha (Supreme Council of Ceylon), (b) Sasana Sangamaya (Sasana Association), and (c) Kruthi-vidhayak-Samsadaya (the Executive Working Committee). While the Uttara Sangha Sabha was to consist only of monks, the other two bodies were to be composed of monks as well as laity. The Uttara Sangha Sabha, it was stipulated, would deal with matters relating to the monastic order ; the other two bodies would deal with matters relating to the clergy as well as the laity.

The Buddha Sasana Council it was suggested, would be an independent body, having powers of a legalised institution such as filing of cases, and the use of a common seal but it was stipulated that the working committee of the respective Nikayas would continue to undertake administrative activities even after the establishment of the Council.[24]

Apart from the Sasana Council, the Commission made provisions for the establishment of ecclesiastical tribunals (Sanghadhikarana) consisting of the ecclesiastical courts of the various sects and a Maha Sanghadhikarana Chief Ecclesiastical Court comprising ten Bhikkhus and a lay secretary, appointed by the Minister of Cultural Affairs. It was proposed that the trial of all major offences should be conducted by the law courts but in the cases of minor offences and in civil cases, where both the parties were Bhikkhus, they should be heard by the Chief Ecclesiastical Court. In cases where one party was Bhikkhu and another a laity, the case should be sent to the ecclesiastical court with the consent of both the parties. It was proposed, however, that all the cases regarding the disputed succession in a temple for the post of Viharadhipati, those involving removal from such offices or disputes over the status of a Bhikkhu to be a monk should be dealt with by

23. Ceylon, *Buddha Sasana Commission Vartava* (Buddha Sasana Commission Report), Sessional Paper 18 of 1959 (Colombo, 1959), pp. 244-6.
24. Ibid., pp. 245-50.

the ecclesiastical courts. These courts should be vested with all powers of the law courts.[25]

The report also envisaged the reorganisation of the temple lands administration and proposed that a new government department for looking after the administration of temple land should be formed. The department and not the individual trustees should look after the temple land administration. It was also mentioned that the paddy fields belonging to the Viharagam and Devalagam should not be bound by the Paddy Land Act.[26]

The Commission felt that as provided earlier, records of the registration of monks should vest not with the Registrar-General but with the Sasana Council. Provision was also made to punish those who were not properly ordained.

Apart from these recommendations, the report also dealt with some of the problems which modernisation had created for the Bhikkhus and which constituted the transgression of Vinaya rules. The use and handling of money by the Bhikkhus was one of many such issues dealt by them. It was proposed that no Bhikkhu should indulge in the production of wealth. Nor should he be appointed to any wage-earning service, without the prior approval of the Buddha Sasana Council. However, as imparting education was one of the duties of the Bhikkhu, he should have the option to join this service. It was specified, however, that apart from the monks who were engaged in teaching when the Buddha Sasana Council was formed, the other monks wanting to be teachers should obtain the permission of the Council. In other words, the proposal was for future appointments only. As such it was not to affect those who were already in the teaching profession. As regards the Bhikkhus' involvement in politics, the Commission maintained that while the monks could give advice on various matters, they should keep away from party politics.[27]

The report thus provided a blueprint for Sangha reform characterised by a moderate tone which, though drawing inspiration from the canonical rules and regulations, recog-

25. Ibid., pp. 188-207.
26. Ibid., pp. 150-70.
27. Ibid., pp. 63-79.

nised the changing social structure of Sri Lanka and suggested reforms which, if implemented, would have brought about radical changes in the structure of the Sangha. Some of the proposals of the Commission, for instance, were unusual innovations. The idea of a Sasana Council vested with legal powers to define the Buddhist position on a number of problems and to get it implemented through the State was unusual for the highly individualistic Theravada Buddhism of Sri Lanka. Similarly, a central pooling of funds was an idea not in consonance with the traditions. On the other hand, in view of the changing nature of the polity from monarchy to democracy, the Commission appeared to look for ways and means bringing the Sangha into closer relation with the laity as well as between the individual and his faith and provide for a greater influence on the day-to-day affairs of the country. Finally, the traditions of old were contained in new forms; proposals were made to bring about structural changes in Buddhism not only through individual or group efforts but also through direct legislative and administrative acts.

Submitted a few months before the assassination of Prime Minister Bandaranaike by a Bhikkhu, the gazetting of the report as a Sessional Paper was suspended for a while. Consequent to the assassination of the Prime Minister, a strong lay reaction against the Buddhist clergy swept the island. Traditional deference to the Bhikkhus either in the buses or elsewhere was done away with and at times they were openly abused. In fact, popular revulsion against the clergy was so great that Mrs. Bandaranaike had to issue an appeal in the name of her late husband to permit the Sangha to participate freely in various rituals consequent to the death of the late Premier. It was only after this appeal that the Bhikkhus were allowed to view the body of the late Prime Minister.[28]

The public reaction also manifested itself in the form of a large number of articles, editorials as well as letters to the editor, demanding the cleansing of the Sangha. The majority of them emphasised the Sasana Commission Report which provided for a definite role of the State to reform the Sangha and

28. Political Correspondent, 'Cleanse the Sangha of Dusseela Monks,. *Ceylon Daily News*, 3 October 1959.

demanded the expulsion of the 'Dusseela' (unprincipled) monks.[29]

While the Sasana Commission Report met with unanimous approval of organisations like the ACBC [30] others like the Sasanaraksha Bauddha Mandalaya felt that its proposals were not radical enough because it had failed to recommend the immediate removal of the Bhikkhus from the order who were earning salaries or were engaged in business and had left scope for Bhikkhus to indulge in party politics.[31]

As regards the Buddhist clergy, the presiding elder of the Ramanna Nikaya immediately announced his Nikaya's decision to accept all the recommendations of the Sasana Commission.[32] The co-ordinated Central Council of the Amarapura Nikaya unanimously decided to accept the report but 'with certain modifications'.[33] As regards the Malwatta and Asgiri chapters of the Siam Nikaya, their presiding officers convened a joint meeting and the Secretary of the Asgiri chapter maintained that in view of their opposition to the appointment of the Commission itself, their stand on the Report remained unchanged.[34]

29. In his paper Donald Smith refers to the press censorship of news relating to the Sangha during October and maintains that this ban was removed in November to be followed by a spate of articles demanding the cleansing of the Sangha. Smith, n. 9, p. 502. However, even during October 1959 a spate of editorials and letters to the editor appeared in the Ceylonese press on the issue. For example see Political Correspondent, 'Cleanse the Sangha of Dusseela Monks', *Ceylon Daily News*, 3 October 1959; Editorial, 'Religion and Politics', *Times of Ceylon*, 5 October 1959; Several letters to the editor in the *Ceylon Daily News*, 7 October 1959.
Some of the articles and editorials which appeared in November 1959 were: Editorial, "Cleansing the Sangha" *Ceylon Daily News*, 12 November 1959; Political Commentary, *Ceylon Daily News*, 14 November 1959; Sirisoma Jayasinghe, 'Let us Cleanse the Sangha', *Ceylon Observer*, 16 November 1959.
30. *Ceylon Daily News*, 12 November 1959, and *Times of Ceylon*, 16 November 1959.
31. *Times of Ceylon*, 2 November 1959, and *Ceylon Daily News*, 27 November 1959.
32. *Ceylon Daily News*, 14 November 1959.
33. For details of these amendments see ibid., 18 December 1959.
34. *Ceylon Observer*, 16 November, 1959.

Elections of 1960 and the Sasana Commission Report

The process of implementing the report, however, had to wait till the elections were over. In the election manifestoes of the various parties, the issue of the Sangha reorganisation appeared with varying emphasis. The SLFP, for instance, maintained that it was pledged to examine the report of the Commission to implement such reforms in accordance with the principles of the Vinaya, and to give legislative sanction and authority to the Sangha for that purpose. The UNP was more cautious. It promised to establish a Sasana Council consisting of the representatives of the Sangha and the laity to work for the welfare of the Buddha Sasana without, however, infringing the autonomy of the Nikayas. In the election manifesto of his newly-formed party, Premier Dahanayake took a stand closest to the standpoint of Malwatta and Asgiri. All the reforms, stated the manifesto of the Lanka Prajatantravadi Pakshaya, must come from the Sangha itself and all steps in this direction would be taken with the approval of the various representative bodies of the Sangha.[35]

The March election, ending in a plurality was followed by another election in July in which the SLFP, headed by Mrs. Bandaranaike, secured a clear majority and announced in its first Throne Speech itself that legislation would be introduced shortly in the Parliament to set up a Sasana Council as a first step towards the implementation of the Buddhist Commission Report.[36]

Implementation : A Fortuitous Effort

Soon after assuming power, the SLFP Government found itself embroiled in the issue of the schools take-over and it was only in 1961 that the question of Sangha reform came to the fore.

Meanwhile, a sub-committee of the Buddhist Advisory Council (a semi-official body of Bhikkhus and lay leaders

---

35. Ceylon Daily News, *Parliaments of Ceylon, 1960* (Colombo, 1960), pp. 191, 198 and 210.
36. *Times of Ceylon*, 17 August 1966.

appointed to advise the Government on Buddhist affairs) had already examined the recommendations of the Commission and had forwarded its report to the Minister of Cultural Affairs, Maithripala Senanayake.[37]

In matters relating to the employment of the Bhikkhus as salaried teachers, the recommendations of the Sub-committee were more far-reaching than those of the Buddha Sasana Commission. Acting on the Commissioner recommendations (which provided for debarring the clergy from holding any government jobs) the Government notified all the departments that a member of the priesthood of any religious denomination should not be employed in the public service, in the local government service or any government-sponsored corporation in any post which could be filled by a layman. It further maintained that any such appointment made on or after 1 June 1961 be terminated.[38]

Elaborating on the subject Maithripala Senanayake maintained that if it became necessary to employ a Bhikkhu for a particular post, then the application to the post should be submitted through the head of the Nikaya to which the Bhikkhu belonged. If a Bhikkhu, after complying with this procedure, was employed in the government service, he would not be paid directly but the amount due to him would be credited to a fund for the welfare of the Bhikkhus. He added that this was one of the recommendations of the Buddhist Commission which the SLFP had decided to implement immediately.[39]

The official decision affected a number of Bhikkhus, particularly the young graduates from Vidyodaya and Vidyalankara Universities who had applied for teaching positions in the schools. But as the schools had been already taken over by the Government in 1961,[40] their applications were turned down. It was reported in the press that when the Government's ban was known, several Bhikkhus informed the Education Department that they had discarded their robes and, therefore,

---

37. For details see *Ceylon Daily News*, 16 December 1959. Also see ibid., 15 May 1961 and 16 June 1961.
38. Ibid., 20 June 1961 and *Daily Mirror*, 7 July 1961.
39. *Ceylon Daily News*, 16 June 1961.
40. On the nationalisation of schools, see Smith, pp. 482-7.

were eligible for the teaching positions for which they had earlier applied.[41]

The notification came under heavy attack from some of the Bhikkhus who, so far, had been ardent supporters of the SLFP. They saw in it a sinister move on the part of the Government to wipe out the Sangha since qualified Bhikkhus would thereby be encouraged to leave the Buddhist order and obtain teaching jobs as laymen.[42] The pressure on the Government was great. Under the circumstances, the ban on the employment of monks was lifted on the recommendation of the Minister of Education.[43] In February 1963. it was disclosed that the majority of the teachers selected by the Education Department during 1962 were Bhikkhus (300 out of 402 appointees).[44] The only positive step taken by the government on the report had to be virtually rescinded.

Several other measures, such as the detailed procedure for the income tax payment on temple lands, the compulsory keeping of accounts by the Viharadhipatis and trustees as well as certain provisions of the Paddy Land Act[45] were the measures which caused consternation to the clergy. But it was the issue of the appointment of Bhikkhus in the public sector, particularly educational institutions, and the question whether their salaries should be paid directly to them or not which made many pro-SLFP monks turn against it. The Sasana Commission report which earlier had the blessings of many of them, was now viewed as an instrument of interference and control of the Bhikkhus' affairs. Consequently, almost overnight, several Bhikkhus holding high positions in the two new Universities of Vidyodaya and Vidyalankara as well as in the various

41. *Ceylon Daily News*, 29 June 1961.
42. See for instance Bambarende Siriseevali Thero, 'Government "Vinaya" Not for Monks', *Ceylon Observer*, 15 July 1961. Also see his speech in *Ceylon Daily News*, 6 September 1961, and the statement of Talpawila Seelawamsa Thero, *Ceylon Observer*, 6 September 1961. Both the monks had earlier been ardent supporters of the SLFP.
43. *Times of Ceylon*, 5 December 1961 and 23 March 1962.
44. *Ceylon Daily News*, 6 February 1963.
45. *Morning Times*, 26 July 1958. These issues are discussed in some detail subsequently.

Pirivenas, who had earlier supported the appointment of the Commission became bitter critics of its recommendations which implied a greater State control over the Sangha. Expediency, thus, brought together the staunch critics of the Commission like Malwatta and Asgiri as well as some of its former staunch protagonists.

In an article entitled "Government 'Vinaya' not for monks", the Dean of the Buddhist Studies, Bambarende Siriseevali Thero declared that no government could tell the Sangha what it should do. "On religion" maintained the Bhikkhu, "we are the sole authorities. We monks have got the training and we are the custodians of our religion." He rejected the Government regulations pertaining to the discipline within the Sangha, the administration of the Buddhist temporalities, the remunerative appointment of the Bhikkhus and their political rights. In another speech he maintained that "though the Bhikkhus had kept away from the earlier two elections, they would once again take their place in the political field as religion and nation are heading towards danger".[46]

Another militant Bhikkhu, Talpavila Seelawamsa Thero, formerly a member of the SLFP Executive Committee and one of the leading figures of the now-defunct Eksath Bhikkhu Peramuna (EBP) announced that he was coming back to politics to fight the proposals of the Cultural Affairs Minister, Maithripala Senanayake, on the report. "We monks", maintained Seelawamsa, "cannot accept Mr. Senanayake as a Buddha. He is now trying to frame rules to punish the monks. These attempts will in no way help uplift the Sasana."[47] The Bhikkhu concluded that in view of the conduct of the present Government, he strongly felt that the UNP was "ten thousand times better" than the SLFP regime. On another occasion, speaking in the meeting organised by the pro-UNP All-Ceylon Bhikkhu Sammelanaya (which had Malevana Gnanissara as its President) the Bhikkhu declared that in the event of the implementation of the Sasana Commission Report, "Bhikkhus

46. Bambarende Siriseevali Thero, "Government 'Vinaya' not for Monks", Ceylon Observer, 15 July 1961, Smith n. 9, p. 507. Also see his speech in Ceylon Daily News, 6 September 1961.
47. Ceylon Observer, 5 July 1961.

would set aside their robes and contest every parliamentary
seat against the SLFP."[48]

The Bhikkhu leader Sinahala Jatika Sangamaya Baddegama
Wimalawamsa Thero (of Sri Lanka Vidyalaya) declared in the
inaugural meeting of the Buddha Sasana Maha Mandalaya
that the Buddha laid down the Vinaya to control the action
of the Sangha. As such, it was ridiculous for a government of
laymen to legislate disciplinary action against the Bhikkhus.[49]
Another Sangha organisation —Lanka Sangha Samvidhanaya
— with its headquarters at Sunetra Devi Pirivena (Colombo)
resolved in its first meeting that there could not be "any
reform of the Sangha except as part of reforming the entire
structure of society economically and socially."[50]

With the earlier standpoint of the Maha Nayakas of
Malwatta and Asgiri chapters vindicated, they lost no time in
augmenting their resources. It was reported that a United
Front of the Siam Nikaya, Udrata Amarapura Nikaya and
certain sections of Ramanna Nikaya would be formed with a
view to protecting temple land and the rights of Sangha against
government action in implementing the Sasana Commission
reports. The Front decided to draw a code itself (Kathikavata)
to regulate the Sangha's activities instead of the government-
appointed Sasana Council doing it.[51]

As has been mentioned already, in 1959 the Chief High
Priests of Ramanna and Amarapura Nikayas had given their
general approval to the report. In the context of this controversy, while the Maha Nayaka of Ramanna held steadfastly
to his earlier position[52], one of the important temples
belonging to the same (Sri Lanka Vidyalaya) had openly
opposed the report. In the case of the Maha Sangha Sabha of
Amarapura Nikaya, it had earlier supported the report with
certain reservations. Now the Sabha, in a secret conclave on
23 July 1961 unanimously rejected the report 'compiled by

48. *Ceylon Daily News*, 8 August 1961.
49. *Times of Ceylon*, 4 July 1961.
50. *Ceylon Observer*, 12 July 1961. Lanka Sangha Samvidhanaya was
    a resuscitation of the old Sinhala Maha Sabha. (For details on
    Sinhala Maha Sabha see Chapters V and VI).
51. *Ceylon Observer*, 15 July 1961; *Times of Ceylon*, 20 July 1961.
52. *Ceylon Daily News*, 5 August 1961.

the Buddhist laity' mainly on procedural grounds and on the plea that it was not 'placed before the Maha Sangha for approval before submission to the government'.[53]

Meanwhile, some of the opposition parties lost no time in exploiting the issue. In a public meeting, the UNP leader Dudley Senanayake maintained that it was absurd of the SLFP Government "to frame disciplinary rules for the members of the Maha Sangha ignoring the laws framed by Lord Buddha."[54] Another UNP leader, J.R. Jayawardene maintained that any reform in the Sangha must come from the Sangha itself and by public opinion created by lay devotees. Referring to the earlier mobilisation of the Bhikkhus by the SLFP in the 1956 elections he alleged that "unfortunately today those who used the Sangha to defeat their political opponents are raising their hands to destroy them because they now disagree with those who were once their colleagues. This is not the way to purify the Sangha."[55] M.P.s like R.G. Senanayake and W. Dahanayake (formerly members of the SLFP) alleged that the government was out to destroy the Bhikkhu Order by enacting the new legislation.[56]

The government tried to counteract the opposition to the report. In her broadcast, Mrs. Bandaranaike tried to assure the Bhikkhus that the government did not in any way intend to interfere with the rules of Vinaya or with regard to matters pertaining to various sects. "All that we propose to do", declared the Premier, "is to implement the recommendations of the Sasana report in consultation with the Sangha for the preservation of the Sasana as was done by the Buddhist Kings of old".[57] However, though in her address she had spoken appreciatively of the Bhikkhus' role in the 1956 elections, she defended the Commission's recommendations that the Bhikkhus should be kept out of politics. According to her, since, in every temple there were Buddhist devotees belonging

53. Ibid., 27 July 1961.
54. Ibid., 28 June 1961. Also see *Ceylon Observer*, 21 September 1961.
55. *Ceylon Daily News*, 29 June 1961.
56. Ibid., 18 September 1961.
57. *Ceylon Observer*, 27 July 1961.

to different parties, it would create disharmony if the Bhikkhus become partisan.[58]

Such an attitude, however, did not seem to satisfy her one-time Bhikkhu protagonists barring a few.[59] No doubt the Commission had the staunch support of the lay organisations like the All-Ceylon Buddhist Congress and Young Men's Buddhist Association[60] but it was obvious that it had failed to evoke the confidence of a large majority of the Bhikkhus, many of whom seemed to have their first bitter taste of the extent of State power on the question of the monk's salaried appointments.

Seeing the intensity of the tides of protest, the government was not in a mood to make it a prestige issue and stake the Bhikkhu support altogether. Soon after, the Cultural Affairs Minister announced that the Commission's recommendations would be modified so as not to harm in any way the honour and dignity of the Sangha. By early 1963 it was reported that all the public memoranda which had been solicited in connection with the Commission's report had remained unattended and the Advisory Council on the Sasana Commission Report had not met for quite some time.[61]

The Report was thus shelved and the question of Sangha reform was left in abeyance. In the elections of 1965, significantly enough, the SLFP manifesto remained silent on the Sangha reform issue. It merely maintained that in compliance with the wishes of the Maha Sangha, the SLFP would set up a Buddhist University at Anuradhapura exclusively for the training of the Bhikkhus. The UNP manifesto, on the other hand, emhasising upon chapter autonomy, declared that it was opposed to the control of the Buddhist Sangha by the Government or the laity. The Buddhist Sangha, it was main-

58. Ibid.
59. E.g., Henepitigedera Gnanaseeha's statement in *Ceylon Observer*, 25 June 1961 and Kalukondayawe Pannasekara Thero, "Sangha Reforms', ibid., 17 July 1961.
60. E.g., G.P. Malalasekhara, 'Why I want Sangha Reforms', Ibid., 14 July 1961; C.D.S. Siriwardene, 'An Intelligent Buddhist's Guide to the Buddhist Problem', *The Buddhist*, Vol 32, October 1961, pp. 38, 40 and 43.
61. Smith, n. 9, pp. 506-8.

tained, must be given such powers as it needed to reorganise itself, with the State giving the Sangha such aid as it needed to fulfil its mission of propagating Buddhism.[62]

During the UNP regime (1965-1970) the proposal of appointing a second Sasana Commission was broached but only in passing. The only issue that seemed to be live during this period was that of the Government legislation with regard to the special ecclesiastical courts to deal with matters pertaining to the Sangha. This was one of the recommendations of the Sasana Commission Report.

In this connection a delegation comprising the members of Malwatta and Asgiri met the Minister of Justice, A.P. Wijemanne, in February 1968 and pointed out various difficulties which would arise in the implementation of the proposed appointment of the judicial court (Sangha dhikaran) as envisaged by the Minister. It was maintained, among other things, that according to the proposal, disputes pertaining to a particular sect could be referred for adjudication only to members of that sect in the judicial body. As the number of that particular sect in the Sanghadhikaran would be small, it was unlikely that that particular sect would accept such a decision as final and binding. Besides, appeals against the judicial body could still be entertained in the ordinary courts of law. As such, it was wondered as to whether such a judicial body could serve any 'useful purpose'.[63]

The attitude of the Karaka Sabha appeared again to be negative. It seemed that it was neither willing to accept the power of such judicial body as final nor keen to delegate it such primacy in judicial matters pertaining to the Bhikkhus. The proposed legislation, thus, in effect, met with the same fate as the Report itself.

In 1970, after coming to power, the United Front took up the issue of Sangha reform again but in a much more subdued manner. It was announced that the Minister of Cultural Affairs, S.S. Kulatilake, had decided to apoint a committee to study the present state of Buddhism and to make its

---

62. Ceylon, *Parliament of Ceylon 1965* (Colombo, 1965), pp. 172 and 177.
63. *Sun*, 28 February 1968.

recommendations with a view to restoring to Buddha Sasana its pristine purity and glory.[64]

Such announcements on the part of the UNP and later of the SLFP could at the best be termed political gimmickry to sidetrack the main issue. Neither party needed to 'study' the state of Buddhism a detailed blueprint of which was already provided in the Sasana Commission Report. As regards the recommendations, they had been studied in some detail by the Buddhist Advisory Councils and their implications analysed. What was needed, thus, was not a report but implementation of certain measures on which a unanimous view needed to be obtained amongst the various chapters of the Sangha.

In the past, Sangha reform in effect was brought about by autocratic Buddhist kings : a job which was not easy for a democratically elected government to do, for, despite its loose structuring, it was obvious that if the necessity arose, the Sangha could get sufficiently organised to resist effectively any change. As regards the lay leaders, the Sangha reform was an issue not critical enough in their overall politics. Also, in terms of political costs and gains, any radical measure by any party on monastic reform was bound to be more 'expensive' than the party could afford.

On the issue of Sangha reform, thus, it was a cluster of Bhikkhu groups and personalities which had succeeded in winning its points. The debate on Sangha reform indicated that while new associations, cutting across the Nikaya lines had come to stay in Ceylonese politics to pressurise the government in their chosen line of action, the pressure tactics of the top leadership of the traditional hierarchical structure had not become altogether redundant and ineffectual in this respect.

BUDDHIST TEMPORALITIES AND THE LEGISLATIVE PROCESSES

The shelving of the Sasana Commission Report brought to naught the appointment of a Buddhist Sasana Council. Meanwhile, several legislative enactments came into being which affected the control of the Bhikkhus over the administration

64. *Daily Mirror*, 19 October 1970.

and control of temporalities in several ways. The response of the Bhikkhus on such measures was varied in view of the extent of the stakes which they had had on the issue. While the Chief High Priests of the viharas with extensive land holdings were, more than often, for the *status quo*, others with small or virtually no land holdings welcomed such State initiative. In the process, new alignments (e.g., the alignments of the EBP and that of the Maha Nayakas of Malwatta and Asgiri) came into being the rationale for which could be explained in interest terms.

A resume of the origins and administration of the Buddhist temporalities has already been presented in Chapter II. It needs to be reiterated that economically a Bhikkhu had no property ; he was an almsman. Tradition endowed upon the Bhikkhu the status of a trustee of the Sanghika property (property of the Buddhist community of Bhikkhus) which was to be actually administered by the laity.

Initially, in the case of viharas with large land holdings such administration was done by the State officials. However, in times of civil wars and external invasions, often the administrative network had a breakdown and the Bhikkhus themselves had to look after the temple land. During the Kandyan period, such a practice was a rule rather than exception so much so that during the British colonial period any legislation which introduced the lay administration over the temple land was resented and opposed by the Viharadhipatis of the Kandyan Province which had the largest extent of temporalities.[65]

Illustrative of this protest, for instance, was a memorandum sent by the Maha Nayakas of Malwatta and Asgiri to King Edward VII opposing the Buddhist Temporalities Ordinance of 1889 which stipulated the appointment of a board of lay trustees to supervise the administration of Buddhist temporalities. "By the laws of Buddha,' contended the memorandum "the laity form no part of religion, they have no proprietary rights in the temples or in the religious endowments. They were never allowed to inerfere in either the internal discipline of the Sangha or in the management of its temporalities. The

65. For details see Chapter II.

Sangha has a perfect organisation within itself to manage all
its concerns including the endowments."[66]

With the enactment of the Buddhist Temporalities Ordinance of 1931, the status of Viharadhipati as the temple
trustee was legitimised. Such Bhikkhu trustees were equal in
status with the lay trustees and were entitled to an honorarium for their services for the temporalities' administration.
Under the item 'remuneration of trustee' a trustee paid himself about five to ten per cent of the total income of the
vihara.[67]

Such a practice was frowned upon by several lay leaders
who maintained that it was "incompatible with their vow of
poverty and inefficient from the administrative standpoint.
Trustees can only lease out the land and collect the proceeds,
and too often the temptation is to obtain more from the
leases than is shown on statement of accounts and other
documents. Such a state of affairs brings discredit on the
entire Sangha and is one of the chief reasons for its internal
weakness and declining prestige today."[68]

While the Buddhist Committee of Enquiry report had
touched on the issue[69], the Sasana Commission had dealt with
it in some detail and recommended that no Bhikkhu himself
should administer temple land; that all the land belonging to
the viharas should be vested with a commissioner and its
management entrusted to a committee appointed by the
Buddha Sasana Council.[70]

In the wake of the enthusiasm which characterised the
Buddhist resurgence in 1956, the public trustee, V.P. Gunaratne,
sent a circular stating that under the item 'remuneration
of trustees', no Viharadhipati would be paid this honorarium.
The reason for such a step was stated to be that it was im-
proper for a Bhikkhu trustee to take any money out of the
income of the vihara for his services rendered to the temple.

Opposing the circular in a meeting held in Kandy in January

66. Ceylon, *Correspondence Relating to the Buddhist Temporalities
    Ordinance IV-1907* (Colombo, 1907), p. 7.
67. *Times of Ceylon*, 24 January 1954.
68. Siriwardene, n, 10, p. 545.
69. The Betrayal of Buddhism, n. 17, pp. 6-40.
70. Ceylon, Buddha Sasana Commission Vartava, n. 23, pp. 281-2.

1957, some Bhikkhus decided to form an organisation of Viharadhipati and Trustees so that 'they might protect their interest.'[71] The President of the Association was Rev. Amunugama Sri Vipassi Thero (Anu Nayaka of Malwatta) and its Secretary was Rev. Palipane Chandananda Thero (Member, Karaka Sabha, Asgiri chapter). The Secrectary claimed a membership of 500 for the Association.[72]

Arguing the case, the Association maintained that the action contemplated by the public trustee was not in keeping with the Temporalities Ordinance of 1931 under which a temple trustee was permitted to claim certain facilities; that the law stated that both the lay and monk trustees were of equal legal status; that the remuneration was not a salary paid by the government but an allowance paid out of the income of the vihara itself; that even traditionally, according to the endowment grants, the monks were allowed the use of any income left after the expenditure on the temple. As such, the circular, connoting lay interference, impinged upon the 'interests' of the monks.[73]

The circular, it seems, was not complied with. Nor did the government take any effective measure for the purpose. Meanwhile, another circular was issued in May 1956 stipulating that every temple trustee shall, when so required by the Public Trustee, prepare a complete inventory of the immovable and movable temple property, a register of the offerings to the temple, a lease rent register, a house rent register, a register of crops, a cash book and an estimate of the probable income and expenditure of the temple.[74]

This circular was opposed by the Viharadhipati Association and was subsequently withdrawn.[75] It, however, reappea-

71. *Times of Ceylon*, 24 January 1957. Also see *Viharadhipati Saha Bharakara Sangamaya Yojna* (Viharadhipati and Trustees Association Proposals, Kandy, 1957).

72. Based on the interview with Rev. Palipane Chandananda on 15 December 1967.

73. Viharadhipati Saha Bharakara Sangamaya, n. 71.

74. For the text of the regulation see 'Buddhist Temporalities Ordinance' *Ceylon Government Gazette,* 8 June 1965, no. 10339 Part 1, Sec (1) General, pp. 1046-8.

75. Information based on the interviews with R.L. Ratwatte on 10 January 1968, and Rev. Chandananda on 15 December 1967.

red in 1961 as part of the Regulations of 1961 (cited as the temporary care custody of property regulation of the temples),[76] in the wake of the incumbency dispute of Kelaniya temple.

A brief resume of the Kelaniya incumbency dispute illustrates the extent to which the State could, if it wished, interfere in the affairs of a vihara on the succession issue and how such interference was resented and ultimately thwarted by the Bhikkhus under the 'rules of the game' of democracy.

It might be recalled that Mapatagama Buddharakhita Thero (belonging to Malwatta chapter), one of the accomplices in the Bandaranaike assassination, decided to renounce his monthood from jail and, by a legally executed deed made his chief pupil Ven. Thalewiia Dhammarakhita Vijitha his successor. Intimating this fact to the Malwatta chapter Maha Nayaka Ven. Purijjala Sri Siddhartha Saranan-kara Thero, he requested that in accordance with the Maha Nikaya laws, Vijitha should be elected as the chief incumbent of Kelaniya vihara.[77]

Ven. Vijitha's right of succession was, however, contested by two other Bhikkhus, one of whom, Mapatagama Sanghara-khhita Thero, claimed his right on the basis of pupillary succession based on kinship. Disputing his claim, the Maha Nayaka maintained that essentially, succession to the Kelaniya temple was decided on the basis of pupillary (Sisyanusisya Param-parawa) and not on pupillary succession based on kinship (Sivura Paramparawa.)

Traditional practices, however, indicated that Sivuru Param-parawa was also in vogue regarding succession to Kelaniya temples. Under the circumstances, the public trustee R.L. Ratwatte decided to withhold the decision of the Maha Nayaka and appointed S.D.S. Somaratne as the provisional lay trustee for the vihara.

However, with Ven. Vijitha already assuming control of

76. For the text of the Regulation see Ceylon, Government Notification, *Ceylon Government Gazette Extraordinary*, no. 12451 of 1961, 31 May 1961, Part 1, Section 1.

77. Details of this controversy in the following paragraphs are based on *Ceylon Daily News*, 21 June 1962; ibid., 21 May 1965 and my interview with R.L. Ratwatte, on 10 January 1968.

the vihara, Ratwatte found it difficult to assume an effective control of the vihara. Consequently, the Regulations of 1961 came into being under which the Public Trustee was invested with far-reaching powers pending the final decision *vis-a-vis* the appointment of the Viharadhipati. Under these regulations, the public trustee or his representative had the powers to enter into the premises of the vihara at any time to inspect the place, take an inventory and seal all or any property belonging to the temple, remove any movable property, including money to any suitable place for safe custody, register all offerings and collections in the collection box and have watchers appointed for the temple.

The issue was immediately taken up by the Viharadhipati and Trustees Association. Calling it an 'obnoxious regulation' which questioned the decision of the Chief Executive Council of the Malwatta chapter and therefore was an affront to its dignity, the Association submitted in March 1965, a memorandum signed by 2,500 members to Premier Mrs. Bandaranaike and demanded its withdrawal.

Meanwhile, the issue of succesion was being negotiated between Vijitha and Sangharakkhita but both seemed to be adamant. In 1964, the Public Trustee referred it once again to the Executive Council of the Malwatta chapter and it upheld its earlier decision in favour of Rev. Vijitha.

Mapatagama Sangharakkhita, however, had threatened to take the case to the court and the Public Trustee could not afford to be a party to the ratification of the Malwatta chapter lest it might be reversed by the court and thereby might make Ratwatte—a government official—a party to it. Ratwatte thus continued to retain the provisional trustee and persuaded Sangharakkhita not to take legal resort. He told him that if he would not file the case in the court in three months, Vijitha (in those favour the Malwatta chapter had already decided) would be legally recognised as the Viharadhipati and the provisional trusteeship of Somaratne would come to an end. As the case was not filed during the next three months, Vijitha's claim was upheld by the Public Trustee.

The incumbency issue of the Kelaniya Vihara was thus settled but not without much heart-burning on the part of the Bhikkhus belonging to the Viharadhipati Association.

The 1961 notification was made much use of in the 1965 elections by the UNP speakers. And soon after the UNP coalition assumed office, the Secretary of Viharadhipati and Trustees Association, Palipane Chandananda Thero appealed to the Minister of Justice to withdraw the regulation. The regulation was repealed in October 1966 and this was the price the UNP paid for the Bhikkhu support.

Apart from the 1961 regulations, the Association also questioned the propriety of the levying of taxes under the provisions of Income-tax Acts, Wealth, Personal and Land Acts in operation in 1962. In a memorandum signed by Amunugama Rajaguru Siri Vipassi (Anu Nayaka, Malwatta chapter) President of the Viharadhipati and Trustee Association, and its Secretary, Palipane Chandananda, presented to the Prime Minister in March 1962, it was alleged that "what the devastating foreign governments out to destroy Buddhist Establishments dared not do, a Government said to be one of the people of Ceylon, which professes its intention of not only preserving Buddhist interests but announces its intention of restoring the lost ones, has committed the most diabolical acts of desecration by the enactment of laws taking the temples."[78]

Quoting the Buddha Sasana Commission (whose legitimacy both the office-bearers had questioned from the beginning), the memorandum maintained that the Commission had clearly recommended exemption of income-tax for those viharas whose income from land, houses, etc., was used for the benefit of the temple as such. It had further maintained that, if any religious organisation or charitable institution employed its funds to promote money-earning trades or profession, such incomes should be taxed.

According to the recommendations of the Sasana Commission, argued the memorandum, the income from the Buddhist temples could not be taxed. The reason was that under the

78. All-Ceylon Viharadhipati and Trustee Association, *Memorial From the All-Ceylon Viharaadhipati and Trustee Association to the Prime Minister and Through Her the Government of Ceylon* (Colombo, 1962), pp. 1-3.

Ordinance of 1931, all the temples with an income exceeding
Rs. 1,000 came under the supervision of the Public Trustee.
And the incomes of such temples were to be utilised for
purposes stipulated under Section 25 of the Ordinance which
"definitely do not include income-earning trades or profession"[79] There was, thus, no room for Buddhist temple
incomes being used for trade and business.

The incomes of temples under the control of the Public
Trustee, demanded the memorandum, must be "exempted
from taxations independent of the fact whether the grants were
made before or after 2. 3. 1815. The Ande share from paddy
lands and share profits of high lands cannot be included as
profits of a business undertaking as is being done today."[80]

An assurance to the Association was given by the Minister
for Industries, Home and Cultural Affairs, Maithripala
Senanayake in a public statement in April 1962. He declared
that all properties donated to the viharas and other religious
institutions before 1815 would be exempted from the tax ;
that the legislation for the same would have provisions to
make allowances of Rs. 4,000 for temple maintenance and
Rs. 20,000 as non-taxable income and that such legislation
would be formulated and executed in the most reasonable
manner.[81]

Such an assurance, however, met the demands of the
Viharadhipati Association only partially, for it insisted on
complete exemption and for all the land donated to the
viharas even after 1815. The issue was brought up again
during the debate on the Inland Revenue Bill and W. Dahanayake, the ex-Premier, took the government to task for levying
taxes on the viharas and thereby imposing hardships on the
temples.[82]

The Government, however, seemed to be in a mood to
accommodate Bhikkhus' demands only up to a point in the
case of legislation affecting the country as a whole. It was,
therefore, no wonder that it had to face tough opposition

79. Ibid.
80. Ibid. It was on 18 March 1915 that the famous Kandyan Conven-
    tion was signed by the British Officials and the Kandyan Chiefs.
81. *Ceylon Daily News*, 11 April 1962.
82. *Times of Ceylon*, 7 March 1963.

from a large number of Bhikkhus in the elections of 1965.

In December 1965, the Nikaya Maha Sangha Sabha (which had supported the UNP in the elections) resolved that the temples should be exempted altogether from income-tax.[83] Similar demands were made by a delegation headed by Amunugama Siri Maha Vipassi which met the Cabinet Ministers in January 1966.[84] Nothing, however, appears to have come out of this. It was one thing for the UNP leader to repeal a regulation under a particular Ordinance which dealt only with temple land ; it was another to bring about changes in the provisions of income taxes which applied to the country as a whole.

The Bhikkhus thus earned the price of support but only in a limited way. Their disillusionment with the Senanayake government was dramatised in even a more significant manner on the government's ambivalence on the Paddy Land Act of 1958 against which the Viharadhipati Association had fought stubbornly in the past but without success.

The Paddy Land Act and the Viharadhipati Association

The Paddy Lands Act which, after a debate for about two years, was enacted in 1959, was the handiwork of Bandaranaike's Marxist Minister of Agriculture, Philip Gunawardane. The Bill presented to the Parliament in 1957 sought, among other things, to secure perpetuity of occupancy and cultivation rights for tenants, and fix land rent payable to the landowner at 15 bushels per acre of production, or one-fourth of the production, whichever was less.

Customarily, the landowner acquired about half of the production as the land rent. In the case of Buddhist temporalities the tenants either paid a certain percentage of production or performed daily services (Rajakaria) to the vihara as well as at the Peraheras or did both.

The Viharadhipatis with large land holdings saw in such legislation not only an infringement on their rights to decide the percentage of production due to the temple by

83. *Ceylon Daily News*, 28 December 1965.
84. Ibid., 19 January 1966.

the tenant-cultivator but also feared that the cultivator, after such an enactment, might not perform the traditional services rendered by him to the viharas.

In October 1957, the Viharadhipati and Trustee Association submitted a long memorandum to Premier S.W.R.D. Bandaranaike requesting him to exempt the temple land from the scope of the Paddy Land Bill.[85] Another memorial, signed by the Maha Nayakas and Anu Nayakas of the Malwatta and Asgiri chapters was submitted to the Governor-General in February 1958.[86] Subsequently, another petition was submitted to the Prime Minister in April 1958.[87]

Reiterating the point raised in the petition of the Viharadhipati and Trustee Association, it maintained that although the draft bill provided for the inclusion of some of the owners in the cultivators' committee, in the act itself, this provision was absent. Because of such an omission, it was pointed out, when collective farms would be formed under the supervision of cultivation committees as envisaged in the Act, the question of ownership would "suffer a terrible fate".[88] The Bhikkhus also objected to clause 4(22) of the Bill under which Bhikkhus were liable to be fined or imprisoned for contravening some provisions of the legislation.[89]

It is significant to note that another group of Bhikkhus which opposed the Paddy Land Legislation was the Eksath

---

85. *Samastha Lanka Viharadhipati Sabha Bharakara Sangamaya* (All Ceylon Viharadhipati and Trustee Association). *Kumburu Panat Gaina Vivechanayak* (Criticism of the Paddy Land Act) Kandy, 1963).

86. *The Memorial of the Maha Nayaka Theros and Anu Nayaka Theros of Malwatte and Asgiri Viharas to His Excellency Oliver Goonetileke, 2-8-1958* (Kandy, 1958). The memorial was signed by Purajjila Sri Siddhartha Saranankara (Maha Nayaka, Malwatta vihara, Yatwatte Dnammakeerthi Sri Sumangala Dh ammaratna (Maha Nayaka, Asgiri vihara), Ambanwella Sri Siddhartha Dhammananda (Anu Nayaka Malwatta vihara) and Udugama Sri Buddharakhita Ratnapala (Anu Nayaka, Asgiri vihara).

87. *Samastha Lanka Viharadhipati Saba Bharakara Sangamaya*, n. 85. Also see *Ceylon Daily News*, 24 April 1958.

88. Ibid.

89. Ibid,

Bhikkhu Peramuna (EBP).[90] And it was primarily on this issue that it was split, with the splinter group founding a new organisation called Lanka Sangha Sabha in May 1958.[91]

The main reason for the EBP opposing the Paddy Land Legislation appears to have been personal. Among the EBP leadership, Buddharakkhita and the Agriculture Minister Philip Gunawardane were opposed to each other. In a speech in the House of Representatives on 6 March 1968, Gunawardane, referring to the Bhikkhu's 'sexy' appearnce,[92] had called him a "buddy racketeer". In his open letters to the Prime Minister, Buddharakkhita had questioned Gunawardane's competence as Food Minister. In the ultimate ouster of the Marxist Minister from the Cabinet Buddharakkhita played a significant role.[93]

There is no doubt that the EBP platform was used to oppose the Paddy Land Legislation. In the process, it also tried to mobilise the support of the religious dignitaries of Malwatta and Asgiri on the issue.[94] They, however, refused to align themselves with the EBP and continued to press the issue through their personal interviews with the Ministers, and by submitting memoranda to the Premier and the other members of the government.

Such protests, either from the Maha Nayakas and Anu Nayakas of the two chapters or by Viharadhipati and Trusteeship Association did not seem to be effective enough to influence the government's decision for several reasons. Firstly, these provisions affected only the rich viharas and not the Bhikkhus as a body. In fact, there were many who felt that the big viharas of Malwatta and Asgiri, controlled to a considerable extent by their respective councils of 20 (virtually each of whom was the chief incumbent of one or more ancient and rich temples), behaved like big landlords ; that

90. For the details of the EBP organisation, see Chapters IV, V and VII.

91. *Times of Ceylon*, 4 June 1958.

92. Ceylon, *Parliamentary Debates: House of Representatives*, Vol. 30, No. 39, 6 March 1958, cols. 3893-5.

93. For details refer to Smith, n. 9, pp. 495-7.

94. *Morning Times*, 12 March 1958.

their affluence gave them considerable power of manipulation; that their excessive hold over the temple land led to a caste-class division of the rich against the poor temples. The incumbents of temples not having sufficient Sanghika property went to the extent of proposing State action to bring about an even re-distribution of temple land among the major chapters/sects. Thus, the efforts of the Agricultural Minister to socialise the agricultural holdings (in which the temple lands had a major share in Central Province), was supported by a segment of the monk community.

Not only this, the Viharadhipati Association, by and large, comprised those whose attitude in the 1956 elections had been interpreted as providing support to the UNP. The identical stand of the EBP and Viharadhipati Association on the Paddy Land Act, however, could not be effective enough to influence the government decision for another reason ; it was on this issue that Buddharakhita was alienated, and according to some monks (who had earlier worked along with him in the EBP), was exposed as a pseudo-socialist. As such, except the Buddharakhita group, the Premier retained the sympathy and support of the Bhikkhus who had been on his side on the promulgation of the socialist measures like the Paddy Land Act.[95]

Thus, nothing came out of the Viharadhipati and Trustees Association presenting an alternate draft bill regulating the administration of paddy land owned by the viharas, to the new Minister of Agriculture, C.P. De Silva, in January 1963.[96]

Nor did the UNP government, which assumed power in 1965, seem to be willing to put the clock back. The disillusionment of the Maha Nayaka of Malwatta, Amunugama Siri Vipassi Thero, was evident from his speech in June 1967 in the inaugural session of a new association called 'Vihara and Dewale Trustee Association.'[97] The Maha Nayaka com-

95. Based on interviews with several Bhikkhus.
96. For details of this proposed draft bill see *Times of Ceylon*, 22 January 1963.
97. Till 1967 the Buddhist Viharadhipatis had kept away from the chiefs of Hindu temples and Rovils. The formation of such an association symbolised an effort on their part to mobilise support

plained that though the Government promised before the
elections to give relief to Buddhist Viharas and Hindu Temples (Dewales) from the Paddy Land Act, there was still no
sign of relief forthcoming.[98]

In February 1970, on the eve of the general elections, the
Bhikkhus, led by the activists in the Viharadhipati Association decided in public a meeting to send a memorandum to
Premier Senanayake and other Cabinet Ministers with a
request to free all the paddy land belonging to the Viharas
and Dewales from the Paddy Land Act. It was also decided
to send similar memorandum to the opposition leader, Mrs.
Bandaranaike, in case the Government did not agree to
accede to the wishes of the incumbents of most of the rich
temples.[99]

However, it is noteworthy that consequent to the 1971 insurgency, when the United Front Government enacted the
land reform legislation in 1972 stipulating a ceiling of 50
acres of land for an 'individual', the Buddhist temporalities,
along with the tea estates of foreign-owned companies and those
belonging to the indigenous-owned corporate sector[100] (not
covered under the term 'individual') remained unaffected. Presumably, the government, with its credibility severely affected
by the insurgency, did not want to alienate the rich segment
of the Buddhist clergy, some of whom had also been its stead-
fast supporters. It, therefore, decided to leave the temporalities undisturbed.

It seemed, thus, that the initiative for change in the status
of Buddhist temporalities was proved infructuous. It was, however, believed by some of the UF leaders that the economic
compulsions might act as a catalyst in this context. Bhikkhus who had no land holdings and who had to depend entirely on the lay patronage for their material needs had

on an issue on which the rich Hindu temples were as much
affected as the affluent viharas.
98. *Daily Mirror*, 12 June 1967.
99. *Ceylon Daily News*, 3 February 1970.
100. However, the government had gazetted a bill in August 1975
     providing for the take-over of the foreign and locally owned tea
     estates. This was subsequently enacted.

begun to feel the pinch of the increasing economic crisis ; patrons could not adequately look after the needs of the Bhikkhus till they had looked after their own mundane necessities. It appears that a group of Bhikkhus had already begun to advocate the idea of a 'temporalities pool' under the aegis of government, earnings from which could provide for the material needs of as many as possible.

By 1975, thus, though vague demands began to be made, their intensity had yet to gain momentum, perhaps partly because of its unorganised nature and partly because the econo mic crisis had not yet been acute enough to provoke opposition from the under-privileged Bhikkhus.

CONCLUSION

The study of the activities of the Bhikkhus in regard to the State measures affecting the monastic order brings into fore certain pertinent points with regard to the organisation and functions. Structurally, the Viharadhipati Association, despite claims by its secrectary of a 500-strong leadership, appeared to be highly unstructured and personalised. From the beginning, its leading lights were Amunugama Siri Vipassi Thero (who subsequently became the Maha Nayaka of Malwatti chapter) and Palipane Chandananda (Asgiri chapter). In its style of functioning, the Association activists took resort to fairly traditional methods, namely, informal lobbying leading to personal contacts with the Cabinet Ministers, Prime Minister and Governor-General and despatch of memoranda to the government officials. In this respect, the Viharadhipati Association lacked the militancy of Bhikkhu organisations like the EBP and Sinhala Jatika Sangamaya.

As regards the effectiveness of its pressure, the Association seemed to depend heavily on the extent to which support could be mobilised. The manner in which the proposal of the Sasana Council met its virtual demise in the 1960s proves the point.

So far as the response of the political decision-makers was concerned, it depended upon (a) the importance of the issue in the priority scale of their overall programme for national development; (b) the cost of conceding to such pressures in

political terms. It was one thing for the UNP or the SLFP,
for instance, to rescind a circular dealing primarily with Bhikkhu affairs but it was quite different to concede to them on
a measure which had nation-wide implications. The Bandaranaike Government, for instance, was not particularly
eager to introduce measures related to the monastic reforms as
a whole. Underlying these considerations was also the awareness of their past, that the greater the degree of control which
the government tended to seek over religious order, the greater
must be the degree of consensus amongst the group concerned
in the very processes of the initiation, formulation and implementation of such regulations. It is in this context that the
power elite of either the SLFP or the UNP in effect, gave
way to their overall efforts to reform the Sangha. If the Bhikkhus themselves did not want Sangha reforms, how could we
impose such measures on them ? This was the tenor of the
arguments during my interviews with several SLFP
leaders.

However, one needs to view this in terms of the cost-gain
factor of politics. In 1962 for instance, in the SLFP national
programme, the Sangha reform was an important issue but
not significant enough to evoke the wrath of even those who
had supported it earlier. A low-posture policy in this respect
could still bring back some of the recalcitrant Bhikkhus in the SLFP fold who still were politically influential,
particularly in rural areas. Political expediency thus demanded the shelving of the Sasana Commission report. Similar
motivations perhaps guided their succumbing to the Bhikkhu
pressure on the question of their remunerative appointments
and presumably, their ambivalence towards temple lands in
1972.

As against this was the question of the Paddy Land Act
or the special exemption sought by the Bhikkhus in the
various legislation pertaining to internal revenue which covered the country as a whole. Economic conditions of the times
made them in fact one of the most crucial measures of their
overall programme. Consequently, despite their continued
efforts, the Viharadhipatis could extract concessions neither
from the SLFP nor from the UNP on such issues.

There is no doubt, however, that such legislation, if implemented effectively, could be seen as the beginning of the end of the affluence and therefore of the power potential of 'monastic landlordism' which had survived from one era to another. In the process it was bound to have Serious repercussions on the monastic organisations, particularly of the rich viharas. As such, it had the potential of affecting the orientations of their inmates in very many ways in the future.

Chapter VII

BHIKKHU PRESSURE GROUPS AND THE POLITICS OF LANGUAGE

INTRODUCTION

An important consequence of colonial rule on the traditional society of plural communities of Sri Lanka was the
emergence of an elite with an identity of interests and outlook.
Operating in a political system which was not wholly exposed
to mass pressures, this elite had little difficulty in accepting
the cultural differentials within itself and in evolving a modus
vivendi which would accommodate each other's distinctiveness.

As it happened, however, in common with the experience
of several other newly emergent independent States, this integrative element in society proved to be far too fragile to withstand the aspiration for power to which a mass of population
beyond the elite had found access. The result was an exacer-
bation of incipient cultural conflicts in a plural society.

One of the principal issues on which this conflict seriously
threatened to impede the process of nation-building of post-
independent Sri Lanka was the question of a status for
the languages of the majority and minority communities.
Briefly, the issue revolved round two questions : should
Sinhala, the language of the majority community, be made the
sole official language of the island ? Or should this status be
accorded also to Tamil, spoken by about a fourth of the
population of the island ?

This problem had confronted the colonial rulers too but

the homogeneity of the elites of the two distinct communities did not create much of a problem and English continued to be the official language of colonial Sri Lanka. This arrangement broke down, however, soon after independence when the emotive potential of the issue in mobilising the exacerbate support of a newly activated element of the population became apparent.

The Sinhalese-Buddhist linkage in Sri Lanka (which has been elaborated elsewhere) imparted to the official language issue heavy religious overtones and drew into the controversy the active participation of a large segment of the Bhikkhus. In the process, this segment emerged initially as an influential electoral factor and consequently, as pressure groups conditioning policy decisions over several issues.

A review of the interaction between the Bhikkhu pressure groups and the institutions of the political system makes intelligible the impact of secular factors on religious groups and conversely, of their influence in political decision-making.

Taking the language issue as a case in point, an attempt is made in this chapter to appraise the structures, functions and roles of the Bhikkhu pressure groups with special reference to (a) those whose membership was confined only to the Bhikkhus and (b) those groups in which, though the membership was open to the Bhikkhus as well as the laity, the effective power rested with some of the Bhikkhus as such. Illustrative of the power was the Eksath Bhikkhu Peramuna (EBP) and of the later Sinhala Jatika Sangamaya (SJS—Sinhalese National Congress).

THE OFFICIAL LANGUAGE ISSUE: SOCIO-ECONOMIC SETTING

The language controversy in the island needs to be considered in the context of several historical factors which heightened the awareness of the minority community of its distinct cultural identity. In its approach to its tradition, the Tamil community was inspired by a historical legacy of a 'core of direction and inspiration', distinct from the native cultures of the land in which it lived. Also, the fact that the Tamil populated northern and eastern provinces of the island were situated almost next to Tamil Nadu across the 22-mile-long shallow strip of the Palk Straits, had given this attitude even a greater intensity. As regards the language, the Tamils not only take pride in its richness and maturity but also in the fact that it is the language of more than 50 million people across the Palk Straits.[1]

The Sinhalese Buddhists, on the other hand, seeking their communal identity in the traditions of their unique Sinhalese Buddhist heritage, are acutely aware of the fact that their language is restricted to Sri Lanka. The survival of their religion and their language depends entirely on the political and social order in Sri Lanka; they cannot look elsewhere for support.

Apart from the emotive overtones, the language issue was of considerable economic consequence also. As long as English was the official language, the Swabhasa (vernacular) educated Sinhalese and Tamils had hardly a chance in the competition for government jobs with the English-educated. Though a tiny minority of less than ten per cent., it was they who competed successfully in public Services and had much wider professional career opportunities than their swabhasa educated counterparts.[2]

Under the circumstances, it was natural that the demotion of English had tremendous emotive appeal and economic implications for a vast segment of the Sinhalese population. In particular, opposition to English was strong amongst the Sinhala-educated school teachers who felt that they were treated as 'second class professionals' and a section of Bhikkhus who had believed that precious little had been done in the first few years of independent Sri Lanka to restore Buddhism to its rightful place and to further the language of the majority community.

The restoration of Sinhala to its 'rightful place' not only necessitated the dethronement of English but also its enthronement as the *only* official language. The history of the pre-colonial past in which Tamil invasions loomed large, coupled with the

1. Howard W. Wriggins, *Ceylon : Dilemmas of a New Nation* (Princeton, 1960), pp. 228-41.
2. Ibid., pp. 241-58.

fear and suspicion of the average Sinhalese *vis-á-vis* the Tamil community, led to a general belief that two official languages would divide the country as neither the Sinhalese nor the Tamils would have any incentive to learn each other's language. Further, if both Tamil and Sinhala were accorded official status as State languages, the former might corrupt the latter. Parity, it was thus feared, might lead to the eventual triumph of Tamil over Sinhala.

Summing up the Sinhalese apprehensions in this context, Bandaranaike claimed in the House of Representatives that the majority of the Sinhalese people felt that "as the Tamil was spoken by so many millions in other countries, and possessed a much wider literature and as the Tamil-speaking people had every means of propagating their literature and culture, it would have an advantage over Sinhalese, which was spoken only by a few million people in this country. They felt that not only in the Northern and Eastern Provinces was there a majority of Tamils, but that there were a large number of Tamil people in the Sinhalese provinces. . . and that. . . all this would create a situation when the natural tendency would be for the use of Sinhalese to shrink and probably in the course of time almost to reach the point of elimination".[3]

Finally, the official status accorded to Sinhala symbolised an assertion on the part of the Sinhalese of their majority status which they believed had been submerged in the past. Even in the Kandyan State, in the heritage of which the Sinhalese took immense pride, the court language under the Nayakkar Kings, they sadly stated, was Tamil. The earlier subjugation of Sinhala, thus, could be remedied only by making it the official language of the island.

Such sentiments found expression in 1956, when, mobilising the support of the rural Sinhalese elites—the Sinhala-trained school teachers, the Ayurvedic physicians and the Bhikkhus—Bandaranaike's MEP won a landslide victory. Bandaranaike's promise that he would make Sinhala the official language within 24 hours of his assumption of office was communicated in no uncertain terms by his political

3. Bandarnaike, S. W. R. D., *Towards a New Era : Select Speeches of S. W. R. D. Bhandaranaike made in the Legislature of Ceylon*, (*1931-1959*) Colambo, (1961), p. 418.

mobilisers who, among others, were a large number of
Bhikkhus. And no one could communicate this message as
effectively as they.

As the custodians of Sinhalese-Buddhist heritage it was
their status in the State which had been jeopardised during
the colonial era. It was they who were the creators of the
Sinhalese language; it was they who had fostered
Sinhalese literature. During the colonial era, the Pirivenas
which were the centres of Buddhist learning and culture and
which were run by the Bhikkhus had suffered a set-back
because of the educational policies of the colonial rulers. It
was time, therefore, that Sinhala was accorded its legitimate
place as the language of the majority community. Such a
status to Sinhala automatically meant greater support to the
Pirivenas and further recognition of the Bhikkhus' expertise
in Sinhala. A logical corollary of the official recognition of
Sinhala as the State language was, consequently, an enhancement of the power and status of the Bhikkhu community.

The Bhikkhu community, as such, seemed to be unanimous
so far as the issue of making Sinhala the only official language
was concerned. Such a view found a group articulation in the
form of the Eksath Bhikkhu Peramuna (EBP) and the Sinhala
Jatika Sangamaya (SJS). Among the lay organisations, its
ardent champions were the All-Ceylon Buddhist Congress
(ACBC) and the Bhasa Peramuna (Language Front)—a group
of Sinhalese enthusiasts which was formed on the eve of
elections and which had joined the MEP. A perusal of the
membership of these organisations indicates the cross-cutting
ties. Members of the SJS were active in the ACBC and Bhasa
Peramuna. Some of the EBP members were also the members
of the Executive Committee of the SLFP.

The most effective and articulate Bhikkhu organisation
which made its impact felt on the decision-making processes
pertaining to several issues, including the official language
question, was the erstwhile EBP. A brief description of its
structure and activities facilitates an understanding of its
power resources and organisational techniques.

THE EBP : ORGANISATION AND ACTIVITIES

Emerging on the eve of 1956,[4] the EBP was the first Bhikkhu organisation which, notwithstanding its Colombo-based leadership, could claim to have a rural network; it had 72 branches and since a branch office could not be started unless it had a certain number of members, it might be assumed that its membership ran into a couple of thousands. A definitive estimate of its membership is not available. During the elections, however, Bandaranaike claimed to have on his side about 12,000 monks; the election observers placed the figures nearer 3,000 [5], and as the EBP was the organised channel of the clergy supporting the People's United Front (MEP) one could perhaps reasonably translate this figure into the EBP membership.

While the actual membership of the EBP may not have been very big, there is no doubt that in 1956 as the vanguard of a 'community association',[6] demanding the 'restoration' of Buddhism as well as the replacement of English by Sinhala as the sole official language, it represented the sentiments and interests of a much larger number of the Bhikkhu community than those who were its actual members. In other words, its appeal seemed to be more widespread than suggested by its actual membership.

Though, as a monk-organisation, the EBP was not expected to have funds, it could command considerable financial resources. As has been mentioned elsewhere, some of its members had money and those in charge of Pirivenas had a well-equipped office. It is on record now that one of the EBP

4. For details on the evolution of the EBP see Chapter V.
5. Wriggins, n. 1, p. 347.
6. Community associations could be defined as 'groups organised on the basis of caste, religion, race, tribe or cultural-linguistic region.' The common concern of all communal organisations is the exclusive concern of each with the interests of a particular segment of society'. Richard D. Lambert, "Hindu Communal Group in Indian Politics", in Richard L. Park and Irene Tinker, eds., *Leadership and Political Institutions in India* (Princeton, 1959), p. 211, and Myron Weiner, *The Politics of Scarcity—Public Pressure and Political Response Groups in India* (Bombay, 1963), p. 39, footnote.

founders, Buddharakhita, contributed a large sum—
Rs. 100,000—to the election fund of the MEP.[7] Whether he did
it in his individual capacity or in his capacity as a members
of the SLFP or as one of the secretaries of the Front is not a
material point. What mattered in 1956 was that the EBP had
shown its political potential; it could provide services and it
had the wherewithal to campaign; it possessed information;
its leaders had an effective access to the political leaders and it
had contributed in no small measure to the victory of
Bandaranaike. This was publicly acknowledged by him in
words as well as in deeds; after the swearing-in ceremony,
Bandaranaike went not to Kandy to pay the traditional
obeisance to the Sangha but to the Kelaniya Maha Vihara,
which was the major centre of the EBP activities and whose
Chief High Priest (viharadhipati) was Buddharakhita.[8]

Intra-EBP Dissensions : The Crisis of Roles

After the dust of the election had settled organisational strains began to surface in the EBP, particularly as its
members had divergent views regarding its future roles and
objectives. In a letter issued by the joint secretaries of the
EBP on 15 May 1956, it was stated that as the limited goal
of the EBP of defeating the UNP in the general elections had
been achieved, it should dissolve itself and should form, under
the aegis of the old organisation, a new body which could
unify the Sangha and could provide the platform for a non-
political central organisation of the clergy.[9] It was also felt by
some of the EBP sponsors that attempts should be made to
bring within the fold of such an organisation not only those
who were neutral towards it but also those who were opposed

7. Judgement in the Court of Criminal Appeal, *Ceylon Daily News*,
   16 January 1962.
8. Refer to L.H. Mettananda's letter in *Ceylon Daily News*,
   4 September 1956.
9. Text of the letter in Sinhalese available at Sunetra Devi Pirivena.
   Also see *Ceylon Observer*, 15 July 1956; *Times of Ceylon*, 14 July
   1956 and 10 September 1956. See also the letter of L.H. Mettananda outlining the history of the EBP in *Ceylon Daily News*,
   4 September 1956, and ibid., 10 September 1956, for a speech of
   S.W.R.D. Bandaranaike on the EBP.

to it. Mention was made that ways and means ought to be found to seek the support and co-operation of the Maha Nayakas of Malwatta and Asgiri who had opposed the EBP's role in general elections right from the beginning.[10]

In a meeting of the Executive Committee of the EBP which was held on 14 July 1956 at Ananda College (Colombo) it was decided to dissolve the Organisation and to form a "Congress of entire Sangha in the island". The task of organising the new Congress of Bhikkhus was entrusted to a ten-monk Special Committee comprising 5 members each from the two major components of the EBP—the Sri Lanka Maha Sangha Sabha (SLMSS) and the Samastha Lanka Bhikkhu Sammela-naya (SLBS).[11]

During the discussions of the Special Committee, a rift among its members regarding the composition and goals became apparent. Majority of the members of the SLMSS seemed to be of the opinion that an organisation of the Bhikkhus had to be non-political to be acceptable to all; that the faction within the EBP led by Rev. Buddharakhita, attempting to revive the EBP, was not in a position to bring the entire Sangha into one organisation because it was 'political minded'; and that it was attempting to impose its politics on the entire Sangha and intended to carry through its political aims under the name of the Sangha.[12] The retention of the old name of Front also did not find favour with some.

Members belonging to the SLBS (along with one secretary of the SLMSS) were, however, emphatic in retaining the old name for two reasons. First, mushroom organisations had sprung up and a new organisation might be mistaken for being one of them and second, the MEP had accepted the Ten Principles (Daasraja Panath) of the EBP. A change of name might not keep the Government obliged to honour its pledge

10. *Ceylon Observer*, 15 July 1956, and *Times of Ceylon*, 15 July 1956.
11. The members of the sub-committee were: Vens. H. Gnanseeha, H. Ratnasara, B. Wimalawamsa, K. Sanghapala and K. Ginananda (All from SLMSS); T. Seelawamsa, M. Buddharakhita, Siriseewali, M. Sri Indasara and S. Punyaratna (SLBS).
12. Pertinax, "Bhikkhu Peramuna-I, Background", *Tribune*, Vol. 3, No. 18, 15 September 1956, pp. 275-6 and 286.

towards the new organisation.[13]

In the following meeting which decided to retain the dissolved EBP's name, the rift amongst its members seemed to be complete by four of its working committee members withdrawing from its deliberations. These members (all of whom belonged to the SLMSS) were openly identified by those present for their "disruptionist activities" against the EBP's attempts to unify the Sangha.[14]

The causes for the rift reflected the dilemma of the Bhikkhus in making up their minds on their future roles; the Buddharakhita faction wanted in the EBP an all-Ceylon organisation of the Sangha which could act as a pressure group and emerge as a powerful force in the country. The SLMSS wanted to achieve a powerful Sangha organisation which was unified first and later, at best, was partly political. A political role for the EBP, according to this group, was not a virtue but a forced necessity.

Besides these differences in emphasis on what was desirable and what was essential, personality factors also seemed important. Buddharakhita and Talpavila Seelawamsa had been with the SLFP since its inception; Buddharakhita's contribution in the 1956 elections was significant; on the other hand, amongst the SLMSS leaders, Rev. Gnanaseeha had been closer to the Senanayakes in the past than to the Bandaranaikes. Thus, Buddharakhita's channels of communication with the Ruling Party and the government were more effective than those of Gnanaseeha—a factor which indirectly strengthened his hands within the EBP.

It was also indicated in the press that since religious unity was not possible among the various sects, some of the EBP sponsors thought of a political organisation of all Bhikkhu sects from which some "progressive monks", inclined towards the left, were to be kept out in order to accommodate the Maha Nayakas of Malwatta and Asgiri. However, the Maha Nayakas not only refused to co-operate with the EBP in any way but also issued an injunction to the members of their chapters asking them not to join or give their support to

13. *Ceylon Daily News*, 25 August 1956.
14. Pertinax, n. 12, p. 285.

"name-changing organisations".[15] In the meanwhile, Premier Bandaranaike had tried to persuade the Maha Nayakas to join the new organisations but had failed. Consequently, the EBP decided to go ahead with its activities without waiting for the "blessings of the Maha Nayaka Theros".

Presumably, the non-cooperation of the Maha Nayakas in the EBP strengthened Bandaranaike's hand in averting an open split in the EBP.[16] This is evident from the fact that the SLMSS group, which was led by Rev. Gnanaseeha and was virtually alienated vis-á-vis Buddharakhita, had anounced to resolve its differences.[17] Notwithstanding this announcement, however, in the subsequent meetings, Rev. Gnanaseeha and a few others continued to keep aloof from the deliberations of EBP.

Programme and Constitution of the EBP

In 1957 the new EBP was born. In a broad outline of the EBP's programme published in January 1957, it was maintained that the EBP aimed to develop and safeguard the rights of the clergy as well as the laity, to start cultural bodies (Sabhas) through provincial Sangha Sabhas, to work for the goal of socialism, to put into action the Daaraja Panath and to implement the Buddhist Committee Report.[18] Again, in March 1957, the EBP's objects were set out : to advise the government on relevent matters, to undertake the propagation of the Buddhist activities and to organise an island-wide social service campaign.[19]

Elucidating its programme, one of the secretaries, Rev. Havanpola Ratnasara, maintained that the EBP was not a political party but was prepared to help any organisation

15. Ibid., pp. 285-6. Also see Ceylon Daily News, 20 July 1956.
16. Cey on Daily News, 10 September 1956 and Morning Times, 18 December 1956.
17. Morning Times, 20 September 1956.
18. Constitution available in Sinhalese in the personal files of Rev. Medagoda Sumanatissa Thero. Also see a letter of the EBP dated 15 November 1957 in Sinhalese, available in the file of Rev. Talpavila Seelawamsa Thero at Colombo.
19. Ceylon Observer, 28 March 1957.

which worked for the advancement of the people and the country on true socialist lines.[20] The EBP also announced that it planned to bring all the Buddhist organisations of the Sangha as well as the laity into one central organisation. This body was to be known as the Samastha Lanka Bauddha Peramuna (All-Ceylon Buddhist Front).[21]

The organisational aspect of the EBP, as specified in its constitution, was that the EBP was to have had a Central Executive Committee (Madhya Karaka Sabha) comprising two representatives for every 25 members in the branches and one member for every 15 non-branch members. It also provided for a Vidhayaka Mandalaya (Committee of Officials) consisting of 21 members appointed by the Central Executive Committee. It was stipulated that the Central Executive Committee should meet once in six months and the Vidhayaka Mandalaya once a month. The meeting of the Maha Sabha—the General Body— was scheduled twice a year. The meetings of the General Body or of the Central Executive Committee, however, does not seem to have taken place. And, though it was generally assumed that the early branch organisations of the EBP were still intact, it is not possible to assess their general membership.

The organisational aspect of the EBP did not seem to merit much attention of the chief sponsors of the EBP either. In fact its three joint secretaries—Rev. Buddharakhita, Rev. Seelwamsa and Rev. Ratnasara Theros (later replaced by Rev. Madelgamuwe Vijitavi) along with the members of the Vidhayaka Mandalaya (e.g., Revs. Siriseevali Thero, Medagoda Sumantissa Thero, Medagoda Dhammajothi Thero, Meewanapalane Wachissara Thero, and Mottune Sri Indrasara Thero) dominated the activities of the Organisation.

By the middle of 1958 virtually all the members of the SLMSS were alienated from the EBP and the Organisation seemed to be virtually run by four Bhikkhus whose political orientations were by no means socialist. As a result some of the Bhikkhus broke away from it on the Paddy Land Bill and formed a new organisation called Lanka Sangha Sabha.

20. *Ceylon Daily News*, 12 February 1957.
21. *Ceylon Observer*, 28 March 1957.

Though dissensions within the EBP led to a process of disintegration, its activities during 1956-59 had given it enough recognition as a force to be reckoned with, though not always respected.

The leading personality behind the EBP was the Chief High Priest of Kelaniya—Buddharakhita—who not only had effective access to the policy-makers but was also well connected with influential people in the Ruling Party (by virtue of his membership in the Executive Committee of the SLFP). He was thus able to 'capture' the EBP by 1957. As an influential member of the EBP, he was in a position to strengthen the organisation by virtue of his ability to persuade authorities to make policy concessions. On the other hand, as one of the EBP, he could claim to represent the decisions of a collectivity.

It is difficult to separate the twin roles of Buddharakhita. However, there is no doubt that the interaction of his dual roles had its effects on the image as well as the effectiveness of the EBP.

EBP as a Pressure Group

In 1956 one of the secretaries of the EBP had declared that it was not a political party. This was true; a brief resume of its activities during 1956-59 makes it clear that it was not a party but a pressure group.

Though the Buddhist Commission Report continued to serve the purpose of the EBP manifesto, the issues which moved the EBP into action were (a) the question of official language, and (b) the Paddy Land Bill. While on the former, virtually all the clergy groups had more or less a unanimous view, on the latter, the clergy was divided, as has already been discussed.

Besides these two issues, the EBP executive met from time to time and considered various other questions[22] such as the proposal for the formation of the Pirivena universities which was endorsed by it.[23] In another meeting in October 1957, it

22. The files at Sunetra Devi Pirivena as well as at Sri Lanka Vidyalaya refer to several letters written to the EBP members to discuss these issues.

23. Letter dated 21 December 1956 in Rev. Sumanatissa's files.

resolved that Assisted Schools should be taken over by the Government as early as possible. In the same meeting, it referred to the 'menace of the illicit immigrants' and the Government was asked to take effective measures to curb their arrival lest, with such an onrush of Indian Tamils, the Sinhalese "become a minority community".[24] Also, in late 1958, when the country was facing a serious economic crisis, the EBP adopted a resolution requesting the Prime Minister either to ban strikes immediately or to resign.

Besides, in the intra-coalition conflicts of the ruling MEP and the intra-SLFP wranglings, some of the EBP Bhikkhus appeared to have played a leading role. During 1958-59 the conservative wing within the SLFP, much to the chagrin of Bandaranaike, seemed to succeed in its political manoeuvres, thanks to Buddharakhita. Whether it was a question of the necessity of new alignments or of new appointments, Buddha-rakkita seemed to carry the day.

In the municipal elections of Colombo, a proposal for a united front with the LSSP and CP was made by the SLFP General Secretary Nimal Karunatillake, who was regarded as the spokesman of the Prime Minister. Apparently, the proposal was inspired by Bandaranaike who wanted to sound the Committee through Karunatillake. The proposal was vehemently opposed by a few lay leaders but it was the Bhikkhus who finally carried the day. "It is no secret", commented an influential daily "that the organiser who put fighting spirit into the right wing was none other than the venerable Budharakhita Thero. Under the inspiration of the revered gentleman, speaker after speaker repudiated the proposal of an alliance with the left."[25]

By the middle of 1959 the break between Buddharakhita (the man behind the EBP now) and Bandaranaike was complete. It was obvious that the EBP was not satisfied with the position accorded to it ; its members wanted more power. One of its members had expected a senatorship (in fact it was openly hinted in certain statements), but in vain ;[26] another had failed

24. Letter dated 20 October 1957 in T. Seelawamsa's files.

25. Donald E. Smith, 'Political Monks and Monastic Reform', in Donald E. Smith, ed., *South Asian Politics and Religion* (Princeton, 1966), pp. 497-8.

26. *Janatha* (Sinhalese), 8 April 1958.

to get official support in an economic venture in which he had an interest, but without success.[27] The members complained that it was neither consulted in the appointment of the Buddha Sasana Commission[28] nor in that of the Buddhist Advisory Council which was formed in 1957. None of the prominent EBP Bhikkhus were members of the Council.

Notwithstanding the discussion with the Prime Minister and his assurance that he would ask the Cultural Affairs Minister to reconstitute the Buddhist Advisory Committee,[29] nothing was done. Its advice to appoint Buddhist ambassadors in Buddhist countries was ignored. In an open letter to the Prime Minister, the EBP wrote: "We must point out that after three years' administration, the people who placed complete confidence in you are living in fear and suspicion...You cannot escape your sole responsibility as the leader of this country dispelling the fear and suspicion in the minds of the people, the majority of whom placed their trust in you. If you ignore or overlook that responsibility we consider it the greatest crime perpetrated on the people of this country".[30]

In June 1959, the Executive Committee of the EBP decided to appoint a committee of three Bhikkhus to find out whether the Government as constituted could provide economic and political stability for long. It was also reported that, if dissatisfied with the performance of the SLFP, the EBP would consider campaigning for any other party or group which could implement the EBP programme.[31]

The EBP's political activities included the use of traditional as well as modern channels of communication. It adopted resolutions and issued press releases and statements. Public meetings were held on various issues to enlighten people of its view and to enlist their support, but often it was through personal, informal mode of communications that issues were settled; sometimes a telephonic conversation brought results.

27. *Ceylon Daily News*, 16 January 1962.
28. Ibid., 15 May 1957, and *Ceylon Observer*, 27 January 1957.
29. *Ceylon Daily News*, 15 May 1957, and *Ceylon Observer*, 6 June 1957.
30. *Times of Ceylon*, 16 January 1959.
31. *Ceylon Observer*, 8 June 1959.

In other cases Bhikkhus would make personal visits to the house of a Minister and, if need be, at his office to press the case for the EBP's line of action. Not only this, the EBP sent general letters to the Cabinet Ministers, as well as specific ones to various Ministries, asking them for the necessary information. They also put forward suggestions on specific issues and the Ministers were asked to expedite the 'matter'. Mostly, these letters were in the form of resolutions adopted by the EBP Working Committee, a copy of which was sent to the Minister or Ministers concerned for necessary action.[32]

Press comments on the EBP's political influence suggested that it had "assumed upon itself the role of a supra-Cabinet.... Stalwarts of the EBP claim that Ministers and even high government officials are at their beck and call; that they promptly reply to any summons from the EBP headquarters; that they are often put on' trial' at EBP headquarters where they explain their action and attitude towards national problems".[33] The extent of the influence of the EBP might be an exaggerated one but the mode of its operation seemed to fit into the general pattern of the monk-laity relationship.

Sinhala Jatika Sangamaya

Another organisation, dominated by the Bhikkhus, which could match the militancy of the EBP and which played an important role on the language issue was the Sinhala Jatika Sangamaya (SJS). This had, in Rev. Baddegama Wimalawamse, a powerful Bhikkhu leader. Conceived in 1954, the SJS was one of the active supporters of the MEP. Most of its members worked in the EBP but after elections, they continued to operate as an independent group. Unlike the EBP, it was a unitary organisa-

32. Letter dated 15 December 1956 for making Sinhalese only as the official language; letter dated 20 October 1957 to the Prime Minister, referring to the menace of the illicit immigrants; letter dated 10 October 1957 regarding the take-over of schools; letter dated 6 May 1956 including its resolution requesting the Prime Minister to appoint only Buddhist ambassadors in Buddhist countries. See the files of Rev. M. Sumanatissa and T. Seelawamsa, at their respective Pirivenas in Colombo.

33. *Times of Ceylon*, 24 March 1957.

tion and the hub of its activities were a few temples in Colombo.

The 51-point SJS programme centered on a demand for the protection of Sinhalese Buddhist values. The programme stipulated the promotion of the "heritage of the Sinhala island, Sinhala nation and Sinhala language irrespective of sects, caste or class differences". It wanted Sinhala to be the sole official language and called for strict measures to save the country from the menace of illicit emigrants. Some of its other demands were : nationalisation of estates and their re-distribution amongst the Sinhalese ; take-over of foreign trading concerns ; more employment for the Sinhalese in defence as well as in civilian services ; the promotion of Sinhalese arts and crafts; parity of salaries between Sinhala teachers and English medium teachers ; a ban on the change of ancient names of towns and villages ; boycott of hotels, cafes and tea boutiques owned by Indians and Pakistanis as well as boycott of Tamil films and Tamil dresses.[34]

The various pamphlets issued by the SJS during 1954-56 broadly conformed to the arguments of the Buddhist Committee of Enquiry. They deplored the pathetic state of affairs in education and criticised the Government for the most favoured treatment meted to educational institutions run mostly by the missionaries. In a ringing tone it exhorted the Sinhalese to come forward to save the Sinhala nation and its language.[35]

There was a distinct emphasis on 'race' in all the publications of the SJS. However, as the issues of race, religion and language were closely related, the promotion of Sinhalese race automatically included the promotion of Sinhalese language. This type of ethnic nationalism was bound to alienate the minority communities which saw in such slogans a threat to their respective traditions and cultures as had developed in the island under the shadow of the Indian Subcontinent.

34. Sinhala Jatika Sangamaya, *Vyavastha Ha Paramartha* (Constitution and Aims), (Colombo, 1959).
35. E.g., see among the SJS publications Rev. Baddegama Wimalawamsa's Bhikkshuvage Anagataya (The Future of the Monk); *Anduwa Ha Missionary Balaya Government and the Missionary Power, Ada Buddhagama* (Buddhism Today) and *Ape Samaja Katayutu* (Our Social Activities).

The SJS, however, was concerned to assert the rights and privileges of the majority community. "Every one speaks of the rights of the minority. How about the rights of the majority community?" queried one of its publications. Elsewhere, it maintained that minority communities could ensure cooperation and sympathetic treatment from the majority community only if they respect the majority views and values. The line of argument that ran through its publication was that it was the majority community in the island which had suffered the tyranny of the minority with its heritage left to the mercies of the minorities and its language relegated to the status of a 'kitchen language'.[36]

Initiated by the monks and laity associated with Sri Lanka Vidyalaya (which was one of the centre of Ramanna Nikaya monks and had operated not only as a Pirivena but also as a coaching institute for various examinations), the SJS summed up the frustrations of the Bhikkhus and laity in educational and cultural affairs. The Organisation had among its presidents and vice-presidents some eminent monks of Ramanna Nikaya. Its executive committee, however, drew Bhikkhus from other Nikayas and chapters as well as lay members belonging to various professions,[37] virtually all of whom were the enthusiasts of 'Sinhala only' as the official language.

THE LANGUAGE ISSUE AND THE BHIKKHU PRESSURE GROUPS

The official language issue came on the political agenda of the State Council as early as in 1944 in the form of a resolution, providing parity of status for Tamil and Sinhala. Till 1954 both the UNP and the SLFP maintained this stand in their statements and publications. The SLFP, for instance, reiterated in its Constitution (drafted in 1951) that: "It is most essential that Sinhalese and Tamil be adopted as official languages immediately so that the people of the country may cease to be aliens in their own land ; so that an end may be put to the iniquity of condemning those educated in Sinhalese and Tamil to occupy

36. Ibid.
37. Sinhala Jatika Sangamaya, n.34, The names of its office-bearers were given on the cover of the pamphlet.

the lowliest walks of life...."[38] Even as late as April 1954, the
SLFP leader, S.W.R.D. Bandaranaike[39] was reiterating this
policy. Speaking at Kalmunai in the eastern province, he maintained that both Sinhala and Tamil should be made the official
languages and that if he ever became Prime Minister he would
see to it that both were accorded the status of national languages.[40]

However, in early 1955, a 'powerful wing' of the SLFP led
by prominent Bhikkhus and laity[41] gave notice for a motion
which sought to amend the Constitution of the SLFP on the
language issue. It demanded that only Sinhalese be made
the official language. Accordingly, a committee comprising
two Tamils, one Muslim, a Bhikkhu and several Buddhist lay
leaders was formed.[42]

Initially, the Committee recommended that the official
language for the northern and eastern provinces should be
Tamil and that Sinhala should be the official language for the
rest of the country. The proposal, however, did not get through
as it was not likely to be acceptable to the majority of the
members of the SLFP. Consequently, when the committee
submitted its final report in September 1955, it recommended

38. Sri Lanka Freedom Party, *Manifesto and Constitution of Sri
    Lanka Freedom Party* (Wellampitiya, 1951), p. 9. The first annual
    conference of the SLFP also resolved in December 1952, "(a) that
    Sinhalese and Tamil be declared the official language of the
    country immediately, (b) that the change-over to the national
    language in the administration be speedily effected; (c) that in
    education Sinhalese and Tamil be adopted as the media of
    instruction without delay, while retaining English as a compul-
    sory second language." *Times of Ceylon,* 29 December 1952. The
    second party conference held in May 1953 at Kandy reiterated
    the same sentiments on the national languages issue. *Times of
    Ceylon,* 28 May 1953.

39. *Ceylon Daily News,* 8 April 1954 and *Ceylon Observer,* 7 April
    1954.

40. For details see Robert N. Kearney, *Communalism and Language in
    the Politics of Ceylon* (Durham, 1967), p. 63.

41. *Morning Times,* 7 February and 29 March 1955.

42. The members of the sub-committee were S.W.R.D. Bandaranaike,
    W.A. de Silva, F.R. Jayasuriya, S. Thangarajah, A.P. Jayasuriya,
    Stanley de Zoysa, A.C. Nadarajah, K.M.P. Rajaratna, Badiuddin
    Mahmud and Talpavila Seelewamsa Thero, see *Ceylon Observer,*
    6 September 1955 and *Ceylon Daily News,* 24 September 1955.

that Sinhala should be the sole official language with 'due recognition for Tamil in legislation, administration and education'.[43] As a protest against the reversal of the earlier recommendation, the Tamil members of the language committee tendered their resignation from the SLFP.

In its annual conference, the SLFP ratified the recommendation of the Committee on language by adopting a resolution. The mover of the resolution was a Bhikkhu—Buddharakhita and the seconder was Badiuddin Mahmud, a Muslim who was also the member of the Language Committee. Bandaranaike did not speak on the resolution.[44]

Meanwhile, the "Sinhala Only" movement seemed to be gradually gaining strength and its protagonists like the Bhasa Peramana and the VLSSP had joined hands with the SLFP.

In this context, the ruling UNP was confronted with a difficult situation as a large number of its influential members wanted the Government to reverse its earlier parity policy for both the languages. Since its inception, the UNP had, as its declared policy, parity of status for Sinhala and Tamil as official languages.[45] In fact, in April 1950, a special meeting of the government parliamentary party had laid down a timetable for "promoting the national languages of the country, i.e., Sinhalese and Tamil...to be the official languages...on terms of equality." Again, in September 1951, the UNP, in a resolution adopted at its National Conference, had approved the appointment by Government of the National Languages Commission to implement its decision to make Sinhala and Tamil the official languages of the country. And in February 1954, the party

---

43. Discussing the Language Committee's report, Bandaranaike maintained that "during the discussion on the parity issue the committee had expressed the fear that gradually the tendency could be for the Sinhala to shrink more and more and Tamil to gain a dominant position at its expense". This was due to two reasons: (1) Sinhala is spoken by only 5-6 million people in this country. Tamil is used not only by Tamils in Ceylon but by many millions in South India. Tamil is thus far more developed. (2) In the Sinalese provinces Tamil traders are to be found not only in dominantly Sinhalese towns but also in rural areas, in addition to the large number of Tamils who are real residents. Ibid.
44. *Ceylon Daily News*, 21 December 1955.
5. *Ceylon Observer*, 18 December 1955.

conference had reiterated in a resolution "its decision to make
Sinhalese and Tamil the official languages of the country in the
shortest possible time."[46]

Thus, though the party had certain members who had
strong views on making Sinhala the sole official language,
the party leadership adhered to its earlier stand till 1954. This
was evident from a statement of Prime Minister Kotelawala at
Jaffna in September 1954 in which he reiterated the parity
approach. His promise to amend the constitution to translate
the UNP promise on language policy into practice, however,
provoked a strong reaction in the South. With pressure mounting within the party on the language issue, the UNP Ministers
and MPs were allowed to express their individual sentiments on
the issue. The result was that although the party's official policy
called for parity, a large number of the UNP's Sinhalese
Ministers and MPs were publicly advocating the policy of
"Sinhala only."[47] By 1955 the UNP leadership had given way
to the mounting public pressure[48] as well as to the pressure of
the protagonists of Sinhala only within the party.

In an effort to dramatise the shift in its language policy at
its annual session at Kelaniya in February 1956, the ruling
party decided to dissolve the Parliament a year earlier than
scheduled and seek an electoral verdict on the issue. Significantly, the UNP did not include any reference whatsoever to
giving Tamil its "due place". Its principal opponents under
the leadership of Bandaranaike, however, maintained that
although they would immediately grant official status to
Sinhala, they did not wish "the suppression of such a mino-

46. In various party conferences and statements of the UNP leaders
    this language parity policy was affirmed during 1952-54. *Times of
    Ceylon*, 11 February 1954; and Premier Kotelawala's and J.R.
    Jayawardane's speeches. *Times of Ceylon*, 30 September 1954, and
    ibid., 11 October 1954. Also refer to the resolutions of the UNP
    at its seventh annual session in Anuradhapura, *Ceylon Observer*,
    27 February 1955.
47. See for instance *Morning Times*, 13 September 1955, and *Times of
    Ceylon*, 11 September 1955 and 29 October 1955. For a criticism of
    the growing Sinhalese militancy on the language issue see the
    editorial in *Times of Ceylon*, 13 September 1955.
48. Kearney, n. 40, p. 76.

rity language as Tamil, whose reasonable use will receive due recognition."[49]

With the electoral victory of the MEP, the process of converting the language promise into public policy was set in motion. However, while the unyielding stand of the Bhikkhus on the language issue was helpful for the MEP during elections, it was soon to become "embarrassing and obstructive".[50]

Immediately after the elections, the EBP took the left parties to task for not supporting the MEP in its policy of making Sinhala the sole official language. It also demanded that the Government which had, as one of its election promises "Sinhalese only in twenty four hours", should expedite the necessary legislation.[51]

In the joint election programme, the MEP had also promised to provide for the "reasonable use of Tamil". The drafting of the legislation on the official language, however, indicated "the forces that were pressing upon the new Prime Minister through non-party interest groups mobilised on linguistic issues."[52]

The first draft bill was prepared by a sub-committee of the parliamentary party which included some prominent non-parliamentary members. It provided for Sinhala as the official language but also contained provisions to ensure that individuals trained in English or Tamil could enter the public services through examinations conducted in these languages till 1967 or

---

49. Howard W. Wriggins, n. 1, pp. 259, footnote. It might be added that as regards the LSSP and the CP, they adhered to their earlier commitment for parity of status for both Sinhala and Tamil. In fact in September 1955 the LSSP leader Dr. N.M. Perera introduced a motion in the House of Representatives seeking constitutional recognition for parity of status for both the languages as official languages. However, the Government decided to adjourn the House before the motion could be discussed. The public meetings of the LSSP and the CP on the language issue in October 1955 were disrupted by the Sinhalese Buddhist mob. For details see *Ceylon Observer*, 13 October 1955; *Morning Times*, 17 October 1955, and *Ceylon Daily News*, 18 October 1955. Also see the editorials in *Morning Times*, 13 October 1955; *Times of Ceylon*, 20 October 1955, and *Ceylon Observer*, 20 October 1955.

50. *Ceylon Daily News*, 7 May 1956.

51. Files at Sunetra Devi Pirivena, Colombo.

52. Wriggins, n. 1, p. 259.

10 years from the passing of the proposed legislation ; that the local bodies had the right to communicate with the Central Government in the language of their choice; and that individuals could communicate with the Government in their own language.

Among the "Sinhala only" enthusiasts, the most vociferous opposition to these provisions came specially from the Bhikkhus who were connected with the EBP[53] and the SJS. They staged demonstrations and their major rally ended at the steps of the House of Representatives with a prominent university lecturer going on a fast within the precincts of the House. Subsequently, the fasting lecturer was invited to present his viewpoint before the parliamentary party group of the SLFP and it appears that his viewpoint evoked a favourable response.

In the face of this agitation, the Cabinet decided to introduce a short bill in the Parliament to declare Sinhala as the official language but leave the specific provisions regarding the reasonable use of Tamil for future legislation.

The "Sinhala Only" Bill, which was introduced in the Parliament in May 1956 and enacted in July the same year, led to a sit-in demonstration of the Tamils which was organised by the Federal Party. Soon after, communal antagonism manifested itself in riots.[54]

During this period, the EBP as well as the SJS desired the Government to adopt a 'hard' line towards the Tamils. After the enactment of the "Sinhala Only" Bill, it was the Sangamaya which requested the Minister of Transport to use

53. Later, in a rejoinder to L.H. Mettananda, Buddharakhita maintained that the Executive Committee of the EBP had made a press announcement, opposing the Jyasuriya fast in view of the fact that it would "have created communal and religious disturbances in the country". *Ceylon Daily News*, 7 September 1956. What is significant in this conetxt is the fact that no newspaper had printed this statement. In view of the importance which the Ceylonese press was giving to the EBP at this time, this seems strange. Besides, Buddharakhita did not touch upon the monks' rally preceding the fast in which some prominent Bhikkhus did participate.

54. For a detailed account of the communal disturbances see Tarzie Vitachi, *Emergency*, 1958 (London, 1958), and Kearney, n. 40, pp. 82-89.

Sinhala characters on the licence plates of the vehicles. Accordingly, the word *Sri* was put on the vehicles all over the island. This led to the anti-Sri campaign (smearing of the Sinhalese name plates by tar) in the Tamil areas which was interpreted by the SJS monks as "not a fight against the letter *Sri* but against the Sinhalese nation".[55] Both the EBP as well as the SJS, reacting vehemently to the Tamil action, threatened the Government that they would take resort to "direct action" if it did not take immediate steps to stop the 'anti-Sri' campaign of the Tamils in the northern province.[56]

The militant mood of the SJS leaders was reflected in their public speeches. In a meeting of the SJS in 1959 hundreds of Bhikkhus vowed to campaign "even unto death" until the Prime Minister heeded to the demands of the Sangha and the masses on public issues. In his Presidential Address, Rev. Baddegama Wimalawamsa, declared that if the Prime Minister would not heed public opinion, the monks would not allow him to continue in office. According to him, if they resorted to drastic action, the Premier would learn "the lesson of his life".[57] Earlier, one of the Executive Committee members of the SJS had publicly declared that if the MEP did not make Sinhala the sole official language, his coalition might have to go the UNP way.

Notwithstanding the expression of such militancy on the part of the Bhikkhus, Bandaranaike decided to go ahead with his plans to implement the second half of his party's electoral pledge—legislative provisions for the reasonable use of Tamil. This had assumed an added urgency in view of the agitation of the FP and its declaration that it would start non-violent direct action (satyagraha) in August 1957 if the demands of the Tamils were not met on the language issue.[58] Under the circumstances, almost a year after the

55. *Morning News*, 13 February 1959.
56. For the summary of the EBP resolution on the anti-*Sri* campaign see *Ceylon Observer*, 27 January 1957.
57. *Times of Ceylon*, 3 April 1959.
58. *Ceylon Daily News*, 20 August 1956.

enactment of "Sinhala Only" legislation, Bandaranaike brought
before the Parliament a four-point proposal.

The plan stipulated that (*a*) persons who wrote in Tamil
would be answered in the same language by governments ;
(*b*) University education would be in Sinhala as well as in
Tamil ; (*c*) Tamils would be examined in their own language
for entrance to the public services, and (*d*) local bodies, which
wanted to transact their official business in Tamil would
be permitted to do so.[59]

The proposals evoked severe criticism both from the
EBP as well as the SJS leadership. In a letter to the Prime
Minister, the SJS maintained that it was opposed to his
four-point proposal on the reasonable use of Tamil on the
plea that the proposal to allow Tamil letters to be answered
in Tamil would require a large Tamil clerical service involving a large expenditure from the Government. The proposal to admit people, ignorant of official language, argued
the SJS would create a group in bureaucracy which might
turn out to be antagonistic to Sinhala.[60] In a public meeting
the SJS leaders maintained further that the four-point proposal would "ultimately lead to parity of status for both
Sinhalese and Tamil."[61]

Instead, the SJS Executive Committee put forward a four-
point proposal as an alternative to Bandaranaike's proposal
on the reasonable use of Tamil. The executive conceded
that the medium of instruction should be in the mother
tongue but proposed that after 1962 the study of Sinhala
should be made compulsory in all the post primary classes.
It further suggested that after ten years, i.e., 1967, those who
did not know Sinhala should not be selected even as pro-
bationers. Finally, it proposed that correspondence between
the central government and local bodies should be in Sinhala
only.[62]

Notwithstanding such pressures, Bandaranaike began
discussions with the FP leader S.J.V. Chelvanayakam on the

59. *Morning Times*, 6 June 1957.
60. Ibid.
61. *Ceylon Daily News*, 9 July 1957.
62. *Ceylon Observer*, 9 July 1957.

basis of his four-point proposal. The discussions ended on
26 July 1957, with the signing of a formal agreement, popu-
larly known as Bandaranaike-Chelvanayakam Pact (BC Pact).
It provided that the 'proposed legislation' on the reasonable
use of Tamil should recognise Tamil as the language of a
'national minority' of Sri Lanka and that along with the
inclusion of the four points of the Prime Minister, provision
should also be made for the recognition of Tamil as the language of administration of the northern and eastern provinces,
without infringing in any way on the Official Language Act
of 1956. It was also agreed that through further legislation,
the Government should provide for the formation of regional
councils with wide powers relating to agriculture, education
and other matters including the selection of colonists for the
Government-sponsored colonisation schemes. This was intended to meet the Tamil Federalists' demands for regional
political autonomy and to stop the Sinhalese colonisation of
Tamil areas.[63]

The Bandaranaike-Chelvanayakam Pact met with
strident opposition from various quarters. The leaders of
Bhasa Peramuna called it an act of 'treachery against Sinhalese nation'.[64] The UNP's Working Committee, in a long
communique issued in August, argued that the Pact virtually
meant Tamil to be the official language of the northern as
well as the eastern provinces and that its provision relating
to regional councils were a step towards the communal
division of the country.[65]

The SJS leader, Rev. Wimalawamsa warned people of the
danger which would befall the country if the BC Pact was
implemented and pledged to lead the people in a campaign
to see that it was not put into effect.[66] Meanwhile, although
it had appeared to be more moderate, the EBP asked the

63. For the text of the Pact see Kearney, n. 40, pp. 144-6. Also see
    Bandaranaike's statement on the subject, *Ceylon Observer*, 15 April
    1958.
64. *Ceylon Observer*, 4 August 1957.
65. For the text of the communique see *ibid;* also refer to J.R.
    Jayawardane's speech on the Pact, *Ceylon Daily News*, 9 September
    1957.
66. *Ceylon Daily News*, 5 August 1957.

Prime Minister to make a full statement on the agreement.[67] However, by September, the leadership of both the groups had joined hands to enlist support for launching the Satyagraha against the BC Pact in October 1957.[68]

The Pact also evoked criticism of the Maha Nayakas of Malwatta and Asgiri. They expressed their deep concern over the Pact as the "first step towards the setting up of a separate state" and called upon the people of the country to assemble at the Dalada Maligawa premises at Kandy on 8 January 1957 to "invoke the blessing and protection of the sacred tooth relic, to prevent the division of their country by the establishment of a separate Tamil State."[69]

While opposition to the Pact was thus mounting in the central provinces and in the south, the Tamils considered these developments to be an affront to them on the part of the Sinhalese Government. Even earlier, the Tamils had protested against the use of the word Sri in Sinhala on the licence plates of the automobiles in northern provinces. In March 1958, when the Ceylon Transport Board's buses bearing the Sri licence plates arrived in Jaffna, the Tamils began to tar the Sinhalese lettering and put Tamil lettering therein. The Sinhalese in the south retaliated by smearing Tamil letters on stores run by Tamils. Communal tension flared up again.

On 9 April 1958, about 500 people, half of whom were Bhikkhus, began a sit-in in front of the Prime Minister's residence. Vehemently criticising the Pact, they demanded its abrogation. Bandaranaike, who had been fighting opposition to the Pact within his own Cabinet on the issue, ultimately gave in. The Bhikkhus got his written pledge that the Pact was abrogated and this was announced soon after by one of his Ministers.[70]

Once again, the Bhikkhus along with the laity, articulating the militant Sinhalese opinion on the language issue, had won.

67. Ibid., 12 August and 27 August 1957.
68. *Times of Ceylon*, 11 August 1957, and *Morning Times*, 17 September 1957.
69. *Times of Ceylon*, 1 September 1957.
70. Smith, n. 25, pp. 477-8.

Subsequently, the EBP declared that it would organise a 'boycott week' from 10 to 17 May 1958 asking the Sinhalese not to have any transactions with the Tamils. It maintained that this move was not conceived in a spirit of anger or jealousy against Tamils but was a symoblic protest against the activities of the FP.[71]

The abrogation of the Pact was followed by another wave of communal outbursts. Consequently, on 27 May 1958, a state of emergency was declared. Several FP leaders as well as the leaders of a small Sinhalese chauvinist group called Jatika Vimukti Peramuna (JVP—National Liberation Front) were arrested.[72]

It was during the state of emergency that Bandaranaike brought before the Parliament the Tamil Language Bill which was enacted in September 1958. The Act provided for the use of Tamil in higher education as well as in public service entrance examination on the condition that those recruited thus should develop proficiency in Sinhala if they were to continue in service and be eligible for promotion. It also provided for the use of Tamil by individuals in their correspondence with the central government as well as local government officials. Finally, Tamil could be used in northern and eastern provinces "for prescribed administrative purposes" and the Prime Minister was authorised to enact regulations to give effect to the provisions of the Act.'[73]

The provisions of the Act had much in common with Bandaranaike's old four-point proposal. But with the emergency in force, no discussion on the Act seemed to be possible. A few weeks before the emergency had been declared, the EBP had announced its intention of convening a conference to discuss the provisions of the Reasonable Use of Tamil Bill on the ground that it would "prejudice the Sinhala Act",[74] but nothing more was heard of it.

Despite the initial opposition to the Government's proposals only to provide some status for the Tamil language, the state of

---

71. *Ceylon Observer*, 22 April 1958.
72. Kearney, n. 40, pp. 86-87.
73. Ibid., pp. 147-9.
74. *Ceylon Daily News*, 10 May 1958.

emergency had enabled the Government to embody the main elements of these proposals in an Act of Parliament. But the possibility remained that further agitational movements might be directed against the implementation of the provisions. It was not until 1966, by which time the Government was a coalition of the UNP and several other parties including the FP, that regulations were promulgated to put the 1958 Act into effect.

The regulations[75], which were enacted on 11 January 1966 provided for the use of Tamil in the transaction of all Government and public business and maintenance of public records as well as for communication between the Tamil provinces and the Centre. The regulations were opposed by the UF, and in a demonstration organised by the opposition, a Bhikkhu was killed by police firing on the demonstrators. But it was possible for the Government to keep the situation under control. This was so because of several reasons. For one thing, the UNP, which had come to power only a few months ago, had received electoral support from many Bhikkhus who had turned against the SLFP because of its coalition with the left LSSP. Also, as the opposition had been organised by the UF, the Sinhalese Buddhist public opinion tended to regard it as a move in which some of the Bhikkhus were being exploited by the left parties.

CONCLUSION

It is clear from the foregoing review that structurally, both the EBP and the SJS were loosely structured, ad hoc in nature and highly personalised in character. Such characteristics were in keeping with the general approach of the Bhikkhus to public life. A monk, from the beginning, was trained to be a leader capable of advising and influencing others. Independence of opinion was thus the hallmark of monkhood. As such, excessive emphasis on the like-mindedness of the clergy corroded the very basis of the source of his power.

However, on issues of public policy the object of such Bhikkhu organisations was almost always confined to obtaining favourable decisions rather than the control of decision-mak-

75. For the text of the regulations see Kearney, n. 40, p. 150.

ing offices as such. This again was inherent in the fact of their being Bhikkhus. Ceylonese monks and laity taking pride in the pure Theravadin character of Sinhalese Buddhism, still felt that while a monk could influence the decision-making process he should not be a decision-maker unless and until he disrobed. Past traditions seemed to be firmly entrenched in the minds of the rural Sinhalese, and this was one of the traditional sanctions which the Ceylonese monk seemed to respect.

As regards their tactics of influence, these were informal as well as formal. Face-to-face communication with the key decision makers was as important as the use of the telephone. Along with the use of the press, publication of pamphlets, adoption of resolutions (copies of which were sent to the Prime Minister and the officials concerned), holding of public meetings, rallies, demonstrations, techniques of non-violent direct action like satyagraha, sit-ins, etc., were also used by them to mobilise public opinion as well as to symbolise a show of their strength so far as the policy-makers were concerned.

The extent of their relative success as a pressure group was partly determined by the objective situation and partly by the extent of support mobilisation from other groups. Thus, during 1954-57, the Bhikkhus, as the defenders of traditional Sinhalese Buddhist heritage, tended to be the most effective exponents of the Sinhalese Buddhist sense of grievance. That virtually the entire Bhikkhu community was in unison on the language issue was a significant factor enhancing the legitimacy of the Bhikku organisations. Further, as an equally articulate section of the Buddhist lay leaders adopted the same attitude towards the issue as the EBP and the SJS, their stand acquired further support.

In 1958, with the communal tension reaching a new high and culminating in the emergency declaration, the normal modes of democratic protest were no longer available. The Bhikkhus and the lay leaders might have succeeded, under normal circumstances, in obstructing the legislation of the Act for the reasonable use of Tamil. But the powers available to the Government under the state of emergency were considerable, and the Bhikkhu pressure groups lacked either the means or the will to sustain the Government's challenge. Looking back, it would seem that, in 1956, the Bhikkhus were using their power and resources for the first time since independence and were, therefore, greatly influential. But it would appear that by 1966 the competition between the two major parties had led to a division of the Bhikkhu community, which was not there to the same degree in 1956. Thus, the fact that the Bhikkhus had operated as pressure groups on various issues was in itself a factor in neutralising their effectiveness. In the past, their views were considered to be, by and large, non-partisan. By 1966 the articulate Bhikkhus were identified with one party or the other. In other words, by 1966 not only were people getting used to the Bhikkhu outbursts on virtually each and every public issue but also tended to regard them not as neutral arbiters but as committed political actors.

The response of the political leadership to the pressure group tactics of the Bhikkhu organisations was determined by the importance which the issue had in its overall policy and programme in terms of its assessment of political costs and gains. This is evident from the fact that on certain issues pertaining to education and cultural spheres, the ruling parties did not let the initiative slip from their hands. The enhancement of grants to the various Pirivenas since 1956, the formation of the Department of Cultural Affairs with special emphasis on Buddhist socio-religious activities, the creation of two new universities with the Sinhala medium as well as a Bhikkhu university at Anuradhapura were expeditious measures on the part of the Government to remedy the Buddhist sense of grievance and conversion of some of their demands into public policies.

Such measures were not difficult to adopt, for they satisfied the majority community without treading on the toes of the other minority communities. This was not so in the case of the language issue. As such, apart from the cost-benefit dimension of the issue, the various measures adopted by the leadership were also partly determined by (a) the perception of its own capability to contain the pressure of the Bhikkhu-laity organisations, or (b) its calculations to exploit it with a view to mobilising its own power base. If Bandaranaike's tenacity to resist the pressure of the Sinhalese Buddhist militants had to

provide for the reasonable use of Tamil (despite his initial
capitulation) symbolised the former, the attitude of the UNP
on the BC Pact as well as that of the UF on the 1966 regulations for the Reasonable Use of Tamil Act, was an apt illustration of the latter.

Chapter VIII

BHIKKHU ORGANISATIONS AND FOREIGN POLICY ISSUES

INTRODUCTION

An analysis of the activities of Bhikkhus and Bhikkhu organisations on some of the foreign policy issues needs to be made in the context of the Theravadin Buddhist legacies of the island (of which the Sinhalese Buddhists show a tremendous pride and awareness) as well as in its pan-Buddhist dimensions. Alongside the long-drawn cultural-religious interaction amongst the people of the Buddhist countries (as is evident, for instance, from the invitation to Bhikkhus from one country to another for the higher ordination ceremony), Bhikkhus had also been going to other countries—Buddhists as well as non-Buddhists—to propagate Buddhism.

This tradition, however, had a serious set-back during the colonial era and soon after independence, efforts were made by the ruling elite of the Buddhist countries like Burma and Sri Lanka to provide a fresh impetus to such an interaction.

The convening of the Sixth Great Buddhist Council (or Synod) at Rangoon in 1954[1] was symbolic of such an effort. This was followed by the lavish celebrations during the Buddha Jayanti year all over the Buddhist world. As regards Sri Lanka, apart from being an active participant in the two-

---

1. The first three Great Councils were held in India, the fourth in Sri Lanka and the fifth in Burma, in 1871. Donald Eugene Smith, *Religion and Politics in Burma* (Princeton, 1965), p. 157.

year long proceedings of the Sixth Buddhist Synod, even
earlier, the government had provided in 1951, a sizeable financial subsidy for specific Buddhist activities to the Burmese
Government. Also at the official level, some of its lay leaders
had taken initiative in forming a world fellowship of Buddhists
as early as in 1950.[2]

The World Fellowship of Buddhists was, however, predominantly a laity organisation. In the Sixties, it was felt that
there was a need for an international Bhikkhu organisation
dealing specifically with the problems of the Sangha. In this
venture again, in 1964, the Sri Lanka Bhikkhus took the
initiative of sponsoring discussions for the convening of a pan-
Bhikkhu organisation. This bore fruit in May 1966 when,
after a four-day deliberation at Colombo among the Bhikkhus
of various countries, the World Buddhist Sangha Council was
formed with its headquarters at Colombo.[3]

The Department of Cultural Affairs provided official patronage to such efforts, and since it had on its agenda the propagation of Buddhism abroad, it sent Bhikkhus to other
countries from time to time to start Buddhist centres and
propagate the Dhamma.[4]

It is also noteworthy that, in the enunciation of its non-
aligned policy, Ceylonese leaders like D.S. Senanayake and
S.W.R.D. Bandaranaike linked it with the Buddhist traditions and tenets. Thus, describing his policy of non-alignment as the policy of the Middle Path, Bandaranaike maintained that such a policy was in harmony with the eternal laws

2. The World Fellowship of Buddhists was sponsored by the All-
   Ceylon Buddhist Congress with Malalasekera as its chairman.
3. For details see World Buddhist Conference, *Sangha Souvenir*
   (Colombo, 1966), and World Buddhist Sangha Council, (*Constitution* (Colombo, n.d.).
4. E.g., two Bhikkhus were selected by the Department of Cultural
   Affairs to propagate Buddhism abroad. *World Buddhism*, Vol. 10,
   no. 2, September 1961, p. 11. In 1963 the Government built a
   Ceylon Hall at the International Institute of Buddhist Studies at
   Rangoon. *Ceylon Observer*, 28 July 1963. In 1967 the Bhikkhus
   were sent to Africa and the USA under official auspices to establish
   Buddhist missions. *Ceylon Daily News*, 17 June 1967, and *Times
   of Ceylon*, 11 April 1967.

of the 'Middle Way' and was best suited to Sri Lanka.[5] Also, in a strife-torn world, the major tenets of Buddhism had great relevance as guiding principles for the promotion and propagation of world peace.[6]

The enunciation of foreign policy objectives and goals needed to be related to the diverse domestic as well as external variables. What needs to be underlined in the context of Sri Lanka is the emphasis on its Buddhist traditions which gave the Government's foreign policy pronouncements an indigenous Sinhalese nationalist slant and at times tended to provide the motivation for its activism on foreign policy issues like Vietnam.

As regards the Bhikkhus and Bhikkhu organisations, a perusal of Sri Lanka's foreign policy since 1948 indicates that they were active only on certain issues. These issues can be classified as : (a) Those in which the Bhikkhus felt concerned as members of pan-Buddhist community, and (b) those in the solution of which, they envisaged a way out for the socio-economic amelioration of the Sinhalese Buddhists at home.

While the issue of Buddhists' plight in Tibet leading to the flight of the Dalai Lama to India in 1959, as well as that of the Buddhists in Vietnam under the Catholic regime of Ngo Dinh Diem in 1963, fall in the former category, the issue with regard to the political status of a large number of persons of Indian origin working on the plantations in the Sinhalese-dominated provinces of Kandy, Uva and Sabargamuva, fall in the latter category.

If the cause of Tibetan refugees was taken up by only one Bhikkhu organisation, the plight of Buddhists and the Maha Nayakas of Malwatta and Asgiri in Vietnam evoked the responses from many. On the issue of the 'Stateless' persons of Indian origin, the response of the Bhikkhus gave an 'inside' view of the manner in which the political parties attempted to elicit the Bhikkhu support to put forward their respective points of view.

5. S.W.R.D. Bandaranaike, *Speeches and Writings* (Colombo, 1963), p. 307.
6. Ibid. Also see Smith, n. 1, pp. 123-4.

BHIKKHUS ON TIBET

According to the 1951 China-Tibet agreement, Tibet, a Mahayanist Buddhist country, had become an Autonomous Region with the right to exercise "national regional autonomy under the unified leadership of the People's Republic of China". The Tibetans, however, resented the increasing Chinese intervention in their internal affairs and attempted to contain it under their spiritual political leader, Dalai Lama. This, however, was met with Chinese antagonism. Consequently, a rebellion against the Chinese administration began in 1959, leading to the flight of the Dalai Lama and some of his associates to India.

The Chinese activities in Tibet led to protests by the All-Ceylon Buddhists Congress[7] as well as by a group of Bhikkhus which included, among others, the Maha Nayakas of Malwatta and Asgiri. In a meeting held at the house of Rev. Malewana Gnanissara Thero, the Maha Nayakas decided to send in April 1959, a deputation of Bhikkhus to present a memorandum to the Chinese Embassy in Colombo protesting against the Chinese military operations in Tibet. The gates of the embassy were, however, closed to the Bhikkhu deputation.[8]

Soon after, some of the Bhikkhus decided to form Sri Lanka Maha Bhikkhu Sangamaya (SLMBS) to support the cause of the Tibetans. The aims of the Association, as spelt out by its president, clearly reflected its ideological orientation. In one of its statements the association declared that its major objective was the protection of the country from Marxism and to help the Dalai Lama, who had been given asylum in India.

In an interview to the Times of Ceylon, the President of the SLMBS, Rev. Gnanissara (a successful Ayurvedic physician at Colombo) declared that a large number of Bhikkhus had decided to assemble in Colombo to protest against the atrocities of the Chinese in Buddhist Tibet, the 'persecution' of the Dalai Lama and the treatment meted to the Bhikkhu deputation, which was refused admittance into the Chinese Embassy in

7. *Morning Times*, 17 April 1959.
8. *Ceylon Daily News*, 11 April, 5 May and 20 May 1959.

Colombo when it went to present a memorandum on Tibet to the Chinese ambassador[9].

In a meeting at Colombo in April 1959, the Bhikkhus adopted four resolutions, condemning the ruthlessness of the Chinese Communists in Tibet and expressed their sorrow at the plight of the Tibetan Buddhists. It applauded the steps taken by the Indian Prime Minister Nehru, to ensure the safety of Dalai Lama and seeking the co-operation of the other Buddhist countries to bring relief to the people of Tibet.[10] It was also decided to send a Bhikkhu delegation to meet the Dalai Lama at Mussoorie in India.

Accordingly, the Bhikkhu delegation led by Rev. Gnanissara went to Mussoorie and presented a memorandum to the Dalai Lama, according to which the 'Sangha of Ceylon' conveyed its deep "sympathy and feeling of brotherhood to the people of Tibet in their terrible sufferings and brutal persecution by the enemies of Dhamma".[11]

The delegation also requested the Dalai Lama to visit Ceylon. Efforts were made by the Association at home to create public opinion in Sri Lanka against the high-handedness of China in Tibet.[12]

In a press statement, Malewana Thero was critical of the 'strange silence' of the SLFP Premier on the Tibet issue.[13] This reproach as well as the efforts of the Association to create a public opinion on the Tibet issue did not seem to be very effective. With the political bias of its President already known, any attempt on his part to present the case of Tibet appeared to be partisan. Besides, Bandaranaike had already expressed his sympathy for the Tibetan plight and had offered his services for mediation if they were needed. After all, argued Bandaranaike, even India had conceded to the suzerainty of China over Tibet. Therefore, as an internal affair of China, the issue could not be raised in the UN. He,

9. Based on interview with Rev. Gnanissara Thero.
10. *Ceylon Observer*, 11 April 1959.
11. *Ceylon Daily News*, 5 May 1959. Also see *World Buddhism*, Vol. 7, no. 11, June 1959, p. 4.
12. *Times of Ceylon*, 16 April 1959, and *Ceylon Daily News*, 20 May 1959.
13. Ibid.

however, hoped that some satisfactory settlement' permitting Tibetans to follow their own way of life under the suzerainty of China would be found soon.[14]

The official stand on the Tibetan issue was to a considerable extent determined by the economic compulsions as much as political expediency. Bandaranaike, trying to build 'bridges' between the Communist and the non-Communist world, had also attempted to shed Sri Lanka's foreign policy of its earlier ideological bias, which was pro-Western, and had established diplomatic and cultural relations with the communist countries in 1956.

Besides, as regards China, Sri Lanka had already concluded a rubber-rice barter agreement under the terms of which Sri Lanka was getting a price higher than the international price current then on the rubber exported to China and was obtaining rice from China at a price lower than that in the world market. Under the circumstances, any action which might alienate China would not have been prudent. Finally, in containing the opposition elements, Bandaranaike's hands were strengthened by Nehru's stand on the issue, that Tibet was an internal matter of China.

Tibet, thus, did not become a live issue in Sri Lanka and the activities of the Sangamaya, in view of the known alignment of its members did not prove to be effective. However, this was the first time that an international question was given religious-cum-ideological bias by certain Bhikkhus in Sri Lanka.

BUDDHISTS IN VIETNAM : THE SETTING

The Vietnamese nationalist movement, after a long-drawn struggle against French colonialism led to the signing of the Geneva Agreement in 1954 under which, the French withdrawal was heralded from the Indo-Chinese peninsula; the 'temporary' division of Vietnam had come to stay. A dominantly Buddhist country of Mahayanist variety, South Vietnam was

---

14. Ceylon, Parliamentary Debates, *House of Representatives*, Vol. 34, 22 April 1959, cols. 2741-44. Also see UN General Assembly, Official Records, Plen. mtg 834, 21 October 1959, p. 528.

ruled over the last two decades by military-civilian regimes which were dominantly Catholic. From time to time Bhikshus and and lay leaders in South Vietnam protested against the high-handedness of the Government on religious and political issues.

This mood of protest found an explosive manifestation in the self-immolation of the 73-year old monk Thich Quang Duc on 11 June 1963 at Saigon. Though the immediate provocation to the act of self-immolation was provided by the refusal of South Vietnam's President, Ngo Dinh Diem, to comply with the five demands of Buddhists, there is no doubt that underneath this provocation was a long drawn and cumulative resentment as well as frustration among the Buddhists in South Vietnam against the policies of its Catholic president.

The Buddhist leadership felt that, though comprising more than four-fifths of its total population, Buddhist interests and rights were being subverted by the 'Catholic Action' in South Vietnam. The Government had favoured the Catholic church against Buddhist pagodas in the grant of land for ecclesiastical purposes. So was also the case in educational policies. Finally, virtually all the key positions, whether in civil or military spheres, were occupied by the Catholics (often refugees from North Vietnam) who comprised a mere 10% of its total population.

It was also contended that the country was, in effect, ruled not by Ngo Dinh Diem, but by his brother Ngo Dinh Nhu, who had, reportedly, a deep-seated antipathy and scorn for Buddhism and its devotees.

The immediate cause for the Buddhist protest came in the wake of a Presidential Order on the eve of the Vesak day (Buddhist New Year Day) in the beginning of May, banning the hoisting of the five-coloured international Buddhist flag. This was followed by the cancellation of a broadcast speech on 8 May 1963 by Ven Thich Thien Khiet, Superior of the General Buddhist Association of Vietnam and the senior Buddhist priest in the country. Protesting against the Governmental action, a peaceful demonstration was held the same day outside the radio station at Hue. The Government retaliated by firing which resulted in the death of nine persons.

Soon after the incident, a Buddhist delegation met the

President with the following five demands:

(1) Cancellation of the Presidential Order banning the hoisting of the Buddhist flag ;
(2) Legal equality for the Catholics and the Buddhists;
(3) End to the arrests of Buddhists;
(4) Free practice and propagation of the Buddhist faith; and
(5) Payment of indemnities to the families of the victims of the Hue massacre of May 8.

These demands were not met to the satisfaction of the Buddhist leadership. Consequently, on 30 May, 400 Bhikkhus and nuns staged a four-hour sit-down strike in front of the National Assembly. The students also joined the Bhikkhus in their protests and, on 3 June 1963, staged a demonstration against the discriminatory religious, policies of the Catholic regime. The self-immolation of Thich Quang Duc followed this demonstration.

The Diem regime tried in vain to suppress the Buddhist revolt. The intensity of the Buddhist revolt, coupled with the gradual disintegration of the official machinery led finally to the army coup and the assassination of Diem in November 1963.

The first phase of the Buddhist crisis was followed by a tussle for power between the army and the civilian leaders. In between, the militant monks and Buddhist lay leaders were provided the opportunity of creating a parallel organisational structure of their own as an alternative to Vietcong ideology. In the process, however, the monks were divided. Thus by 1965, when political power was taken over by the armed forces led by General Nguyen Cao Ky, the monks' appeal had lost its former emotive and unified appeal to the masses. All through this period, two external factors, the US involvement in Vietnam and the infiltration of Vietcong, continued to aggravate the civil strife in the country.

In March 1966, the United Buddhist Asssociation (a political organisation of monks and laity founded in 1964) demanded the restoration of civilian rule and the return of the Generals to the barracks. Its confrontation with the Generals led the country to the verge of a civil war. In comparison to the Buddhists crisis of 1966, the Buddhist revolt against Diem was a "gentle prologue". At that time, the Buddhists had begun to sense their influence with the masses. But in 1966, the Buddhist leadership, sparked by the militant monk Tri Quang, carried on a furious and violent campaign to throw out Premier Ky from power. In this confrontation, the "Buddhist movement was split between moderates and militants".[15]

It is in the context of this brief narrative of political developments in Vietnam that the reaction of the people of Sri Lanka to the Buddhist crisis in Vietnam needs to be analysed.

Ceylonese Response to the Buddhist Crisis in Vietnam

It is noteworthy that unlike the Tibetan issue, no new Bhikkhu organisation was brought into being in Sri Lanka, to espouse the cause of Buddhists in South Vietnam. The Bhikkhus' response on the issue was highly personalised and fairly diffused. They did speak at various meetings and also held rallies of Bhikkhus but without any political label. The major reason for this seemed to be virtually unanimous sympathy of the Bhikkhus as well as the lay leadership for the Buddhists in Vietnam which cut across partisan barriers. The attitude of the UNP in opposition and that of the SLFP in power, for instance, was virtually identical on the issue.

In its resolutions, the executive committee of the UNP condemned the 'persecution of the Buddhists in Vietnam';[16] the SLFP Government, sharing the UNP, sentiments tried to mobilise world opinion, particularly in the Buddhist countries,

15. For the background on Vietnamese Buddhist crisis see Thich Nhat Hanh, *Vietnam—The Lotus in the Sea of Fire* (London, 1967); for a detailed account of political developments during 1963-66 and the role of Bhikkhus therein see Jerrold Schecter, *The New Face of Buddha : Buddhism and Political Power in South Asia* (London, 1967), pp. 166-252.

16. For the text of the UNP resolution see *Ceylon Daily News*, 26 June 1963.

so that the issue could be brought before the United Nations.[17] Such activities of the Government were further facilitated by the initiative and drive of Dr. G.P. Malalasekera, then Ceylon's High Commissioner in the UK, and subsequently the Permanent Representative at the UN,[18] who also played a significant role in the fact-finding mission of the UN in Vietnam.[19]

In fact, not only the Buddhists but even some Hindu organisations in Sri Lanka came out with statements protesting against the action of the Catholic regime in South Vietnam.[20] In fact, public sentiments on the issue ran so high that for the first time in the history of the island, the Governor-General's Throne Speech was amended with unanimous consent to include a paragraph on Vietnam.[21]

Unlike Tibet, the Vietnam issue had a special emotive appeal for the Sinhalese Buddhists, some of whom had already raised their voice against the Catholic Action in the country. Though the most vocal anti-Catholic Action organisation was Bauddha Jatika Balavegaya (BJB) which had, amongst its active members, educationists, government officials and politicians, there is no doubt that even organisations like the ACBC and eminent Bhikkhus like Kalukondayawe Pannasekera Thero and Madihe Pannaseeha Thero envisaged in it a serious threat for Buddhism and the right of the Buddhists.

Commenting on the condition of the Buddhists in Vietnam, the Vice-President of BJB, Ronnie de Mel, maintained that the events in Vietnam offered several lessons for Sri Lanka. If such a situation could arise in South Vietnam with 80% Buddhist population, it could also arise in Sri Lanka which had only 70% of Buddhist population and that too divided in

17. For details of Ceylon Premier's talks with the envoys of other countries as well as the UN Secretary-General see *Ceylon Observer*, 17 July 1963; *Ceylon Daily News*, 15 August 1963; *Ceylon Observer*, 18 and 22 August 1963.
18. *Ceylon Observer*, 21 June 1963; *Ceylon Daily News*, 12 July 1963.
19. *Ceylon Observer*, 13 October 1963. Also see Dhirendra Mohan Prasad, *Ceylon's Foreign Policy Under the Bandaranaikes*, 1956-65 (Delhi, 1973), pp. 107-8.
20. *Times of Ceylon*, 21 September 1963.
21. *Ceylon Daily News*, 15 August 1963.

many ways.[22] The BJB also submitted a memorandum on Catholic Action to the Premier in which it stated that what was happening to the Buddhists in Vietnam today could "happen to the Buddhists of this country tomorrow"[23]

Such statements were reiterated in the speeches of Bhikkhus like Pannaseeha and K. Pannasekera Theros. In a speech at a public meeting, the latter declared that apart from supporting the Buddhists in South Vietnam, it was also necessary for them to examine the extent to which the Catholic Action had gained ground at home.[24]

Apart from the individual utterances of the Bhikkhus like Bambarende Siriseevali;[25] Kalukundayawe Pannasekera, Madihe Pannaseeha and Narada Theros[26] on Vietnam, the Bhikkhus also organised a march through the streets of Colombo to participate in religious ceremonies. These ceremonies were to offer merit to Thich Quang Duc Thero who had burnt himself to death at Saigon.

In the meeting, which was presided by Rev. Kiriwaththudewe Sri Praganasara Thero (Vice-Chancellor of Divyalankara University) at Ananda College, on 21 June 1963, the following resolutions were adopted:

(1) "The Buddhist monks have assembled here to express their deep sympathy and dissatisfaction at the inhuman and atrocious treatment meted out to the Buddhists by the government of South Vietnam headed by the Catholic President, Ngo Dinh Diem, who has denied the Buddhists of that country their religious freedom and right of hoisting the Buddhist flag.

(2) "We request the Government of United States of America and its President, Mr. John F. Kennedy, to stop all military aid and to help Buddhists to enjoy their religious freedom.

22. *Ceylon Observer*, 22 May 1963 and *Ceylon Daily News*, 13 June 1963.
23. Ibid., 14 June 1963.
24. Ibid., 27 May 1963.
25. For Siriseevali's statement, see *Ceylon Daily News*, 16, 23 and 25 August 1963.
26. For the discussion between Prime Minister Senanayake and Ven. Narada Thero see *Ceylon Daily News*, 26 May 1965.

(3) "This meeting of the Buddhist monks also requests the Prime Minister, Mrs Srimavo Bandaranaike, the US President and all the heads of other countries to give all necessary co-operation at the United Nations Organisation in its endeavour to ease this situation."[27]

It was, thus, obvious that so far as the Vietnam issue was concerned, virtually all the politically articulate Bhikkhus were exercised over the happenings, irrespective of their alignments with one group or the other. The initiative for evoking popular support on the issue, however, was taken not by the Bhikkhus but by lay leaders belonging mainly to the ACBC, the BJB and the staunch Sinhalese Buddhist political groups like the Jatika Vimukti Peramuna (JVP) headed by K.M.P. Rajaratna.[28] In other words, the Bhikkhus joined the protest campaign; they did not initiate it.

Even during the latter phases of the Buddhist crisis in Vietnam, it was only one Bhikkhu—Rev. Narada Thero—who reported the situation in Vietnam to the Premier Senanayake in 1965. In many ways the pattern of Buddhist reponse to the Vietnam crisis in 1966 remained more or less the same; the ACBC approaching the government and persuading it to take the matter to the UN,[29] the Premier assuring the Congress leaders of his maximum co-operation and assurance to initiate action on behalf of the Buddhists in Vietnam.[30]

The only new Bhikkhu group which asked 25 Buddhist nations to move into the matter was the World Buddhist Sangha Organisation with its headquaters at Colombo. However, apart from issuing an appeal to the various Buddhist countries, the World Sangha Organisation remained ineffective.[31]

The World Sangha Organisation was formed after a meeting of Bhikkhus from various Buddhist countries in Colombo

---

27. *Ceylon Daily News*, 21 and 22 June 1963.
28. For the speeches of the JVP leaders see *Ceylon Observer*, 14 and 20 May 1963 and 2 July 1963. See Also *Ceylon Daily News*, 3 August 1963.
29. For the summary of the ACBC resolution during 1963 and 66 on Vietnam see *Ceylon Daily News*, 27 May and 29 August 1963 as well as 3 December 1966.
30. *Ceylon Daily News*, 25, 28 and 30 May 1966.
31. *Ceylon Daily News*, 30 May 1966.

from May 9-11, 1966. Comprised Bhikkhus from the Hinayana and Mahayana Schools, the Organisation was considered to be the first move towards unifying the Bhikkhus of Theravada and Mahayana schools.

Though several Bhikkhus in the Conference had expressed the hope that the World Sangha Council, apart from propagating Dhamma abroad and bringing to the minimum the inter-sectoral differences, would also advise the various States on Buddhist issues, it seemed that soon after its inception, its office-bearers were not keen in involving it in 'politics'. As such, apart from alerting the Buddhist nations, the only other action taken by its Secretary-General Rev. Pimbura Sorata was that of sending a message to Tri Quang, the militant leader of Vietnam (whose lieutenant, Thich Tam Chav had incidently represented South Vietnam in the May conference of the Council), stating that the Council was prepared to render any help to safeguard Buddhists in Vietnam.[32] Nothing more was done, however, on this score by the Sangha Council.

In view of the political leadership taking a prompt initiative on Vietnam the Bhikkhus' role remained ancillary to that of the lay leadership on the issue.

BHIKKHUS ON THE 'INDO-CEYLON' QUESTION : THE SETTING

The 'Indo-Ceylon Question' dealt, in the main, with the political status of those persons of Indian origin in Sri Lanka who had migrated from South India to the island during the British colonial period to work on tea plantations. Soon after attaining independence, the Government of Sri Lanka had enacted certain citizenship legislation under which, most of the Tamil estate labourers failed to qualify for Sri Lankan citizenship. As they did not apply for Indian citizenship, they fell into the category of 'stateless persons'.

By the beginning of the 1960s, the number of such 'stateless persons' had swelled approximately to one million—about one tenth of the total population of the island—with a large number of them being resident of the Central Province which was formerly the core of the erstwhile Kandyan Kingdom.

32. Ibid.

If colonial policies militated against the Sinhalese-Indian Tamil integration, historical legacies did not help it either. During the pre-European colonial period Sri Lanka was continuously invaded either from or via South India. In fact, before the advent of the Portuguese, it had been even ruled from time to time by some of the South Indian kings. Such historical memories had been nurtured by the Sinhalese Buddhist Chronicles prepared by the Bhikkhus. The Sinhalese-Tamil confrontation was envisaged in these Chronicles as a subversion of the national identity, religion and culture of the Sinhalese.

During the colonial period, the British policy of isolating the estate workers from the Sinhalese living in adjacent villages led to the retention of two parallel cultures—the Tamils, perched on the hill tops following South Indian customs and usages in their socio-cultural life and the Sinhalese following the traditional Buddhist culture. Besides, as the Tamil estate workers kept their socio-cultural economic links with the mainland across the Palk Straits, it was felt by the Sinhalese leadership that they were 'birds of passage', that their emotional, cultural and economic ties continued to be with the country of their origin and, as such, they had not made Sri Lanka their 'permanent' home. Consequently, the Sinhalese leadership argued (during the last phase of the colonial period) that, in view of their inability to make Sri Lanka their permanent home, they had continued to remain aliens who, by continuing to stay in the island, were depriving the indigenous Sinhalese population of employment avenues. Under the circumstances, only those who could prove their bonafides by fulfilling the criteria provided in the citizenship legislation were entitled to be treated as Ceylonese citizens. Others should go back to India.

The contention of the Indian leaders was that as these labourers had stayed there for about a century and had sweated and toiled for the prosperity of the island, they had a claim on the country of their adoption. If they applied for Indian citizenship, India was willing to accept them but if they did not, it implied that they wished to stay in the island and had all the intentions of making Sri Lanka their permanent home. As such, they ought to be Ceylonese nationals.

The details of the controversy has been the subject of many studies.[33] Notwithstanding the legal debate on the issue, the Governments of India and Sri Lanka were acutely aware of the necessity of a solution of the problem which would be mutually acceptable. It was necesasry for India to find a solution because of its 'sentimental' interests in the political future of these persons who emigrated from India. A solution was also necessary for the leaders of Sri Lanka as these labourers were residents on the island. The uncertainties of the political future had led to a certain patterning in the political behaviour of those who had already achieved citizenship.

It was pointed out that the tendency of the estate labourers to vote en bloc in the general elections reflected their uncertainty about their own political future, particularly in the context of the unsolved issue of the political status of the rest. The 'stateless' question was, thus, as much a question of the domestic politics of Sri Lanka as of its foreign policy. Further, the issue became an irritant in the bilateral relationship of the countries which their respective leaderships wanted to remove as early as possible.

After several futile efforts, it was only in October 1964 that the Prime Ministers of both the countries were able to come to an agreement. Under the agreement signed by the Indian Premier, Sri Lal Bahadur Shastri and the Sri Lanka Premier, Sirimavo R.D. Bandaranaike, a numerical formula was devised under which out of a total number of about 9,75,000 'stateless' persons, 5,25,000 were to be granted Indian citizenship, 300,000 were to be granted the citizenship of Sri Lanka in the ratio of 7:4 and the future of the residents was to be decided later on. In January 1974, the Premiers of both India and Sri Lanka decided to halve the residue to settle finally the numerical allocation.

As has been mentioned already, the Kandyan province which had the largest concentration of the 'Indian Tamils' had also been the headquarters of Malwatta and Asgiri chapters.

---

33. E.g, see S.U. Kodikara, *Indo-Ceylon Relations Since Independence* (Colombo, 1965), and Urmila Phadnis" "The Indo-Ceylonese Pact and the Stateless Persons in Ceylon', *India Quarterly*, Vol. 23, no. 4, October-December 1967, pp. 362-407,

While the Bhikkhus did not raise the issue of 'Indian Tamils' as such during the first 15 years of the island's independence, there is no doubt that perceiving themselves as the torch-bearers of the Sinhalese culture and language, they found irksome the presence of the 'Indian Tamils' in the Central Province and treated them and with a certain degree of distrust.

The question of the political future of the Indian Tamils, however, came on the agenda of the Bhikkhus only after the 1964 agreement. This was understandable. As long as the dispute was in its controversial stage, the Bhikkhus saw no reason to intervene as the Government's attitude did not vary with their own. Even after the Sirimavo-Shastri Pact, the Bhikkhus backed the Government.

Soon after the signing of the agreement, in a meeting orga-nised by the Samastha Lanka Bhikkhu Mandalaya, the Prime Minister was congratulated for finding the solution of the problem. The main speakers in this meeting were the Vice-Chancellors of the Vidyodaya and Vidyalankara Universities as well as some of its Bhikkhu faculty members separately.[34] The Maha Nayakas of Malwatta and Asgiri also issued a joint statement which was along the same lines.

Hailing Prime Minister Sirimavo Bandaranaike's 'bold step' in solving the problem of the persons of Indian origin in Ceylon, the Maha Nayakas maintained : "Action to have the Indians in Ceylon sent away should have been taken long ago. If action had been taken to solve this issue earlier, the prob-lem would not have been aggravated to what it is today." "At a time" continued the statement, "when the problem of employment, housing and other needs of the indigenous popu-lation had reached a critical stage, the action taken to solve the Indian issue was a most timely one."[35]

In a subsequent meeting with the SLFP leader, Felix R. Dias Bandaranaike and N.Q. Dias, the Maha Nayaka of Malwatta chapter, Ven Amunugama Rajaguru Sri Vipassi endorsed the SLFP stand on the Indo-Ceylon question and stated that there were many areas in the hill country where the Sinhalese did

34. *Ceylon Daily News,* 6 November 1964.
35. Ibid., 12 November 1964.

not have an inch of land. Land bought cheap by the British was now changing hands and was being transferred to the Tamilians.[36]

Whatever be the substance of the Maha Nayakas' allegations, it did project the image of the Tamils as interlopers in the Sinhalese-dominated Kandyan province.

As has been mentioned elsewhere, unlike the earlier Maha Nayakas, Amunugama Sri Vipassi (who was elevated from Anu Nayakaship to Maha Nayakaship in 1965) had actively and openly campaigned in the elections of 1965 against proposals of the ruling SLFP-LSSP for free toddy tapping and governmental control over the biggest newspaper monopoly—the Lake House. Besides, even before 1965, the Bhikkhu had been fairly active alongwith Palipane Chandananda Thero of Malwatta chapter, on the question of legislation regarding an increasing governmental control over the Buddhist temporalities. He was, thus, one of those few Bhikkhus in the Kandyan province who had been articulate on certain political issues.

It was, therefore, not surprising that when the UNP Premier Dudley Senanayake decided to enact legislation to put into effect the Sirimavo-Shastri Pact, the SLFP which had certain differences with the ruling coalition over some of the clauses of the Indo-Ceylon (Implementation) Bill,[37] decided to mobilise the support of the Kandyan clergy. Apart from the SLFP, certain Sinhalese chauvinist groups, prominent among which was Bhasa Peramuna (Language Front) under the leadership of R.G. Senanayake, also made a move to mobilise the Bhikkhus and had meetings with them for the purpose.[38]

Soon after the conclusion of Sirimavo-Shastri Pact, the Prime Minister, Mrs. Bandaranaike, had announced that the new citizens under the 1964 Pact would be placed on a separate electoral register. This announcement was viewed by the Indian Prime Minister with dismay who felt that such a separate electoral register miligated against the spirit of the agree-

36. Ibid., 16 July 1965.
37. The SLFP-UNP differences over the Bill have been discussed in some detail in Phadnis, n. 33, pp. 393-402.
38. *Ceylon Daily Mirror*, 6 April 1967.

ment as it gave the newly franchised stateless Tamils the status of a second class citizens.

The matter, however, was not pursued as elections had intervened. The Indo-Ceylon (Implementation) Bill made no mention of the separate electoral register. The incorporation of a clause stipulating it within the Act became an insistent demand of the Bhasha Peramuna as well as that of most of the Bhikkhus.

Beside this, the Bill did not correlate the earlier stipulated ratio 7:4 with the repatriation of the Indian citizens but with the grant of citizenship of both the countries. The opposition members of the SLFP, along with the Bhasha Peramuna, however, insisted that the tie-up of 7:4 was between the grant of Ceylonese citizenship and repatriation to India. In other words, the grant of Ceylon's citizenship was to be proportionate, not with the number of persons registered as Indian citizens, but with the number of Indian citizens repatriated.

On both these matters, the Maha Nayaka of Malwatta took a firm stand during the debate on the Bill. He maintained that (a) the stateless Tamils enfranchised as Ceylon citizens should be put on a separate register till they had integrated themselves with the Slnhalese, and (b) for every 12 persons given Ceylonese citizenship 21 should be repatriated to India.[39]

During March-July 1967, when the debate on the Bill was on, the Maha Nayaka issued several statements and made many speeches.[40] He also demanded that the Standing Committee B of the Parliament, which was appointed to hear the people's petitions and received memoranda to appraise popular opinion on the question, should come to Kandy to take his evidence. The Committee, however, decided that, as of tradition such committees had operated within the precincts of the Parliament, and could not go outside the Parliament to hear the views of anyone. Such a declaration of its

---

39. See for instance the various memoranda presented by the Maha Nayaka to the Standing Committee B, dated May 6, 1967 (cyclostyled), summary given in *Sun*, 12 May 1967.

40. E.g., Maha Nayaka's letter to the Senate, *Sun*, 17 June 1967 and his letters to the Prime Minister, *Ceylon Daily News*, 27 May 1967. Also see his press statement, ibid., 18 May 1967.

Chairman, who was a Muslim, met with a severe indictment from the Maha Nayaka who had already sent detailed comments on the Bill to the Committee.[41] In some of his speeches the Maha Nayaka also alleged that in the formulation of the Bill, the UNP Premier seemed to be guided by his Tamil partners in the Coalition—the Federal Party and the Ceylon Workers' Congress.

In a letter to the Maha Nayaka, Prime Minister Senanayake sought to clarify some of the issues raised by him and assured him that ample safeguards would be incorporated for a just and fair treatment of the Sinhalese in the Kandyan Province.[42] Similar assurances were given to certain other prominent Bhikkhus also who had raised a similar doubt regarding the future of the Kandyan peasantry (in the event of the enactment of the Bill) in political and economic spheres.[43]

Soon after the enactment of the Bill the Maha Nayaka expressed his apprehensions in an interview with a correspondent of *Sun*. "Mark my words", said the Maha Nayaka, "ten years from now we will have a Tamil kingdom over the territory of the Kandyans......This legislation is a crime against the Sinhala people. My present sorrow is that the helpless Kandyans are for the second time being sold over the country."[44]

The Maha Nayaka's reference to the 'second time' referred to the advent of the British and their policies of bringing in the indentured Tamil labour in the midst of the Kandyan peasantry. Concluding his statement, the Maha Nayaka maintained: "Our own people helped the British in 1815 in wiping out the Sinhala Kingdom. You might ask yourself who is doing what against whom in helping the Indians now to dominate our country."[45]

However, hardly had the ink dried on the Indo-Ceylon (Implementation) Act, that the Maha Nayaka issued another state-

41. For the text of the Maha Nayaka see *Sun*, 12 May 1967.
42. *Ceylon Daily News*, 14 May 1967.
43. E.g., Press statement of Madihe Pannaseeha Thero, *Ceylon Daily News*, 29 May 1967 and correspondence between Ven. Wellatota Pannadassi and the Premier, *Sun*, 12 and 30 May 1967.
44. *Sun*, 6 June 1967.
45. Ibid.

ment which urged the people "to assist in the implementation
of the Indo-Ceylon Bill on the basis of the provisions therein
and the assurances given by the Prime Minister".

Explaining the apparent change in his stand, the Maha
Nayaka maintained that as the Bill had become law, any
attempt to obstruct its implementation might "cause unneces-
sary trouble which would not be beneficial to the people of
the country". Secondly, he felt that many 'good provisions' in
the Bill which, if enacted properly with due regard to the
interests of the Sinhalese people in the Kandyan areas, might
benefit them. In the light of the reiterated assurances of the
Premier in this respect, it was "our duty to assist him and the
government to achieve his objectives without causing unneces-
sary disruption".[46] And here the matter rested so far as the
issue of the stateless persons *vis-a-vis* the Maha Nayaka was
concerned.

CONCLUSION

The review of the responses of Bhikkhus on some of the
select foreign policy issues make it obvious that unlike on
Sasana reform or the language, the Bhikkhus did not go out
of their way to pressurise the Government. Nor did they form
any special Bhikkhu organisation (except in one case) to
espouse their viewpoint. Foreign policy, in their overall perspective of political issues, remained peripheral and was
more than often, in response to the initiative of lay organisations, both political as well as non-political. Thus, on the
Vietnam issue, it was under the auspices of the ACBC that the
Bhikkhus were activised. The Bhikkhus' role in foreign policy
was ancillary to that of the lay groups and even in cases like
the Indo-Ceylon Question, notwithstanding the excepted
statements of Bhikkhus like the Maha Nayaka of Malwatta,
one could clearly discern the close resemblances which such
statements had with those of R.G. Senanayake's Bhasa Peramuna as well as of the SLFP, on the Indo-Ceylon Bill of
1967.

46. For the text of the statement see *Ceylon Daily News*, 30 June
    1967.

So far as political parties and groups were concerned, they did not show much interest in mobilising the Bhikkhus on foreign policy questions. Thus, the issue of Tibet came up when SWRD Bandaranaike's 'Middle path' of non-alignment was politically popular and when the country had several other matters to be excited about. Moreover, the stand of Bhikkhus like Malewana Gnanissara on the issue was known to be partisan to make an appeal.

On Vietnam, on the other hand, there was a national consensus and both the SLFP and the UNP had a bipartisan approach. As such, there was no need for either party to woo the Bhikkhus; the utterances of the Bhikkhus thus merely contributed to the national consensus.

The Indo-Ceylon (Implementation) Bill, however, fell in a different category. The SLFP and the UNP had differences on certain major points, and in view of the emotional susceptibilities of the Kandyans on the question, the support of the clergy could be sought.

However, what needs to be noted in this context is the fact that the dispute between the UNP and the SLFP on the 'Indo-Ceylon' problem was not on the numerical formula but on the modalities of its implementation. It was not surprising, therefore, that most of the Bhikkhus did not feel called upon to become unduly agitated.

The exception to this was, of course, the Maha Nayaka of Malwatta whose utterances were at times highly critical of the UNP Government on certain aspects of the Bill. This was particularly significant in view of his overt support to the UNP during the 1965 elections. It can be explained in the context of his ambitions, articulate and fairly politicised personality as a Bhikkhu (a) the boost to such traits after 1965, (b) his anger at the Standing Committee's refusal to come to Kandy to take his evidence, and (c) his Maha Nayakaship itself—a position which he had acquired only a few months ago.

The Maha Nayaka's role on the problem thus could be viewed as that of a religious patriarch who, maintaining earlier traditions, felt responsible for the well-being of the Kandyan-Sinhalese Buddhists. As such, the Maha Nayaka felt a special sense of responsibility towards the interests of the indigenous population and deemed it necessary to excercise his influence to the utmost. However, after the opposition had lost the parliamentary battle on the issue, the Maha Nayaka thought it prudent to put his weight behind the Government's decision and let the matter be set at rest.

The foreign policy issues thus indicated once again that the participation of Bhikkhus on political questions had become ancillary to that of the parties. To a considerable extent, politics had resulted in the neutralisation of their power potential and, in the process, had led to a gradual diminution to the political ascendancy of the Bhikkhus which had made a significant beginning in the elections of 1956.

Chapter IX

CONCLUSION

An analysis of the patterns of interaction between the professional religious elites and the present-day political system
in Sri Lanka reveals a process of mutual accommodation to
contemporaneous pressures and pulls which have ensured a
historical continuum. The identification of the critical phases
of this process and of the elements which made such an
accommodation possible leads to an understanding of the
present-day correlation between the two distinct, but not
divergent, social phenomena, namely, the religious and political.
This also provides an insight into the responsive relationship
between the two and the likely nature of their interaction in
the future.

In its historical perspective, thus, Buddhism represents
the simultaneous and cumulative processes of adaptation,
confrontation and conciliation between worldly and other-
worldly aspects. For instance, the religious ideals of Buddhism
(as provided in the canonical texts), incorporated the rituals
of magical animism and certain systemic features of Hinduism.
Such a religious syncretism of Sinhalese Buddhism, as it
emerged over centuries was as much a response to the
'plebeian' social needs as a convergence to the politico-economic systems of the old days.

The impulses for religious syncretism seem to be an universal
phenomenon in the context of the world religions of traditional societies. This appears to be so whether it be Hindu,
Buddhist, Islamic or Catholic societies, which, through this syn-
cretic process, absorbed the socially relevant features of various

other religious ideologies and movements experienced by these societies from time to time.

Notwithstanding this similarity of the historical processes, what needs to be underlined is the fact that though deriving their ideological moorings from the respective founders of world religions as well as their subsequent interpreters, the religious systems in these societies evolved certain characteristics distinct from each other.

The explanation for this is not far to seek whether it be a Buddhist, Hindu, Islamic or Christian system; the religious system of a particular society is a facet of its total culture which permeates other institutions as much as it is affected by them. Thus, in contrast with other Theravadin countries like Burma and Thailand, the Buddhist Sangha in Sri Lanka is marked by caste divisions and kinship ties. Such a canonical feature of Sinhalese Buddhism has been a reflection of its socio-political order which, notwithstanding its dominant Buddhist ethos, was caste-ridden. On the other hand, the Sinhalese-Buddhist Sangha, extolling in its pure Theravadin character, has not favoured the occasional disrobing and enrobing—a phenomenon very common in Burma.

Coupled with such structural variations, one also finds a sharp emphasis on the religious-cultural legacies within a specific territory. Thus, notwithstanding the Theravadin dimension of Sri Lankan, Burmese or Thai societies, their distinctive national identity was maintained. This 'indigenisation' has been a feature as much of Buddhist societies as of Hindu, Islamic or Christian. Thus, in a discussion of religion and politics of various traditional societies, one needs to underline their distinctiveness as much as their common traits.

To illustrate further, unlike the Buddhist Sangha which formed an organic part of Buddhism itself (as is evident in the invocation of the triple gems)[1], or the Christian Church, which had become a distinct entity long before its close associations with the political authority of the Roman Empire, the idea of an exclusive religious organisation as such

---

1. Every Buddhist laity had to invoke the triple gems—the three sacred symbols—which were: 'I take refuge in Buddha; I take refuge in the Dhamma (Doctrine); I take refuge in the Sangha.'

was absent in Islam. It was the sacred law—the 'Shariah'—
which was the corpus of the Prophet's commands and
prohibitions were deduced from the sacred Kuran and
the Sunnah. However, there needed to be a group of learned
men, the Ulema, who devoted their time and energy in the
understanding as well as in interpreting the sacred law.

Though they did not develop an autonomous ecclesiastical
structure comparable to the Buddhist Sangha or the Catholic
Church, the Ulema did acquire some of the characteristics of
a clerical class as legal interpreters and judges of the Muslim
sacred law and as educationists. In Hinduism, Brahmins
enjoyed a similar status but within a secular institution—the
caste system which tended to be the cornerstone of the traditional Hindu social order.

In sum, whatever be the sources, in all the religions a
dominant status group emerged in their respective religious
systems which was the harbinger and interpreter of religious
norms and values. In due course, these professional religious
elite could draw upon their social power, religious precepts
and/or traditional sanctions as the social activists.

The role performance of these elites necessitated the support
of the State authority. On the other hand, the political elites
needed their backing for the legitimization of their authority,
for the maintenance of order and stability in the country. It is
not surprising thus to find a wide range of Hindu, Buddhist,
Muslim and Catholic kingdoms sharing a basic notion of
the sacred nature of the Government. The ruler was either
the God on earth or his agent.

Such a conceptualisation of political authority having certain
attributes of divinity was provided primarily by the professional religious elites. They legitimised the kingship and the
kingship in turn provided them with the necessary material
wherewithal. The pattern of interaction between the religious
and political authorities thus was characterised by mutuality of
interest and a role complementary to each other.[2] When new

2. The comments of Ivan Vallier on the pattern of relationship between the Catholic Church and the State in Latin America highlights
   these similarities notwithstanding the late advent of Catholicism
   in South America. According to him: "The Church entered Latin
   America under the protection and sponsorship of the Spanish

religious groups emerged and various kingdoms came into conflict, there were disruptions, but behind such disruptions the basic impulses for such inter-dependence of the religious and political systems remained more or less unchanged. And the religious elites provided a 'normative consensus'[3] on the individual's relationship with the State and the State's relationship with the society. In the process, the religious elites performed a significant integrative function by legitimising the social and political base of the kingship.

One major factor which became functional at one time and dys-functional in this interaction at another, was that of 'monastic landlordism'; the endowments given to the clerical order or a segment of it by the royalty. There were times when some of the 'monastic landlords' provided support for the perpetuation of a particular political order favourable to them but others discerned a threat to their power and survival in the continuance of a particular ruler and some of his policies. They, therefore, tried to find ways and means of combating it. European history of the 16th-18th century as well as that of South and South-East Asia during the pre-colonial and colonial periods is replete with such incidents.

COLONIALISM, NATIONALISM AND CLERICAL GROUPS

Stretching over 350 years, Western colonalism in Asia and elsewhere triggered a spurt of nationalist movements.

Crown, becoming one of the main instruments of conquest and a permanent fixture of the entire system of social control. The civil rulers were held responsible for the welfare of the Church and for the Christianization of the indigenous peoples. In turn, the secular rulers expected the Church to support the Crown's policies and to accept certain decisions regarding episcopal appointments, financial arrangements, and the establishment of ecclesiastical jurisdiction. The symbiotic patterns that evolved led, in the era of independence revolts, to a transference of the 'civil rulers' rights over the Church to the leaders of the new republics". Ivan Vallier, *Catholicism, Social Control, and Modernisation in Latin America*, (New Jersey, 1970), pp 33-34.

3. E.g. M.S. Agwani, 'Religion and Politics in Egypt', *International Studies*, Vol. 13, no. 3, July-September 1974, p. 388.

Though several economic, social and political factors accounted for the origin and growth of such movements, there is no doubt that religious symbols and groups also played a noteworthy role in this process. It is not without significance that it was in religious revivalism that the beginnings of nationalist movements can be found. Clerical groups also provided leadership. Thus, if the Ulema played an important role in the nationalist struggle against imperialism in countries like Indonesia, Algeria and Egypt, the Buddhist clergy gave an impetus to the Buddhist renaissance and nationalist sentiments in Burma and Sri Lanka.

The contribution of the clerical leadership to the nationalist movement cannot be quantified in view of the multi-dimensional causes of nationalism in these countries as well as the divergence in the organisation and orientations of the clerical leaders. This is evident from a comparison of the activities of the clergy in Sri Lanka in the 19th century and Burma in the early 20th century.

In Sri Lanka, the Bhikkhus worked in close collaboration with the lay leadership and did not spell out wide encompassing socio-political roles for the Bhikkhus as the fiery and charismatic Bhikkhu of Burma, U Ottuma did in 1923.[4] However, what is common in the case of both was their reaction to the attitude of the Christian missionaries and their strong feeling that colonial policies—secular as well as religious—were subverting their status and power in educational and religio-cultural spheres.

As the symbols of their respective country's cultural traditions, it was easy for them to rally mass support and evoke nationalist sentiments. The first wave of nationalist

4. In a speech, Ottuma advised the Sangha not to rest content with its role as preachers and as competent interpreters of Buddhism. He exhorted them to read the history of various Burmese dynasties as well as to study the Indian Penal Code and British administration so that the Sangha could explain the implications of such colonial measures to the laity. Not only this, he asked the Sangha to critically examine the various other colonial legislations to enable them to enlighten the laity regarding the oppressive economic implications of such colonial measures. For details see Fred R. Von der Mehden, *Religion and Nationalism in Southeast Asia* (London, 1968), pp. 213-14.

resurgence in Burma was, for instance, on the issue of
Europeans walking with sandals in the Buddhist pagodas.
In Sri Lanka, the religious reformation and revivalism made
its beginning in the wake of the religious controversies
between the Bhikkhus and Christian priests regarding the supremacy of one religion over the other. In India, on the other
hand, while the precursors of social reforms were the lay
leaders, the impetus for its initiation was the same.

However, while the activism of clerical groups had its
ebbs and flows in the nationalist movement, there is no
doubt that their participation fostered the development of a
group identity, binding people together in opposition to
certain policies of the colonial rulers. Not only this,
there were cases where religion provided legitimation
for resistance to the foreign rule. Thus, the Islamic tradition
favouring alongside obedience to the Muslim rulers, whatever
his moral and administrative failings were, also stipulated
the Ulema's formal declaration of a Holy war (*Jehad*) against
an 'infidel'. The 'foreignness' of the colonial ruler thus proved
to be a powerful legitimation of national revolt.[5]

This legitimation appeared in a slightly different form in
the nationalist resurgence of the Theravada Buddhist countries like Burma and Sri Lanka where it was stipulated that
an 'alien' was incapable of propagating Buddhism which had
had State patronage before the advent of the European
rulers. The resuscitation of the 'national' religion necessitated
the expulsion of the foreign rulers.

Though this study focusses on the organisation and role of
professional religious groups in the political processes it may
also be mentioned that while Islam provided the focal point
of the national identity and State consciousness of Pakistan[6]

5. Donald Eugene Smith, ed., *Religion, Politics and Social Change in
   the Third World—A Source Book* (London, 1971), p. 96.
6. However, in the case of Islam, the concept of nationalism connoting the loyalty of the individual as highest to the nation created
   other problems in view of the traditional concept of Ummaah,
   (Islamic community ruled by Caliph) which was trans-national in
   character. The critical response of the Ulema of Deoband school
   in India about the creation of Pakistan as a separate nation was,
   for instance, patly due to this reason.

it tended to be one of the triple 'gems' of Sukarno's ideological creed, the other two being nationalism and socialism. As against this was the Turkish experience leading to the abolition of the Caliphate and later of the Shariah which was a revolt as much against the content of the traditional law as of an attempt to affirm the supremacy of the State authority over the religious hierarchy. A Similar variation of experiences can be witnessed in the case of Latin American countries. If, for instance, in Chile, the Catholic Church and State had a peaceful but separate co-existence, in Mexico, the national revolution was characterised by militant anti-clericalism.

In sum, the interaction of religious groups and political leadership has taken diverse forms from close co-operation to sharp confrontation reflecting the divergence in the patterns of interaction between the social, economic and political systems, as much as the nature, tenor and the tenure of colonial rule. Notwithstanding such diversities, it is necessary to note the role which religion, religious symbols and professional religious elites played in mass mobilisation and the rousing of nationalist awareness in the country during the colonial period.

PROFESSIONAL RELIGIOUS ELITES IN THE POST-COLONIAL ERA

As in the pre-colonial period, a segment of professional religious elites have continued to play a noteworthy role in the processes of mass mobilisation and nationalist awareness in many states during the post-colonial era. The role of Bhikkhus in Sri Lanka and Burma in electoral politics and that of a segment of the Ulema in the Pakistani elections of 1965 illustrate this. It might be underlined again that the role of secular agencies like parties, interest groups, government, as well as ideologies like Marxism and Nationalism have been, at times, more significant agents towards the processes of democratisation and social change. The religious factor, however, (as rightly pointed out by Donald Smith) is of special significance in view of the fact that rooted in the traditional past, its influence on a segment of the population is still apparent, affecting at times its political behaviour to some extent.

That religious elites have played a diverse and complex role in the political processes of many countries is a point well emphasised. However, case studies on the mode and tenor of their behaviour and their impact on electoral politics as well as in the processes of the formulation of public policies in the post-independent polities of the third world countries, are far and few. Similarly, except for a few studies on the Catholic Church in Latin American countries,[7] the impact of secular forces on the organisation and orientation of the clergy also needs a deeper probe and more empirical studies.

Many questions suggest themselves in this context. If electoral politics evoke the interest of the clergy, why is it so? What sort of issues encourage it to assume the role of interest groups ? What have been the religious elite's strategies and styles in this context? In what ways does such participation itself affect their organisation and role-perception ? What are the other agencies—religious and secular, national and international—which impel them to introduce changes within the religious system or maintain the status quo.

Such questions, however, need to be qualified in one respect. To view any religious system—be it Christianity or Islam or Buddhism—as monolithic either ideologically or structurally—is a travesty of facts as they are already divided and subdivided into various divisions and sects. Organisationally even if the Catholic Church appears to be a monolith, in effect it is not so as is evident in the Latin American countries.

In terms of its orientations, the clergy has been differentiated as fundamentalist, traditionalist and modernist. Similarly, as regards its attitude to politics, the clergy has tended to be political, a-political or anti-political, raising at times the basic issue of the relevance of politics to religion. This manifested itself in the controversy on the word 'politics' in 1946 in Sri Lanka. However, the electoral processes in the island also indicate the induction into politics of a number of a-political Bhikkhus. This was particularly so in the Sixties as was evident from the larger number of Bhikkhus participating in elections and responding to public issues.

7. See for instance Vallier, n. 2.

Such an increasing political socialisation of the Bhikkhus has been due to several factors. The changing educational system, the influence of the politically active Bhikkhus on the others, the efforts of the political leadership to draw them in its fold and harness their socio-religious resources for political support, have been some of the major factors. Besides, the pluralist character of the societies and the policies of a ruling elite belonging to a minority religion has also tended to be a catalyst in the political socialisation of the religious elites. This is evident from the internal revolt in South Vietnam in the Sixties, in which the Bhikkhus (representing the hopes and aspirations of the Buddhists having a relative sense of deprivation as a majority community) played a significant role.

In Sri Lanka, too, the 'national revolution' of 1956 was born out of a similar sense of grievance on the part of the majority community. However, unlike Vietnam, the politics of Sri Lanka treading the path of parliamentary democracy, succeeded in assuaging this feeling of the majority community through legitimised political process. The assertion of the 'majority status' of the dominant community led to the communalisation of the political processes for a while. This lead to the minority racial and religious communities—the Tamils, the Hindus and the Christians (particularly the Catholics)—to viewing such developments as an infringement of their cultural autonomy and a subversion of their linguistic-educational rights.

With the past legacies of Sinhalese-Tamil confrontation and the Tamil concentration in the two provinces adjacent to India's Tamil Nadu, the relationship between the two communities continues to be strained. On the other hand, it appears that the Catholics (comprising a lion's share of its Christian community of 8.4%) have after initial opposition to the Government policies of taking over the schools (a large number of which were earlier run by the missionaries), not only come to terms with the aspirations of the majority community but have made overt efforts to present an indigenous version of Catholicism in Sri Lanka.

The stand of some of the missionaries on the issue of Poya days being made the weekly holiday instead of Christian Sunday, has been significant; it underlined the fact that even in observing the Sabbath, the religious sensitivity of the majority community ought to hold precedence. Further, Sabbath was made for men and not men for Sabbath. As such, it was necessary that Christians should be able to respond to the changing mores of the social structure and adjust themselves accordingly.[8]

As against this is the case in India where, while the Nehru Government succeeded in bringing about certain far-reaching measures in Hindu laws pertaining to inheritance, succession and marriage, it preferred to leave the Muslim law untouched lest it antagonise the largest minority community of the country and thereby corrode one of the support bases of the Congress. As such, one discerns an interesting situation. The 'theocratic' State of Pakistan has succeeded in bringing about much more radical changes in Islamic laws than secular India.

A proposition may be put forward here: in countries operating within the parliamentary democratic framework, the interaction between the religious and political system has been, much more consensual and conservative than in other regimes— revolutionary, military or para-military, at least in the initial phase of such political change.

Thus, in Sri Lanka, notwithstanding the initial efforts on the part of the State to initiate structural changes in the Sangha, the SLFP beat a hasty retreat when it was confronted with the concerted opposition of a large number of Bhikkhus. Further, in its latest land reform legislation it has preferred to leave ambivalent the monastic and temple land issue. In Burma, on the other hand, U Nu, the leader of Anti-Fascist People's Freedom League, had a special rapport with the Sangha and finally promulgated Buddhism as the State religion in 1961 (which was one of the major planks of the party manifesto in the 1960 elections).

Under the military regime of the Ne Win since 1962, the earlier constitution was prorogued and along with it went the special position accorded to Buddhism therein. "More than that, the military moved to diminish the influence of the

---

8 Fred R. Von der Mehden, 'Secularisation of Buddhist Polities : Burma and Thailand', in Donald Eugene Smith, ed., *Religion and Political Modernisation* (London, 1974), p. 61.

Sangha, which was the last legal organised group that could offer opposition to the new regime. In the succeeding twelve years there have been numerous clashes between military men and the Sangha and the Ne Win regime has continued its secular policies."[9]

Similar trends can be seen in Islamic countries like Algeria, Turkey, Pakistan and Egypt. Soon after the revolution of 1952, President Nasser curbed the power of the Muslim Brotherhood (which was a broadbased religio-political organisation of a fundamentalist nature), when it seemed to be one of the organised groups having the potential to challenge military authority. The religious endowment system was nationalised, the Shariah courts abolished and the administration of Al Azhar University (the most esteemed mosque university of the country) was secularised to a great extent.[10]

In Pakistan, on the other hand, the constitution-making process in the 50s underlined the role of the Ulema who propagated the enthronement of the traditional Islamic law and formulation of an exhaustive legal code drawing its inspiration from the Shariat. The Constitution of 1956, which was primarily oriented to the modernist Islamic view (with its emphasis on the universal ethical values of Islam, i.e., equality, social justice, democracy etc.) did forbid the enactment of laws repugnant to the Shariat. During this period of parliamentary democracy, though certain far-reaching changes were recommened, they were kept in abeyance and it was under the military regime of Ayub Khan that the Family Laws Ordinance of 1961 was promulgated introducing far-reaching changes.

The Latin American countries present a highly diversified and complex pattern of interaction. Mexico is an instance of strong anti-clerical traditions but in Chile there has been a peaceful co-existence between Church and State. In Peru, on the

9. Unfortunately full-fledged studies on the political behaviour of the Church in Sri Lanka have yet to be undertaken. I have done an elementary exercise in this context in 'Political Profile of a Religious minority in Ceylon : Negombo—A case study" in M.S. Rajan, ed., *Studies in Politics, National and International* (Delhi, 1971), pp. 270-97.

10. For details see Daniel Crecelius, 'The Course of Secularisation in Modern Egypt', in Smith, n. 8, pp. 85-90.

other hand, the military regime has the support of the Catholic
Church and has introduced several radical socio-economic
reforms. This indicates that in countries where the changed
political order has regarded the clerical group as a threat to
its political power, systematic action has been taken to undermine the influence of this organised interest group. However,
when these groups coalesce with the governing elite, they
become part of the governing mechanism and, more than often,
are ancillary to it.

It should also be noted that alongside the diminution of
power of a clerical group, the governing lay elites utilise religious
symbols as well as religious groups (as and when possible) to
legitimise their own ideology and actions: the utilisation of the
services of the Ulema for the propagation of family planning by
President Ayub; the solicitation of formal legal opinion from
the Ulema on the entire range of its government's activities
like land reforms, birth control, nationalisation, and scientific
research in Egypt indicates the efforts on the part of Nasser to
give formal religious sanctions to his secular policies. However,
the point to underscore in Egypt is that it is the 'regime, not
the ulema, that inevitably introduces Islam into the political
debate".[11] Nasser's concept of 'Socialist Islam' on the basis of
reinterpreted Islamic principles, for instance, is another device
to use religious ideologies and symbols for the benefit of a
military regime.

Referring to the role of religion as legitimiser of traditional
politics, Donald Smith wrote thus in 1971: "Reilgion, that
traditional legitimiser of social, economic and political structures, once again presented itself as a qualified candidate for
the job. The choice was between secular modernization of
society and religious legitimation of polity". This stand[12]
however, can be questioned. In effect, the political leadership
has not only oscillated between two alternatives but more than
often has tended to use simultaneously secular as well as
religious symbols and forces.

11. Ibid., p. 90.
12. Smith, n. 5, p. 3. This stand, however, is modified by Smith in his
    subsequent edited study, n. 8, pp. 8-9.

The clash between the two, as and when it has arisen, has been due to the religious groups emerging as contenders for political power. On the other hand, instances are not wanting when the political leadership has succeeded in using the support base of these groups to legitimise and aggregate its own power. Meanwhile, it has also pursued policies and adopted measures which have strengthened the processes of secularisation. Smith's subsequent characterization of this stage as political process of secularisation, i.e., the relative "decline in political salience and influence of religious leaders, religious interest groups, religious political parties, and religious issues" as well as a gradual "weakening of religious identity and ideology of political actors as a consequence of participation in political process"[13] is an appropriate description of this phenomenon.

THE PROFESSIONAL RELIGIOUS ELITES AS
INTEREST GROUPS : SOME PROPOSITIONS

How does the clergy perceive its roles ? The answer to this obviously depends upon its divergent attitude and orientation towards society and polity. In the case of Sri Lanka, for instance, we find that Bhikkhus and Bhikkhu organisations like the Kandy Seminary are purely religious, engaged in disseminating the tenets of Buddhism in Sri Lanka and abroad. On the other hand, we have seen the proliferation of Bhikkhu organisations functioning as religio–political interest groups and influencing the public policies in different degrees.

In this context it is necessary to recapitulate certain propositions raised regarding Bhikkhu pressure groups and the decision-making processes on pages 207-208 and elucidated in Chapters VI-VIII. Unfortunately, detailed case studies on the political behaviour of the professional religious elites as pressure groups are meagre for comparative purposes. As such, this study can merely appraise these propositions, which will need to be tested further through other case studies.

To begin with, it has been suggested that in a democratic framework the greater the emphasis on the part of the State on welfare services, the greater is the scope for the proliferation of

13. Smith, n. 8, p. 8.

social groups emerging as interest groups. This is amply vali-
dated by political activities of increasing the number of
Bhikkhus and the proliferation of their groups.

It is also argued that the more differentiated the governmental structures are, the greater are the opportunities for
success of such groups through their patron-client relationship with the leadership at various levels and in different
departments. Our data, however, necessitates a slight modifica-
tion in this proposition. No doubt the greater the differentiation in the political structure the larger are the 'access' poinis
for the Bhikkhu interest groups to influence the decision-
making process. However, in view of the nature of the party
system of Sri Lanka, such 'access' points being open to all the
Bhikkhus, their chances of success depend upon the 'issue'. If
the majority of the politically oriented Bhikkhus are in unison
on a particular issue then the chances of their success are in any
case high. But if the Bhikkhu organisations have divergent
and partisan views on a particular issue, the multiplication of
'access' points may in effect lead them to a situation where the
extent of their influence may get virtually neutralised.

This, in fact, brings us to our next proposition namely, that
the more favourable the contextual factors (for example
political parties, public opinion, and other interest groups). the
brighter are the chances for the effectivity of the tactics adopted
by the Bhikkhu organisations to influence the course of the
decision-making process on a public issue in their favour as
pressure groups.

Structurally, the Bhikkhu pressure groups fall in the category
of 'non-associational interest groups' with the potentiality of a
fairly high standard of organisation which is corporate and at
the same time highly autonomous and personalised. As regards
the political capabilities of such groups, they seem to be often
greater than that of the religious hierarchical structure and the
religious patriarch therein. In fact, they have not only existed
parallel to the traditional religious hierarchy but often have
cut across Nikaya, sectoral and regional differences.

The strategies and tactics of these groups are an amalgam
of the traditional and the modern in electoral politics as well as
the decision-making processes, stretching in techniques from
behind-the-door or open 'advice' to mass action such as

demonstrations, sit-in, threats of fasts and strikes. Also, apart from informal, face-to-face contacts with the elites and masses, the Bhikkhus have harnessed the modern public media for espousing their viewpoint on a particular issue. News-sheets and pamphlets are printed, statements are issued and public meetings are organised and addressed by them.

The implications of such participation in electoral politics as well as in debates on public policies, as indicated earlier, has tended to be a double-edged weapon. No doubt some of the Bhikkhus may emerge as 'political influentials' for a while but this position itself has the risk of corroding the very basis of their social resources as religious elites in view of their public image turning from a neutral to a partisan one.

PROFESSIONAL BUDDHIST ELITES IN SRI LANKA : THE PROSPECTS

In the context of the third world countries, can one envisage the demise of the clergy as a body or a shrivelling of its roles as an institution? The present warrants an answer in the negative in the new states, like Sri Lanka, which are struggling to have some sort of a variant of democracy as the basic ideology of their respective polities and yet have to remain in a transitional stage of development. These necessitate the harnessing of all social resources on the part of its ruling elites to aggregate their power. Religious groups thus are bound to continue and proliferate in these States, though as ancillaries to the parties. The influence may be mercurial, depending upon the political climate of the country but there is no doubt that they have come to stay and will continue to do so.

In the context of a Buddhist country like Sri Lanka, it may also be added that the Buddhist religious system in the island, with the pluralistic overtones of its value system and structure also make it, in certain respects, congruent with the pluralist structures of democracy. Traditional Buddhist elites of Sri Lanka thus may continue to be an important segment of its political life for decades to come unless and until the major premises of its present political system themselves undergo a metamorphosis.

Granting the continuance of *status quo*, however, necessitates certain amount of heart searching on the part of Bhikkhus on their future roles specially in view of the fact that 1976 is not 1956; that Buddhist sense of grievance as it surfaced in 1956 has been more or less met; that a bi-partisan approach on Buddhist issues has found 'demand-solution' of the majority community through various measures.

As regards the young Bhikkhus, presumably such an awareness exists already. This further necessitates an attempt on their part to appraise their future roles in view of certain characteristics which differentiate them from the older Bhikkhus regarding their political orientations and attitudes to politics.

It is significant to note that in Sri Lanka of the 1970s many 'old guards' of the 'political' Sangha are either dead or too old to be effective or are too discredited to ensure respect and mobilise support. As regards the new generation of the Bhikkhus, it seems to have lived only partly under the old Pirivena milieu. Many Pirivenas and the university campuses are hardly different in terms of their curriculum and ethos from a secular school or a university. (The University of Bhikkhus at Anuradhapura, it is a well known fact, does not attract the 'cream' of the Bhikkhus). Coupled with this change in the education and its orientation, the young generation of the Bhikkhus has grown up in a highly politically saturated ethos in which (along with their lay counterparts and age group) they have not only influenced the verdict of the ballotbox in favour of one party or the other (as new voters comprising about 20% of the total electorate in the 1970 elections) but some of them have also showed their disenchantment with the present political system by participating in the insurgency of 1971.

Can one envisage a radical change in the Buddhist religious system of Sri Lanka ? The answer seems to be in the negative at least in the near future for several reasons. To begin with, the radicalisation of the religious system has been, historically speaking, coterminus with similar pace of changes in the politico-economic structure. In fact, they have *followed* them, not *preceded* them. Secondly, as long as the economic basis of the Sangha organisation remains intact with the perpetuation of the vested interests therein, the 'revolt' in the temple may take a long time unless supported by the lay leadership. That the present Government does not want to stir the hornet's nest by bringing the temple land within the purview of its Land Legislation Act of 1972 is already an indication of its circumspection.

One, however, cannot rule out the possibility of the young and 'non-affluent' Bhikkhus demanding the extension of the governmental policies of 'egalitarianism and social justice' to the Bhikkhu community as a whole by vesting the temple land in the State and giving the grants to all of them for the upkeep and maintenance of the viharas. But there does not seem to be much intensity in such demands. However, it is only when the initiative for such changes comes from within— from a segment of the Sangha—that the democratic leadership of Sri Lanka may react.

It appears that the more intense the economic crisis becomes the greater are the chances for socio-political upheavals in the island. And it is in the wake of such upheavals that the economic resources of the Sangha may also tend to be more widely distributed. Unlike the Catholic Church in Latin America, with its few centuries of historical traditions and with internal as well as 'external' impulses operating to facilitate changes in the pattern of interaction between Church and State,[14] the Sangha organisation in Sri Lanka has maintained certain continuities in its structures which are too deep rooted in its history to be uprooted so soon. Nor can one discern the 'external' impulses for change (as in Catholic Church) emanating in the case of Sangha in Sri Lanka for, unlike the Catholic Church, Buddhism did not have an international patriarch. As such, structurally, the Sangha in Sri Lanka may tend to continue to be highly autonomous but fairly fragmented.

As regards their future roles, the Bhikkhus in Sri Lanka seem to be at cross-roads. Will they rest content with their role as social missionaries and/or interest-group activists? Or are they going to join the group of the new revolutionaries ? If history is any indicator, they may continue to perform all the three roles, with one group having as its primary activity the propagation of the Dhamma at home and abroad, the other indulging in interest-group activities and still others joining those propagating a new 'political religion'.

14. For details on the role of the Vatican hierarchy in Church reformation in various countries see Vallier, n. 2, pp. 61 and 85.

AMARAPURA NIKAYA : VARIOUS DIVISIONS

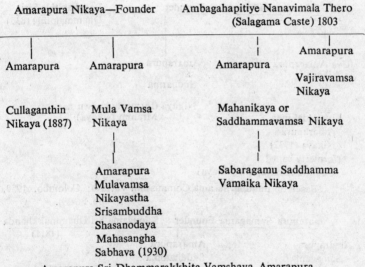

Amarapura Nikaya—Founder		Ambagahapitiye Nanavimala Thero (Salagama Caste) 1803	
Amarapura	Amarapura	Amarapura	Amarapura Vajiravamsa Nikaya
Cullaganthin Nikaya (1887)	Mula Vamsa Nikaya	Mahanikaya or Saddhammavamsa Nikaya	
	Amarapura Mulavamsa Nikayastha Srisambuddha Shasanodaya Mahasangha Sabhava (1930)	Sabaragamu Saddhamma Vamaika Nikaya	

Amarapura Sri Dhammarakkhita Vamshaya Amarapura
(Founder Attudave Dhammarakkhita (1812 or 2356 BV) (Durava- caste)

(Mihirapanne) Nikaya

(Recently the Nikaya has branched off into several groups)

(Based on Buddha Sasana Commission Vartava Sessional paper 18
of 1959, Colombo, 1959, pp. 34-36).

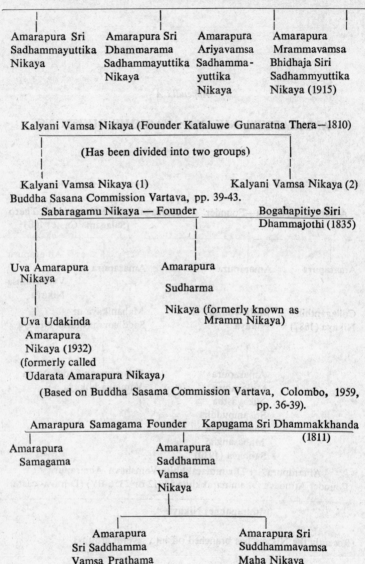

Amarapura   Siri   Sadhammayuttika   Matara   Nikaya (I841)

Amarapura Sri Sadhammayuttika Nikaya	Amarapura Sri Dhammarama Sadhammayuttika Nikaya	Amarapura Ariyavamsa Sadhamma-yuttika Nikaya	Amarapura Mrammavamsa Bhidhaja Siri Sadhammyuttika Nikaya (1915)

Kalyani Vamsa Nikaya (Founder Kataluwe Gunaratna Thera—1810)

(Has been divided into two groups)

Kalyani Vamsa Nikaya (1)   Kalyani Vamsa Nikaya (2)
Buddha Sasana Commission Vartava, pp. 39-43.

Sabaragamu Nikaya — Founder   Bogahapitiye Siri
                                                          Dhammajothi (1835)

Uva Amarapura   Amarapura
Nikaya
                              Sudharma

                              Nikaya (formerly known as
Uva Udakinda   Mramm Nikaya)
Amarapura
Nikaya (1932)
(formerly called
Udarata Amarapura Nikaya)

(Based on Buddha Sasama Commission Vartava, Colombo, 1959,
                                                               pp. 36-39).

Amarapura Samagama Founder   Kapugama Sri Dhammakkhanda
                                                                (1811)
Amarapura   Amarapura
Samagama   Saddhamma
                              Vamsa
                              Nikaya

            Amarapura   Amarapura Sri
            Sri Saddhamma   Suddhammavamsa
            Vamsa Prathama   Maha Nikaya
            Maha Nikaya

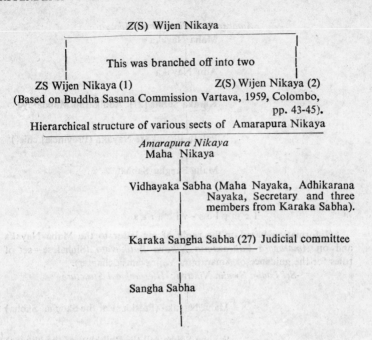

Z(S) Wijen Nikaya

This was branched off into two

ZS Wijen Nikaya (1)   Z(S) Wijen Nikaya (2)
(Based on Buddha Sasana Commission Vartava, 1959, Colombo,
pp. 43-45).

Hierarchical structure of various sects of Amarapura Nikaya

Amarapura Nikaya
Maha Nikaya

Vidhayaka Sabha (Maha Nayaka, Adhikarana
Nayaka, Secretary and three
members from Karaka Sabha).

Karaka Sangha Sabha (27) Judicial committee

Sangha Sabha

Based on the *Amarapura Nikaya Vyavastha* (Constitution of Amarapura Nikaya—Sinhalese typescript—and on interview with Rev. M.
Sasanaratna, Professor of Philosophy, Vidyalankara University, on
12 October 1967).

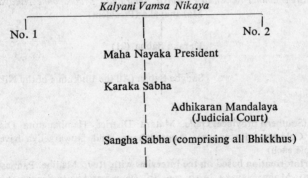

Kalyani Vamsa Nikaya

No. 1   No. 2

Maha Nayaka President

Karaka Sabha

Adhikaran Mandalaya
(Judicial Court)

Sangha Sabha (comprising all Bhikkhus)

V i h a r a s

(Information based on the reply to a letter addressed to Maha
Nayaka dated 25 October 1967)

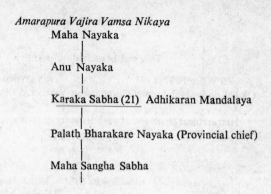

Amarapura Vajira Vamsa Nikaya
Maha Nayaka

Anu Nayaka

Karaka Sabha (21)   Adhikaran Mandalaya

Palath Bharakare Nayaka (Provincial chief)

Maha Sangha Sabha

Temples-viharas

(Information based on the reply of my letter to the Maha Nayaka
and on *Amarapura Vajiravamsa Nikaya Katikavata* (Sinhalese—set of
rules for the guidance of Amarapura Vajiravamsa chapter).

Sri Lanka Swajin Nikaya : Hierarchical Structure

Maha Nayaka (President of the Sangha Sabha)

Sangha Sabha (all the Bhikkhus of the Nikaya)
                                Adhikaran Mandalaya
                                (3 Bhikkhus)

(Information supplied by the secretary of the Nikaya in May 1967)
Sri Dhamma Rakkhita Vamsaya Amarapura Mihirapanne Nikaya
Mahanayaka (President)

Karaka Sabha (21)

Sangha Sabha (All the Bhikkhus of the Nikaya)

(Southern province, Galle, Matara Dlstrict, Hambanatota District
and Colombo. Ratnapura, Anuradhapura and Nuwaraeliya have one
temple each)

(Information based on the interview with Rev. Madihe Pannaseeha
Thero, Maha Nayaka. Also see Sri *Dhammarakkhita Sangha Sabhave
Vyavastha*—Constitution of Sri Dhammarakkhita Sangha Sabha (Type-
script).

GENERAL QUESTIONNAIRE

General

1. Did religion play any role in the nationalist movement of Ceylon? Who were the pioneers?
2. Did lay Buddhist organisations like B.T.S. and Y.M.B.A. play any role in the nationalist movement?
3. What roles have the lay Buddhist organisations/monks— individually or collectivelly—played in the politics of the country since independence?
4. Were there monks in the pre-1948 era who were politically active? Who were they?
5. What was their socio-economic background? Did they belong to any particular Pirivena/temple? Will you say that they were young urban monks? Were all of them highly educated? Why did they come to politics?
6. Were the monks brought into the arena of election of 1931, 1936 and 1947 by the politicians?
7. Did some of them participate in the election campaign? Who were they? Could you name them?
8. Did the monks vote in the elections of 1931, 1936, 1947 ? What were the major issues in these elections?
9. Did you vote in these elections? Whom did you vote for ?
10. What was the U.N.P. policy towards Buddhism under D.S. Senanayake?
11. What was the attitude of the UNP towards Buddhism under Dudley Senanayake and Kotelawala?
12. What has been the SLFP policy towards Buddhism ?

13. What were the major issues in the 1952 elections. Did monks play any role individually or in groups therein ?

14. What were the major issues in the 1956 elections? What prompted the monks to participate in these elections? Who were they? Could you name some of the monk leaders and their organisations? Who organised the E.B.P.?

15. Do you think that S.W.R.D. Bandaranaike would have won even without the support of monks? How crucial was their support ? What other factors contributed to his victory?

16. Did you vote in 1952 and 1956? Whom did you vote for ?

17. What role did the Maha Nayakas of Malwatta, Asgiri and Maha Nayakas of other sects play in the elections of 1947, 1952 and 1956 ? Did any of them issue a statement?

18. What were the issues during the election of March and July 1960? Did the monks participate in the elections? Did you vote in these elections ? Whom did you vote for ?

19. What were the organisations of monks which actively participated in the 1965 elections ? Could you name them? What were the major issues in this election? What was the attitude of the Maha Nayakas of Malwatta/ Asgiri, Amarapura and Ramanna Nikaya towards the election?

20. Did you vote in 1965? Whom did you vote for ?

21. Could you recollect instances of monks who disrobed themselves to come to politics?

22. Should monks participate in politics? If yes/no why?

23. Is it in consonance with the precepts/goals of Buddhism?

24. Can they do their duty without getting themselves involved in politics?

25. How to draw a line between the involvement of a monk in social-religious-political affairs ? What is political and what is not ?

26. Are the following actions, if taken by monks, political or non-political:

    (a) Issuing of statements, pamphlets, participation in the writing of reports (like Sasana Commission or Buddhist Commission).

    (b) Membership of various Sabhas, Committees, Commissions; Government organisations: (Radio Broadcasting Corporation).

    (c) Reference to political issues in the temple;

    (d) Accepting presidentship of a meeting, say, on Vietnam;

    (e) Expressing views on issues like Paddy Land Act, Poya Day as holiday, Press take-over, language question, Indo-Ceylon Bill, toddy regulations etc;

    (f) Canvassing in the election, and

    (g) Fasting.

Sangha and State

27. What has been the traditional role of the Sangha *vis-a-vis* the State?

28. What role has the State played traditionally in reforming and unifying the Sangha?

29. Do you think that the traditional pattern of roles should/could still be followed ? If not, what changes do you suggest ?

30. Should the State have powers of legislation over the Sangha? In what spheres ?

    (a) Temporalities ?

    (b) Ecclesiastical Courts ?

    (c) Any other sphere ?

31. What do you think of the recommendation of the Buddhist Commission (1955) regarding State control over Sasana?

32. What is your view about the composition, and recommendations of the Buddha Sasana Commission of 1959 ? What do you think about its proposal regarding Sasana Council ?

33. Could you tell me as to how organisations (like E.B.P. and others) and individuals like the Maha Nayakas as well as other monks reacted to the proposal regarding the Sasana Council?

34. What was the attitude of your party organisation regarding the recommendations of the Sasana Commission ?

35. Should the State have a Buddhist Sasana Department ?

36. What do you think of the proposal regarding the incorporation of Ramanna Nikaya? Could you throw some light on it?

37. Why is it that several attempts by the Maha Nayaka of Asgiri to reform Siam Nikaya have simply remained on paper? State reasons.

Sangha and the Laity

38. What has been the relationship between the Buddhist monks and Buddhist organisations like YMBA, ACBC, BTS etc?

39. Do you think that the relationship between the laity and the monks has been more/less close since 1948 ? Do you find any differences in urban/rural areas in this context?

40. Could you name some organisations where both the monks and the laity are associated ?

41. Could you enlighten me about the various sub-sects of the three major sects i.e. Siam, Amarpaura and Ramanna Nikayas ?

42. When did they come into being ?

43. What was the reason for the split ?

44. How many sub-sects in Siam/Amarapura, Ramanna Nikayas ?

45. What is the relationship between Karaka and Dayaka Sabhas at Village/District/Province level ?

46. What are their powers and jurisdiction respectively ?

47. Where is the centre of power ? In Dayaka or Karaka Sabha?

48. Do members of the Karaka Sabha influence the decision of the priest ? In what way ?

49. How is the Chief Maha Nayaka elected ? Tell me in particular about the Nikaya you belong to ? Who elects them? Does for instance, the village priest, belonging to Siam Nikaya play any role, say, in the election of the Nayaka and Maha Nayakas ? Could you describe the process in detail ?

Monkhood

50. What prompted you to become a monk? Was it your decision?

51. Is the number of the monks increasing or decreasing in the island?

52. Is their a tendency amongst the monks to disrobe themselves since the inception of the two new universities?

53. How much has the outlook of the monks been affected because of the University education?

54. Could you tell me something about the succession process in the temple ? Is it always pupillary ? Were you related to your Chief Priest ?

55. Could you give me some details about your temple/ pirivena.

56. How many monks are living in your temple ?

57. If Pirivena—how many students—lay and monk ?

58. What are the activities of the temple ? How much is the income of the temple ?

59. Who is the chief incumbent? Has there been any dispute regarding succession in your temple at any time ? If so, give details.

60. Could you tell me something about the Vinayawardhana Movement.

LETTER SENT TO THE MAHA NAYAKAS OF VARIOUS CHAPTERS IN CEYLON IN 1967

1. How many sub-sects/chapters are there in Siam and Amarapura Nikaya? Please give names.
2. When did your Nikaya/sub-sect come into being? Who was its founder ?
3. What were the reasons for its inception? Did it originate due to caste conflict ?
4. What are the main temples of your chapter? Please give their names.
5. Do you have an Adhikarana Sabha in your Nikaya/sub-sect? If so, what are its powers and functions?
6. How is it appointed? What is the tenure of office of its members? How is the Karaka Sabha appointed ? What is the tenure of its office-bearers?
7. Where does the highest ordination ceremony of your Nikaya/subsect take place?
8. How many Bhikkhus are there in your Nikaya?
9. How long have you held the position of Maha Nayaka? Did you hold any other office before ?
10. Have you expressed your opinions regarding the following questions?
    (a) Raising the status of the Vidyodaya and Vidyalankara Parivena to the University status;
    (b) Language issue;
    (c) Paddy Land Act;
    (d) Poya holidays;
    (e) Indo-Ceylon question.

If you have written on any of these issues please send me a copy of the same.

11. How many novices and Bhikkhus are there in your temple? Are there any lands belonging to your temple?

12. Finally, could you please give me your bio-data on the following :

(a) Date of birth;

(b) Place of birth;

(c) When did you become a priest ? When were you ordained?

(d) Why did you become a monk ? Was it a decision of your parents or your own wish?

(e) Are you related to the Maha Nayaka?

(f) What are your educational qualifications?

(g) To which Caste do you belong?

(h) Have you been to any Buddhist country? If so, when? How long did you stay there?

QUESTIONNAIRE TO THE STUDENTS OF THE VIDYALANKARA UNIVERSITY ON 6 JANUARY 1968

Rev. Sir,

I am a lecturer at the Department of South Asian Studies at the Indian School of International Studies, New Delhi. I have come to Ceylon to collect data for my book entitled 'Religion and Politics in Ceylon'. I will be most grateful to you if you kindly fill this form and thereby help facilitate my research work. Please hand over the form to Rev. Ratanasara Thero after completing it.

1. Have you obtained higher ordination? If so, when ?
2. Why did you become a Bhikkhu?
3. To which Nikaya does your temple belong ?
4. Why were you ordained in this temple ?
5. Are you related to your preceptor? What is his age ?
6. Are you the most senior of his students? How many pupils does he have?
7. Why did you think of entering the University? Was it on your own accord ? How did your preceptor react to it?
8. Who is spending on your education ?
9. There was an election for the selection of members to the student's council. Did you compete for any post? Why did you compete?
10. Did you help any candidate? For what reasons? In what way did you help the candidate?
11. What are your plans for the future? After obtaining your degree, do you intend:

(a) going back to the temple;

(b) teach;

(c) take up any other employment.

12. In Burma every layman enters the order for a certain period of time. Do you think that it is suited to the order of the Sangha in Ceylon?

13. Do your benefactors (Dayakas) look after the daily needs of your temple ?

14. Were you a voter in the 1965 elections? Did your preceptor take part in the elections ? Did you help any member of a particular party? If so, in what way ?

15. During the elections, politicians try to get the support of the Bhikkhus. How did the people in your area react in this matter ? Do they like the idea of monks taking part in political meetings and political discussions?

16. What role should a Bhikkhu play in the present social set-up in Ceylon?

17. Should a Bhikkhu use money?

18. What are the educational, social and political services done by the Bhikkhus during the past 20 years?

19. What are the duties performed by your Dayakas? Does your temple have a pirivena?

20. Where do you spend your holidays;

(a) In the temple?

(b) Sangharamaya?

(c) With your friends?

(d) With your relatives?

21. What do you think of the proposed Bhikkhu University ? Will this fulfil the objectives of monkhood ?

22. Do you think that any reforms should be made in the Sangha organisation ? What reforms do you suggest?

23. Date and place of birth, village and region.

24. Caste.

25. Who do you think has done greater service to the Bhikkhus? The UNP or the SLFP?

26. Should a Bhikkhu, teaching in a university or in a School receive salary?
27. Should a Bhikkhu participate in politics?
28. What role did the Bhikkhu play in the 1956 and 1965 electlons?
29. Name and class.

DECLARATION OF THE VIDYALANKARA PIRIVENA

The Buddha permitted Bhikkhus to change minor rules of the Vinaya if they so desire. Nevertheless, there is no historical evidence to show that the bhikkhus of the Theravada school have on any occasion actually changed the rules of the Vinaya. Likewise, we do not say that even now they should be changed.

But it has to be admitted that the political, economic and social conditions of today are different from those of the time of the Buddha, and that consequently the life of bhikkhus today is also different from that of the bhikkhus at that time.

In those days the ideal of monks generally was to realise Nibbana in their very lifetime. In later times their ideal was to exert themselves to the best of their ability in activities beneficial to themselves and other with a view to realising Nibbana in a future life.

It is clearly seen that as a result of this very change, a great many other changes not known in the earlier days took place in the life of bhikkhus in later times.

The extent to which the life of monks today has undergone changes can be clearly gauged when we take into consideration the prevailing conditions of life in temples, monasteries and pirivenas, the teaching and learning of Sinhalese, Sanskrit and such other subjects, the present system of examinations, the editing and writing of books and journals, conferring and accepting Nayakaships and such other titles, participation in various societies and being elected as office-bearers in them. It has to be accepted, therefore, that although the rules of the

Vinaya have remained unaltered, the life of monks has undergone change and that this change is inevitable.

We believe that politics today embraces all fields of human activity directed towards the public weal. No one will dispute that to work for the promotion of the religion is the duty of the bhikkhus. It is clear that the welfare of the religion depends on the welfare of the people who profess the religion. History bears evidence to the fact that whenver the Sinhalese nation—which was essentially a Buddhist nation—was prosperous, Buddhism also flourished. We, therefore, declare that it is nothing but fitting for bhikkhus to identify themselves with activities conducive to the welfare of our people—whether these activities be labelled politics or not—as long as they do not constitute an impediment to the religious life of a bhikkhu.

We cannot forget that from the earliest days the Sinhalese monks, while leading the life of a bhikkhu, were in the forefront of movements for the progress of their nation, their country and their religion.

Even today bhikkhus by being engaged in education, rural reconstruction, anti-crime campaigns, relief work, temperance work, social work and such other activities, are taking part in politics, whether they are aware of it or not. We do not believe that it is wrong for bhikkhus to participate in these activities.

We believe that it is incumbent on the bhikkhus not only to further the efforts directed towards the welfare of the country, but also to oppose such measures as are detrimental to the common good. For example, if any effort is made to obstruct the system of free education, the great boon which has been recently conferred on our people, it is the paramount duty of the bhikkhu not only to oppose all such efforts but also to endeavour to make it a permanent blessing.

In the ancient days, according to the records of history, the welfare of the nation and the welfare of the religion were regarded as synonymous terms by the laity as well as by the Sangha. The divorce of the religion from the nation was an idea introduced into the minds of the Sinhalese by invaders from the West, who belonged to an alien faith. It was a convenient instrument of astute policy to enable them to keep the people in subjugation in order to rule the country as they pleased.

It was in their own interests, and not for the welfare of the people, that these foreign invaders attempted to create a gulf between the bhikkhus and the laity—a policy which they implemented with diplomatic cunning. We should not follow their example, and should not attempt to withdraw bhikkhus from society. Such conduct would assuredly be a deplorable act of injustice, committed against our nation, our country and our religion.

Therefore, we publicly state that both our bhikkhus and our Buddhist leaders should avoid the pitfall of acting hastily, without deliberation and foresight, and should beware of doing a great disservice to our nation and to our religion.

K. Pannasara
Principal, Vidyalankara Pirivena
Tripitaka. Vagisvaracarya Upadhyaya
Chief High Priest of the Colombo
and Chilaw Districts.

13.2.1946
Vidyalankara Pirivena

This declaration was unanimously passed by the staff of tie Vidyalankara Pirivena on Wednesday the 13th of February 1946.

GLOSSARY

In the preparation of the glossary, I have drawn heavily on Rhys Davids, T.W., and Stede, William, ed., The Pali Text Society's Pali-*English* Dictionary (*Surrey,* 1921)

Abbhidhamma Pitaka	:	Basket of Philosophy
Adhikarana Lekhaka	:	Judicial Secretary
Adhikarana Mandalaya	:	Ecclesiastical Board
Adhikarana Nayaka	:	Attorney-General, chief high priest administering justice
Adhyapana Mandalaya	:	Board of Education
Agganu Vijjaka Mandalaya	:	Highest Ecclesiastical Board
Anunayaka	:	Deputy Supreme Chief Monk
Aramika	:	Rest House
Ayatana	:	Monastic College
Bana	:	Sermon
Basnayke Nilame	:	Temple Lords
Bhasa Peramuna	:	Language Front
Bhikkhu	:	Buddhist Clergy
Buddha Pujava	:	Worship of the Buddha
Chandaya Jayantı	:	Election Jayanti
Dasa Panatha	:	Ten Principles
Dayaka	:	Patron—Benefactor, Person who looks after the material needs of the Sangha
Dewala	:	Shrine
Dhamma	:	Doctrine
Dhammadipa	:	The Island of Buddhist Doctrine
Dhammapada	:	Verses of the Buddhist Doctrine
Dhasa Raja Dharma	:	Ten Buddhist Principles
Digha Nikaya	:	Longer Dialogues of the Buddha
Duka	:	Suffering
Durava	:	A Caste group
Eksath Bhasa Peramuna	:	United Language Front

Ekasath Bhikkhu Pera-muna	:	United Monks Front
Gamavasin	:	Village Dwellers
Gana	:	A meeting or a chapter of Bhikkhus living in one communion or a large congregation of monks living in several monasteries
Ganadetu	:	Leader of the Gana
Ganthadhura	:	The one pursuing the doctrine of Books
Grantha	:	Learning
Jatakas	:	Stories of the former lives of Buddha
Jatika Vimukti Pera-muna	:	National Liberation Front
Jyestha Anuvijjaka Mandalaya	:	Senior Ecclesiastical Board
Kappiyakaraka	:	One who by offering any thing to a Bhikkhu, makes it legally acceptable
Karma	:	Law of Action or Retribution
Karmavagga Cariyan	:	Monk-teacher in a particular branch of Buddhist dispensation
Karaka Sabha	:	Executive Committee
Katayutu Pilibanda Lekhaka	:	Educational Secretary
Katikavata	:	Set of rules prepared for the guidance of monks
Lanka Eksath Bhikku Mandalaya	:	Ceylon Union of Bhikkhus
Laukika	:	worldly
Lekam	:	Secretary
Lobha	:	Attachment
Lokottara	:	Other worldly
Lanka Sangha Sam-vidhanaya	:	Ceylon Organisation of Bhikkhus
Madhya Karaka Sabha	:	Central Executive Cammittee
Magul Bera	:	Ceremonial Drumming
Mahajana Eksath Peramuna	:	People's United Front
Mahajana Sewak	:	Servant of the People
Maha Lekhaka	:	Chief Secretary
Maha Nayaka	:	Supreme Chief Monk
Maha Sanghadhikarana	:	Chief Ecclesiastical Court
Maha Sangha Peramuna	:	Bhikkhu Front
Mahasami	:	Patriarch
Maha Vihara	:	The Great Monastery
Mahimi	:	Patriarch
Mulas	:	Monastic Colleges

Nayakas	:	Chief Monks
Nikaya	:	Fraternity of the Bhikkhus
Nikaya Maha Sangha		
Sabha	:	General Body of a particular fraternity of Bhikkhus
Nildhari Mandalaya	:	Board of Control for the general body of Bhikkhus; committee of officials
Nirodh	:	Extinction of Desire
Nirvana	:	Salvation
Palak Maha Sangha		
Sabha	:	Central Legislative Body, Board of Control for the General Body of Bhikkhus
Parshwaya	:	Branches
Paritta	:	Protective Charm
Paritta Pota	:	The book of Paritta
Pirivena	:	Monastic College
Patipatti	:	Practice
Pativedha	:	Penetration, comprehension, attainment, insight, knowledge
Pav	:	Sin
Pin	:	Good
Pinkama	:	Merit
Poya Day	:	Day connoting phases of the moon
Poyamalu	:	The main centre of Bhikkhu village dwelling
Pradeshik Anuvijjaka	:	Provincial Divisional Ecclesiastical
Mandalaya	:	Court
Pradeshika Sasanaraksha	:	Provincial Council for the protection
Samiti		of Buddhist Religious societies
Pratipatyaraksha	:	Matters relating to the issues dealing with canonical issues
Punyakheta	:	Merit field
Rajakariya	:	The obligations to work for the King
Ramanna Vamsa	:	Ramanna Chronicles
Sabhapati	:	President
Samanera	:	Novice
Samantakuta	:	Adam's peak
Samastha Lanka		
Buddha Peramuna	:	All-Ceylon Buddhist Front
Samastha Lanka		
Bhikkhu Sammela-		
naya	:	All-Ceylon Bhikkhu Congress
Samvega	:	Religious Emotion caused by contemplation on the misery of the world

Sangha	:	Community of Buddhist Monks
Sanghadhikarana	:	Ecclesiastical Tribunals
Sangharaja	:	Patriarch
Sangha Sabha	:	General Body of all the Bhikkhus
Sanghika Dana	:	Alms given to the community of monks
Sangrahaya	:	Collection, set
Sanna Lekhaka-chariya	:	Registrar-General
Sansara	:	Temporal world
Sasana	:	Instruction, Order, totality of Buddhist institutions in an unbroken succession from the time of the Buddha
Sasanarakaha Samitis	:	Protection of Buddhist Religious Societies
Shariah	:	Traditional Law
Silavat Samagama	:	Fraternity of the Pious
Sima	:	Boundary
Sinhala Jatika Sanga-maya	:	Sinhala National Congress
Sisyanusisya Paramparawa	:	Pupillary succession
Sri Lanka Eksath Bhikkhu Bala Mandalaya	: :	Sri Lanka United Bhikkhu Organi-sation
Sri Lanka Maha Bhikkhu Sangamaya	:	All-Ceylon Congress of Bhikkhus
Sri Lanka Maha Sangha Sabha	: :	Conference of the Maha Sangha of Sri Lanka
Sri Lanka Sangha Samvid-dhanaya	:	Sri Lanka Organisation of Monks
Sivuru Paramparawa	:	Pupillary Succession based on kin-ship
Suttas	:	Sermons
Sutta Pitaka	:	The book of Sermons
Sthvira	:	Elder Bhikkhu
Ulema	:	Islamic scholars
Ummah	:	Islamic Community
Upaddhyaya	:	Monks officiating in ordination ceremony
Upasampada	:	Higher Ordination ceremony
Upasampada Karaka Sabha	:	Executive Committee for higher ordination ceremony
Up Lekhaka	:	Deputy Secretary
Up Sabhapati	:	Vice-President
Vanavasin	:	Forestdwellers

Vamsa	:	Chronicles
Varan	:	Warrants
Vassa	:	Observance of Lent
Vesak Day	:	Buddhist New Year Day
Vidhayaka Mandalaya	:	Committee of officials
Vidyodaya Pirivena	:	Name of a monastic college
Vihara	:	Monastery
Viharagama	:	Monastic village
Vtharadhipati	:	Chief abbot, principal Bhikkhu of the monastery
Vinaya	:	Buddhist monastic discipline
Vinaypitaka	:	The Basket of Discipline
Vinischaya Karaka Sabha	:	Panel of judges
Vipassana	:	Meditation
Vippasanadhura	:	One pursuing the vocation of meditation
Vyavastha	:	Constitution, code

BIBLIOGRAPHY

This is a highly select bibliography. For a detailed bibliography on religions and political systems in Sri Lanka, the reader should refer to the relevant sections in H.A.I. Goonetilleke's **A Bibilography Of Ceylon** *(Switzerland, 1972), 2 vols.*

Documents : Official Publications

Ceylon, *Administration Report of the Public Trustee,* 1948-71 (Colombo) (Annual Publication).

———, 'Buddhist Temporalities Ordinance', *Ceylon Government Gazette,* pt. 1, sec. (1) General, no. 10339, 8 June 1956, pp. 1046-8.

———, *Buddha Sasana Commission Vartava* (Buddha Sasana Commission Report),, Sessional Paper 18 of 1959 (Colombo, 1959.)

———, *Buddhist Temporalities, Interim and Final Reports of a Commission appointed to enquire into the Working of Buddhist Temporalities Ordinance No 8 of 1905* (Colombo, 1920).

———, *Buddhist Temporalities, Report of the Commissioner appointed under Ordinance No. 15 of 1919* (Colombo, 1923).

———, *Constitution of Sri Lanka* (Colombo, 1972).

———, *Correspondence Relating to the Buddhist Temporalities IV 1907* (Colombo, 1907).

———, *The Government and the People* (Colombo, 1959).

———, Government Notification, *Ceylon Government Gazette Extraordinary,* no. 12451 of 1961, pt. 1, sec I, 31 May 1961.

———, *Report of the Commission Appointed to enquire into the Administration of the Buddhist Temporalities,* Sessional Report 17 of 1876.

————, *Report of the Commission on Constitution Reform* (London, 1945).

————, *Report of the Commission on Tenure of Lands of Viharagam Dewalagam and Nindagam* (Colombo, 1956).

Ceylon, *Report of Special Commission on the Constitution* (London, 1928.)

————, *Report to His Excellency the Governor-General By the Commission Appointed in Terms of the Commissions of Enquiry Act to enquire into and Report on certain matters connected with the Assassination of the Late Prime Minister Solomon West Ridgeway Dias Bandaranaike,* Sessional Paper III-1965 (Colombo, March 1965).

————, Department of Cultural Affairs, *Administrative Report of the Director of Cultural Affairs for the Financial Year,* 1957-71 (Colombo) (Annual Publication).

————, Department of Cultural Affairs, *Viharastha Sasanara-kshaka Samiti Saha Pradeshika Sasanarakshaka Mandalaya* (Sinhalese Temple Societies for the Promotion of Buddhism) (Colombo, 1959).

————, Department of Census and Statistics, *Census of Ceylon 1946* (Colombo, 1952).

————, Department of Census and Statistics, *Census of Ceylon 1953* (Colombo, 1953).

————, Department of Census and Statistics, *Statistical Pocket Book of Ceylon*—1970 (Colombo, 1970).

————, Department of Elections, *Report on the Parliamentary Elections* (Colombo, 1962), Sessional paper 11 of 1962, 19 March & 20 July 1960.

————, Department of Elections, *Report of the Sixth Parliamentary General Elections of Ceylon* (Colombo, 1966), Sessional paper 20 of 1966, 22 March 1965.

————, Department of Elections, *Report on the Seventh Parliamentary General Election in Ceylon* (Colombo, 1971,) sessional paper 7 of 1971, 27 May 1970.

————, Department of Elections, *Results of Parliamentary General Elections in Ceylon, 1947-1970* (Colombo, 1971).

————, House of Representatives, *Parliamentary Debates,* 1948-74 (Colombo).

Documents : Unofficial, Unpublished

Amarapura Saddhamma Vamsa Maha Nikaya Vyvavastha Sangrahaya (Amarapura Saddhama Vamsa Maha Nikaya Code).

Ames, Michael M., Religious Syncretism in Ceylon (Thesis, Ph.D., Harvard University, 1962).

Dhammavisuddhi, Yatadolawatta, 'Buddhist Sangha in Ceylon, *Circa, 1200-1600* (Thesis, Ph.D., London University 1970).

Fernando, Tissa, "Arrack, Toddy and Ceylonese Nationalism: Some Observations on the Temperance Movement, 1912-1921' (Ceylon Studies Seminar 1969-70 series, no. 9, 7 June 1970) mimeo.

Gunasinghe, Newton, Buddhism and Economic Growth with Special Reference to Ceylon' (Master's Thesis, Department of Anthropology and Sociology, Monsah University, 1972).

Green, Arnold L., 'Sangha and King : The Structure of Authority in Mediaeval Ceylon' (Paper read at a symposium on the Problems in the Sociology of the Theravada Buddhism, Honolulu, 22 August 1967), mimeo.

Gombrich, Richard F., 'Buddhism in the Ethics of Sinhalese Villagers : Theory and Practice' (University of Ceylon, Ceylon Studies Seminar 69-70 series, no. 5, 1 February 1970) mimeo.

Gunavardhana, R.A.L.H., *The History of the Budhist Sangha in Ceylon from the Region of Sena I to the Invasion of Magha (800-1215).* Thesis, Ph.D., University of London, 1965).

Jayasinghe, Karunasena, Hewawasan, *The Extension of the Franchise in Ceylon with some Consideration of their Political and Social Consequences* (Thesis, Ph.D., London School of Economics and Political Science, University of London, 1965).

Malalagoda, K., *Sociological Aspects of Rivival and Change in Buddhism in Nineteeth Century Ceylon* (Thesis, Ph.D., Oxford, 1970).

Panabokke, Gunaratne, *The Evolution and History of the Buddhist Monastic Order with Special Reference to the*

   Sangha in Ceylon (Thesis, Doctoral, Lancaster University, 1969).

Roberts, M., 'The Political Antecedents of the Revivalist Elite within the MEP Coalition of 1956' (*Ceylon Studies Seminar*, 1969/70, Department of Sociology, Peradeniya, cyclostyled doc.) no. 11.

Roberts, Michael, 'Reformism, Nationalism and Protest in British Ceylon, The Roots and Ingredients of Leadership' (Paper read at the School of Oriental and African Studies, University of London, 1974), mimeo.

Roberts, M., 'Variations on the Theme of Resistance Movements: The Kandy Rebellion of 1817-18 and later day nationalisms in Ceylon' (*Ceylon Studies Seminar*, 1970/72, Department of Sociology, Peradeniya) no. 9, mimeo.

Seneviratne, H.L., 'The Sacred and the Profane in a Buddhist Rite' *Ceylon Studies Seminar*, 1969/70, series, no. 7, University of Peradeniya, mimeo.

Vajirganana, P. (Rev.), 'The Contemporary Ceylonese Sangha' (Department of Philosophy, University of Ceylon Peradeniya). Typed article.

Wachissara, Kotagama, *Valivata Sarannakara and the Revival of Buddhism in Ceylon* (Thesis, Ph.D., School of African and Oriental Studies, University of London, 1951).

Books and Pamphlets

Adikaram E.W., *Early History of Buddhism in Ceylon* (Colombo, 1953).

All-Ceylon Buddhist Congrsss, *Buddhism and the State Resolutions and Memorandum of the All-Ceylon Buddhist Congress* (Colombo, 1951).

————, *Presidential Address of Sri Lalita Rajapaksa*, 30 December 1961 (Colombo, 1962).

All-Ceylon Viharadhipati and Trustee Association, *Memorial From the All-Ceylon Viharaadhipati and Trustee Association to the Prime Minister and Through Her The Government of Ceylon* (Colombo, 1962),

Almond, Gabriel A and Powell, Bingham, G., *Comparative Politics : A Developmental Approach* (Boston, 1966).

Arasaratnam, Sinnapah, *Dutch Power in Ceylon, 1658-1687* (Amsterdam, 1958).

Ariyapala, M.B., *Society in Mediaeval Ceylon* (Colombo, 1956).

Baker, C.J. and Washbrook D.A., *South India : Political Institution and Political Change. 1880-1940* (Meerut, 1975).

Bandaranaike, SW.R.D., *Speeches and Writings* (Colombo, 1963).

————, *Towards a New Era : Select Speeches of S.W.R.D. Bandaranaike made in the Legislature of Ceylon, 1931-1959* (Colombo, 1961).

Baddha Jatika Balavegaya, *Catholic Action—A Reply to the Catholic Union of Ceylon* (Colombo, 1963).

————, *Catholic Action According to Balavegaya* (Colombo, n.d.).

Bellah, R.N., *Religion and Progress in Modern Asia* (New York, 1965).

————, *Tokugawa Religion—The Values of Pre-industrial Japan* (Glencoe, 1957).

Bliss, Kathleen, *The Future of Religion* (Harmondsworth, Middlesex, 1969).

Bendix, Reinhard, *Nation Building and Citizenship* (Berkeley, 1969).

Bentley, Arthur F., *The Process of Government* (Evanston, 1949).

The Buddhist Committee of Enquiry, *The Betrayal of Buddhism: An Abridged Version of the Report of the Buddhist Committee of Enquiry* (Balangoda, 1956).

Castles, Francis G., *Pressure Groups and Political Culture* (London, 1967).

The Catholic Union of Ceylon, *Companion to the Buddhist Commission Report—A Commentary on the Report* (Colombo, 1957).

————, *Education in Ceylon according to the Buddhist Commission Report : A Commentary* (Colombo, 1957).

————, *The Church, the State and Catholic Action* (Colombo, n.d.).

Ceylon, Daily News, *Parliament of Ceylon 1947* (Colombo, 1947).

————, *Parliament of Ceylon 1956* (Colombo, 1956).

Ceylon Daily News, *Parliaments of Ceylon, 1960* (Colombo, 1960).

———, *Parliament of Ceylon, 1965* (Colombo, 1965).

———, *Seventh Parliament of Ceylon, 1970* (Colombo, 1970).

Copleston, R.S., *Buddhism, Primitive and Present in Magadha and in Ceylon* (London, 1908).

Dahl, Robert A., *Polyarchy—Participation and Opposition* (London, 1971).

Dearlove, John, *The Politics of Policy in Local Government : The Making and Maintenance of Public Policy in the Royal Borough of Kensington and Chelsea* (Cambridge, 1973).

De Silva, Colvin, R., *Ceylon Under the British Occupation, 1795-1833* (Colombo, 1953),

De Silva, K. M., *Social Policy and Missionary Organization in Ceylon, 1840-1855* (London, 1965).

———, ed., *History of Ceylon from Beginning of the 19th Century to 1948* (Colombo, 1973), vol. 3.

Dewaraja, Lorna Srimathi, *The Internal Politics of the Kandyan Kingdom, 1707-1760* (Colombo, 1972).

Dhanapala, D.B., *Eminent Indians* (Bombay, 1943).

Dharma Vijaya (Triumph of Righteousness) or *The Revolt in the Temple* (Colombo, 1953).

Dias, N. Q., *Rajya Sewakayange Bauddha Katayutu Ha Ehi Prativipaka* (Buddhist activities of the government servants and their consequences) (Colombo, 1965).

Dissanayake, T. B. and de Soysa, Colin A. B., *Kandyan Law and Buddhist Ecclesiastical Law* (Colombo, 1963).

Dowse, Robert E. & Hughes, John A., *Political Sociology* (London, 1972).

Durkheim, Emile, *The Elementary Forms of Religious Life*, trans. Joseph Ward Swain (New York, 1915).

Dutt, Sukumar, *Early Buddist Monarchism* (Bombay, 1960).

———, *Buddhist Monks and Monasteries in India : Their History and Contribution to Indian Culture* (London, 1962).

Duverger, Maurice, *Party Politics and Pressure Groups—A Comparative Introduction*, trans. by Robert Wagoner (London, 1972).

Eckstein, Harry, *Pressure Group Politics—The Case of the*

British Medical Association (London, 1960).

Eisenstadt, S. N., *Modernization : Protest and Change* (New Delhi, 1969).

Eckstein, Harry and Apter, David, eds., *Comparative Politics: A Reader* (New York, 1963).

Eldersveld, S. J., *Political Parties : A Behavioural Analysis* (Chicago, 1964).

Ensor, R.C.K., *England 1870-1914* (London, 1936).

Evers, Hans-Dieter, *Monks, Priests and Peasants : A Study of Buddhism and Social Structure in Central Ceylon* (Leiden, 1972).

Farmer, B.H., *Ceylon : A Divided Nation* (London, 1963).

Finer, S. E., *Anonymous Empire* (London, 1969), edn. 2.

Geertz, Clifford, *The Religion of Java* (Illinois, 1960).

———, ed., *Old Societies and New States : The Quest for Modernity in Asia and Africa* (New Delhi, 1963).

Geiger, Wilhelm, *Culture of Ceylon in Mediaeval Times*, ed. by Heinz Bechert (Wiesbaden, 1960).

Gerth, H. H. and Mills, Wright C., eds., *Max Weber, Essays in Sociology* (New York, 1958).

Glassenapp, Helmuthvon, *Buddhism : A Nontheistic Religion* (London, 1970).

Gnanissara, Malewana, *Hal Sairu deka denna Keseda*? (How can the two measure of rice be given?) (Colombo, n.d.).

Gnanissara, Malewana and Amaramansa, Devamottawe, *Kokad Hari-Hath Havula? Tun Havula* (Which is Right? Six-Party Front of the Three-Party Front ?) (Colombo, n. d.).

Gombrich, Richard F., *Traditional Buddhism in the Rural Highlands of Ceylon* (London, 1971.)

Goonewardene, Leslie, *A Short History of the Lanka Sama Samaja Party* (Colombo, 1960).

———, *What We Stand for* (Mardana, 1959).

Guruge, Ananda, ed., *Return to Righteousness : A Collection of Speeches, Essays and Letters of Anagarika Dharmapala* (Colombo, 1965).

Hanh, Thieh Nhat, *Vietnam—The Lotus in the Sea of Fire* (London, 1967).

Hardy, Rev., R. Spence. *Eastern Monarchism* (London, 1850).

Harper, Edward B., ed., *Religion in South Asia* (Seattle, 1964).

Hayward, Max and Fletcher, William C., eds., *Religion and the Soviet State : A Dilemma of Power* (London, 1969).

Houtart, Francois, *Religion and Ideology in Sri Lanka* (Bangalore, 1974).

Humphrey, Christian, *A Popular Dictionary of Buddhism* (London, 1962).

Jayawardane, J. R., *Marxism and Buddhism* (Monograph, Colombo, n. d.).

Jayawardena, Visakha Kumari, *The Rise of the Labour Movement in Ceylon* (Durham, N.C., 1972).

Jeffries, Charles Sir, *Ceylon—The Path to Independence* (London, 1962).

Jennings, W.I., *The Constitution of Ceylon* (Bombay, 1953).

John, Christian, *What is Catholic Action* ? (Colombo, 1964).

Kearney, Robert N., *Communalism and Language in the Politics of Ceylon* (Durham, 1967).

————, *Trade Unions and Politics in Ceylon* (New Delhi, 1971).

Keuneman, Pieter, *25 Years of the Ceylon Communist Party* (Colombo, 1968).

Knox, R., *An Historical Relation of Ceylon 1617* (Colombo 1958).

Kochanek, Stanley A., *Business and Politics in India* (Berkeley, 1974).

Kodikara, S.U., *Indo-Ceylon Relations Since Independence* (Colombo, 1965).

Kothari, Ranji, ed. *Caste in Indian Politics*, Delhi, (1973).

The Lanka Bauddha Mandalaya, *An Event of Dual Significance* (Colombo, The Ministry of Home Affairs, n. d.).

Lanka Sama Samaja Party, *Election Manifesto* (Colombo, 1952).

————, *Election Manifesto of the Lanka Sama Samaja Party, July 1960* (Mardana, 1960).

————, *Parliamentary General Elections 1956 : Manifesto of the LSSP* (Colombo, n. d.).

Lankananda, Abugama, *Jayawardana Pur Kotte Sri Kalyani Samagri Dharma Maha Sangha Sabha* (Colombo, n.d.).

Lasswell, Harold D. and Cleveland, Harlan, eds., *The Ethic of Power : The Interplay of Religion, Philosophy and Politics* (New York, 1962).

Leach, E. R., ed., *Aspects of Caste in South India, Ceylon and North-West Pakistan* (Cambridge, 1960).

———, *Pul Eliya* (Cambridge, 1961).

Ludowyk, E.F.C., *The Footprint of the Buddha* (London, 1958).

Malalasekera, G. P., *The Pali Literature of Ceylon* (Colombo, 1958).

Malalasekera, G. P. and Jayatilleke, K. N., *Buddhism and the Race Question* (Paris, 1958).

The Memorial of the Maha Nayaka Theros and Anu Nayaka and Anu Nayaka Theros of Malwatta and Asgiri Viharas to His Excellency Oliver Goonetilleke, 2-8-1958 (Kandy, 1958).

Mendis, G.C., *Ceylon Today and Yesterday—Main Currents of Ceylon History* (Colombo, 1963), second revd. edn.

———, *The Colebrook Cameron Papers* (Colombo, 1956), 2 vols.

Michels, Robert, *Political Parties* (New York, 1959).

Millen, Bruce H., *The Political Role of Labour in Developing Countries* (Washington, D.C., 1963).

Morgon, Kenneth, ed., *The Path of Buddha* (New York, 1957).

Mosca, Gaetano, *The Ruling Class*, trans. by Kaan, Hannah D., ed. & revised. with an Introduction by Arthur Livingstone (New York, 1939).

Muelder, Wallace R., *Schools for a New Nation : The Development and Administration of the Education System of Ceylon* (Colombo, 1962).

Mueller, Max F., ed., *The Sacred Books of the East* (Delhi, 1967), vol. 35.

Namasivayam, S., *The Legislatures of Ceylon* (London, 1951).

Nash, M., ed., *Anthropological Studies in Theravada Buddhism* (New Haven, 1966).

Neumann, Sigmund, ed., *Modern Political Parties : Approaches to Comparative Politics* (*Chicago, 1956*).

Nicholas, C.W. and Paranantana, S., *A Concise History of Ceylon* (Colombo, 1961).

Nyanatiloka, *Buddhist Dictionary and Manual of Buddhist Terms* (Colombo, 1956),

Obeyesekere, Ganannath, *Land Tenure in Village Ceylon : A Sociological and Historical Study* (Cambridge, 1967).

Pareto, Vilfredo, *The Mind and Society*, ed. by Livingstone Arthur (New York, 1935).

Perera, Horace L.H. and Ratnasabhapathy, M., *Ceylon and Indian History* (Colombo, 1954).

Park, Richard L., and Tinker, Irene, eds., *Leadership and Political Institutions in India* (Princeton, 1959).

Pieris, P.E., *Ceylon and Portuguese* (Tellipallai, 1930).

Pieris, Ralph, *Sinhalese Social Organisation : The Kandyan Period* (Colombo, 1956).

———— ed., *Some Aspects of Traditional Sinhalese Culture* (Peradeniya, 1956).

Prasad, Dhirendra Mohan, *Ceylon's Foreign Policy Under the Bandaranaikes, 1956-65* (Delhi, 1973).

Ponniah, S., *Satyagraha and the Freedom Movement of the Tamils in Ceylon* (London, 1963).

Rahula, W., *Bhikkuvage Urumaya* (The Heritage of Bhikkhus) (Colombo, 1946).

Rahula, Walpola, *History of Buddhism in Ceylon : The Anuradhapura Period—3rd Century B.C. to 10th Century A.D.* (Colombo, 1956).

Rajan, M.S., ed., *Studies in Politics—National and International* (Delhi, 1971).

Ratnapala, Nandsena, *The Katikivatas : Laws of the Buddhist Order of Ceylon from the 12th Century to the 19th Century* (Critically edited, translated and annotated) (Munchen, 1971).

Robertson, Ronald, ed., *Sociology of Religion* (London, 1965).

Roberts, T.W., *Problems of Public Life in India and Ceylon* (Colombo, n.d.).

Ruberu, Ranjit T., *Education in Colonial Ceylon* (Colombo, 1963).

Ryan, B., *Caste in Modern Ceylon : The Sinhalese System in Transition* (New Brunswick, 1953).

Ryan, Bryce, *Sinhalese Village* (University of Miami Press, 1958).

Samastha Lanka Viharadhipati Sabha Bharakara Sangamaya (All-Ceylon Viharadhipati and Trustee Association) *Kumburu Panat Gaina Vivechanayak* (Criticism of the Paddy Lands Act) (Kandy, 1963).

Sarkisyanz, E., *Buddhist Backgrounds of the Burmese Revolution* (The Hague, 1965).

Sasanatilake, Matale, *Ramanna Vamsa* (Ramanna Chronicles), (Colombo, 1964).

Schecter, Jerrold, *The New Face of Buddha* : *Buddism and Political Power in Southeast Asia* (London, 1967).

Singer, Marshall R., *The Emerging Elite—A Study of Political Leadership in Ceylon* (Cambridge, MIT, 1964).

Sinhala Jatika Sangamay, Vyavastha Ha Paramartha (Constitution and Aims), (Colombo, 1959)

Siriwardene, C.D.S., *Tax Exemption and Religious Bodies* (Colombo, 1955).

Smith, Bardwell L., ed., *Tradition and Change in Theravada Buddhism* : *Essays on Ceylon and Thailand in the 19th and 20th Centuries* (Leiden, 1973).

Smith, D.E., *Religion and Political Development* (Boston, 1970).

Smith, Donald Eugene, *Religion and Politics in Burma* (Princeton, 1965).

———, *Religion, Politics and Social Change in the Third World* (New York, 1971).

———, *Religion and Political Modernization* (New Haven and London, 1974).

Smith, Donald Eugene, ed., *South Asian Politics and Religion* (Princeton, 1966).

Smith, Wilfred Cantwell, *Islam in Modern History* (New York, 1957).

Spiro, Melford E., *Buddhism and Society* : *A Great Tradition and its Burmese Vicissitudes* (London, 1971).

——— ed., *Symposium on New Approaches to the Study of Religion* (Washington, 1963).

Sri Lanka Ekasath Bhikkhu Bala Mandalaya, Prakashanaya Publication (Colombo, 1970).

Sri Lanka Freedom Party, *Manifesto and Constitution of the Sri Lanka Freedom Party 1951* (Wellampitiya, 1951).

Tennent, Sir James Emerson, *Christianity in Ceylon* (London, 1850).

Thani Nayagam, Xavier S., *Language and Liberty in Ceylon* (Colombo, 1956).

Truman, David B., *The Governmental Process* (New York, 1951).

United Left Front Agreement (Colombo, 1963).

UNP, *Communism Suppresses Religion—What Dr. Colvin R. de Silva Saw in Russia* (Colombo, n.d.).

UNP (Matara Branch), *Buddha Sasanaya Ruka Gama, Yahi Maha Nayaka Semi tada vary Avavada Karati* (Protect Buddha Sasana—Advice of the Maha Nayakas) (Matara, 1952).

United National Party, *Fourth Anniversary Celebrations, Kandy 29th and 30th September 1951* (Colombo, 1951).

———, *General Election, 1956, Manifesto of the United National Party* (Colombo, 1956).

———, *Progress Through Stability : United National Party Manifesto* (Colombo, n.d.).

———, *What We Believe* (Colombo, 1963).

Vaithianathan, Sir Kanthiah, *Catholic Action and Thirukethee-swaram* (Colombo, 1964).

Vallier, Ivan, *Catholicism, Social Control and Modernization in Latin America* (California, 1970).

Vittachi, Tarzie, *Emergency '58* (London, 1958).

Vimalananda, T., *Buddhism in Ceylon Under the Christian Powers*, Colombo, 1963).

Von der Mehden, Fred R., *Religion and Nationlism in Southeast Asia* (London, 1968).

Wasby, Stephen L., *Political Science—The Discipline and its Dimensions* (Calcutta, 1970).

Weber, Max, *The Religions of India : The Sociology of Hinduism and Buddhism*, ed. and trans. Gerth, Hans. H. and Martindale Don T. (Illinois, 1958).

Weerawardana, I.D.S. *Ceylon General Election 1956*—Colombo, 1960).

———*Government and Politics in Ceylon 1931-1946*) (Colombo 1951).

———*Ceylon General Election* (Colombo, 1960).

Weiner, Myron, *The Politics of Scarcity—Public Pressure and Political Response in India* (Bombay, 1963).

Wickramasinghe, Martin, *Buddhism and Culture* (Ceylon, 1964).

Wickramasinghe, M., *Aspects of Sinhalese Culture* (Colombo, 1958).

Wimalasama, Baddegama, *Ada Badaggma* (Bnddhism Today),

(Colombo, n.d.)

————, *Anduwa Ha Missionary Balaya* (Government and the Missionary), (Colombo, n.d.).

————, *Ape Samaja Katayutu* (Oor Social Activities), (Colombo, n.d.).

————, *Bhikkshuvage Anagataya* (The Future of the Monk), (Colombo, n.d.)

Woodehouse, George William, *Sissiyanu Sissia Paramparawa and other Laws relating to Buddhist Priests in Ceylon* (Tellippalai, Ceylon, 1916).

Woodward, Calvin A., *The Growth of a Party System in Ceylon* (Rhode Island, 1969).

Woodward, E.L., *Age of Reform 1815-1870* (New york, 1938)

World Buddhist Sangha Conference, *Sangha Souvenir* (Colombo, 1966).

World Buddhist Sangha Council, *Constitution* (Colombo n.d.).

Wotton, Graham, *Interest Groups* (New Jersey, 1970).

Wriggins, Howard W., *Ceylon : Dilemmas of a New Nation* (Princeton, 1960).

Yalman, N., *Under the Bo Tree, Studies in Caste, Kinship and Marriage in the Interior of Ceylon* (California, 1967).

Articles

Agwani, M.S., 'Religion and Politics in Egypt', *International Studies*, vol. 13, no. 3, July-September 1974, pp. 367-88.

Ames, Michael, 'Ideological and Social Change in Ceylon', *Human Organization*, vol. 22, no. 1, Spring 1963, pp. 45-53.

Ames, Michael, M., 'Buddha and the Dancing Goblins : A Theory of Magic and Religion', *American Anthropologist* vol.66, no.1, February 1964, pp. 75-82

————, 'Magical-animism and Buddhism : A Structural Analysis of the Sinhalese Religious System', *Journal of Asian Studies*, vol. 23, no. 3, June 1964, pp. 21-52.

————, 'The Impact of Western Education on Religion and Society in Ceylon', *Pacific Affairs*, vol. 40, nos. 1-2, Spring and Summer 1967, pp. 19-42.

Bechert, Heinz, 'Theravada Buddhist Sangha : Some General Observations on Historical and Political Factors in its

Development', *Journal of Asian Studies*, vol. 29, no. 4, August 1970, pp. 761-58.

————, 'Sangha, State, Society, "Nation" : Persistence of Traditions in "post-Traditional" Buddhist Societies' *Daedalus*, vol. 102, no. 1, Winter 1973, pp. 85-95.

B.M., 'A People's Government : Social and Political Trends in Ceylon', *World Today*, vol. 12, no. 7, July 1956 pp. 281-91.

de Silva, K.M., 'The Development of British Policy on Temple Lands in Ceylon, 1840-55", *Journal of the Ceylon Branch of the Royal Asiatic Society*, New Series, vol. 8, pt. 2, 1963, pp. 321-29

Dharampala, Anagarika, 'A Message to the Buddhist Boys of Ceylon', *Mahabodhi and the UBM*, vol, 29, no. 18, October 1921, p. 351.

Evers, Hans-Dieter, 'Buddhism and British Colonial Policy in Ceylon, 1815-1875', *Asian Studies*, vol. 2, no. 3, December 1964, pp. 323-33.

————, 'Magic and Religion in Sinhalese Society', *American Anthropologist*, vol. 67, no, 1, February 1965, pp. 97-99.

————, 'Kingship and Property Rights in a Buddhist Monastery in Central Ceylon' *American Anthropologist*, vol. 69, no. 6, December 1967, pp. 703-10.

————, 'The Buddhist-Sangha in Ceylon and Thailand", *Sociologus*, vol. 18, no. 1, 1968, pp. 20-35.

————, 'Buddha and the Seven Gods : The Dual Organization of a Temple in Central Ceylon', *Journal of Asian Studies*, vol. 27, no. 3, May 1968, pp. 541-50.

————, 'Monastic Landlordism in Ceylon : A Traditional System in a Modern Setting", *Journal of Asian Studies*, vol. 28, no. 4, August 1969, pp. 685-92.

Hobbs, Cecil, 'The Political Importance of the Buddhist Priesthood in Burma', *Far Eastern Economic Review*, vol. 21, no. 19, 8 November 1956, pp. 586-90.

Jayatillaka, D.B., 'Sinhalese Embassies to Arakan', *Journal of Royal Asiatic Society* (Ceylon Branch), vol. 35, no. 93 1940, pp. 1-6.

Jennings, W.I., 'Ceylon General Elections of 1947', *University of Ceylon Review*, vol. 6, no. 3, July 1948, pp. 133-95.

Kitagawa, Joseph M., 'Buddhism and Asian Politics', *Asian*

Survey, vol. 2, no. 5, July 1962, pp. 1-11.

Kodikara, S.U., 'Communalism and Political Modernization in Ceylon', *Modern Ceylon Studies*, vol. 1, no. 1, January 1970, pp. 94-114.

Leach, E.R., 'Pulleyar and the Lord Buddha : An Aspect of Religious Syncretism in Ceylon', *Psycho-analysis and Psycho-analytic Review*, vol. 49, no. 2, 1962, pp. 80-102.

'Notes and Comments on Some Aspects of Buddhist Revival', *Ceylon Historical Journal* vol. 1, no. 2, October 1951, pp. 73-77.

Obeyesekere Gananath, 'The Great Tradition and the Little in the Perspective of Sinhalese Buddhism', *Journal of Asian Studies*, vol. 22, no. 2, February 1963, pp. 139-53.

———, 'Religious Symbolism and Political Change in Ceylon', *Modern Ceylon Studies*, vol. 1, no. 1, 1970, pp. 43-63.

Paranavitane, S., 'Mahayanism in Ceylon', *Ceylon Journal of Science*, Section G, vol. 2, 1928-33, pp. 35-71.

Peiris, Edmund, 'Sinhalese Christian Literature of the XVIIth and XVIIIth Centuries', *Journal of Royal Asiatic Society* (Ceylon Branch), vol. 35, no. 96, 1943 pp. 163-81.

———, 'Tamill Catholic Culture in Celon', *Tamil Culture*, no. 3, and 4, September 1953. pp. 229-44.

Pertinax, 'Bhikkhu Peramuna—I, Background', *Tribune*, vol. 3, no. 18, 15 September 1956, pp. 275-6 and 286.

Phadnis, Urmila, 'The Indo-Ceylonese Pact and the Stateless Persons in Ceylon', *India Quarterely*, vol. 23, no. 4, October-December 1967, pp. 362-407.

———, 'Federal Party in Ceylon : Towards Power or Wilderness ?' *Economic and Political Weekly*, vol. 4, no. 20, 17 May 1969, pp. 839-43.

———, 'Buddhism and State in Ceylon Before the Advent of the Portuguese', *Asian Studies*, vol. 8, no. 1, April 1970, pp. 120-34.

———, 'Insurgency in Ceylonese Politics : Problems and Prospects', *The Institute of Defence Studies and Analyses*, vol. 3, no. 4, April 1971, pp. 582-616.

———, 'Trends in Ceylon Politics', *India Quarterly*, vol. 27, no. 2, April-June 1971, pp. 122-39.

———, 'The UF Government in Ceylon : Challenges and

Responses' *World Today*, vol. 27, no. 6, June 1971, pp. 267-76.

————, 'Politics of Coalition Governments in Ceylon', *Tribune*, vol. 17, nos. 1-3, 39 June 1971, pp. 26-98, and vol. 17, no. 4, 14 July 1971, pp. 12-13.

————, 'Republic of Sri Laka : Crisis of Consensus', *Weekly Round Table*, vol. 1, no. 24, 16 July 1972, pp. 24-26.

————, 'Sri Lanka Today', *Current History*, vol. 63, no. 375, November 1972, pp. 210-13.

Rudolph, Llyod I, and Rudolph Susan Hoebar, 'The Political Role of India's Caste Associations', *Pacific Affairs*, vol.33, no. 1, March 1960, pp. 5-22.

"Sociology and Anthropology of Religion in Sri Lanka", *Social Compass*, vol. 20, 1972-73. (The whole issue in devoted to the title mentioned above and has several contributors).

Tambiah, H.W., "Buddhist Ecclesiastical Law", *Journal of the Ceylon Branch of the Royal Asiatic Society*, New Series, vol. 8, pt. 1, pp. 71-107.

————, "Kingship and Constitution of Ancient and Mediaeval Ceylon", *Journal of the Ceylon Branch of Royal Asiatic Society*, New Series, vol. 8, part 2, pp. 291-311.

Tambiah, S.J., "Ethnic Representation in Ceylon's Higher Administrative Services, 1870-1946" *University of Ceylon Review*, vol. 13, vols. 2 and 3, April-July 1955, pp. 113-34.

Thapar, Romila "Ethics, Religion and Social Protest in the First Millenium B.C. in Northern India", *Daedalus*, vol. 104, no. 2, Spring 1975, pp. 119-32.

Totten, George O., "Buddhism and Socialism in Japan and Burma", *Comparative Studies in Society and History*, vol.2, 1959-60, April 1960, pp. 293-304.

Weerawardane, I.D.S., "The General Elections in Ceylon, 1952", *Ceylon Historical Journal*, vol. 2, nos. 1 and 2, July and October 1952 (Special Supplement), pp. 111-208.

Wilson, A.J., "Ceylon Cabinet Ministers 1947-1960 : Their Political, Economic and Social Background", *Ceylon Economist*, vol. 5. no. 1, March 1960, pp. 1-54.

Wishwawarnapala, W.A., "The Formation of the Cabinet in Sri Lanka : A Study of the 1970 United Front Cabinet",

Political Science Review, vol. 12, nos. 1 and 2, January-June 1973, pp. 121-33.

——, "Composition of Cabinets 1948-60", *Young Socialist*, vol. 2, no. 5, pp. 267-72.

Wriggins, Howard W., "Ceylon's Times of Troubles, 1956-1958", *Far Eastern Survey*, vol. 28, no. 3, March 1959, pp. 33-39.

——, "Impediments to Unity in New Nations : The Case of Ceylon", *American Political Science Review*, vol. 55, no. 2, June 1961, pp. 313-20.

Yalman, Nur, "Ascetic Buddhist Monks of Ceylon", *Ethnology*, vol. 1, pp. 315-28.

Other Newspapers and Periodicals Referred to in the study

Buddhist (Colombo) (Monthly)
Ceylon Daily News (Colombo) (Daily)
Ceylon Observer (Colombo) (Daily)
Daily Mirror (Colombo) (Daily)
Guardian (London) (Daily)
Jayanti (Colombo) (Monthly)
Kalaya (Sinhalese) (Weekly)
Morning Times (Colombo) (Daily)
Patriot (New Delhi) (Daily)
Peramuna (Sinhalese, Colombo) (Daily)
Silumina (Sinhalese, Colombo) (Weekly)
Siyarata (Colombo) (Weekly)
Sun (Colombo) (Daily)
Times of Ceylon (Colombo) (Daily)
UNP Journal (Colombo) (Weekly)
World Buddhism (Colombo) (Monthly)

INDEX*

Index prepared by Shri Hari Om, Librarian, Hindustan Times,
    New Delhi.